PROSTHETIC
TERRITORIES

POLITICS & CULTURE

Avery Gordon and Michael Ryan, *editors*

Politics and Culture is a serial publication that publishes material from a diverse number of disciplinary perspectives, from literature to law, from anthropology to political science, from cultural studies to sociology. The serial is concerned with the political significance of cultural forms and practices as well as with the cultural character of social institutions and political formations.

Prosthetic Territories: Politics and Hypertechnologies,
edited by Gabriel Brahm Jr. and Mark Driscoll

After Political Correctness: The Humanities and Society in the 1990s,
edited by Christopher Newfield and Ronald Strickland

Body Politics: Disease, Desire, and the Family,
edited by Michael Ryan and Avery Gordon

3

POLITICS AND CULTURE

PROSTHETIC TERRITORIES

Politics and Hypertechnologies

edited by

GABRIEL BRAHM JR. &
MARK DRISCOLL

WESTVIEW PRESS

Boulder • San Francisco • Oxford

Politics and Culture 3

Copyright © 1995 by Westview Press, Inc.

Published in 1995 in the United States of America by Westview Press, Inc., 5500 Central Avenue, Boulder, Colorado 80301-2877, and in the United Kingdom by Westview Press, 12 Hid's Copse Road, Cumnor Hill, Oxford OX2 9JJ

Library of Congress Cataloging-in-Publication Data
Prosthetic territories : politics and hypertechnologies / edited by
    Gabriel Brahm Jr. & Mark Driscoll.
      p.   cm. — (Politics and culture ; 3)
    Includes bibliographical references and index.
    ISBN 0-8133-2368-1 — ISBN 0-8133-2369-X (pbk.)
    1. Cybernetics—Social aspects.   2. Technology and civilization.
3. Politics and culture.   4. Information society.   I. Brahm,
Gabriel.   II. Driscoll, Mark.   III. Series.
HM221.P74   1995
306.4'6—dc20   95-1100
                                                                                    CIP

Printed and bound in the United States of America

The paper used in this publication meets the requirements
of the American National Standard for Permanence of Paper
for Printed Library Materials Z39.48-1984.

10   9   8   7   6   5   4   3   2   1

Contents

Acknowledgments

The editors wish to thank, first and foremost, Michael Ryan. Without his patience and generosity this book wouldn't exist. Hayden White provided sage advice at the planning stage. Wendy Brown's "Feminist Hesitations, Postmodern Exposures" originally appeared in *Differences: A Journal of Feminist Cultural Studies* 3.1 (1991)—thanks for permission to reprint with changes, and to Jenny Anger for kind assistance in obtaining proofs. Thanks to Tera Martin for invaluable technical assistance.

Gabriel Brahm Jr.
Mark Driscoll

PROSTHETIC
TERRITORIES

Introduction

GABRIEL BRAHM JR.

T HE STAKES IN [what has traditionally been conceived as a] border war between organism and machine have been the territories of production, reproduction, and imagination," writes Donna Haraway.[1] What, then, is at stake when
these borders collapse?

The essays in this volume all offer arguments that lend support, in different
ways, to Haraway's own recommendation for those she terms "cyborgs." A good
cyborg will at once take "*pleasure* in the confusion of boundaries" and demand
"*responsibility* in their construction."[2] The question becomes how to celebrate the
decentering, liberating effects of technologically driven border crossings while
combating the irresponsibility of state and corporate centers of power.

A cyborg is part human, part machine (a *cyb*ernetic *org*anism). Where these
"parts" meet and intermingle, confusion necessarily arises as to the nature of
older boundaries between the organic and the inorganic, the "cybernetic" and the
"organism." In this confused space a new kind of "territory" emerges. There production, reproduction, and imagination always already coexist. Hence the cyborg
is itself an image and a metaphor—as well as an embodiment—of transgressed
borders, confused boundaries. In an age of "hypertechnology" (computerization,
mass media), this metaphor suits most of us, and our view-screens. We're all cyborgs now.

As reflected in this volume, new movements (against racism, male-dominant
capitalism, ideologies of progress, individualism, and the appropriation of labor
and the earth as mere "resource" or raw material) tend not to pause in dispute
over the (im)purity of these regions. Nor do they agonize much over outmoded
divisions between "theory and practice." Rather, they begin by assuming hybridity in all things. In an attempt to provisionally name this new terrain of political
and cultural struggle, we have dubbed these hybrid spaces of theory-practice
"prosthetic territories." A "prosthesis" can be defined as "a foreign element that

reconstructs that which cannot stand up on its own, at once propping up and extending its host. The prosthesis is always structural, establishing the place it appears to add to."[3] When the border between the "foreign" and the "native"—the cultural and the natural, the political and the cultural, the social and the political—can no longer be readily justified or perhaps even maintained, we have entered "prosthetic territory."

Though contributions differ in the relative emphasis placed on one or the other of Haraway's twin imperatives (pleasure/responsibility in boundary confusion/construction), each essay unites with the others in assuming the necessity and desirability of both. For in each of the chapters that follow, technology, text, built environment, and body interpenetrate on a plane of immanence common to all. Such phrases as these seem to echo one another: "technology of writing," "corporeal city," "cartographic self," "geography of the body," "words as ligatures," "battleground of bodily form," "semiotic guerrilla warfare," "veil of print," "text of the veil," "textual architecture," "materiality of the printed text." It would be wrong to conclude from these echoing terms that this is a book "about" poststructuralism, however. Rather, this is a book that assumes certain poststructuralist tenets as standard equipment for operations involving feminism, cyborgism, Marxism, postcolonial studies, queer theory, and the critique of racism and technique. "Writing" and "text," therefore, in these essays, include broadly what Jacques Derrida has called "the entire field covered by the cybernetic program."[4] This is the field of cyborgs, androids, and aliens—a horizontal plane crisscrossed by multiple zones of engagement, which are known (henceforth) as *prosthetic territories.*

NOTES

1. Donna Haraway, "A Manifesto for Cyborgs: Science, Technology, and Socialist Feminism in the 1980s," *Socialist Review* no. 80, 15.2 (March-April 1985): 66. The article is reprinted in Donna J. Haraway, *Simians, Cyborgs, and Women* (New York: Routledge, 1991).

2. Ibid., 66.

3. Mark Wigley, "Prosthetic Theory: The Disciplining of Architecture," *Assemblage,* no. 15 (1991): 9. Cited in Jennifer A. González, "Autotopographies" (this volume).

4. Jacques Derrida, *Of Grammatology,* trans. Gayatri Spivak (Baltimore: Johns Hopkins University Press, 1984), 43.

PART ONE

TERRITORIES: THE POLITICS OF SPACE & THE SPACE OF POLITICS

1

The City in Pieces

VICTOR BURGIN

IN HER BOOK about Walter Benjamin's Paris arcades project, Susan Buck-Morss tells the story of how, in 1924, Benjamin traveled to Italy: "in order to bring to paper his [thesis] *The Origin of German Tragic Drama,* with which he hoped to secure an academic position at the University of Frankfurt."[1] This was the year of Lenin's death and the year of the first surrealist manifesto. An eventful year in politics and art, it was no less eventful for Benjamin's personal life. In Italy he met and fell in love with Asja Lacis, "a Bolshevik from Latvia, active in post revolutionary Soviet culture as an actress and director, and a member of the Communist Party since the Duma revolution."[2] In 1928, having failed to win the approval of the university, *The Origin of German Tragic Drama* was nevertheless published.[3] Benjamin dedicated it to his wife, from whom he separated that same year. Also in 1928 Benjamin published *One Way Street,*[4] a montage of textual fragments in which he juxtaposes observations on everyday life with descriptions of his dreams. One of the longer fragments is titled "Teaching Aid—Principles of the Weighty Tome, or How to Write Fat Books."[5] *One Way Street* is not a "weighty tome." No academic monument, it has more the appearance of a city plan: Avenues of open space cross its pages between compact and irregular blocks of text. Benjamin's dedication to *One Way Street* reads:

> This street is named
> Asja Lacis Street
> after she who
> like an engineer
> cut it through the author

∾   ∾   ∾

When, in 1924, Benjamin first told Lacis about the academic thesis he was working on, her horrified response was, "Why bury oneself with dead literature?"[6] In Benjamin's subsequent production, funerary construction gives way to a lighter and more open textual architecture. When, in 1925, he and Lacis wrote an essay together about the city of Naples, the central image (which Susan Buck-Morss tells us was "suggested by Lacis") is that of "porosity." Naples rises where sea meets cliff. Lacis and Benjamin write: "At the base of the cliff itself, where it touches the shore, caves have been hewn. ... As porous as this stone is the architecture. Building and action interpenetrate in the courtyards, arcades, and stairways. In everything they preserve the scope to become a theater of new, unforeseen, constellations. The stamp of the definitive is avoided. No situation appears intended forever, no figure asserts its 'thus and not otherwise.' This is how architecture, the most binding part of the communal rhythm, comes into being here."[7] Benjamin and Lacis find that "Buildings are used as a popular stage. They are all divided into innumerable, simultaneously animated theaters. Balcony, courtyard, window, gateway, staircase, roof are at the same time stage and boxes."[8] Or again, "Housekeeping utensils hang from balconies like potted plants. ... Just as the living room reappears on the street, with chairs, hearth, and altar, so, ... the street migrates into the living room."[9] The permeability that Lacis and Benjamin saw in the streets of Naples is also to be found in *One Way Street*, a street that will eventually lead to the *Passagen-Werk*. We will remember that Benjamin named this street Asja Lacis Street, "after she who, like an engineer, cut it through the author." Just as Benjamin recounts his dreams in *One Way Street*, so his laconic dedication to the book is itself a dream image: the image of a book that is a city street cut through the body of the author by his lover. Benjamin's written body is penetrated by Lacis just as the body of what might have been *his* text on Naples became porous, translucent, permeable to *her* voice. The lapidary inscription commemorates an erotic event in which the categorical distinctions that separate body, city, and text dissolve.

The (con)fusion of representations of body and city has a history. In the third book of Vitruvius, dedicated to the design and construction of temples, the Roman architect describes how the outstretched limbs of a "well-formed man" subtend the circle and the square. The purpose of the description—the basis of a widely known drawing by Leonardo da Vinci—is to urge that buildings display the same harmonious relation of parts to whole as Vitruvius found in the human form.[10] The body is not simply that which is to be contained by a building; the body *contains* the very generating principle of the building. In an article of 1974,[11] Françoise Choay describes how, in the work of Alberti and other architect-theorists of the Italian Renaissance, the Vitruvian doctrine was woven into a mythology of origins. For example, Humanist authorities wrote that the first men derived their units of measurement from the palms of their hands, their arms, and their feet. Or again, that Adam, driven from the Garden of Eden, protected himself from the rain by joining his hands above his head—a gesture that subsequently led him to construct the first roof. That the human body is seen as the origin not only of the building but of the entire built environment is apparent from the descriptions and drawings of anthropomorphized cities that appear in illustrated books during the Renaissance. Choay describes an image from a book by Francesco di Giorgio Martini as showing "a personnage whose head is adorned with a fortress which he supports with his arms. His body is inscribed in a rectangle marked *città*. His legs are spread, and his feet and elbows are figured by towers. His navel marks the center of a circular public place, on the periphery of which is situated the principal church."[12] Such fantasy constructions were already implied in the writings of Alberti, who had found that "the city is like a large house and the house like a small city"[13] but that ultimately, "every edifice is a body."[14]

If in Renaissance Italy the city could be conceived of as a body, it was because the city had recently coalesced from a condition in which it was virtually undifferentiated from the countryside. In a book of 1974, translated in 1991 as *The Production of Space*, Henri Lefebvre observes: "The city in Vitruvius is conspicuous by its absence/presence; though he is speaking of nothing else, he never addresses it directly. It is as though it were merely an aggregation of 'public' monuments and 'private' houses. ... Only in the sixteenth century, after the rise of the medieval town (founded on commerce, and no longer agrarian in character), and after the establishment of 'urban systems' in Italy, Flanders, England, France, Spanish America, and elsewhere, did the town emerge as a unified entity—and as a *subject*."[15] The text in which Alberti inaugurates the concept of the corporeal city[16] postdates, by about fifteen years, his treatise on painting, *De Pictura*, which contains the first written description of a method of drawing in linear perspective. Perspective provided, quite literally, the "common ground" on which the identification of architectural space with corporeal space could "take place." In the Renaissance, the inaugural act in constructing a painting was to lay out the horizontal plane that united the illusory space of the image with the real space of the viewer. This is the familiar grid of receding squares accelerating toward a vanishing point, which in many paintings rises to the finished surface thinly disguised as a tiled floor. The side of each square in the underlying perspective grid represented a common unit of measurement, the *braccio*, equivalent to one-third of the height of a standing man. By this means, the correct stature of a depicted figure could be determined relative to any point in the illusory depth of the represented space. The size of all other objects—not least the built environment—could then be determined by reference to this common corporeal measure. Man, here, is literally "the measure of all things." For all that the erect male body may have been at the origin of this space, however, it quickly ceded its place to its disembodied metonymic representative—the eye—in what Lefebvre has called "the spiriting-away or scotomization of the body."[17] As a consequence, as Luce Irigaray remarks, "man no longer even remembers that his body is the threshold, the porch of the construction of his universe(s)."[18]

At the dawn of modernity, disembodied geometric and mathematical principles came to dominate all visual representational practices. The same abstract order that informed painting and architecture was brought to enhance the instrumentality of such things as navigational charts, maps, and city plans. In conform-
ity to the exigencies of a militant and expansive mercantile capitalism, the image
of the convergence of parallel lines toward a vanishing point on the horizon became the very figure of Western European global economic and political ambitions. This optical-geometric spatial regime—the panoptical-instrumental space
of colonialist capitalist modernity—would govern Western European representations for the ensuing three centuries. It has been widely remarked that this representational space, inaugurated in the Renaissance, entered into crisis in the early
part of the twentieth century. We have become familiar with the arguments from
industrialization, urbanization, and technology: Fordism and Taylorism, factory
town and garden city, steam train and airplane, telephone and radio, all were implicated in a changed "common sense" of space. On the basis of the "artistic" evidence, also, few would disagree that the early twentieth century was a time of major change in Western representations of space, and space of representations.
Exhibits presented in evidence here typically include such things as analytical
cubism, the twelve-tone scale, jazz, and Bauhaus design. It is in terms of such arguments that I understand Lefebvre when he writes: "Around 1910 a certain space
was shattered. It was the space of common sense, of knowledge (*savoir*), of social
practice, of political power, ... the space, too, of classical perspective and geometry ... bodied forth in Western art and philosophy, as in the form of the city and
town."[19] Lefebvre also observes, however, that "'common sense' space, Euclidean
space and perspectivist space did not disappear in a puff of smoke without leaving any trace in our consciousness, knowledge or educational methods."[20] A certain space was shattered, but nevertheless it did not disappear. The "nevertheless"
does not signal that disjunction between knowledge and belief to which Freud
gave the term *Verleugnung,* "disavowal." For our terminology here, we might better turn to Mao Tse-tung: The relation between the existing instrumental space of
political modernity and the emergent space of aesthetic modernism is one of
"nonantagonistic contradiction."

∾   ∾   ∾

Benjamin and Lacis, themselves out of place in Naples, found all things in Naples to be dis-located, as when "the living room reappears on the street." This particular image, retrospectively determined by a short history of surrealism, returns
in Benjamin's long essay of 1938 about Paris at the time of Baudelaire. Here, Benjamin remarks on the tendency of the *flâneur* to "turn the boulevard into an
intérieur." He writes: "The street becomes a dwelling for the *flâneur;* he is as much
at home among the façades of houses as the citizen is in his four walls. To him the
shiny, enameled signs of business are at least as good a wall ornament as an oil

painting is to a bourgeois in his salon."[21] This passage, in retrospect, helps to reveal a fundamental ambiguity both in Lacis and Benjamin's essay about Naples and in Benjamin's dedication to *One Way Street*. The *flâneur* who turns the street into a living room commits an act of transgression, which reverses an established distinction between public and private spaces. Whereas Benjamin and Lacis saw the porosity of urban life in Naples as the survival of precapitalist social forms that had not yet succumbed to the modern segregation of life into public and private zones. Again, Benjamin's terse dedication to *One Way Street* pictures a fusion of spaces in the same instant that—through the image of penetration—it asserts the individual integrity of those spaces. Like an arrested filmic lap-dissolve, which refuses to decide either origin or destination, the image forms through condensation. It also forms through displacement to, or from, the image of Haussmann's infamous *percements,* which ripped through working-class districts of Paris like the cannon fire they were designed to facilitate.[22] An ambivalence inhabits this textual fragment: as if two different spaces—one sealed, the other permeable—compete to occupy the same moment in time. In both the essay on Naples and the dedication to *One Way Street,* the metaphor of porosity competes with a dialectic of interior and exterior that belongs to a different register. This ambivalence marks the representational space of modernism in general.

One of the most visible images of the modern dialectic of interior and exterior is the wall of steel and glass, of which the glass and iron structures of the Paris arcades are a prototype. We may take the specific example of the administrative office for a model factory complex built by Walter Gropius and Adolf Meyer for the Werkbund exhibition in Cologne in 1914. As Richard Sennett describes it, "In this building you are simultaneously inside and outside. … From the outside you can see people moving up and down between floors. … You can see through walls, your eyes move inside to outside, outside to inside. The confines of the interior have lost their meaning. … Gropius and Meyer have used glass in and around the doors so that you can literally look through the building to people entering from the other side. … Inner and outer become apparent at once, like the front and side of a cubist portrait."[23] It is no doubt this sort of "image of the modern"[24] that Benjamin has in mind when he celebrates "the twentieth century, with its porosity, transparency, light and free air."[25] The modernist architect to whom he pays explicit homage, however, is not Gropius but Le Corbusier, the designer of the "radiant city."[26] Le Corbusier's project of 1930 for the Ville Radieuse is the source of the now clichéd perspectivist vision of urban modernity as made up of evenly spaced towers rising from a limitless expanse of parkland. The project evolved from Le Corbusier's plan for the Ville Contemporaine—a city to contain 3 million people—which was exhibited in Paris in 1922. Kenneth Frampton describes the Ville Contemporaine as "an élite capitalist city of administration and control with garden cities for the workers being sited, along with industry, beyond the 'security zone' of the green belt encompassing the city."[27] We may remember, then, that as

much as modernity is the locus of transparency in architecture, it is also at the origin of the social isolation in and between high-rise apartment houses, the death
of the street as a site of social interaction, and the practice of "zoning," which
establishes absolute lines of demarcation between work and residential areas, and
between cultural and commercial activities. The transparent wall, used by such
socialist modernists as Gropius to unite interior with exterior, was destined to become the very index of capitalist corporate exclusivity.

∾   ∾   ∾

Lefebvre finds both that, around 1910, "a certain space was shattered" and that
"it did not disappear." The phallocentric abstract space of capitalist modernity
survived to inhabit the representational space of aesthetic modernism. Indeed, it
survives to the present day. It is not that one spatial formation was replaced by another. It is rather as if a superior "layer" of spatial representations itself became
permeable, "porous," and allowed an inferior layer to show through. Lefebvre
himself supplies the appropriate analogy. He notes that early in the genesis of a biological organism, "an indentation forms in the cellular mass. A cavity gradually
takes place. ... The cells adjacent to the cavity form a screen or membrane which
serves as a boundary. ... A closure thus comes to separate within from without, so
establishing the living being as a 'distinct body.'" This "closure," however, is only
ever relative: "The membranes in question remain permeable, punctured by
pores and orifices. Traffic back and forth, so far from stopping, tends to increase
and become more differentiated, embracing both energy exchange (alimentation,
respiration, excretion) and information exchange (the sensory apparatus)." Closure, then, rather than belonging to the natural order, is a creation of the social
order. Thus, Lefebvre writes: "A defining characteristic of (private) property, as of
the position in space of a town, nation or nation state, is a closed frontier. This
limiting case aside, however, we may say that every spatial envelope implies a barrier between inside and out, but that this barrier is always relative and, in the case
of membranes, always permeable."[28] The transgressional magic of the *flâneur* is to
make the interior appear on the "wrong side" of its bounding wall, the wrong side
of the façade. Certainly, the transformation is an illusion, but then the interior itself is an illusion—in a double sense. First, Benjamin points out that the bourgeois interior emerges into history, in the nineteenth century, as a reified fantasy:
"For the private person, living space becomes, for the first time, antithetical to the
place of work. ... The private person who squares his accounts with reality in his
office demands that the interior be maintained in his illusions. ... From this
springs the phantasmagorias of the interior. For the private individual the private
environment represents the universe. In it he gathers remote places and the past.
His drawing room is a box in the world theatre."[29] In an essay about the domestic
architecture of Adolf Loos, Beatriz Colomina writes: "In Loos's interiors the sense
of security is not achieved by simply turning one's back on the exterior and be-

coming immersed in a private world—'a box in the world theatre,' to use Benjamin's metaphor. It is no longer the house that is a theatre box; there is a theatre box inside the house, overlooking the internal social spaces, so that the inhabitants become both actors in and spectators of family life—involved in, yet detached from their own space. The classical distinctions between inside and outside, private and public, object and subject, are no longer valid."[30] It is not, however, that these distinctions are no longer valid, it is rather that they have been displaced—as in the Paris arcades, which pierce the façade only to reproduce the façade in the form of glass entrails within the body of the building.[31] Further, Lefebvre's example of the biological organism would indicate that, in any real sense, the absolute distinction between interior and exterior can never be valid. It will always belong to "reality," never to the order of the Real. Here, then, is the second sense in which the interior is an illusion. Extending the analogy of the biological organism to the social space of the built environment, Lefebvre reminds us that an apparently solid house is "permeated from every direction by streams of energy which run in and out of it by every imaginable route: water, gas, electricity, telephone lines, radio and television signals, and so on," and that similar observations apply in respect of the entire city. Thus, he writes: "As exact a picture as possible of this space would differ considerably from the one embodied in the representational space which its inhabitants have in their minds, and which for all its inaccuracy plays an integral role in social practice."[32] If the built environment is conceived of in terms of the body, then a different body is at issue here.

An Arnold Newman photograph from 1949 shows the components of a prefabricated house laid out on what appears to be the concrete runway of an airfield. Every shape in the intricate pattern of this carpet of components is equally visible. No hierarchy, formal or functional, governs the relations between the parts. Contiguity alone links wood, metal, and glass; frames, planks, and pipes. This is nothing like a house, yet nothing but a house. If the houses destined to be its neighbors had been laid out alongside, it would have been impossible to tell where one ended and the other began. At the beginning of his book of 1974, *Économie Libidinale*, Jean-François Lyotard similarly lays out the surfaces of the body. In a long and violent passage glistening with mucus and blood, he unfolds not only that which is seen, "the skin with each of its creases, lines, scars, ... the nipples, the nails, the hard transparent skin under the heel," but also the most intimate and deep interior linings of the body. Moreover, as nothing but proximity links one surface to another, we pass indiscriminately to other contiguous bodies. We pass, for example, from these lips to other lips, and to the lips of others. We pass from the palm of the hand, "creased like a yellowed sheet of paper," to the surface of an automobile steering wheel. Even further, Lyotard reminds us, we must not forget to add colors to the retina or to add to the tongue "all the sounds of which it is capable," including "all the selective reserve of sounds which is a phonological system." All of this, and more, belongs to the libidinal body. This "body" bears no allegiance to what Lyotard terms the "political economy" of the organic. The "political body" is a hierarchically organized assembly of constituent organs—jointly ruled by mind and heart—which seeks to resist death and to reproduce itself. It is a body clearly differentiated from other bodies, and from the world of objects. It is this body under the Law that may become the site of "transgression"—illustrated for Lyotard by a Hans Bellmer drawing in which a fold in a girl's arm stands in place of the crease of the vulva. It is not such transgressive metaphor that is at issue, but a more corrosive metonymy. Lyotard writes: "We must not begin with transgression, we must immediately go to the very end of cruelty, construct the anatomy of polymorphous perversion, unfold the immense membrane of the libidinal 'body,' which is quite the inverse of a system of parts." Lyotard sees this "membrane" as composed of the most heterogeneous items: human bone and writing paper, steel and glass, syntax and the skin on the inside of the thigh. In the libidinal economy, writes Lyotard, "all of these zones are butted end to end ... on a Mœbius strip, ... a mœbian skin [an] interminable band of variable geometry (a concavity is necessarily a convexity at the next turn) [with but] a single face, and therefore neither exterior nor interior."[33]

Gropius and Meyer's design for the 1914 Werkbund exhibition may render interior and exterior mutually visible, but it does not thereby abolish the hierarchical distinction between the two: It is, after all, an administration building. The glass walls of the corporate towers that follow may be transparent, but they are no more porous than are their "glass ceilings." Such façades retain their classical function[34] of both leading the eye toward a vanishing point, or point of interest, and marking a *boundary*. Lefebvre seems to leave the transparent wall out of account when he notes: "A façade admits certain acts to the realm of what is visible, whether they occur on the façade itself (on balconies, window ledges, etc.) or are to be seen *from* the façade (processions in the street, for example). Many other acts, by contrast, it condemns to obscenity: these occur *behind* the façade. All of which seems to suggest a 'psychoanalysis of space.'"[35] The façade of which Lefebvre speaks here is opaque. By his account, if nothing is concealed then there is no need for psychoanalytic theory. This would be to reduce psychoanalysis to a theory of repression, but modern psychoanalysis is no more *necessarily* concerned with repression than the modern façade is necessarily opaque. Lefebvre's observation about the façade is the only passage where he suggests the possibility of a psychoanalysis of space. There are nevertheless many points in Lefebvre's complex and densely argued book where his ideas invite development in terms of psychoanalytic theory. Most fundamentally, he writes that space is "first of all *my* body, and then it is my body counterpart or 'other', its mirror-image or shadow: it is the shifting intersection between that which touches, penetrates, threatens or benefits my body on the one hand, and all other bodies on the other."[36] The full psychoanalytic implications of such a remark—most obviously in relation to Lacan's idea of the "mirror stage"—remain to be developed. Indeed, insofar as they apply to considerations of space, they are as yet little developed within the field of psychoanalysis itself.

∾   ∾   ∾

The problematic of space is encountered from the beginning of Freud's thera-peutic practice and metapsychological theory: both in real terms, as in the ques-tion of the therapeutic setting, and in metaphorical terms, as in his topographical models of mental processes. It is perhaps because of this early ubiquity that the topic of space as such came to receive little, and late, direct consideration in psy-choanalysis. To my knowledge, Paul Schilder's 1935 essay "Psycho-Analysis of Space"[37] is the first to address the topic explicitly and exclusively. Schilder finds that "space is not an independent entity (as Kant has wrongly stated) but is in close relation to instincts, drives, emotions and actions."[38] His remarks here an-ticipate an isolated work note made by Freud in 1938: "Space may be the projec-tion of the extension of the psychical apparatus. No other derivation is probable. Instead of Kant's *a priori* determinants of our psychical apparatus. Psyche is ex-tended; knows nothing about it."[39] Schilder's findings in respect to psychical space emerge from his work on—in the words of the title of his book of 1935 (a book that is one of the sources of Lacan's idea of the mirror stage)—"the image and appearance of the human body."[40] In "Psycho-Analysis of Space" Schilder writes: "There is at first an undifferentiated relation between an incompletely de-veloped body-image and the outside space. Clearer differentiations take place around the openings of the body. There is a zone of indifference between body and outside world which makes distortions of body-space and outside-space by projection and appersonization possible."[41]

"Appersonization" is the process in which "we may take parts of the bodies of others and incorporate them in our own body-image."[42] In a pathological setting, such interchange of body parts is a characteristic of the "psychoses." Among what Freud calls the "defense psychoses" autism and schizophrenia bear most directly on the corporeal relation to external reality. In her book of 1972, *Autism and Childhood Psychosis*, British psychoanalyst Frances Tustin notes that "the com-mon psychiatric division of psychotic children [is] into those suffering from Early Infantile Autism and those suffering from childhood Schizophrenia."[43] Tustin finds this distinction "too rigid." For expository clarity however, outside of a clin-ical setting, it is convenient to retain the distinction. Schematically, the terms "au-tism" and "schizophrenia" name the opposing extremities of a continuum of modes of psychocorporeal relation to external reality. The middle range of this schematic continuum would encompass "normal" socially acceptable ways of re-lating to the world. At one extreme limit, autism represents a total closing down of that relation: The autistic subject may appear "dead to the world." At the oppo-site extreme, schizophrenia represents a total opening of the relation to the extent that the schizophrenic body is scattered in pieces throughout its world. Both autism and schizophrenia are normal states of very early infancy, the time when there is as yet little substantive distinction between an outer world of "real" objects and the inner world of those "objects," which are the psychical representations of sensations from, primarily, bodily organs and the mother's body. Pathological autism and schizophrenia represent a fixation at, or regression to, such early object relations. We should, however, remember that, as Freud remarks, "the frontier between the so-called normal states of mind and the pathological ones is to a great extent conventional, and ... is so fluid that each one of us probably crosses it many times in the course of a day." As Octave Mannoni succinctly puts it, "we are all more or less healed psychotics."[44]

A book of drawings by Antonin Artaud, published in France in 1986,[45] is accompanied by an essay by Jacques Derrida that is, in effect, an extended reflection upon the rarely used French word *subjectile*—a word that appears, appropriately rarely, in Artaud's writings. The 1978 edition of the *Petit Robert* dictionary defines *subjectile* as "surface serving as support (wall, panel, canvas) for a painting." This is not how the term functions for Artaud. Rather, as Derrida notes, the *subjectile* is that which lies "between the surfaces of the subject and the object."[46] It is the place where may be traced "the trajectories of the *objective*, the *subjective*, the *projectile*, of the *introjection*, the *interjection*, the *objection*, of *dejection* and *abjection*, etc."[47] Derrida describes a graphic work by Artaud in which "with the aid of a match, Artaud opens holes in the paper, and the traces of burning perforation are part of a work in which it is impossible to distinguish between the subject of the representation and the support of this subject, in the *layers* of the material, between that which is above and that which is below, and thus between the subject and its outside, the representation and its other."[48] Reading this, I was reminded of a recurrent television news image: the image of a house, or apartment, whose walls have been pierced by rocket fire, or shells. For all its repetitions, the image never fails to "pierce" me. This has nothing to do with Roland Barthes's *punctum* or the *studium*. This is neither a private nor an ethical reaction. Something quite different is at issue. Discussing the child's anxiety at being separated from its mother, Freud notes that at the origin of the distress is the child's perception of the mother as the one who will satisfy its needs. Thus, rather than being reducible simply to object loss, "the situation ... which [the child] regards as a 'danger' and against which it wants to be safeguarded is that of a ... *growing tension due to need*, against which it is helpless" (italics in the original). Even more fundamentally, regardless of need, anxiety derives from "the economic disturbance caused by an accumulation of amounts of stimulation which require to be disposed of. It is this factor ... which is the real essence of the 'danger.'"[49] In the contemporary environment of mass media, particularly television, we are all of us subject to anxiety arising from, among other things, exposure to pain we are helpless to alleviate. The helplessness and distress we may feel—comparable to infantile 'transitivism'—bears witness to the congenital instability of psychocorporeal boundaries, which is at the source of both empathy and jealousy, compassion and aggression. It indicates the fragility and permeability, the porosity, of the layers between one embodied subject and another. In the physical encounter, the porosity is of the boundary of skin that contains the body ego, the "skin ego."[50] In the mediatic encounter, there is permeability between "layers," such that interior and exterior, here and there, are simultaneously affirmed and confused. I am thinking of the corneal and retinal layers, which both receive and transmit the image; the phosphor-coated layer of glass, which in receiving the bombardment of electrons that encode the image effectively pierces the layer, the screen, that is the wall of my living room; the pierced layer of the wall *in* the image within or behind the television screen within that building, behind that wall, where someone in their living room perhaps once watched television.

∾   ∾   ∾

The Paris arcades of which Benjamin spoke, and the modernist buildings they presaged, did not mark the emergence of a historically unprecedented space. Such examples rather represent the imperfect partial development of an image of space latent in all of us: the preœdipal, maternal, space: the space, perhaps, that Benjamin and Lacis momentarily refound in Naples. In this space it is not simply that the boundaries are "porous" but that the subject itself is *soluble*. This space is the source of bliss and of terror, of the "oceanic" feeling and of the feeling of coming apart, just as it is at the origin of feelings of being invaded, overwhelmed, suffocated. The generation of Europeans to which I belong grew up in a world of fixed borders, of glacial boundaries frozen, it seemed for eternity, by the Cold War. Now, in the time of thaw, borders everywhere are melting, sliding, submerging, reemerging. Identities—national, cultural, individual—are experiencing the exultant anxieties that accompany the threat of dissolution. Benjamin's Europe was one of strong borders, a fact that was to prove tragically fatal to Benjamin himself. Today's national borders are largely inconvenient to world capitalism; they have long been routinely ignored by transnational corporations and by a money market become a global computer network operating at the speed of light. As weak and emergent nations struggle to maintain their faltering identities by drawing their borders more tightly around them, stronger established nations are losing the political will to effectively police their uncertain limits. The boundaries of today's Europe are increasingly porous. The recent history of Germany is an example. A space in transition, it represents the economic and political equivalent of "osmosis"—the movement of a fluid through a semipermeable membrane from the weaker to the stronger solution. However, as "The Wall" crumbled inside Germany, osmosis at Germany's borders—fluid transmissions from the weaker to the stronger economy—revived a pathological horror of mixing, the modern history of which has been so effectively cataloged by Klaus Theweleit.[51] The rhetoric of neofascism, by no means unique to Germany, sounds familiar, but it now re-sounds in a different space. Rhetoric, we may remember, was originally an art of space—of gesture and of staging—as well as an art of speech. The space of the stage, the Antique source of perspectival space, has changed.

In explaining the principle of drawing in perspective, Leonardo da Vinci asked his reader to imagine looking through a window and tracing the outline of what he saw upon the surface of the glass. Virilio describes the television screen as "an introverted window, one which no longer opens onto adjoining space."[52] Today, the perspectivist's "window on the world," and proscenium arch, remain the habitual frames of our representations—even in television. But such means of circumscribing the mise-en-scène appear out of their time; dislocated remnants from another time, a sort of nostalgia. The truth of this is nowhere better seen than in the images of computer-generated "virtual" realities with which we have recently become familiar. Their impeccably Euclidean "wire-frame" spaces invoke nothing so much as illustrations from seventeenth-century treatises on perspective, creating much the same uncannily nostalgic effect as a polystyrene bowl that has been molded to bear the impression left in wet clay by a potter's fingers. Benjamin remarked that the arrival of photography in the nineteenth century "gave the moment a posthumous shock." Much of this shock was the shock of the uncanny: the strangeness of the automaton, the android, the replicant; the shock of the unfamiliar familiarity of this new old representational space. The photograph, we are now accustomed to observe, lends itself easily to fetishism: that psychical structure which is the preferred commodity form of capitalism, the most favored psychoaesthetic currency in which modernity and "postmodernity" alike are traded. Photographs, therefore, are most amenable to "disavowal" as the mechanism by which we may defend ourselves against their more distressing (un)realities. As Mannoni expresses the form of disavowal, "I know very well, but nevertheless":[53] "I know very well that this (unpleasurable) reality exists/existed, *but nevertheless* here there is only the beauty of the print."[54] Since Laura Mulvey's influential essay "Visual Pleasure and Narrative Cinema,"[55] we have also become accustomed to the idea that fetishism is also a predominant psychosexual structure of cinematic representation. The television image is rarely "beautiful" in the way of a photograph or a cinematic shot,[56] nor does its evanescent mobility allow the petrification necessary for fetishistic investment. The regressive unconscious defense mechanisms invoked by television as it funnels suffering and excitation into our box in the world theater, as it pours all the world's broken cities into our *interior,* are different from those invoked by photography and cinemaphotography. They produce a different space.

For all its "thick-skinned" stupidity, television is also a fragile permeable membrane of near-global extension. Its web of instant mutable satellite links, indiscriminately crossing fixed meridians and old frontiers, has turned global space from a graph paper into a palimpsest. Paul Virilio has remarked that both Benjamin and René Clair compared architecture to cinema in that both address what Benjamin termed "simultaneous collective reception."[57] What Virilio finds of particular interest in this comparison is the implicit recognition of a historical transition from the representational priority of "surface" to that of "interface." Benjamin notes that Baudelaire described the inhabitant of the modern city as "a *kaleidoscope* equipped with consciousness" and that with the coming of film, "perception in the form of shocks was established as a formal principle."[58] The subsequent arrival of television—also, like architecture, a technique of "simultaneous collective reception"—has massively consolidated this principle. In his essay of 1936, "The Work of Art in the Age of Mechanical Reproduction," Benjamin wrote: "Our taverns and our metropolitan streets and offices and furnished rooms, our railroad stations and our factories appeared to have us locked up hopelessly. Then came the film and burst this prison-world asunder by the dynamite of the tenth of a second, so that now, in the midst of its far-flung ruins and debris, we calmly and adventurously go traveling."[59] Today, for more anxious, less adventurous, armchair travelers, the "far-flung ruins and debris" of exploded towns is routinely projected into our living rooms through the aperture of television. Television, "the box," is today's "box in the world theater"—so often a theater of war. For Virilio, it is television that has definitively marked the end of perspectival space, the orderly concatenation of façades. He writes: "The blind alley disappears into the superimposed vision of a ... television that never turns off, that always gives and receives ... all surfaces and all the pieces of a tele-topological puzzle."[60] All the surfaces and all the pieces of the body form a complex puzzle we were once required to solve in order to become human. Like the elements of a building, the completed puzzle-picture holds together more or less provisionally: Here, cracks may run wild under a calm façade; there, they may shatter a transparent carapace; and other structures may endure only in mute and fearful isolation. Today, the autistic response of total withdrawal, and the schizophrenic anxiety of the body in pieces, belong to our psychocorporeal forms of identification with the teletopological puzzle of the city in pieces.

NOTES

1. Susan Buck-Morss, *The Dialectics of Seeing: Walter Benjamin and the Arcades Project,* Cambridge and London, MIT, 1989, p. 8.

2. Ibid., p. 11.

3. Benjamin submitted his completed dissertation in 1925 and was "advised to withdraw his petition ... rather than suffer the embarrassment of rejection." Ibid., p. 22.

4. In Walter Benjamin, *Reflections,* New York and London, Harcourt, 1978.

5. It lists seven items of advice—advice that I suspect is to this present day widely offered to graduate students. For example, the first item advises that "the whole composition must be permeated with a protracted and wordy exposition of the initial plan"; the final item

urges: "A number of opponents all sharing the same argument should each be refuted individually" (Walter Benjamin, "One Way Street," in *Reflections*, p. 79).

6. Asja Lacis, *Revolutionär im Beruf: Berichte über proletarisches Theater, über Meyerhold, Brecht, Benjamin und Piscator*, Munich, Regner & Bernhard, 1971, pp. 43–44; quoted in Buck-Morss, *The Dialectics of Seeing*, p. 15.

7. Walter Benjamin and Asja Lacis, "Naples," in *Reflections*, pp. 165–166.

8. Ibid., p. 167.

9. Ibid., p. 171. So, for example, "if the father of a family dies or the mother wastes away, close or distant relatives are not needed. A neighbour takes a child at her table for a shorter or longer period, and thus families interpenetrate in relationships that can resemble adoption" (p. 172).

10. We may, moreover, recall that the circle and the square are the diagrams of, respectively, the *orbis terrarum* and the *castrum*—the subject territories of the Roman Empire and the Roman military camp.

11. Françoise Choay, "La ville et le domaine bâti comme corps dans les textes des architectes-théoriciens de la première renaissance Italienne," *Nouvelle Revue de Psychanalyse*, no. 9, Spring, 1974.

12. Ibid., p. 248.

13. Ibid., p. 244.

14. Indeed, the Renaissance idea of the corporeal city included not only the external appearance of a body seen in Vitruvian terms of harmony of proportions but also the idea of the body as an ensemble of mutually dependent organs; albeit, Choay remarks, no part of the city is seen as equivalent to the genitals.

15. Henri Lefebvre, *The Production of Space*, Oxford and Cambridge (Mass.), Basil Blackwell, 1991, p. 271.

16. Alberti, *De Re Aedificatoria*, written about 1450 and published, after his death, in 1483.

17. Lefebvre, *The Production of Space*, p. 201.

18. Luce Irigaray, *Éthique de la différence sexuelle*, quoted in Margaret Whitford, *Luce Irigaray: Philosophy in the Feminine*, London and New York, Routledge, 1991, p. 53.

19. Lefebvre, *The Production of Space*, pp. 25–26.

20. Ibid.

21. Walter Benjamin, *Charles Baudelaire: A Lyric Poet in the Era of High Capitalism*, New York and London, NLB, 1978, p. 37. (This "essay" is actually part of Benjamin's larger, unfinished, Paris arcades project. At the time of its completion, in 1938, Benjamin intended that it should form part of a longer book about Baudelaire, which he planned to extract from his *Passagen-Werk*.)

22. It might be objected that Benjamin would not write about Haussmann until the *Passagen-Werk*, but Benjamin himself reminds us that for historians, as for psychoanalysts, what comes before may be determined by what comes after.

23. Richard Sennett, *The Conscience of the Eye: The Design and Social Life of Cities*, New York, Knopf, 1990, p. 104.

24. Benjamin saw the Paris arcades as "the mold from which the image of 'the modern' is cast."

25. Walter Benjamin, *Gesammelte Schriften*, Frankfurt am Main, Suhrkamp Verlag, 1972–, v. 5, p. 292, quoted in Buck-Morss, *The Dialectics of Seeing*, p. 303.

26. "How are we to imagine an existence oriented solely toward Boulevard Bonne-Nou-velle, in rooms by Le Corbusier and Oud?" Walter Benjamin, "Surrealism: The Last Snap-shot of the European Intelligentsia," in *Reflections*, p. 189.

27. Kenneth Frampton, *Modern Architecture: A Critical History*, London, Thames and Hudson, 1987, p. 155.

28. Lefebvre, *The Production of Space*, pp. 175–176.

29. Benjamin, *Reflections*, p. 154.

30. Beatriz Colomina, "Intimacy and Spectacle: The Interiors of Adolf Loos," *AA Files*, 20, 1990.

31. My thanks to Peter Wollen for suggesting this metaphor.

32. Lefebvre, *The Production of Space*, p. 93.

33. Jean-François Lyotard, *Économie Libidinale*, Paris, Éditions de Minuit, 1974, pp. 10–11.

34. That is, they retain it in the perspectival "prospect," which in the Renaissance be-came the dominant form of organization of urban space.

35. Lefebvre, *The Production of Space*, p. 99.

36. Ibid., p. 184.

37. Paul Schilder, "Psycho-Analysis of Space," *International Journal of Psychoanalysis*, v. 16, 1935.

38. Ibid., p. 295.

39. *The Standard Edition of the Complete Psychological Works of Sigmund Freud*, London, Hogarth, 1953–1974, v. 23, p. 300.

40. Paul Schilder, *The Image and Appearance of the Human Body*, New York, Interna-tional Universities Press, 1950.

41. Schilder, "Psycho-Analysis of Space," p. 295.

42. Schilder, *The Image and Appearance of the Human Body*, p. 172.

43. Frances Tustin, *Autism and Childhood Psychosis*, London, Science House, 1972, p. 106.

44. Octave Mannoni, "La Part du Jeu," *L'Arc*, no. 69 (special issue on Donald W. Winnicott).

45. Paul Thévenin and Jacques Derrida, *Antonin Artaud—Dessins et portraits*, Paris, Gallimard, 1986. My thanks to Lindsay Waters for having brought this essay to my atten-tion.

46. Ibid., p. 79.

47. Ibid., p. 63.

48. Ibid., p. 70.

49. Sigmund Freud, "Inhibitions, Symptoms and Anxiety" (1926), in *The Complete Psy-chological Works of Sigmund Freud*, v. 10, p. 137.

50. See Didier Anzieu, *The Skin Ego*, New Haven, Yale University Press, 1989.

51. Klaus Theweleit, *Male Fantasies*, Minneapolis, University of Minnesota Press, 1987, v. 1; 1989, v. 2.

52. Paul Virilio, *Lost Dimension*, New York, Semiotext(e), 1991, p. 79.

53. Octave Mannoni, "Je sais bien, mais quand même," in *Clefs pour l'imaginaire ou l'autre scène*, Paris, Seuil, 1969.

54. Victor Burgin, "Photography, Phantasy, Function," in Victor Burgin (ed.), *Thinking Photography*, London, Macmillan, 1982, pp. 190–191.

55. Laura Mulvey, "Visual Pleasure and Narrative Cinema," (1975), in *Visual and Other Pleasures,* London, Macmillan, 1989.

56. I am thinking of the type in which a Sternberg frames a Dietrich.

57. Virilio, *Lost Dimension,* pp. 69–70.

58. Benjamin, *Charles Baudelaire,* p. 132.

59. Walter Benjamin, "The Work of Art in the Age of Mechanical Reproduction," *Illuminations,* London, Fontana, 1973, p. 238.

60. Virilio, *Lost Dimension,* p. 71.

2

Slackspace:
The Politics of Waste

PATRICK DURKEE

N THIS ESSAY I theorize the social space inhabited by *slackers*. By "slacker," I mean the downwardly mobile, more or less college-educated, mostly white, middle-class people in their twenties who make it their business to hang around cities and college towns. At this moment, when the permanent wartime economy fails to support the massive middle class it created, slackers have a special relationship to the many kinds of waste produced by consumer capitalism. On the one hand, they are waste. As the leftovers of a fifty-year party of production and consumption, they are themselves the detritus of the culture of abundance. On the other, slackers make good use of the culture of waste that has been thrust upon them. By slacking off from the obligation to produce and consume, slackers interrupt the infiltration of social space by commodity culture. Piecing together styles of living, forms of community and personal identities, out of both the material and ideological waste of the postwar United States, the slacker's practice of ostentatiously doing very little illustrates the possibilities of resistance left to a culture in which the logic of the commodity relentlessly colonizes social space. Indeed, slackers are a paradigmatic example of such conditions because the social space they inhabit is largely the product of the postwar economic boom. Slackers manage to create a politics of waste; this sort of politics is, to a great extent, dependent upon the consumer culture that produces human, material, and ideological waste. The most insightful interpretation of the culture and politics of slack is Richard Linklater's 1990 film *Slacker*, which details the myriad ways in which slackers attempt to frustrate the commodification of everyday life in and around the neighborhood of the University of Texas at Austin. Through an explication of *Slacker*, as well as observations recorded during my own habitation of slackspace, I examine conspicuous consumption and its discontents, considering the possibilities as well as the limitations of resisting and rerouting the commodification of social space through slack.

"Conspiracy-a-Go-Go":
Cognitive Mapping and Symbolic Exchange in Slackspace

Slackers are themselves the human waste of consumer culture and do their best to remain such; the ideological waste of postwar culture also figures crucially in slackspace. Just as they continually piece together provisional social bonds around the last dregs of the largess of the society of abundance—that is, low-tuition, state-funded universities and the lazy college towns that go with them—so slackers represent the larger society around them through a bricolage of narratives and characters that bear at best only a peripheral significance to actual events. This tendency is exemplified in Linklater's film through the several characters who are Kennedy-assassination freaks, UFO nuts, and the like. Such fringe characters are, of course, naturally drawn to milieus such as slackspace where the instrumental function of knowledge is not valued particularly highly, but their fantastic attempts to make meaning of waste represent something more significant than simple fantasy: the attempt to produce from within slackspace a *cognitive map* of the world using only the waste materials at hand.

Paranoid narratives such as conspiracy theory can represent the impossibility of sufficiently conceptualizing real conditions. According to Fredric Jameson, "Conspiracy, one is tempted to say, is the poor person's cognitive mapping in the postmodern age; it is a degraded figure of the total logic of late capital, a desperate attempt to represent the latter's system, whose failure is marked by its slippage into sheer theme and content."[1] The assassination nut's obsession with who killed Kennedy certainly misses the big picture, but we may yet detect in such fancies an *allegorical* function. Though real conditions may be too complex and obscure to be properly representable, this "absent cause, one that can never emerge into the presence of perception ... can find figures through which to express itself in distorted and symbolic ways" (*CM*, 350).

To take an example from the film, when the character known simply as JFK Buff chatters excitedly about an episode in which Oswald "was supposed to go up the street, up Beckly Avenue—it was in Oak Cliff, you know—to go to the Steak and Egg Kitchen where he was supposed to meet with J.D. Tippet and have their 'breakfast of infamy,'"[2] his intense relationship with this worthless information expresses, in a distorted way, the utopian desire for authentic political agency. Conspiracy theory envisions a corrupt government manipulated by forces that are not conceivable within the framework of American liberal ideology. It is the negative expression of the need for meaningful political associations in a world in which it is impossible to imagine who is pulling the strings or what kind of politics might be appropriate to the mysterious atmosphere of multinational capital.

Moreover, the joy JFK Buff takes in "keeping up with my JFK assassination theories" (S, 71) indicates another crucial characteristic of the contemporary American political scene: the way in which politics function as spectacle. Whether we have in mind the Gulf War or the endless representations of the life and death of Kennedy, the first made-for-television president, JFK Buff's pleasure in consuming such representations points to the way in which spectacle substitutes for real participation in democratic activity. As he tells a friend how gratified he is to have "located this wonderful JFK memorial booklet: 'His Life, His Words, His Deeds'" and looks forward to completing his collection with "the Jackie Kennedy issue that's got those wonderful articles like 'How I Told the Children' and 'Why the Eternal Flame?'" (S, 71), JFK Buff's otherwise inexplicable enthusiasm expresses, in an allegorical fashion, the way in which the morbid spectacle of the Kennedy myth is offered to Americans in place of the social progress and justice the Kennedy era was supposed to promise.

Jameson argues that cultural production in the era of postmodernity must be read allegorically because the attempt to grasp "the absent global colonial system" results in "a situation in which we can say that if individual experience is authentic, then it cannot be true; and that if a scientific or cognitive model of the same content is true, then it escapes individual experience" (CM, 349). I have shown two examples of the way in which allegories of the true reside in individual experience. JFK Buff also illustrates exactly why individual experience cannot be *authentic* and *true* at the same time. His experience of a world of conspiracy is, indeed, authentic precisely because he has the paranoid's ability to foreclose any point of view or outside agency that threatens to disturb the smooth coherence of the narrative he imposes on the world. This facility is beautifully illustrated in the film by JFK Buff's tendency to assume everyone around him is as equally steeped in JFK lore as he himself is. To an acquaintance encountered in the conspiracy section of a bookstore, who has already protested, "I really don't know too much about this. ... I was kind of just flipping through," he speaks familiarly of obscure Kennedy assassination trivia such as "the testimony of Sam Holland, you know, the Prince of the Puff of Smoke" and "all the head-snap stuff" (S, 71–72). Thus, the very authenticity that JFK Buff's paranoia lends to his view of the world guarantees his alienation from others. This effect, of course, ensures not only that his experience cannot be "true" but also that it cannot be valuable to any kind of politics because, by definition, it cannot be shared with others. This instance of ideological bricolage demonstrates the limitations of cognitive mapping from the outposts of waste.

Whereas JFK Buff is a good example of the failure of one form of bricolage to provide the sort of imagination Jameson calls for in his essay, I wish to argue that, though slackspace may not produce forms of knowledge that are both authentic and true (in Jameson's global-historical sense), many kinds of resistances to commodity culture are staged there through networks of anticommodifying *symbolic exchange* created from the waste products of the consumer economy. Slackers assiduously avoid work and its pretext, conspicuous consumption; they make the odd material and ideological artifacts of the world of production and consumption that drift into their space the occasion for forms of community that are played out over and above the logic of commodity exchange.[3] A paradigmatic example of this technique from *Slacker* is a scene in which two motorheads identified in the script as GTO and Nova discuss their modifications to their 1960s-era muscle cars:

> GTO: So you put that 383 bore kit back in here, huh?
> NOVA: Yeah, I got the pop-up pistons, got the block bored over 30, 400
>   crankshaft, 400 harmonic balancer … it's practically a big block now.
> GTO: You mill the heads?
> NOVA: No, didn't mill the heads.
> GTO: Stock manifolds, though … (*S*, 75–76)

The specialized nature of the knowledge traded by these two customizers is similar to that of JFK Buff's; the crucial difference is that their transformations of old Chevrolets, at once the most material and the most typical waste product of postwar America, produce a sense of community and a basis for symbolic exchange between them. Such relations resist the logic of commodity exchange because the arcane knowledge circulated among initiates of a subculture such as car customizing is simply nonexchangable: although it may *circulate* among those in the know, it may not be *exchanged* in the manner of commodities because it emerges strictly from the combination of individual expertise, particular moments of automotive bricolage, and the willingness of one gearhead to share with another the mysteries of the craft. That the emergence of community from the manipulation of America's junk is the meaning of symbolic exchange in slackspace is illustrated as GTO and Nova continue their day picking over dead cars at the junkyard.

"I May Live Badly, But at Least I Don't Have to Work to Do It": Putting the Slack in Space

The previous example shows how forms of anticommodifying social relations may arise from waste, but the phenomenon of waste itself is not, of course, hostile to capitalism. Indeed, the production of waste is one essential function of the consumer economy. Therefore, slackers carefully reformulate the significance of waste in order to avoid being reintroduced into consumer culture. A more detailed understanding of the slacker's relation to waste begins with Thorstein Veblen's history of *conspicuous consumption*.[4] According to Veblen, waste first emerges in the Western world as the *leisure* affected by the aristocratic class in precapitalist society. Hence, a "standard of decency" (*TLC*, 92) is created and maintained by the gentleman's conspicuous abstention from work. The conspicuous consumption of goods replaces leisure as the preferred method of waste as social distinction in the transition to the modern era, in which "the means of communication and the mobility of the population now expose the individual to the observation of many persons who have no other means of judging of his reputability than the display of goods ... which he is able to make while he is under their direct observation" (*TLC*, 86). Hence, for Veblen, consumption is a symbolic form of leisure: "The utility of both alike (conspicuous consumption and leisure) for the purposes of reputability lies in the element of waste that is common to both. In the one case it is a waste of time and effort, in the other it is a waste of goods. ... The choice between them is a question of advertising expediency simply" (*TLC*, 85).

Veblen's vision of leisure transformed into consumption presents a version of the "democratization of luxury" in which rising standards of living and ready access to goods produced by a capitalist economy present the opportunity for unprecedented numbers of people to take part in the pleasure and distinction of leisure as commodity consumption. Accordingly, Veblen's critique of commodity culture falls in the area of elucidating the social inequity inherent in consumer culture: The social stratification that produces leisure, once plainly present in the form of a shamelessly idle leisure class, is now obscured by luxury's apparent democratization.

Veblen's critique of capitalism is important for an analysis of slackspace because he affirms that waste is an essential component of capitalist production. Indeed, for Veblen, it is the desire to attain the social distinction of waste that guarantees the middle class's enthusiastic participation in the economy: "It is by no means an uncommon spectacle to find a man applying himself to work with the utmost assiduity, in order that his wife may in due form render for him that degree of vicarious leisure which the common sense of the time demands" (*TLC*, 81). There is, however, another chapter in the history of leisure that informs the dynamics of slack in late capitalism. In the contemporary United States, the previously described separation between categories such as work and leisure, production and consumption, is far from clear. Veblen anticipated the way in which consumption itself may be considered work because it fuels the economy; later critics of mass society such as Max Horkheimer, Theodor Adorno, and Guy Debord theorize much more extensively the affinities between work and leisure in the full-blown consumer economy. It is when consumption is technologized, they argue, that leisure becomes structured with the rationalized and dispiriting character belonging to factory work. When leisure is converted to *entertainment* and the conspicuous squandering of goods is converted to the consumption of *spectacle,* the space of leisure (nonwork) is colonized by the logic of work. Leisure is no longer an activity that provides a social space over and above work, but rather leisure simply reproduces work in the form of "fun." If consumption is production, then leisure is work.[5]

Michel de Certeau formulates the problem of resistance to such administered leisure as one of *space*. He affirms that, indeed, the proliferation of "cultural techniques that camouflage economic reproduction" means that there is no longer any social space that is not structured by the logic of consumption and production: "Cut loose from the traditional communities that circumscribed their functioning, (consumers) have begun to wander everywhere in a space which is becoming at once more homogeneous and more extensive. Consumers are transformed into immigrants. The system in which they move about is too vast to be able to fix them in one place, but too constraining for them ever to be able to escape from it and go into exile elsewhere. There is no longer an elsewhere."[6] For de Certeau, resistance in this atmosphere in which escape is not possible takes the form of "tactics" (*PEL*, 34), a style of inhabiting social space that deforms and obstructs the commodifying tendency of its structure. Such styles are the tactics of slack. The way in which slack deforms the administered leisure of social space is exemplified in *Slacker* by the following exchange:

> VIDEO INTERVIEWER: So, did you vote in the most recent election?
> HITCHIKER: Hell no. ... I've got less important things to do.
> VIDEO INTERVIEWER: What do you do to earn a living?
> HITCHIKER: You mean work? To Hell with the kind of work you have to do to earn a living. All that does is fill the bellies of the pigs that exploit us. Hey, look at me. ... I'm making it. I may live badly, but at least I don't have to work to do it. (*S*, 79)

Hitchiker not only refuses the obligation to produce and consume, but by contentedly declaring that he "lives badly," he disavows the consumer economy's most powerful strategy of all, the injunction to have a *lifestyle*. Veblen defined leisure as a conspicuous abstention from work; Hitchiker knows that in the atmosphere of late capital, the only respite from work is *slack*, the conspicuous abstention from leisure. Hence, Hitchiker's refusal to vote represents the way in which slackers decline to take part in "cultural techniques that camouflage economic reproduction" (*PEL*, 40). The tactical evasion of identities that play into the logic of production and consumption, the slacker's mode of what de Certeau calls "making do," causes a loosening in social space. The commodifying structure of social space is deformed as the slacker's conspicuous abstention from work and leisure causes it to go slack.

"Housecooling": The Dangers of Slack

The tactics of slack sabotage social space in order to salvage authentic waste from the domain of leisure; this form of making do poses a problem for the creation of symbolic exchange. The difficulty is that the cool and lackluster stance required for an effective resistance to work and leisure bleeds into the slacker's cathexis of positive communal relations assembled from the transfigured waste of slackspace. The current practice of "housecooling"[7] illustrates this dynamic. Simply the opposite of housewarming, housecooling is done when it is time to move out. De Certeau notes that since *tactics* must always operate by short-circuiting the given structure of social space rather than staking out a space of their own, such resistance, "operates in isolated actions, blow by blow. It takes advantage of 'opportunities' and depends on them, being without any base where it could stockpile its winnings" (*PEL,* 37). The notion that a house must be properly cooled before it can be vacated is a recognition that sites of community and meaning are always provisional in the space transformed by tactics: The warmth produced by social bonds is neither something that can endure for long where it emerges nor something that a house's inhabitants will carry with them in the future. Infusing social space with slack means that the forms of community created in the process are bound for rapid dissolution.

The phenomenon of associations rapidly forming and dissolving in the form of a house full of roommates is due in large measure, of course, simply to the fact that young people without steady jobs are highly mobile. But the interruption of communal bonds among slackers is directly linked to the practice of studied laziness required by an abstention from leisure. This problem is demonstrated by a scene from *Slacker* in which a group of roommates in a co-op house puzzle over a roommate who has disappeared without warning, leaving only a cryptic, autobiographical story written on a series of postcards. The narrative reads, in part, "He rents a room in a large house and rarely sees the people he lives with. One is called Frank something and he thinks there are some more, but he can't be sure. ... Last summer he thought about sticking his index finger in a fan. Someone told him his fingerprints are unique, but he believes there's too much direct evidence against uniqueness. He thinks the differences are minor compared to the similarities. All of his days are about the same: He wakes up at eleven or twelve, eats cereal or toast, reads the newspaper, looks out the front door, takes a walk" (*S,* 51–52). By rejecting the notion of uniqueness, this departed roommate resists the ideology of lifestyle and the attendant injunction to consume one. Like Hitchiker, he creates slack in the social space he inhabits by not bothering to "get a life." But the sense of anonymity produced by this tactic erodes the departed roommate's sense of connection to others, whose singular identities, signified by their names, he cannot recall. Hence, the style of living that resists commodification also undermines sociality. The coolness that frustrates the imposition of reified consumerist identities in turn produces a different sort of anomie: One can slack off so much that he or she falls outside the networks of anticommodifying community (such as cooperative living arrangements) created in slackspace. This continual drift between assembling and dismantling communal associations structures slackspace with what may be called a *dialectic of tightening and slackening.*[8] Tightening-up on sites of symbolic exchange, community, and meaning always entails slacking-down into the dissolution of such sites.

"Let's Put Squeaky Fromme on the One-Dollar Bill": How "Political" Is Slack?

The dialectic of tightening and slackening illustrates the limits of the political uses of slack. If the basis of slack is primarily the negation of the obligation to produce and consume, then slack is always itself produced by the consumer economy. Although slack powerfully rearranges the social space produced by this system, it still always remains part and parcel of late capitalism. Therefore, although slacking off may produce endless local instances of noncommodified social relations, it cannot envision modes of association that truly challenge the economic structures that produce slackspace as their waste.

The limits set to the social imagination of slack in this way are exemplified in *Slacker* by the character Old Anarchist. Of all the characters in the film, Old Anarchist has the most cohesive political vision. He affirms the broad political significance of slackspace's superlocalized forms of resistance by eulogizing Leon Czolgosz, the assassin of William McKinley: "He was an unknown Polish emigre who happened to be an anarchist of the 'propaganda by the deed' variety. If there were a hundred like him around today, they could change the world" (*S*, 84). Yet this vision of multiple eruptions of political sabotage bringing down the government is undercut by Old Anarchist's sense of how such political action might unfold in his own social space: He enthusiastically explains to an acquaintance his plan to "pull ... a 'Guy Fawkes' on the Texas Legislature—just blow the damn thing sky-high." He complains that "Texas is so full of all these so-called modern-day Libertarians with all their goddamn selfish individualism. Just the opposite of real anarchism—they don't give a damn about improving the world. But now Charles Whitman ... there was a man" (*S*, 85). Not bothering to distinguish between Leon Czolgosz, a political activist motivated by the doctrine of "belief put into action" (*S*, 84), and Charles Whitman, an insane gunman of the disgruntled postal worker variety, Old Anarchist shows how a politics that affirms any and all deformations of administered social space fails to produce a vision that reaches beyond random instances of rebellion.

To conclude, the advantages and disadvantages of slack for politics may be weighed by considering the presence of marginal figures such as Whitman in Linklater's film. The possibilities and the limits of fashioning a politics of waste are enacted by characters who, throughout the film, attach the greatest historical importance to strange and obscure personalities. This tendency is demonstrated by one lighthearted conspiracy theorist who responds to the suggestion that American history is controlled by a Freemason conspiracy (including "the Warren Commission ... a Shriner's convention without go-carts") by declaring, "Exactly ... the slate of American history needs to be wiped clean ... let's put Squeaky Fromme on the one-dollar bill. At least we ought to get that Masonic pyramid bullshit off the back" (*S*, 109). Fromme is a perfect emblem for the political dynamic of slack because her famous moment of political intervention is at once utterly nonsensical and heavily fraught with meaning. Her attempt at "propaganda by the deed" exhibits the limits of slack precisely through its ephemerality. Just as it was only seconds before Squeaky went down in a pile of Secret Service agents, so the deformation of social space she created disappeared as soon as she achieved it. Squeaky is the archetypal flaky teenager driven insane by the alienating conditions of Southern California's consumer wasteland; her quixotic political gesture typifies the way in which the resistance offered by slackspace, itself made possible by the system of production and consumption, is not ultimately dangerous to that system. Nevertheless, the figure of Squeaky, along with Johnny Ace, Jack Ruby, and others, provides the occasion for symbolic exchange in slackspace through the circulation of their parahistories among those in the know. The elevation of Lynette "Squeaky" Fromme in the slack imagination embodies the politics of waste.

NOTES

1. Fredric Jameson, "Cognitive Mapping," in *Marxism and the Interpretation of Culture*, Laurence Grossberg and Cary Nelson, eds. (Urbana: University of Illinois Press, 1988), p. 356; hereafter cited in the text as *CM*.

2. Richard Linklater, *Slacker* (New York: St. Martin's Press, 1992), p.72; hereafter cited in the text as *S*.

3. My sense of "symbolic exchange" is a fairly broad one. I define the term as simply any moment in which a sense of unique community and meaning is produced through the exchange of specialized knowledge, know-how, or ritual. The idea that the circulation of such "symbolic capital" resists the principle of exchange, which is the core of the commodity form, I derive from Jean Baudrillard's essay "For a Critique of the Political Economy of the Sign," condensed in *Jean Baudrillard: Selected Writings*, Mark Poster, ed. (Stanford: Stanford University Press, 1988).

4. Thorstein Veblen, *Theory of the Leisure Class* (New York: Penguin, 1979); hereafter cited in the text as *TLC*.

5. The way leisure is converted to work in the contemporary First World "information society" is described in Max Horkheimer and Theodor W. Adorno's "The Culture Industry: Enlightenment as Mass Deception," in *The Dialectic of Enlightenment*, John Cumming, trans. (New York: Continuum, 1969); and Guy Debord's *Society of the Spectacle* (Detroit: Black and Red, 1983).

6. Michel de Certeau, *The Practice of Everyday Life*, Steven Randall, trans. (Berkeley: University of California Press, 1984), p. 40; hereafter cited in the text as *PEL*.

7. The practice of "housecooling" is something I have observed firsthand.

8. This phrase was suggested by Gabriel Brahm during a series of conversations on slack in which many of the ideas discussed in this essay were conceived collectively.

3

Under Western Eyes:
The Media in the Gulf War

MAHMUT MUTMAN

Middle Easterners get much of their information through their senses of smell and touch, which require a close approach; Americans rely primarily on visual information, backing up in order to see an intelligent picture.

—*San Francisco Chronicle,* January 13, 1991

Now dark with shadows, now beaming forth an excess of light as it waits to be disposed in new landscapes. In hollow, in lack or excess, man would perceive and receive nothing except from his own eye.

—Luce Irigaray, *Marine Lover,* 1991

THE CRISIS IN the Gulf once again demonstrated the strong association between *Western* interests and *world* peace. The U.S. invasion of Panama received the same legal response and official condemnation from the United Nations as did Iraq's occupation of Kuwait. However, the former action incurred remarkably little public criticism. Perhaps this is why very few people are actually familiar with the U.N. resolutions in the case of Panama. On December 23, 1989, just eight months before the official U.N. condemnation of Iraq, which was passionately supported by the U.S., the same U.S. government vetoed a U.N. Security Council resolution condemning the invasion of Panama. Six days later, on December 29, the U.N. General Assembly issued another resolution demanding the withdrawal of the "U.S. armed invasion forces from Panama" and calling the invasion a "flagrant violation of international law and of the independence, sovereignty and territorial integrity of states."[1] However, in the domain of what is called the international public sphere, nobody has accused the United States of "nefarious aggression," "monstrosity," or "blood thirstiness,"[2] those signifiers of an imperial, primitive, despotic, and therefore by definition illegitimate and irrational desire to eat up small and defenseless countries. On the contrary, the media and the respectable public seemed to unanimously agree that the United States is the only power capable of enforcing international law against such aggression. The war's legitimacy was a case of severe amnesia.

My aim in this essay is to examine some of the significations, discourses, and images in the media during the war in 1991: the "legitimation process," as it is called in the sociological literature. By the notion of legitimacy, I understand something more (and something different) than a relationship of consent between the ruler and the ruled. Although what I am going to say necessarily addresses the question of popular consent to a certain extent, by "legitimation" I understand the way that a position is constructed as legitimate by the subject who takes such a position, hence the very process of the *production* of the subject itself. What I hope to do is bring a set of uneven and separate historical, political, and economic fragments together so that we will be able to see the Gulf War in a different way. First, I want to refer to orientalism as a condition of the discourse of war. Second, I will refer to the economic and historical roots of crisis in the Middle East and the new situation imposed by the global conjuncture. Third, I will talk about the figure of woman in the war. I will then examine the figure of Saddam Hussein, and finally I will attempt to show that Saddam Hussein's "face" can be seen as the constitutive metaphor of the war.

Orientalism

The association between Western interests and world peace demonstrated that the "world" is not just a place where we happen to be, or a just place, but it is a world that is already *worlded* by power, already coded into the grand narrative of the West. The worlding of the East, and the Middle East in particular, was studied by Edward Said in his monumental work *Orientalism*.[3] By criticizing a narrow reading of orientalism as simply consisting of orientalist books, Said's argument referred to a larger *text*, a *relational web* in which the necessarily forgotten discourse of orientalism was placed. He called attention to all those institutions (not only universities and research institutes but also colonial institutions, media, the economy) to which orientalism essentially contributed, and to texts (geography, history, sociology, literature) that it made possible by writing itself on their margins. In Said's definition, orientalism is not simply a name for an academic field or a system of ideas but a historically specific *discursive move* that makes "an epistemological and ontological distinction between the West and East."[4] Orientalism is thus the production of the text or inscription of places and directions, a "worlding" in Gayatri Spivak's words.[5]

Orientalism is hegemonic not simply because it is a dominant idea consented to by people but because it is a *signifying force* that is multiplied and reproduced in different texts and contexts to such a degree that it is not even recognizable as a separate entity; it is *elaborated* in the Gramscian sense and diffused in the culture at large. Elaboration means that the marking of the Orient as Other occurs on multiple levels (academic, political, epistemological, literary, cultural, popular, moral) and that its continuity is not simply a totalization but a continuity that is possible only through discontinuity and dissimulation. Orientalism does not bring different discursive spheres and modes together, it dissimulates itself, changes and transforms itself through them. It thus disappears into the culture at large, and its name is forgotten there. This is why, whatever methodological differences there are between Said and Foucault, Said's work appears as truly archaeological in Foucault's sense, for it discovers an "Orientalist layer" in the history of *production* of the Western subject, or "man," the subject of humanism. If several different places are homogenized under the sign of the Orient, such a homogenization does not inscribe the Orient only; this inscription *centers* the West as the privileged or dominant pole of an epistemological and ontological opposition. This is exactly how orientalist discourse is related to the Western *hegemonic investment* and the colonial/imperial *apparatus of power* that embodies it. The West constitutes itself as universal and sovereign subject by marking the different as Other and by thus *dissimulating* its forceful appropriation of peoples, lands, and resources. Such a dissimulation is the symbolic violence of orientalism as knowledge or truth of the Orient.

The first quotation with which I opened this article is a banal, everyday, media version of the epistemological and ontological distinction between the West and East, or *the centering of the Western self* (the one who backs up in order to have an "intelligible picture," a "horizon"). What is important is the speed with which such stereotypes came to surface during the war. The reason we have to go back to Said's analysis in the face of such a blatant instance of racism is precisely to see that it is not as banal as it may seem. Such a banality will always be denied and fixed by the epistemological and ontological measures of the *larger* imperial and humanist project of coding and decoding cultures and knowing, understanding, and liberating others. This is the true meaning of Gramsci's notion of *elaboration*. To give another banal example, although we now criticize a discourse called orientalism in an emergent discipline or field called "cultural studies," we tend to forget that those whom we criticize (media, politicians, writers, other academics like ourselves, etc.) do not even, or no longer, use the word "Orient."[6] This is because the "world" is already coded into the grand narrative of the West. This is the *factual result* of orientalism that the United Nations *empirically demonstrated* in practice by legally sanctioning a violator to act as the law enforcer against another violator. If so, however, our task is *not simply* to show how the media images of the Middle East during the Gulf War were continuous with orientalist and colonial stereotypes but also to show how this continuity itself is always discontinuous, how orientalism's continuity depends on the forgetting of a fundamental act of division and violation that repeats itself in this very forgetting.

Crisis

The energy question is never seen as an issue in international trade but rather as a question of *national security* in the United States and Europe. In this context, Simon Bromley defines oil as a "strategic commodity."[7] James O'Connor explains in detail how essential oil is for the contemporary capitalist economy. It is important for the production of capital, value and surplus value, and the circulation of capital in general. In his words, there is "no capitalism without oil."[8] How did oil come into this important place that it occupies in capitalist world economy today? I would like to stress here the historical connection between decolonization and oil.

Although oil was discovered in the United States during the early nineteenth century and the demand took off in the early twentieth century, it gained its real politico-economic significance in the postwar world. Using Deleuze and Guattari's terminology, we might say that the new postwar hegemonic project led by the United States corresponded to a new phase of *deterritorialization* in the development of capitalism.[9] Decolonization was expected to lead to a system of independent nation-states held together by the abstract unity of the world market. Removal of the European political zones would displace the politically sanctioned, closed economic circuits and would open these regions to penetration by internationally mobile productive capital. Of course, an essential element of the project was the transnationalization of U.S. capital. The breakup of old "territorial" political units and the reproduction on an enlarged scale of the economic space of oligopolistic competition would lead to an expansion of the scope of the world market.[10] The program of classical, "territorial" imperialism depended on a modern overcoding of (Foucaultian) disciplines according to principles of ancient imperial regime—those "neoarchaisms" of modern Europe from Bonaparte to the United *Kingdom*. In the new hegemonic project led by the United States, however, the exercise of national self-determination was necessary in order to enter into the abstract design of a global market order.[11] The regulation of the world market would be achieved through the international hegemony of the dollar, trade liberalization, and U.S. control over international oil. This last point, the necessity to control oil, already demonstrates that this new abstraction or deterritorialization would not be achieved without some significant degree of reterritorialization (another series of neoarchaisms). Indeed, the political and ideological aspects of the new model were the military unity of the capitalist world (NATO) vis-à-vis the Eastern bloc and a strong anti-Communist discourse. To be sure, decolonization was not created by the new hegemonic project. On the contrary, there would be no decolonization without the resistance struggles of the peoples of the colonized countries and the national liberation movements that they established. The defeat of the fascist-imperialist project was another important factor. But it is important to stress that the process of decolonization did not occur outside the new hegemonic project that aimed to capture and articulate it.

Within the framework of this new hegemonic model, oil played a crucial role. It became a "strategic commodity" with the Truman Doctrine–Marshall Plan, which embodied the project.[12] Middle Eastern oil was controlled by U.S. transnational capital in the form of major oil companies (called "majors" in the literature of political economy). As the Cold War made intercapitalist unity vis-à-vis communism necessary, there was also the urgent need to reconstruct postwar Europe. Western Europe and Japan became strategically and economically dependent on the United States. Low-cost oil supplied to Europe and Japan by the "majors" was central to the postwar capitalist boom. The restructuring of industry in Europe and Japan required a massive influx of oil.

The rise of a radical Arab nationalism and the foundation of the state of Israel complicated the U.S. hegemonic project, but they did not change its basic outlines. The U.S. managed to fight against Arab radical nationalism on the one hand and control Middle Eastern oil on the other. In this, the so-called twin-pillar policy played a key role. Instead of a direct military presence, close alliances with two Muslim countries, Saudi Arabia in the peninsula and Iran in the Gulf (in addition to the other two allies, Israel and Turkey), helped the United States to exercise considerable power and control in the region. Iran and Saudi Arabia thus became dependent on U.S. military power.[13] With the withdrawal of Britain from the emirates, these newly independent small countries too would become dependent on the United States.

This postwar hegemonic system in the region continued without major interruption until the 1973–1974 oil crisis. The oil crisis came as a reaction by producer states against the unilateral reduction of "posted," or tax-reference, prices of crude oil by metropolitan countries.[14] The resolution of the crisis meant a reunification of the world market and a consolidation of the nation-state system. But it also meant some loss of control for the United States. As Edward Said shows, this new politico-economic situation imposed its own cultural rule in the form of bringing the *image* of Islam into the American media, whereas before "one saw and heard of Arabs and Iranians, Pakistanis and Turks, rarely of Muslims."[15] The political culture of the Western world experienced an intensified return of the orientalist themes of old territorial imperialism, and once more, Islam became one of those major Oriental figures by which the Westerners, especially Americans, defined themselves: The new enemy Other was seen as inversely equal and opposite to "us"; order was opposed to chaos, civilization to backwardness, dynamism and democracy to despotism and stagnation. The Islamic revolution in Iran and a radical religious-political discourse that emerged out of the double crisis of Arab nationalism and socialism made this opposition even more rigid. The postcrisis conjuncture was thus characterized by an entirely new structuration of the relations between the United States and the Middle East. The Gulf states gained a further political significance, for the U.S. hegemonic role "came to depend on the connections established to the Gulf producers and especially to Saudi Arabia."[16] Any threat to the integrity of Gulf states is regarded as a direct challenge to the United States. In the present conjuncture created by the collapse of Stalinist regimes in Eastern Europe, the United States managed to use this hegemonic connection to its (at least provisional) advantage. The urgent need to reaffirm its own leadership position was now maintained by a unilateral control of oil supply, which was guaranteed with the victory.[17]

After a detailed discussion of two different theories of war—the economic theory, which emphasizes the importance of the control of Gulf oil and oil revenues,[18] and the political theory, which stresses the exigencies of the Middle East and the imperatives of the national security state—O'Connor reaches the following conclusion: "Oil and U.S. power, the nature of the economy and U.S. foreign policy, are at stake, as is the leading role of the military industrial complex. Oil can now be seen as the means to economic and imperialistic ends. Politics, the Pentagon and military-industrial complex, and the banking system are in their own ways means to the end of oil. Threaten oil and you threaten the national security state and U.S. 'credibility.' Threaten the Pentagon and the military-industrial complex and you threaten oil. Economics and politics thus collapse into an *almost impenetrable black hole*" (emphasis added).[19]

In what follows I will read this "almost impenetrable black hole" as a metaphor for the crisis of the Western subject whose *subject* position is constructed by practices such as orientalism. I am referring to the sovereign and supreme white male seen on TV every day during the Gulf crisis, always firm, always in control: President Bush, Mr. Baker, Dan Rather. (I should nevertheless specify that I am not referring to the male subject only. As my following argument makes clear, there are subject positions available for both male and female Western subjects in the discourse of the war.) The system of subject formation that I will discuss here can be described as one that *produces* "black holes." The Gulf crisis itself can be considered as a metaphor of this system of subject formation: The Gulf is the trouble spot in metropolitan society's everyday life that Edward Said mentions. I will now examine a set of images and representations and then make an overall evaluation in which I want to show the media's strategic function.

Difference: Woman

In this section, I want to focus on the representation of Arab woman in the war. I approach this representation within a problematic of sexual difference, which is, as a problematic of difference, always in articulation with other codes and systems of difference (economic, political, cultural, ethnic, etc.).

Abouali Farmanfarmaian develops a comprehensive analysis of the U.S. national fantasy in the Gulf War.[20] Farmanfarmaian's account of the articulation of sexual, racial, and cultural difference is an important contribution to the more mainstream social scientific accounts of the *crisis* of the national security state, for it offers a historical and analytic explanation of what the national security state might look like on the level of the *unconscious* inscription of its subject position. I will take his analysis as a starting point for my own. According to Farman-farmaian, by means of the fantasy machine that was built around the stories of rape, looting, infanticide, and torture of Kuwaitis by Iraqis and by means of the metaphor of the "rape of Kuwait" and the definition of the Middle East as a "culture of rape," and so on, the white male soldier tries to escape his castration. But the paradoxical result of his sexualization of the world is indeed castration.[21] For Farmanfarmaian, this fantasy machine is rooted in the mythical narrative of the "black rapist vs. white woman." In other words, the war was fought for the white woman against the black rapist. Farmanfarmaian stresses the fluidity of the military and racist consciousness for whom Saddam Hussein and Rodney King are the same.[22] Although I agree with his analysis in its general lines, I have two important reservations that might change the character of his psychoanalytic account.

The first one has to do with the equivalence of Saddam Hussein and Rodney King. Such an equivalence is clearly readable in the discourse of the police officers Farmanfarmaian quotes. In order to prevent an overinvestment in the very economy of sameness that we criticize, it seems important to me to note that the Arab, the African American, and the African are the same from the perspective of the castrating and castrated white male colonizer. The acknowledgment of the fictional nature of this sameness is not necessarily a fall into a theory of false consciousness but is an awareness of the multiple articulations of otherness and difference and of the complexity of the economy of sameness. In war against a Third World dictatorship, Rodney King can well be an alibi.[23]

Second, it also seems that the place of the native woman remains rather limited in Farmanfarmaian's narrative. He describes woman's role in the early imperialist (colonial) economy: The white woman constituted the *ideal* of womanhood and the native woman was assigned the chores. However, it is not clear why one should take the early colonial narrative as the model for the recent war. Not only does Farmanfarmaian's account seem to depend on a mythical narrative of origins, but also, the hegemonic system might be much more intricately established. The hegemonic system does not simply deny the value of the oppressed but rather assumes value in order to be able to extract it from her.[24] Farmanfarmaian chooses to focus on the myth of white woman–black rapist instead of focusing on what he himself describes, in the context of the sexualization of the colonized, as "the continued and consistent assault on black women by *constructing* them as promiscuous initiators of any sexual act."[25] This choice is interesting especially if we think that in the same context he refers to Malek Alloula's study of the *Algerian* postcards sent by the French soldiers.[26] Alloula's study shows not only *Algerian woman's* construction as the "promiscuous initiator of any sexual act" (the assumption of an excess sexuality necessary to extract affective value) but also, and much more important in the context of a war in the *Middle East,* the strange association between *the veil and the European male's sexual fantasies.* Alloula's work provides a more convenient model to think about the recent war's discourse, fantasy, and imagery in terms of sexuality. Indeed, Fanon had already pointed to the significance of the veil in the context of French colonization in Algeria: Conquering Algeria was identical to conquering its woman, unveiling her.[27] In this sense, Farmanfarmaian's account becomes really an account of an American myth *in America* rather than in the neocolonial context. If, as Farmanfarmaian suggests, Saddam Hussein was unconsciously seen as identical to a black rapist, the one who is protected or liberated was the *other woman.* Indeed, this war might offer us the possibility of questioning the complexity of the system of patriarchy—a system that constitutes woman as the site of an ambiguity and undecidability whose complex inscription always requires the *other* woman.

Such an identification in the context of the recent war might be important because, within the textual problematic of orientalism, the United States occupies a "strategic location" in Said's sense: "an author-position in a text with regard to the Oriental material he writes about."[28] The U.S. government and media can also be seen as authors writing the text of their own intervention. When the Muslim woman is identified as the object of a strategy,[29] there is the opportunity to construct a language of liberation, progressive influence, and so on. I am drawing attention to this language not simply because it is obviously politically profitable but because such political profit is even more complex than it seems. For instance, the strategic choice of Muslim woman probably gives the middle-class *Western women* a sense of being liberated and a feeling of obvious superiority compared to the women in the hands of those despotic Orientals. The Western self that orientalism constructs is man, but in the larger and complex hegemonic project, Western woman has a role to play because what is at stake in this project of subject formation is also the construction of her "self."[30] The Muslim woman was one of the strategic "signs" that was "worth marking" during the crisis. "Islam," too, was mediated through her. The war would not have been as legitimate as it was without her embodiment of the metaphor of oppression. This is why we cannot understand the American project with models based on the early colonial period or the context of Nazi discourse.[31]

During the period of crisis, we have heard, watched, and read numerous accounts of the situation of women in Muslim and Arab countries. Her rights and well-being were taken as the *measure* of the backwardness of Islamic or Arabic culture. And we saw almost every day the image of a veiled woman. These images were mobilized by a neoorientalist discourse, always accompanied by a fixed story line that transformed American presence into a progressive mission in a foreign and backward land of Oriental despots. The veil was a constant obsession and a proof of the darkness and backwardness of culture. A report from *Time* magazine is a typical example:

> The modernization and enrichment of Saudi life produced by the oil-price boom of the 70s and 80s may one day look like a mere twitch compared with the convulsions to come. ... Ripping the veil off their closely shrouded ties with the U.S., the Saudis offered their territory as the base for the greatest concentration of American troops since the Vietnam war. A land that forbids women *to drive, to travel unaccompanied, to wear Western garb or to expose anything more than a scant flash of eyes and cheekbones* is now host to thousands of rifle-toting, jeep-driving female G.I.s clad in fatigues.[32] (Emphasis added.)

If oil is a *strategic commodity* of global capitalism, the Muslim woman, as the measure of "progress" and "democracy," emerges as the *strategic target-subject* of the neoorientalist discourse of the new world order. A political value is extracted from the representation of her (strategically useful) identity as oppressed/woman.[33] Donna Pryzbylowicz and Abdul JanMohamed referred to a moral surplus gained in the recent war that overcame the moral deficit produced by the unsuccessful Vietnam War.[34] To this, we may add political and even future economic surpluses. The Muslim woman stands where the political, the economic, and the cultural "values" meet: Her culturally specific embodiment is the commodity that is exchanged with other commodities. During the war, these (mostly middle-class) Saudi women were constructed as ready at any moment for "liberation," as we see in a photo in *Time* magazine: Two veiled, dark silhouettes hold colorful Benetton shirts in their hands, already burning with desire to consume, to *have* "looks." (Let me add that I do not mean that these woman are not oppressed by the feudal and semifeudal structures of Saudi Arabian society—a feudalism that is reinforced and reproduced by the place of Saudi Arabia in the global capitalist division of labor. Surely, we also read stories of street demonstrations by Saudi women. I simply draw attention to the fact that their struggle is captured and articulated by a specific project—hence the complexity of such struggles.)

In Figure 3.1 we find the same strategic opposition (veiled vs. liberated) in the contrast between the sunny background of a marketplace and the woman's veiled dark silhouette; this is a scene that is inscribed as "natural" (in other words, inscribed as "uninscribed") in photographic space.[35] This is the space, we should remember once again, in which one "backs up in order to see an intelligent picture." If the quote from the *San Francisco Chronicle* that begins this chapter is a condensed, packaged, consumable *elaboration* of the grand narrative of evolution, this picture manifests its *black hole*. In the postcards Alloula studied, the relationship with the Algerian woman was romanticized, eroticized, and sexualized; she was constructed as "licentious other," belonging to an Other space where she was imprisoned by the Oriental despot. But she was, or would be, accessible and would be appropriated once that space was liberated/colonized. In these post-

FIGURE 3.1

cards, she was unveiled, often half-naked.[36] During the war, however, there was a strong emphasis on the *darkness of the veil.* The veiled woman in the picture with her dark, faceless presence and her hood is an embodiment of death. How to read the desire for this picture?

"Saddam"

Now I want to examine a series of images that are all Saddam Hussein faces in close-up (Figures 3.2, 3.3, 3.4, 3.5). We know the significance of Hussein's face from the war rhetoric; it is *the face that should not be saved.* And now we understand why: As we see in these pictures, *Saddam's face has to be veiled.* We can read these pictures as a demonstration of the structural role that sexual difference plays in the signification of cultural difference. The formula of fetishism is applicable here. Freud defined fetishism as a mechanism of "disavowal," that is, the displaced persistence of a belief despite the contrary perception.[37] "We know that he is not a woman, but nevertheless ..." The tabloid story is always consumed as just a story (Ella Shohat writes): "The cover of a *National Examiner* (March 12) featured 'Saddam Hussein's Bizarre Sex Life: A Recent CIA Report Reveals' with an image of *Hussein the crossdresser in a mini skirt.*"[38] With Saddam Hussein, we have not left

FIGURE 3.2

woman. Indeed, it would not be an exaggeration to say that *during the war, the woman was everywhere, as the veil, as the metaphor of truth, and as the truth.*[39]

As a moment of Otherness, the moment of fetishism is also a moment of *ambiguity* and *displacement*. During the crisis, the media kept asking one question every night in the news, in every single TV program: *What is in Saddam's mind?* We are of course reminded of the question that Freud articulated: What does woman want? Slavoj Zizek argues that racism is determined by the Freudian and Lacanian libidinal economy. As an example he mentions the question that was asked about Jesse Jackson in the 1988 elections: What does Jesse Jackson want?[40] According to Zizek, this question is related to the structure of racist fantasy: The Other's actions are always suspected of being guided by a hidden motive. The point, therefore, becomes to know his hidden desires, his hidden plans, his hidden weapons. *The whole of Iraq was (is still) covered with a huge veil.* The media, the experts, and

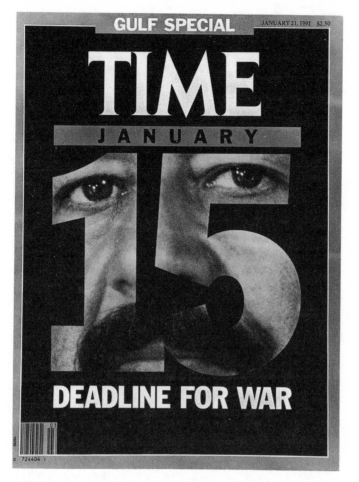

FIGURE 3.3

the inspectors were never tired of searching for plans, plants, weapons—remember those cold faces on television, always in control and always pointing to their little black holes on photos and maps! Following Lacan, Zizek argues that it is this assumption of the Other's hidden *surplus* enjoyment that keeps racist fantasy going. Let us also remember that one fundamental argument for the war was *to stop Saddam Hussein*, not just to liberate Kuwait. Here are a few descriptions of this new villain: "Armed and audacious, Saddam Hussein takes Kuwait—and *no one knows how to stop him*"; "Iraq's dictator seems to be *capable of doing anything* to get his way"; "Ruthless Saddam Hussein seizes tiny Kuwait—and *no one is sure where his ambition will end*"; "*Just how far* will Saddam Hussein's lust for power

FIGURE 3.4

carry him?"; "*No one can be very sure,* what if any message will derail his ruthless drive to be the paramount power in the Persian Gulf?"; "Of course Saddam has *more in his mind* than money."[41]

But why the obsession with Hussein's *face?* His face is veiled, we see *his eyes,* he is looking at us. *Time* correspondent Dan Goodgame wrote: "On meeting him, a visitor was first struck by his eyes, crackling with alertness and at the same time cold and remorseless as snake eyes on the side of dice. They are the eyes of a killer."[42] According to Lacan, who provides us with a psychoanalytic theory of the subject, the *fantasy space* is constituted by the split between the eye and the gaze.[43] The subject can see another person's eyes or his eyes in the mirror but cannot see the gaze, that is, the place from which he is looked at or the place from which he would look at himself to be able to have himself before himself. He therefore *assumes* the gaze in the field of the Other. The gaze assumed in the field of the Other is called "stain" by Lacan: "that which always escapes from the grasp of that form

FIGURE 3.5

of vision that is satisfied with itself in imagining itself as consciousness."[44] Saddam Hussein's gaze is an embodiment of this no-thing, or black hole, of the luminous, enlightened Western subject, that is, the necessary possibility of a place from where he is looked at, caught in the act. The excessively dark veil, the dark, snake eyes, the face that should not be faced: In Saddam, there is more than Saddam. "Saddam" is the *object petit a*, that is, the source of enjoyment or *jouissance* of the racist subject.[45]

The notion of Saddam Hussein's demonization is therefore not sufficient because what is at stake is much more, and much more complex. Hussein's look signifies a *reversal* of the Western imperial subject's own control, an "always already possible" possibility of his own failure. This reversal of the utopia of the rational, scientific eye is the backward, all-seeing, omnipotent, Oriental-despotic evil eye who controls everything and from whom the Western subject extracts an immense amount of political profit compensating his failures (recession, public approval). Saddam Hussein came to fulfill this function of the Other in the Western game of ruling the world. To be sure, *he fulfilled such a function as the real person that he is*. But given the support that was given to him in the past, he was not only a cause but also a result, a product. Or to follow Lacan, "There is cause only in something that doesn't work."[46] The causes, the trouble spots, the black holes, are created by a *system* whose perverse enjoyment is to substitute one trouble for another: Khaddafi, Khomeini, Noriega, Hussein. In this respect, what was important in the war was the Middle Easterner's closeness to "us" (Hussein in close-up), to the imperial subject's controlling eye, and to the abstract space of coding (petrodollars) and lifestyle (cars). As Said already said for the image of Islam, it is something that we hear about every day, something close yet entirely alien. As Larry King of CNN expressed it, "The power thing is awkward for me because I still feel the Brooklyn kid in me. But yeah, I realize the effect the show can have. I'm aware that I am being watched—like Bernard Shaw called in and talked to my guest, President Reagan, and we both realized that Saddam Hussein might be watching. That's extraordinary to know. We're watched worldwide."[47]

A number of analysts and critics have stressed the narrative organization of the war discourse. Of course what is at stake is not a simple or straightforward indoctrination (as, for instance, in Nazi propaganda) but rather, as the Frankfurt School also clearly saw, in the capitalist system of production for the market it is a matter of selling. "Saddam" sells as the new serial drama. Stuart Ewen writes: "In the ratings game, the news—out of economic necessity—must be transformed into a drama, a thriller, an entertainment."[48] Following Ewen, Hammer and McLaren stress the relation between prior mass cultural narrative and the narrative of the war: "Especially with reference to the CNN coverage of the war, a kindred range of films and videos dealing with war at a distance (*Top Gun, Iron Eagle*, etc.) tacitly co-ordinated the reception of many viewers to the aerial shots of 'precision' hits through a superimposition of images and forms of emplotment— memories from postmodern war's electronic and celluloid Hollywood archive— transforming the war coverage into a type of palimpsest blending the discontinuity of war with the continuity of Western narratives about it."[49]

This palimpsest can be read in Derrida's words as "a depth without bottom, an infinite allusion, and a perfectly superficial exteriority: a stratification of surfaces each of whose relation to itself, each of whose interior, is but the implication of another similarly exposed surface."[50] Layers of preserved inscription constantly evoke frames of perception that are rewritten by fresh inscriptions. If desire for war is mobilized in the model of the mass narrative of Hollywood (the hero Bush, the villain Saddam),[51] this should cover a vast field from cowboy movies to Cold War spies to the genre of adventure, but one that is itself modeled on what we might call "colonial discourse." It is the "white hero versus the Other (race or culture, the villain" opposition that is traversing and racially charging these different genres. As I shall argue, this narrative structure itself is enacted politically. It is in such a field that we can pose questions of the complex relations between the political and the cultural, the ways these two distinct fields *feed into* each other. It is also in this sense that we can talk about a discursive space that refers only to itself but perhaps hides such self-referentiality precisely because what is simulated is always simulated in a different field.[52]

Primitive Accumulation

I began this essay by referring to the contradiction embodied in the institution of the United Nations (allowing a violator according to its own decisions to enforce the law against another violator). But such a "contradiction" is perhaps a functional necessity of the world order. In other words, there is not first law, then violation, but many violations, one of which enforces itself as the law.[53] In our world, the law is embodied by those privileged members of the U.N. who have veto power.

Where do we find this law of the world order in the cultural domain? In his thoughts on the recent war, Fredric Jameson refers to the Latin American genre of the great dictator novels, which express a repressed admiration of sadistic tyrants such as Hitler and Stalin.[54] But perhaps we should look for this law in the most international and most popular of arts in the twentieth century: the mass narrative of Hollywood. What is the model of the mass narrative of Hollywood, of this fascinating hegemonic apparatus? Could it be what Marx called primitive accumulation? In relation to the specific character of state violence, Gilles Deleuze and Felix Guattari argue that "it is very difficult to pinpoint this violence because it always presents itself as preaccomplished."[55] They refer to Marx's observation that "there is a violence *that necessarily operates through the State,* precedes the capitalist mode of production, constitutes the 'primitive accumulation' and makes possible the capitalist mode of production itself."[56] This, however, means that primitive accumulation ("colonial plunder") is not a stage that is accomplished once and for all, "before" the capitalist mode of production in an evolutionary logic. Since it is preaccomplished, primitive accumulation or state violence (the process of capturing bodies, land, and resources) never leaves us, it is forever accomplished. In the words of Deleuze and Guattari, "It is a violence that posits itself as preaccomplished, even though it is reactivated everyday. This is a place to say it, if ever there was one: *the mutilation is prior, pre-established.* However, these analyses of Marx should be enlarged upon. For the fact remains that there is a primitive accumulation that, far from deriving from the agricultural mode of production, precedes it: as a general rule, there is primitive accumulation whenever an apparatus of capture is mounted, with *that very particular kind of violence that creates or contributes to the creation of that which it is directed against,* and thus presupposes itself."[57]

Deleuze and Guattari name this particular violence, characterized by the creation of what it is directed against—"lawful violence." If the Gulf War is an instance of preaccomplished violence, Saddam Hussein's occupation of Kuwait can be considered as what Deleuze and Guattari call "crime." They define this as another form of violence: "a violence of illegality that consists in taking possession of something to which one has no 'right,' in capturing something one does not have a 'right' to capture."[58] Given the U.N. resolutions about the U.S. invasion of Panama, is the U.S. action not criminal violence as well? But there is a law that is preaccomplished, already accomplished before this crime is committed. If, as Foucault shows, the modern punishment system punishes the criminal rather than the crime, if, in other words, the criminal is Other (somebody different from us, somebody with a different psyche and constitution, on the other side of a strict line), then such a position can best be fulfilled by all the Others of grand ideological narratives such as racism, orientalism, or class narrative (the subproletariat).[59] What matters is *the power to construct, the power to inscribe reality, events, facts—the power to create that which you are acting against.* The preaccomplished nature of lawful violence works in the capacity to sanction violence as law, which is to inscribe what is criminal. (Butler gives a parallel example from the language of war: Colin Powell's description of the sending of missiles as "'the delivery of an ordinance' figures an act of violence as an act of law.")[60]

We should ask, then, Whom is this violence directed against? Against Saddam Hussein the dictator? The aim of lawful violence is not to exercise violence itself but rather to capture people or to appropriate land and resources (primitive accumulation). Since Hussein was not captured, we perhaps need to ask who was. In the immediate aftermath of the liberation of Kuwait, the Kuwaiti police captured immigrant Palestinian workers who were suspected of collaborating with the Iraqi military during the occupation. These Palestinians appeared a couple of times on TV; there was some discussion and some worry about their possible fate, and then they disappeared. I want to argue that they were, in a strange way, the real targets, however unimportant they may seem.

But at this point, we need to turn back to Saddam Hussein's face. Everything that I have said so far about it presupposes the argument that this face is *made, produced.* In their approach to questions of semiotics and subjectivity, Deleuze and Guattari refer to a "desiring machine" that appears at the intersection of "significance" ("signification" in their terminology) and "subjectification." This machine produces faces, though it is itself not a face but a "white wall/black hole system." They call it the "abstract machine of faciality." "Concrete faces can not be assumed to come ready made. They are engendered by an *abstract machine of faciality* (*visagéité*), which produces them at the same time as it gives the signifier its white wall and subjectivity its black hole. Thus the black hole/white wall system is, to begin with, not a face, but the abstract machine that produces faces according to the changeable combinations of its cogwheels. Do not expect the abstract machine to resemble what it produces, or will produce."[61]

Therefore we should not assume that the Palestinians have come there ready made. *Is this not the question of language, the question of where to speak from and how?* Because "it is absurd to believe that language as such can convey a message. A language is always embedded in the faces that announce its statements and ballast them in relation to the signifiers in progress and subjects concerned. Choices are guided by faces, elements are organized around faces."[62] Palestinians, Arabs, were *facialized, given the face of Saddam Hussein,* which was itself produced by a distribution of black holes on the white screen of the hyperreal electronic media (which connected itself to the infamous abstract machine of faciality).[63]

According to Deleuze and Guattari, facialization does not mean simply the production of a face but also the "overcoding" of the body by the face: "an operation worthy of Doctor Moreau: horrible and magnificent. Hand, breast, stomach, penis and vagina, thigh, leg and foot, all come to be facialized. Fetishism, erotomania, etc., are inseparable from these processes of facialization."[64] We may read Hussein's feminization in the tabloid press as the facialization of the woman's body. But what triggers this machine? Deleuze and Guattari write:

> the maternal power operating through the face during nursing; the passional power operating through the face of the loved one, even in caresses; the political power operating through the face of the leader (streamers, icons and photographs), even in mass actions; the power of the film operating through the face of the star and the close-up; the power of television. It is not the individuality of the face that counts but the efficacy of the ciphering it makes possible, and in what cases it makes it possible. This is an affair not of ideology but of economy and the organization of power (*pouvoir*). We are certainly not saying that the face, the power of the face (*la puissance du visage*), engenders and explains social power (*pouvoir*). *Certain assemblages of power (pouvoir) require the production of a face,* others do not.[65]

The military and cultural apparatus of imperialism is one that requires the production of a face, a face that should not be saved, not because it belongs to an individual but because it makes possible a reading. This is a face that is made of so many powers/faces: the maternal power (mother's face), the power of the film (the face of the star, the face of the villain, always in close-up), the political power (the face of the president, Stormin' Norman, Hussein's other face on the walls of Baghdad), the passional power (the tearful, proud loved ones left behind), the power of television (TV faces, Dan Rather, Ted Koppel, Larry King, or when you switch it off, the TV's other, dark face in your room), the face of the magazine, and so on. All these faces run into a white wall/black hole system, making lines, dots, circles, pipelines, holes, spaces, curves; drawing, writing, inscribing one face, the face on the surface of the palimpsest; and repressing and stratifying other surfaces, other faces: "Saddam, the Butcher of Baghdad, with his snake eyes, the New Hitler!"[66]

It was certainly a power operation, and his face was all over the United States (and Europe), circulating in society: TV showed a group of young white males who turned over and kicked an *old American car* on which they drew Saddam Hussein faces (the face of the car); there was a Saddam Hussein voodoo doll sold in chain drugstores—it had a brutal, malicious face. Again TV showed people practicing their aim with Hussein's face as the target (somebody said it helped to release the tension). The Hussein shown on TV hardly ever spoke. He did say, "This will be the mother of all battles," which proved that he did not even know how to speak, unlike Hitler (who spoke a lot on the radio). He was kissed and hugged by a lot of males, he looked at us and smiled with his snake eyes. Hussein as the agenda was the facialization of Palestinians and Arabs. His face represented the silence of their voices, implying a certain accent in their speech even before they spoke. In this way lawful violence creates the violence it is then used against. It inscribes the name and makes the face (It's an Oriental! It's an Arab! It's a Jew! It's a lunatic!) that dissimulates its own horrific violence: "The State can in this way say that the violence is 'primal,' that it is simply a natural phenomenon the responsibility for which does not lie with the state, which uses violence only against the violent, against 'criminals'—against primitives, against nomads—in order that peace may reign."[67]

Such is the grand narrative of oil, orientalism, insofar as the Middle East is concerned. It is by these techniques that human bodies are captured, facialized, and made to do what they are *assumed* to be capable of, that is, producing *more* than what is necessary for their subsistence. The ironies surrounding the war—the violator United States as the police, the United States in a war against a regime it had supported against the fundamentalist Iranian regime, which now understandably gave support to the anti-Iraqi coalition by remaining neutral—demonstrated the West's power to do what it wants to do. The faces and images are substitutable and absolutely necessary in this new order. (I do not say they are easily substitutable.) What is at stake now is a "neoorientalism" or neocolonial discourse in which lawful violence against created Third World criminals and dictators is an essential element of the cultural and political writing of global capitalism.

Conclusion

By way of a conclusion, I want to refer to two different articles, one by Barbara Harlow, the other by Gayatri Spivak. In a discussion of the literary articulations of decolonization and partition, Harlow refers to the Palestinian novelist Ghassan Kanafani's work. Kanafani's first novel, *Men in the Sun* (1956), is the story of three poor Palestinian refugees who try to enter Kuwait from Iraq in order to find work in that oil-rich country. Harlow writes:

After having been bartered, bargained over and overcharged by the Iraqi brokers and traders in Palestinian labor, [they] meet Abul Khaizuran. This Palestinian, once a political leader in the community, agrees to transport the three refugees across the border in the empty water tank of the truck he drives for a Kuwaiti merchant. The fate of the three migrant workers of *Men in the Sun*, silently suffocated in their water tank while the truck driver listens to the obscene jokes of the Kuwaiti border guards, is well-known, even legend, in Palestinian litero-political history, and the question posed by Abul Khaizuran at the story's end has long resounded through that history: "Why didn't they bang the walls of the tank? Why? Why? Why?" Kanafani's story was written prior to the formation of an organized, independent, Palestinian national resistance, and the narrative critique that it elaborates across Arab borders and through its fractured plot and interrupted characterizations, addresses both a wanting Palestinian leadership and the trading in the Palestinian cause by existing Arab regimes. Those emergent Palestinian democratic aspirations to national liberation and self-determination of the early 1960s, still spurned today by regimes but become popular and exemplary throughout the Arab world and around the globe, were threatened with extinction once again, and again on the Iraq-Kuwait border, not in an empty water tank but over disputed burning oil fields.[68]

The three Palestinians who could not bang the walls of that tank while crossing the border illegally were the victims of an already accomplished, lawful violence. Their stories, their faces, were made across borders, through fractured plots, interrupted characterizations, under the threat of extinction.

My second example comes from Gayatri Spivak. In her reading of Salman Rushdie's *Satanic Verses* (both the "text" and the "event"), Spivak refers to the case of Shahbano, a Muslim Indian woman who went to the Supreme Court to demand an allowance from her divorced husband, but, following a political conflict between the Muslim minority and the Indian government, denounced the Supreme Court judgment in her favor against Muslim law and went back to her community by reclaiming her religious identity.[69] In India, Shahbano became an occasion for the creation of a Muslim collective agency, which would also influence Rushdie's fate. But she was easily forgotten. Spivak finds in Shahbano the difficult case of a notion of "agency" that cannot depend on free will. She compares Shahbano's disappearance with the rise of Khomeinei's "monolithic face, this construct, with the piercing eyes under the iconic turban." In conclusion, she writes: "Whenever they bring out the Ayatollah, remember the face that does not come together on the screen, remember Shahbano. She is quite discontinuous with Salman Rushdie's fate as it is being organized on many levels. ... When the very well-known face is brought out, remember the face that you have not seen, the face that has disappeared from view, remember Shahbano."[70]

Certainly these are different cases. But still, in a similar way, I would like to suggest that whenever they bring out Saddam Hussein, we should remember the immigrant Palestinians in Kuwait, the Palestinians in the occupied territories, whose fate is, generally speaking, a metaphor for all subaltern Arab and Muslim peo-

ples—especially those in the Middle East, who because of oil have been the victims of a severe humiliation, oppression, and exploitation and are produced in
the images of their bloodiest leaders, who are no more than the reverse images of
those who produce them.

As conditions like the recent war force us to speak in the discursive mode of
ideology-critique, we should also remember that what is behind or before the face
is not always a true identity but often a captured body in resistance. We should
turn the facialization of those bodies into a moment of questioning the production of our own "faces," our own "selves," a moment of questioning the complexities and complicities of our being *in* the world. We should turn our bodies into
the "probe-heads" that Deleuze and Guattari demand and turn that moment of
horrific violence into a moment of re-searching and re-making the connections
that we have to the people who live and die *elsewhere.*

NOTES

I would like to thank Stephen Heath, Victor Burgin, James Clifford, and Meyda Yegenoglu
for their useful suggestions and comments on earlier versions of this chapter.

1. Noam Chomsky, "Nefarious Aggression," *Magazine Z* (October 1990), p. 20.

2. The people who use such words against the U.S. invasion of Panama are *normally* regarded as extremists.

3. Edward Said, *Orientalism* (Harmondsworth: Penguin, 1978).

4. Ibid., pp. 2, 12–13.

5. Spivak explains her notion of textuality as follows: "As far as I understand it, the notion of textuality should be related to the notion of the worlding of a world on a supposedly uninscribed territory. When I say this, I am thinking basically about the imperialist
project which had to assume that the earth that it territorialised was in fact previously
uninscribed. So then a world, on a simple level of cartography inscribed what was pre-
sumed to be uninscribed. Now this worlding actually is also a texting, textualising, a making into art, making into an object to be understood." Gayatri Chakravorty Spivak, *The
Post-Colonial Critic: Interviews, Strategies, Dialogues,* ed. S. Harasym (New York and London: Routledge, 1990), p. 1.

6. Except in the oldest institutions of colonialism such as the British School of Oriental
and African Studies.

7. Simon Bromley, *American Hegemony and World Oil: The Industry, the State System
and the World Economy* (London: Polity Press, 1991). See especially pp. 82–84.

8. James O'Connor, "Murder on the Orient Express: The Political Economy of the Gulf
War," *Capitalism Nature Socialism* 2, no. 7 (June 1991), pp. 1–17.

9. G. Deleuze and F. Guattari, *Anti-Oedipus: Capitalism and Schizophrenia,* vol. 1, trans.
R. Hurley, M. Seem, and H. R. Lane (Minneapolis: University of Minnesota Press, 1983),
pp. 222–262.

10. Bromley also refers to Giovanni Arrighi, "A Crisis of Hegemony," in *Dynamics of
Global Crisis,* eds. S. Amin, G. Arrighi, A. G. Frank, and I. Wallerstein (London: Macmillan, 1982). See especially pp. 92–98.

11. Communist-led national liberation movements (Korea, Vietnam, Cambodia) complicated this project.

12. Bromley, *American Hegemony and World Oil*, p. 82.

13. See Fred Halliday, *Arabia Without Sultans* (Harmondsworth: Penguin, 1979), pp. 71–74.

14. Bromley, *American Hegemony and World Oil*, pp. 121–123.

15. Edward W. Said, *Covering Islam: How the Media and the Experts Determine How We See the Rest of the World* (New York: Pantheon Books, 1981), pp. 33–34.

16. Simon Bromley, "Crisis in the Gulf," *Capital and Class* 44 (Summer 1991), p. 13.

17. For further analyses, see Samir Amin, "U.S. Militarism in the New World Order," *Polygraph* 5 (1992), pp. 13–37; Immanual Wallerstein, "The Persian Gulf War: What Gain for the United States?" *Polygraph* 5 (1992), pp. 38–45. Amin emphasizes imperialist rivalry and different U.S. hegemonic projects ("maritime" and "coalitionist"). Both authors think that the Third World is an important area of conflict in the present conjuncture.

18. O'Connor, "Murder on the Orient Express," p. 6. O'Connor stresses that petrodollars are integral to the health of U.S. finances. As he explains, the fact that oil is priced in dollars helps it maintain its position as the world's reserve currency. He adds to this general principle the conjunctural questions of capital shortage and decreasing exports in the United States, which made the petrodollar an urgent issue for U.S. finances, and, by implication, global financial stability.

19. O'Connor, "Murder on the Orient Express," p. 16.

20. Abouali Farmanfarmaian, "Sexuality in the Gulf War: Did You Measure Up?" *Genders*, no. 13 (Spring 1992), pp. 1–29. Another interesting account of national fantasy can be found in Jochen Schulte-Sasse and Linda Schulte-Sasse, "War, Otherness and Illusionary Identifications with the State," *Cultural Critique*, no. 19 (Fall 1991), pp. 67–95.

21. Farmanfarmaian, "Sexuality in the Gulf War," pp. 13–14.

22. Ibid., p. 12.

23. Is it a coincidence that *Dances with Wolves* was given an Oscar in the same year?

24. I am trying to think through Gayatri Spivak's complex formulation: "Work in gendering in principle sees the socius as an affectively coded site of exchange and surplus. The simple contentless moment of value as it is gender coded has historically led to the appropriation of the sexual differential, subtracted from, but represented as, the theoretical fiction of sexual identity." "Poststructuralism, Marginality, Postcoloniality, Value," *Literary Theory Today*, ed. P. Collier and H. Geyer-Ryan (Oxford: Polity Press, 1990), p. 227. For the production of political value or "speech," see Spivak's "Reading the Satanic Verses," *Third Text* 11 (Summer 1990), pp. 52–53. Speaking of the famous case of Shahbano, Spivak writes: "In the sphere of the production of political value, the mute as articulate in the service of 'orthodoxy' (to borrow Gita Sahgal's word)—a discontinuous naming of collective agency in the name of the 'sacred' rather than the 'profane' (in the other coding called 'secular,' 'national')—is more spectacularly muted because so abundantly audible." Ibid., p. 53.

25. Ibid., p. 13.

26. Malek Alloula, *Colonial Harem* (Minneapolis: University of Minnesota Press, 1986).

27. Franz Fanon, "Algeria Unveiled," in *A Dying Colonialism*, trans. H. Chevalier (New York: Grove Weidenfield, 1965), pp. 35–67.

28. Said defines orientalism's strategic formation as "the relationship between texts and the way in which groups of texts, types of texts, even textual genres acquire mass, density

and referential power among themselves and thereafter in the culture at large" and strategic location as "the author's position in a text with regard to the Oriental material he writes about." *Orientalism*, p. 20.

29. For the definition of strategy, see Michel de Certeau: "I call a strategy the calculation (or manipulation) of power relationships that becomes possible as soon as a subject with will and power (a business, a city, an army, a scientific institution) can be isolated. It postulates a place that can be delimited as its own and serve as the base from which relations with an exteriority composed of targets and threats (customers or competitors, enemies, the country surrounding the city, objectives and objects of research, etc.) can be managed." *The Practice of Everyday Life*, trans. S. Randall (Berkeley: University of California Press, 1988), pp. 35–36. See also Michel Foucault, *The History of Sexuality*, vol. 1, trans. R. Hurley (New York: Vintage Books, 1980), pp. 100–102.

30. See Meyda Yegenoglu, "Supplementing the Orientalist Lack: European Ladies in the Harem," *Inscriptions*, no. 6.

31. See, for instance, K. Theweleit's psychological analysis of German fascist soldiers: *Male Fantasies*, vols. 1, 2 (Minneapolis: University of Minnesota Press, 1989).

32. *Time*, September 24, 1990.

33. See Spivak's formulation in note 24.

34. D. Pryzbylowicz and A. JanMohamed, "Introduction: The Economy of Moral Capital in the Gulf War."

35. Here, by photographic space, I am very loosely referring to what Henri Lefebvre calls abstract space in his presentation of the mythical grand narrative of the visual sense (which gained hegemony over all the other senses by defeating them in the historical process). Henri Lefebvre, *The Production of Space*, trans. Donald Nicholson-Smith (Oxford and Cambridge, Mass.: Basil Blackwell, 1991), pp. 285–287. Lefebvre sees abstract space as an amalgam of three elements: geometric (Euclidian) space, optical space, and phallic space. Abstract space is susceptible to rational operations, it is luminous and is a space of images, and lastly it is a space that is produced by violence, instituted by the state apparatus and military. I also read Lefebvre's text as an exposition of the mythical grand narrative.

36. Alloula, *Colonial Harem*. Fanon's formulation of unveiling Algeria can be read in terms of the body of the woman signifying the body of the earth for the colonizer. See Fanon, *A Dying Colonialism*, pp. 35–67. See also Meyda Yegenoglu, "Veiled Fantasies," *Cultural Studies* (forthcoming). I am drawing on Yegenoglu's analysis.

37. In Freud's words, "In the situation we are considering, on the contrary, we see that the perception has persisted, and that a very energetic action has been undertaken to maintain the disavowal. It is not true that, after the child made his observation of the woman, he has preserved unaltered his belief that women have a phallus. He has retained that belief, but he has also given it up. In the conflict between the weight of the unwelcome perception and the force of his counter-wish, a compromise has been reached, as is only possible under the unconscious laws of thought in the primary processes. Yes, in his mind the woman has got a penis, in spite of everything; but this penis is no longer the same as it was before." Sigmund Freud, *Standard Edition*, vol. 21, p. 154.

38. Emphasis added. Ella Shohat, "The Media's War," *Social Text*, no. 28 (1991), p. 136.

39. Perhaps we should think of all this with the concept of "womb-envy," which Gayatri C. Spivak proposes in *In Other Worlds* (London and New York: Routledge, 1989), p. 81.

40. See Slavoj Zizek, *Sublime Object of Ideology* (London: Verso, 1989), p. 114. Once more I am in agreement with Abouali Farmanfarmaian insofar as such connections are concerned, but what I want to emphasize is the difference between Jesse Jackson and Rodney King, and/or Saddam Hussein, and/or the immigrant Palestinian worker in Kuwait, and so on.

41. *Time*, August 13, 1990.

42. Ibid.

43. See Jacques Lacan, *The Four Fundamental Concepts of Psychoanalysis*, ed. J. A. Miller, trans. A. Sheridan (New York and London: W. W. Norton, 1977), pp. 67–119.

44. As Jacques Lacan puts it, "That in which the consciousness may turn back upon itself—grasp itself, like Valéry's Young Parque, as seeing oneself seeing oneself—represents mere sleight of hand. An avoidance of the function of the gaze is at work here." *The Four Fundamental Concepts of Psychoanalysis*, p. 74.

45. In a similar way, and following Slavoj Zizek's framework, Jochen Schulte-Sasse and Linda Schulte-Sasse argue that Saddam Hussein can be seen as a negative embodiment of the American national fantasy, an embodiment whose counterpart is "the flag, the president or Stormin' Norman." See "War, Otherness and Illusory Identifications with the State," pp. 91–92. I want to emphasize the *production* of such "negativity."

46. Lacan, *The Four Fundamental Concepts of Psychoanalysis*, p. 22.

47. Larry King, "Interview with Larry King," *TV Guide*, July 25, 1992.

48. Stuart Ewen, *All Consuming Images* (New York: Basic Books, 1988), quoted in Rhonda Hammer and Peter McLaren, "The Spectacularization of Subjectivity: Media Knowledges, Global Citizenry and the New World Order," *Polygraph* 5 (1992), pp. 49–50.

49. Hammer and McLaren, "The Spectacularization of Subjectivity," p. 50.

50. Jacques Derrida, "Freud and the Scene of Writing," in *Writing and Difference*, trans. A. Bass (Chicago: University of Chicago Press, 1978), p. 224.

51. See, for instance, Shohat, "The Media's War"; J. B. Childs, "Notes on the Gulf War, Racism, and African American Social Thought"; and Fredric Jameson, "Thoughts on the Late War."

52. For the notion of hyperreal, see Jean Baudrillard, *Simulations* (New York: Semiotext[e], 1983). See also the interesting analysis by Mark S. Roberts: "Iraq: Inventing the Event," *Art and Text*, no. 39 (May 1991), pp. 54–59.

53. For a similar account of law in the Hegelian and Lacanian problematics, see Slavoj Zizek, "The Limits of the Semiotic Approach to Psychoanalysis," *Psychoanalysis and … ed.* R. Feldstein and H. Sussman (New York and London: Routledge, 1990), especially pp. 92–99.

54. Fredric Jameson, "Thoughts on the Late War," p. 146.

55. G. Deleuze and F. Guattari, *A Thousand Plateaus*, p. 447.

56. Ibid., 447. For primitive accumulation, see Karl Marx, *Capital*, vol. 1, trans. B. Fowkes (New York: Vintage, 1977), ch. 31.

57. The last emphasis is added. Deleuze and Guattari, *A Thousand Plateaus*, p. 447.

58. Ibid., p. 448.

59. "The delinquent, the strange manifestation of an overall phenomenon of criminality, is to be found in quasi-natural classes, each endowed with his own characteristics and requiring a specific treatment, what Marquet-Wasselot called in 1841 the 'ethnography of the prisons'; 'The convicts are … another people within the same people; with its own hab-

its, instincts, morals.'" Michel Foucault, *Discipline and Punish: The Birth of the Prison*, trans. A. Sheridan (Harmondsworth: Penguin, 1977), pp. 252–253. Foucault's notion of "useful delinquency" has obvious implications for inner cities, drug wars, and crime in the United States. Although it cannot simply be appropriated for a critique of Western production of Third World dictators, his approach constitutes an important beginning point in this area as well, in terms of its implications for the "use- and/or exchange-value" of crime.

60. J. Butler, "Contingent Foundations," p. 157. Butler further argues that "it figures the missile as command, an order to obey and is thus a certain act of speech which not only delivers a message, i.e., get out of Kuwait, but effectively enforces that message through the threat of death and through death itself. Of course, this is a message that can never be received, for it kills its addressee, and so it is not an ordinance at all, but the failure of all ordinances, the refusal of a communication. And for those who remain to read the message, they will not read what is sometimes quite literally written on the message" (ibid.). But if this leads to "massive and violent contestation," in Butler's words, then in some strange sense, they do read the message and receive the command. I have argued elsewhere that fundamentalist Islam can be seen as a Western command. See my "Under the Sign of Orientalism: The West vs. Islam," *Cultural Critique* (Winter 1993). Jameson puts this paradox in a different way in his discussion of the imperialist notion of setting an example: "The problem is the familiar paradox of of time-travel generally, namely, that you thereby try to influence a future which is however itself profoundly modified by the very act of trying to do so, so that the putative warning is no longer valid for the new situation in which it exists as a bloody fact." "Thoughts on the Late War," p. 144.

61. Deleuze and Guattari, *A Thousand Plateaus*, p. 168.

62. Ibid., p. 179.

63. I should stress that according to Deleuze and Guattari, the face is in fact Christ, or the ordinary white man's face. Other races are evaluated according to their degree of deviation from the white man's face. They argue that racism does not work by exclusion, by designating someone as Other, but "by the determination of degrees of deviance in relation to the White-Man face." *A Thousand Plateaus*, p. 178. As they themselves put it, however, the logic of facialization or Christianization requires that "there are only people who should be like us and whose only crime it is not to be" (p. 178, emphasis added). I am trying to think of this particular "crime" in the context of primitive accumulation/lawful violence, that is, as "the creation of that which it is used against" (p. 448, emphasis added).

64. Ibid., p. 170.

65. Ibid., p. 175.

66. Many critics emphasized the pronunciation of this name, the connotations it had: sodom, satan. But this is nothing compared to the production of a face!

67. Deleuze and Guattari, *A Thousand Plateaus*, p. 448.

68. Barbara Harlow, "Drawing the Line: Cultural Politics and the Legacy of Partition," *Polygraph*, no. 5 (1992), p. 104.

69. Gayatri C. Spivak, "Reading the Satanic Verses," *Third Text*, No. 11 (Summer 1990), pp. 41–60. For a detailed account of this famous case, see Zakia Pathak and Rajeswari Sunder Rajan, "Shahbano," *Signs* 14, no. 3 (Spring 1989), pp. 558–582.

70. Spivak, "Reading the Satanic Verses," p. 60.

4

The Subject of
Imperial Geography

BRUCE AVERY

I N THIS ESSAY I describe two phenomena: the social forces that contributed to the rise of the map as a form of territorial description and its subsequent absorption into perceptions of territory that contribute to the formation of the subject. This description requires a brief detour through the historical development of cartography out of narrative itineraries, whose formal properties are open and multivalent in opposition to the totalizing perspective of cartography. After this detour the essay centers on the nineteenth century and Rudyard Kipling, whose immensely popular novel *Kim* absorbs the cartographic perspective into its landscapes and then deploys it to reconcile contradictions between racial and territorial identities. For Kipling and his contemporaries, as well as for English imperialism, geography becomes the expression of racial destiny, and the map is the lens through which the blurry muddle of colonial identity becomes clearly visible.

Medieval Mappaemundi

In the medieval period, before classical theory reemerged to create modern cartography, the most significant form of cartography was the *mappamundi*, which was an attempt to show Christians the significant events in the history of their religion in spatial terms. Maps such as the Ebstorff mappamundi portrayed the earth as part of the body of Christ with Jerusalem in the center, and events widely spaced in time were made to appear simultaneous and hence timeless, coherent, and logical within the unifying Corpus Christi. These mappaemundi differ from narratives of Christian history in the way maps differ from itineraries: They ignore temporal distinctions and linearity and arrange events by spatial location. It is important to note, however, that the Christian event gives significance to the location and not vice versa. Thus space coheres according to its relevance to Christianity and the religion is naturalized because territory appears to be the stage of Christian drama; territory beyond the Christian viewer's experience becomes comprehensible as the location of some familiar event from the Christian narrative.

Portolan Charts and the Compass Rose

Commercial concerns provided the impetus for the technological innovations that produced more accurate maps and led to their increasing importance in daily life. To reach markets, merchants needed ships capable of navigating across oceans instead of merely, as Greek ships did, following the coastline. The combination of an accurate compass and the portolan sea chart enabled sailors to cross oceans with some sense of accuracy. Historian G. R. Crone points out that these charts are a "a good instance of the response of technicians to a new social demand, in this case the need of the commercial communities of Italy to develop communications with their expanding markets."[1] Moreover, the sailor discovered that with a tool of science and a parchment he could achieve some measure of control over the hostile sea around him, although the new technology also, with its web of lines that had to be followed, achieved some measure of control over him. This sense of being above the earth and in control of it differs significantly from the narrative sense of moving through territory, of being among objects and unable to see the end point of the journey through them.

Core and Periphery in the Development of Cartography

Cartography then, like exploration itself in the early modern period, was advanced by the emerging institutions of nascent capitalism and the need to conquer the space separating capital from markets. In such a context landscape description is important because landscapes seen from the cartographic perspective reinforce structures of exploitation inherent in colonialism. By contrast landscapes associated with premap, precolonial technologies of representation—narrative itineraries, for example—might enable anticolonialist perspectives on territory.

The rise of the map in early modern culture was part of the evolution from a feudal to a market economy. With this evolution came the commodification of land, and so it makes sense that accurate depiction and quantification of land was necessary. More important, as many anthropologists from Marcel Mauss to Pierre Bourdieu have demonstrated, social and economic relations differ in traditional and market economies.[2] Briefly, in traditional economies economic relations are embedded in social relations. The principal mode of exchange under these circumstances is the gift, which disguises divisions of labor in redistribution economies. Karl Polanyi notes that "in the ethnically stratified societies of Africa it sometimes happens that the superior strata consist of herdsmen settled among agriculturalists who are still using the digging stick or the hoe. The gifts collected by the herdsmen are mainly agricultural—such as cereals and beer—while the gifts distributed by them may be animals, especially sheep or goats."[3] In this exchange the social act covers an economic symbiosis that benefits both groups. In practice the time lag between gifts can be manipulated in order to maintain the appearance of a social relation; if gifts are not exchanged immediately, one for the other, the participants can avoid the appearance of pure economic barter. In Western Europe the symbiosis was more clearly exploitative, but nonetheless the economic relation of tenant and lord was embedded in social acts of tribute paid to the lord in exchange for protection, tribute that itself was embedded in such terms as loyalty, care, and responsibility. Ultimately, as Polanyi notes, in the traditional economy "the production and distribution of goods is organized in the main through collection, storage, and redistribution, the pattern being focused on the chief, the temple, the despot, or the lord."[4]

The market economy, however, involves the opposite relation: "The market pattern ... being related to a peculiar motive of its own, the motive of truck or barter, is capable of creating a specific institution, namely, the market. ... It means no less than the running of society as an adjunct to the market. Instead of economy being embedded in social relations, social relations are embedded in the economic system."[5] In practice this meant the commodification of labor, of money, and of land. Labor needed to be free to follow the market; land needed to be freed up to obey the market for rents. Since both of these things are impossible under the feudal system, the transformation to a market economy meant the disruption of the traditional relation of the farmer to both his lord and the land. In early modern culture, then, there was a dynamic process: Certain economic relations were emerging from containment in social structures while certain traditional social relations were subsumed under the relations of the market. This evolution is relevant to this study because it created conditions under which the map became a popular medium of representation: In the midst of social flux emerged a new form of territorial description that functioned to realign identifications away from tenant to lord and toward citizen and territory.

J. B. Harley, in an essay that suggests this very phenomenon, speculates that the early modern map functioned as a "cartographic *lingua franca* helping to fashion mental geographies at a variety of territorial scales away from the limited 'eyewitness' experience of individual observers."[6] Mapmakers developed codes, or keys, to aid interpretation, and as these keys were common to maps of all the different shires, a resident of Warwickshire could see in a map of Surrey the same hills, rivers, forests that he knew by sight. As an aid to the imagination, these map codes invoked "landscape elements which were universal rather than particular."[7] In this they helped spur a sense of national identity. Harley argues that "the image, in short, mediated the features of the unknown county with the viewer's own experience of the English landscape."[8] By the early twentieth century, nationalism and geography were thoroughly intertwined with the imperial project, and with individual identity. This complex formation is the subject to which I now turn.

Curzon's Proper Public Man

On May 20, 1912, at the annual dinner of the Royal Geographic Society, Lord Curzon, Earl of Keddleston, president of the society, and former viceroy of Her Majesty's Indian Empire, rose to give a characteristically long-winded toast. Comfortable among his fellows, Curzon began: "Surely we may say that our science of geography is the most cosmopolitan of all sciences, and that there is no individual whom it does not touch at some point or another of his public or private life."[9] Curzon's fond possessive—"our science"—suggests the degree to which the Royal Society, a group that included the prime minister, the archbishop of Canterbury, and most leading members of Parliament, knew geography to be in fact "their" subject, the science that helped them control the far-flung empire on which their economy depended.

Yet Curzon's subsequent words suggest that he and the rest of the public men in the room that night were subject to geography as much as it was their subject:

> We recognize geography as the handmaid of history. Without geography you cannot understand, much less can you write, history. Geography, too, is a sister science to economics and politics; and to any of us who have attempted to study geography it is known that the moment you diverge from the geographical field you find yourself crossing the frontiers of geology, zoology, ethnology, chemistry, physics, and almost all the kindred sciences. Therefore we are justified in saying that geography is one of the first and foremost of the sciences: that it is necessary for a proper conception of citizenship, and is an indispensable adjunct to the production of a public man.[10]

He goes on and on, but we may take it from Curzon, one of the foremost imperialists of any age, that a public man adventures across the borders of academic disciplines much as he does across the borders of nations. Note the progression: From the strife-filled world of policy and exchange we escape into nature, geology, and zoology, from which pastoral space we can explore the territory of humans in their primal state, the land of ethnology. From there we range into the place called chemistry, where the elements that make the world coagulate and pulse, and onto the pathway leading to the microworld of physics, where indiscernible but essential particles incorporate to form the larger world.

I exaggerate here to draw attention to the spatial metaphor with which Curzon plots the location of his pet discipline among the others. As we telescope downward from the big geographic perspective to the most minute study of the smallest particle, we reinforce the position of geography as the broad picture, the frame that allows us to situate the partial vision produced by the other sciences.

Curzon's image of geography walking hand in hand with history, and alongside economics and politics, makes sense at a time when England wrote its history at the same time it wrote its capitalistic designs on ever-larger sections of the globe. No wonder, then, that to Curzon a proper sense of citizenship requires a sense of one's nation as primarily a geographic entity. This sense enables a public man to know that history unfolds spatially as his nation establishes, preserves, or expands borders and that the imperial explorer fulfills his historical destiny by crossing frontiers. As he moves beyond them into uncharted space, the explorer achieves global knowledge of alien cultures; he locates the territory of the Other, helps to define his own nationality, and so helps to define himself. For Curzon, then, there can be no proper British subject without the subject of geography and the knowledge it produces of the alien subject as an occupant of an alien space.

I pun on the word "subject" to indicate the role geography plays in the constitution of the ego in the peculiar landscape of imperialism. The word "subject" as I use it here refers to the idea that the ego achieves psychic unity only in and through language.[11] It follows that since geography offers a particular vocabulary and inflects the locatives in grammatical structure in a certain way, geographical awareness affects the constitution of the subject. In other words, because the self must define itself in relation to the Other in language, a set of concepts and words that dictate identity in terms of place names and spatial location will in part structure self-knowledge as an aspect of geography.

There is, then, a "discourse" of geography, a particular, specialized domain of language use. That discourse circulated widely in the culture surrounding Curzon; it did indeed touch all individuals at "some point or another of [their] public or private life." One of its effects was the achievement of the spatialization of national and racial identity, the culmination of a process we have seen begin in the early modern period. For the purposes of this analysis, then, let the term "subject of geography" extend in two directions, to a primary and to a secondary function. The definition of the primary subject is the institutionalized study of territory with borders both natural and fictional, bodies of water, sites of inhabitation, minerals and other resources, maps, and charts; the definition of the secondary subject is the particular human consciousness structured through a language that has as some of its circulating components ideas and concepts produced by the domain of knowledge described in definition one. The primary subject evolved over centuries and is the product of Greek geography, Christian spatial history, Gerardus Mercator, and the Dutch, Spanish, Portuguese, and English imperialism I discussed earlier; the secondary subject is the individual whose consciousness of itself and of others is structured in part by the emergence of the primary subject into general knowledge and public discourse. Individuals who occupy historical moments in which geography has great importance will of course be more subject to the discourse of geography. Curzon was one of those individuals; as we shall see, Kim is another.[12]

Kim and the Geographic Education

Rudyard Kipling's novel *Kim* opens with an orphan at play on an old cannon that locals believe to symbolize military superiority over the Punjab in India. That orphan is Kim, and the first few lines introduce the themes that will dominate the narrative—military conflict and an ambiguity about the identity of the subject of the sentence: "He sat, in defiance of municipal orders, astride the gun Zam-Zammah on her brick platform opposite the old Ajaib-Gher—the Wonder House, as the natives call the Lahore Museum."[13] Then we move to the second paragraph, and the narrator's voice sounds gently satiric: "There was some justification for Kim—he had kicked Lala Dinanath's boy off the trunnions." The narrative describes a small world, after all, a world without much significance: the world of child's play. Yet immediately the narrator qualifies that notion: "since the English held the Punjab and Kim was English." In this book, then, child's play has resonance in the big world of imperialism. So within these three sentences we have a tension between childhood and maturity in the imperial conflict, and one between play and war. These tensions increase later when we discover that the spies in the Secret Service call the imperial conflict "The Great Game"—the interminable jousting between England and Russia over Afghanistan—and that the child Kim will have a big role to play in that game. The narrator also suggests something about Kim's character by asserting first that he defies municipal orders, then telling us that Kim is English. The English always told themselves they were in India to establish order, not to defy it. The exemplary Englishman serving in India most often portrayed in popular fiction was a straight arrow, heroic, stern but kind, and obedient—not to mention white, which brings us to the next sentence: "Though he was burned black as any native ..." Clearly, then, Kim is not the ordinary hero of Anglo-Indian popular fiction.

The question of just what he is drives the narrative as it follows him across the subcontinent. The story concerns itself with Kim's search for the destiny his father, a former soldier, prophesied for him before his death, using his regimental flag as an icon, a red bull on a green field. When he finds that flag, says his father, he will find his home among people who will know his true identity and will bring him up as an Englishman. Meanwhile he lives with an Indian woman and to all appearances is an Indian boy. Shortly after the novel begins Kim hooks up with a Tibetan monk, Teshoo Lama, who is tracing the footsteps of Buddha Sakyamuni in search of the River of the Arrow. Immersion in this river, says the Lama, will cleanse him of all sin. This dual quest—Kim for his father's regiment, the Lama for his river—forms the first part of the narrative. The second part follows Kim as he finds his father's regiment, is introduced to the rigors of English education, and is adopted by the Secret Service for espionage. The foci of his education are the practice of surveying and the art of map drawing. A by-product of this education is Kim's confusion about his own identity. He is caught between his childhood as an Indian street urchin who thinks and speaks in Hindi and the insistence of his British educators on his genetic English identity. In the final part of the novel Kim attempts to work out his conflict, which is dramatized when Kim falls four times into a reverie, at crucial points in the plot, in which he repeats, "I am Kim. But what is Kim?" (166, 233, 273, 331).

In answer to that question, Abdul JanMohamed has argued that Kipling's novel indeed offers its hero only two possible identities: Indian or Englishman. JanMohamed notes that there appears to be a struggle between Kim and the narrator: "Every time someone suggests that he is white, Kim denies it vehemently and even insists that he will die if he is removed from his beloved Indians."[14] JanMohamed writes that the narrative burdens Kim with a genetic identity that must be fulfilled. Kipling compromises by giving the orphan Kim two sets of de facto parents, some Indian, some British. Kim has an emotional allegiance to the Indians and a rational allegiance to the British. By this compromise, says JanMohamed, the book reinscribes Kim within "the Manichaean allegory," according to which the East is emotional and sensuous and the West is rational and scientific.

As satisfying as JanMohamed's analysis is, it misses something I believe to be important. The figure of Hurree Chunder Mookerjee, M.A., more often referred to as "the Babu," complicates the dyadic model of identifications JanMohamed has constructed out of the Manichaean philosophy. The Babu does not fit neatly along the left-hand wall where JanMohamed places the Indian characters, and although he certainly does not line up on the right with the British, he certainly wishes he could.[15] Furthermore, Kim's relation to the Babu is emotional, but I would hardly call it an allegiance—antipathy is more accurate. For reasons I shall articulate, the Babu uses Kim's antipathy; he manipulates it in a way that suggests Kim's subject formation is much less a dyadic affair than JanMohamed says it is. The question of Kim's subjectivity involves more than an analysis of the discourses produced by the racial theories of imperialism, more than mute historical forces, although these are part of it. Likewise it involves more than pre- and postoedipal male psychology, though these too play a part. It is instead a product of *both* an imperial structure *and* psychological drives manifested as a sequence of aggressive and defensive moves in the relationship between Kim and the Babu.

As I hope I have made clear by now, major components of that imperial structure are the discourse and institutions produced by the subject of geography. The discourses include ideas about racial identity that derive from spatial origin; the institutions include the Royal Geographic Society, the schools that teach geographic knowledge, and the military, in whose secret surveys Kim participates. In this context it makes sense that the narrator attempts to dragoon Kim, the British, and the Indian characters into a single visual orientation toward an imperial representation of India, a representation that supports and reflects the structure of imperialism. That representation posits either a British or Indian identity on the basis of a genetic inheritance that derives its originary status from geographic conceptions of identity and nationality (though these terms are often muddled in nineteenth- and twentieth-century discourse). Those who trace their genes from inside the borders of India are Indian; those who trace them from without, from England, are English. In other words, Kim's subject position is produced not exclusively from a particular attachment to any other characters, as JanMohamed argues, but also from a particular way of looking at his relationship to territory and borders. This inscription of racial essence on particular geographic entities, from whence racial identity is then picked back out, is a feature of Curzon's definition of citizenship. But although Kipling's novel reflects this contemporary structuration of national identity, his narration of the relationship between Kim and the Babu dramatizes at the same time something else: the disenchantment with the Curzonian notion that one's identity stems *naturally* and only from the intersection of geography and genetics.[16] Kim becomes a subject of geography as much out of a psychological need to avoid the fate of the Babu as through some deterministic force of history or birth.

Eastern and Western Visual Perspectives

Others have noted that the novel flirts with the Eastern concept of maya, or illusion.[17] The theme finds its textual anchor in the Lama's wheel of life, a Tibetan *tangka* that represents a Buddhist map of the cosmos. Teshoo Lama uses the wheel to help him interpret the chaos of daily life in relation to the eternal world of the gods beyond appearance. I will here define the tangka as a map because it fulfills a similar function: It offers a way for the subject to position itself in relation to the surrounding visual field. As it happens, the tangka purports to form the subject's vision in such a way as to project it beyond the world of appearance, the world of cause and effect, whereas the geographic map positions the viewer above the visual field.

According to our narrator, Kim has a profound attachment to Teshoo Lama, though it seems clear he has no investment in the Lama's metaphysics. If he had, he probably would not take such glee in joining with the Babu to manipulate the old man into the mountains for the purposes of the Great Game when the Lama has made it abundantly clear that the river of his healing lies on the plains (although one of the touches of irony in this narrative is that the Lama cannot see his river because he has accepted a pair of good Western eyeglasses from the English museum curator, and so his gaze is directed to the sharp clear outlines of the world of illusion).[18] But Kim's repressed deceit returns to haunt him later when they return from the mountains, and he breaks down sobbing, complaining to the Lama that he has "walked thee too far: I have not picked always good food for thee; I have not considered the heat; I have talked to people on the road and left thee alone. ... I have—I have ... Hai mai! But I love thee ... and it is all too late. ... I was a child. ... Oh, why was I not a man?"(320) Notably Kim's self-abusing confession halts in ellipsis just when he might have admitted his complicity in the Babu's plan to lead the Lama into the mountains. He then translates his failure into terms of maturity: Were he a man he would have served the Lama better. Kim has internalized the voice of the Babu, who structures "maturity" as the achievement of departmental status within the practices of the Great Game. During Kim's education, he is continually referred to a time in the future when he will achieve departmental stature, and it is the Babu who brings Kim the first tidbit of departmental praise that thrills him. Thus the Babu helps construct a scenario for Kim in which his relations with the Lama play out as lack, or failure, or—worse yet—adolescence, and his relations with the British work out as professional success and the achievement of mature identity. This is related to the structure of the narrative, in which the narrator's ironic distance from Kim reduces as Kim grows more Anglo. The Babu's strategy echoes a commonplace of colonial discourse in which the colonized were depicted as children to the adult Europeans.[19]

In one of his more subtle lessons the Babu shows Kim how a rosary the Lama uses to escape the world can be used instead for a productive engagement with, and interpretation of, that world—namely to make maps. This is significant because time and time again, the narrator notes the presence of the Lama in a scene by marking the clicking beads of his rosary. The rosary becomes a synecdoche for both the Lama and his metaphysics, since the clicking beads signify that he is in meditation, far removed from the worldly, chaotic hurly-burly in which the narrator and Kim glory. But Hurree Babu explains to Kim that "as it was occasionally inexpedient to carry about measuring chains a boy would do well to know the precise length of his own foot pace. ... To keep count of a thousand paces, Hurree Chunder's experience had shown him nothing more valuable than a rosary of eighty-one or a hundred and eight beads, for 'it was divisible and sub-divisible into many multiples and sub-multiples'" (211). The Babu appropriates a talisman of the East and uses it as a tool in the service of European domination. It becomes a fetish object, overvalued and compensating for the purported lack of objectivity in Eastern mysticism. The Babu also assumes the identities of various "characters" from Indian street life, under the cover of which he collects his information and serves the imperial state. One way to think of this is to see the Babu as a master of a general tendency to appropriate social formations and symbols in such a way as to make them appear to speak "normally"—that is, in an enchanted fashion—to the naive subject but to also speak for the strategic purposes of the disenchanted imperialist. At the same time a system of correspondences is set up in which a succession of displacements occurs. The Babu can displace his own powerlessness and despair onto the characters he plays; the narrator and the reader can observe him doing so and displace their own disenchantment onto him.[20] For an example, here is the Babu, explaining some of the secrets of espionage to Kim:

You say: "I am Son of the Charm." Verree good.

"I do not understand quite. We must not be heard talking English here."

"That is all raight. I am only Babu showing off my English to you. All we Babus talk English to show off," said Hurree, flinging his shoulder-cloth jauntily. (231)

To the native observer the Babu is speaking according to the form: All babus speak to show off their English. But he manipulates that form to conceal important information for the maintenance of the empire. As I hope to show in a moment, there is a another set of codes here as well, signifying in the register where Kim and the Babu play their psychological game. These codes show Kim how to use a constructed subject position or identity in the service of the empire but also show up the fictionality of that position. In the less-than-great game the Babu is playing with Kim's psyche, this is a disenchanting move. The strategy works, both as the fulfillment of the Babu's professional duty and as psychological aggression, and so he can tell himself he is just doing his duty even as he tries to make Kim hurt in the same way he himself hurts.

Kim's reaction is this: "Here was a new craft that a man could tuck away in his head and by the look of the large wide world unfolding itself before him, it seemed that the more a man knew the better for him" (211). Clearly the message has gotten through to Kim that first, there are different ways of interpreting the visual field and that second, if he learns mapmaking he can interpret the wide world to his own benefit. Curzon echoes here. We can see Kim's emerging geographic consciousness in the participle "unfolding" as it modifies "world." We get the sense that Kim is, for the first time, seeing more and more territory beyond the horizon, ripe for describing, surveying, mapping. This metaphor has a certain thickness to it, as well, since "unfold" is something the world does when you open up a map. The phrasing that describes the world as wide, huge, and needing interpretation will recur later in an important context, but for now I want to emphasize the use of the Lama's rosary as a tool for the drawing of the imperial map, for interpreting the world in such a way as to facilitate British domination. The Babu uses Kim's position as disciple of the old man to insert him into situations where he can serve the state: Who would suspect that a *chela* (disciple) trailing his holy man, ticking off beads on his rosary, might actually be pacing off distances between fortifications to aid the army of the imperial power?

In short, the Babu wants Kim to learn to see India from the British perspective, from the perspective of the map. But this perspective places Kim at odds with his chosen mentor, the Lama, for whom soldiers and spies are "bound upon the Wheel, [and] go forth from life to life—from despair to despair ... hot, uneasy, snatching" (102). The Lama is on to something: Despair indeed motivates the Babu to take a paternal interest in Kim. When I say he despairs I mean that he wants something badly and also knows he will never have it. As for what he wants, it seems clear to me that the Babu wants to be on the outside of India, looking in. We are told he wants to be a member of the Fellows of the Royal Society of Ethnographers, which means he wants to be an Englishman studying Indian culture (222). The Babu knows he has done horrible things to get what he desires, such as help oppress and subjugate his countrymen, and so he has a contempt for himself that causes him to seek out punishment. In this reading the Babu's behavior in a crucial scene with the French and the Russian spies, in which he delivers himself up to them though he knows they will beat him, becomes more clear to us than it does to Kim. Kim shows perplexity at the Babu's behavior: "He makes them a mock at the risk of his life—I never would have gone down to them after the pistol shots—and then he says he is a fearful man ... and he is a fearful man" (331). And, we might add, he propels himself into his fear, the beatings and mockery of the foreigners, because they will, in a sense, punish him for his duplicitous deeds.

The other part of the cycle of despair is aggression against others, and that aggression motivates the relationship between the Babu and Kim. Their interactions constitute a series of offensive and defensive moves contending over which of the available subject positions Kim will occupy: Indian or English? naive or disenchanted? The Babu has a stake in this question. If, by the time he reaches maturity within the paternal structures of the Secret Service, Kim is a disenchanted Briton, the Babu will have won the psychological game between them, and Kim will be prey to the same despair that motivates the Babu. The Babu's methodology in this game involves a kind of self-display in which he shows Kim that he always knows that he is enacting a role self-consciously. Consider the following exchange in Kim's indoctrination. The Babu has come to Kim and has complimented him on his first triumph in service to the state:

> For the first time in his life Kim thrilled to the clean pride (it can be a deadly pitfall, none the less) of Departmental praise—ensnaring praise from an equal of work appreciated by fellow-workers. Earth has nothing on the same plane to compare with it. But, cried the Oriental in him, Babus do not travel far to retail compliments.
> "Tell thy tale, Babu," he said authoritatively.
> "Oah it is nothing. Onlee I was at Simla when the wire came in about what our mutual friend said he had hidden, and old Creighton—" He looked to see how Kim would take this piece of audacity.
> "The Colonel Sahib," the boy from St. Xavier's corrected. (268)

Kim responds in the way the Babu wants him to. The audacity is calculated—the narrator clues us by noting that the Babu is watching Kim's response—to provoke Kim to assert his position as a sahib, educated at one of the sahib's best schools, St. Xavier's. Kim responds to the Babu "authoritatively" in picking up the challenge to departmental discipline, and after some minutes with the glib Babu, comes finally to assert, "looking up at the broad, grinning face, 'Babuji ... I am a Sahib'" (269). I think it important that Kim asserts his British identity—something he has resisted for years—just as he looks into the face of the Babu. What is more, I think, this is the response the Babu wants. It means his project to make Kim a Briton in spite of his history has worked. For the other part of his project, to make of Kim a *disenchanted* Briton, he relies upon the display of his own ambiguous subjectivity—at times playing the "Babu to his boot heels" (330), at other times showing Kim how he is playing himself as a babu, in effect emptying out his ambiguous, compromised subject position and displaying for Kim the fictionality of it.

It might work: Three of Kim's four lapses into reveries of self-doubt come immediately following his conversations with the Babu. The two have been equated by one of the important Englishmen in the book, Lurgan (209). Like the Babu, Kim's social background would orient him toward the pole opposite his genetic identity. He is, we are told and shown often enough, quite satisfied with his lot in life as an Indian. The Babu, however, by pushing Kim into a position similar to his own—one assigned according to genetic origin instead of social and psychological background—can put someone else in his predicament, can share the misery, as it were.

But on the brink of learning the language of despair—"I am a fearful man, but somehow or other, the more fearful I am the more dam'-tight places I get into," says the Babu (330)—Kim stops talking, stops thinking, and tries to reenter the world. He returns as well, or tries to return, to his other mentor, the Lama:

> He tried to think of the Lama ... but the bigness of the world, seen between the forecourt gates, swept linked thought aside. Then he looked upon the trees and the broad fields, with the thatched huts hidden among crops—looked with strange eyes unable to take up the size and proportion and use of things. ... All that while he felt, though he could not put it into words, that his soul was out of gear with his surroundings.
>
> "I am Kim. I am Kim. And what is Kim?" His soul repeated it again and again. (331)

To read this passage, and to suggest what it means for Kim to occupy the British subject position, recall the distinction I made earlier between tangkas and maps. In an effort to get some interpretive control over the amorphous "bigness of the world," Kim first adopts and then discards the Buddhist perceptual system as a place from which to define himself. This is the vision the tangka tries to produce, a vision that rejects the false world of cause and effect, or "linked thought," as the narrator has it. He looks on the world with "strange eyes" because, according to the narrator, he is a British subject and thus the vision produced by this way of seeing must be alien. In this vision the perceptual categories of size and proportion, and the economic category of use value, have no place. In this condition as well Kim is outside of language, and the narrator assumes descriptive control, telling us that Kim is "out of gear with his surroundings." Clearly the narrator does not think the tangka is the right sort of map for Kim, and just where the narrator ends and Kim begins is difficult to know in this instance, which suggests that Kim has come very close to the Anglo position occupied by the narrator. Yet Kim *is* uncomfortable as he resorts to his mantra "What is Kim?"—always a sign of confusion.

The Signifying Gaze

In order to imagine himself, to answer that question "What is Kim?" successfully, that is, in a way that allows him to fulfill his racial destiny as Victorian ideology demands yet also in a way that avoids the fate of the disenchanted Babu, Kim must adopt a perspective and think through a language that tells him he is a sahib not in terms of relation or opposition to another subject but in relation to space and borders. When he does, "with an almost audible click he felt the wheels of his being lock up anew on the world without. Things that rode meaningless on his eyeball an instant before slid into proper proportion. Roads were meant to be walked upon, houses to be lived in, cattle to be driven, fields to be tilled, and men and women to be talked to" (331). In this moment, when Kim answers the question, "What is Kim?" I want to focus on the narrator's conspicuous use of the passive voice. It allows Kim to deposit into the "natural" a structured interpretation of the world as soon as he accepts that interpretation as his own. The passive voice removes the agent of the verb "to mean" and thus naturalizes the interpretation that endows the objects in the visual field with meaning. Furthermore, the grammatical construction renders these objects as subjects of passive verbs: houses, for example, are "to be lived in." This structure further removes human agency from the visual field, to the extent that ultimately men and women are "meant to be talked to" and thus made passive subjects in wait of hailing by an absent interpreter whose address will give their existence significance. So Kim adopts a subject position that removes his own agency from his visual field and that sees the world through precisely the kind of vision engendered by geography and imperialism, where the landscape lies passively awaiting the surveyor's signifying gaze. This is, furthermore, Kim's strategy to avoid the fate of the Babu. The geographic perspective allows Kim to reenchant his relation to the world in such a way as to avoid seeing the constructedness of his position and his own agency in that construction. At once he solves the issue of his own identity in a way that conforms to Victorian ideology and yet avoids the Babu's efforts to disenchant him—for the nonce, at least. At the same time the narrator eliminates the ironic distance that had produced a coherent perspective on Kim as he was achieving his identity, and so the narrator attempts a direct identification with Kim as an Anglo subject in the geographic sense I outlined at the beginning of this essay.

By way of contrast, note the narrative, ground-level perspective of Kim's earlier journey along the Grand Trunk Road:

> The Grand Trunk at this point was built on an embankment to guard against winter floods from the foothills, so that one walked, as it were, a little above the country, along a stately corridor, seeing all India spread out to left and right. It was beautiful to behold the many-yoked grain and cotton wagons crawling over the country roads: one could hear their axles, complaining a mile away, coming nearer, till with shouts and yells and bad words they climbed up the steep incline and plunged on to the hard main road, carter reviling carter. It was equally beautiful to watch the people. (111)

This is the perspective of the itinerary; the narrative space is organized by the passage of agents through it. The details noted are attributes of individuals, and their activities take precedence in the grammar of description. That is, in the quotation previous to this one the physical objects of the visual field took precedence and agency was removed from that field; in this passage agency takes precedence because it creates the visual field. The gazing subject is present in the grammar, and the objects of the gaze do not sit passively awaiting that gaze. Instead they actively compel its attention. Yet this vision does not, despite its claim, encompass "all of India" in an organized, clear representation. Therefore it is insufficient for the imperial enterprise. Its revelations are personal, its spaces flexible and inconstant. For Kipling's narrator it is not the unifying vision necessary to encompass the diverse and fractious perspectives that make up India. Such perspectives require the "cartographic lingua franca" maps provide.

In *The Practice of Everyday Life* Michel de Certeau establishes the relationship between maps and narrative itineraries in terms of a distinction between place and space. His terms provide a useful insight into the superiority of maps for the purpose of colonial representation. Place is static, passive; its elements are located in "proper" configurations. Space, however, is a "practiced place."[21] It "has none of the univocity or stability" of a proper place. Space is subject to the transformations of time; agents construct it by movement, by practice. In formal terms, the map represents place; the narrative itinerary, space. De Certeau notes that the narrative itinerary is the origin of the pictorial map but that over time, "the map has slowly disengaged itself from the itineraries that were the condition of its possibility."[22] That is to say, the ships, exotic creatures, and other semiotic material that signified the colonialist origins of the cartographic enterprise gradually disappeared from the maps it produced, thus allowing it to be absorbed into structures of perception as a purchase on the real in the way I have outlined here.

The Cartographic Lingua Anglica

Kipling labors hard to show us how attached to the Lama Kim really is because the connection between the two is an important element in the reality effect that makes Kim an endearing little boy. How is Kim to reconcile with the Lama when he manages to discover his identity only by forgetting him? The narrator solves this problem by incorporating the Lama into the imperial perspective. The Lama, in search of his river, goes out to meditate. After fasting, he falls into a nondescript river, where he is rescued by the Babu. Later, he interprets for Kim his experience as the long-awaited encounter with the River of the Arrow:

> Yea, my Soul went free, and, wheeling like an eagle, saw indeed that there was no Teshoo Lama nor any other soul. As a drop draws near to water, so my Soul drew near to the Great Soul which is beyond all things. At that point, exalted in contemplation, I saw all Hind, from Ceylon in the sea to the Hills, and my own painted Rocks at

Such-Zen; I saw every camp and village, to the least, where we had ever rested. I saw them at one time and in one place; for they were within the Soul. (337)

What interests me is what the Lama's vision becomes in retrospect, when he renders it into language. Then the vision becomes a bird's-eye view of the subcontinent, a view made possible by the maps the Lama first saw in the Museum of Lahore early in the novel.[23] The narrative here incorporates the Lama into the imperial gaze, adjusting his vision to conform to the perspective of the imperial map. In that vision the individual subject disappears, replaced by a vision of territory where what becomes important is the record of the mapping subject's passage over it, but with the interpreting subject itself absent from that space, just as what the Lama sees is every camp and village where he and Kim rested on their travels, but with "no Teshoo Lama nor any other soul" in those places.

Finally, the reconciliation of Kim and the Lama, and the resolution of the narrative in the Victorian manner, do not result from Kim asserting his Indian nurture at the expense of his British nature. Instead they come when the Lama adopts the imperial view of India. The record of his religious pilgrimage becomes another kind of map, much like one Kim might draw or study at St. Xavier's, a bird's-eye view of the whole territory, imagined as a homogeneous space subject to the imperial gaze. The usefulness of the imperial gaze for Kim is that it allows him to imagine his Other spatially, as a territory and not as the discomfiting, grinning face of Hurree Chunder Mookerjee, M.A., a very fearful man, a man in whose face Kim might have had to see pain, fear, despair, and his own future. Through the imperial gaze made possible by the *primary* subject of geography, Kim can look into that face and see not a disenchanting conundrum, not even a Babu, but an Indian. That makes his own identity, and finally the narrator's identity, much less problematic. He has taken his place as a *secondary* subject of geography and become one of Curzon's "proper public men."

NOTES

1. G. R. Crone, *Maps and Their Makers* (London: Hutchinson, 1968 [1953]), p. 38.

2. Pierre Bourdieu, *Outline of a Theory of Practice* (Cambridge: Cambridge University Press, 1977); and Marcel Mauss, *The Gift* (London: Routledge, 1990).

3. Karl Polanyi, *The Great Transformation* (Boston: Beacon Press, 1957), p. 52. Polanyi has been criticized for "being unable to do more than describe the shifting place of the economy in various societies, without ever really being able to pose the theoretical problem of its effect upon the functioning and evolution of societies, and therefore of its role in history." Maurice Godelier, *The Mental and the Material* (London: Verso, 1986), pp. 200–201. Although Polanyi's notions of value and commodification, among others, may not be deeply theorized or deeply Marxist, his point that the shifting place of the economy affects the structure of society, and that changes in the structure cause real pain and real fear, are borne out by the texts under consideration here.

4. Polanyi, *The Great Transformation*, p. 52.

5. Ibid., p. 57.

6. J. B. Harley, p. 25.

7. Ibid.

8. Ibid.

9. George Nathaniel Curzon, "Geography," in *Subjects of the Day* (New York: MacMillan, 1915), p. 155.

10. Curzon, "Geography," p. 156.

11. I am indebted to Kaja Silverman's *The Subject of Semiotics* (New York: Oxford, 1983) for my understanding of this concept.

12. "Kim, the self-possesed orphan of Rudyard Kipling's creation, found himself drawn into the adventurous, sometimes clandestine operations of the Survey of India. Kim had what it took. ... Though fictional [he was] true to the life of British India in the most colorful era of the Survey, a mapping service with one of the longest and proudest traditions." So begins a chapter in John Noble Wilford, *The Mapmakers* (New York: Vintage, 1981), p. 161. Wilford notes that *Kim* is obviously a product of a culture fascinated by maps.

13. Rudyard Kipling, *Kim,* ed. Edward W. Said (Harmondsworth: Penguin, 1987 [1901]), p. 49. All subsequent references to this text are included parenthetically within the essay.

14. Abdul JanMohamed, "Colonialist Literature," in *Race, Writing, and Difference,* ed. Henry Louis Gates Jr. (Chicago: University of Chicago Press, 1986), p. 98.

15. Said traces back to the drama of Aeschylus and Euripedes a topos of representation of Asia: Europe, strong and victorious, Persia, defeated and despairing. A habit of thought begun in medieval times was to view Mohammed as an impostor of Christ, and from this was built a vision of the representative Oriental as a crude, poor mimic of the Westerner— hence, here, the Babu figure as a mimic. See Edward Said, *Orientalism* (New York: Vintage, 1979 [1978]), pp. 56–57.

16. Perhaps here a brief definition of the term "disenchantment" is in order. By this I simply mean the recognition of the man-made character of something previously considered "natural" or transcendent.

17. JanMohamed, "Colonialist Literature," p. 97.

18. I am indebted to Professor John Jordan for this insight.

19. Said, *Orientalism,* p. 40, and JanMohamed, "Colonialist Literature," p. 87, have noted this persistent tendency of colonialist literature. It serves as a legitimizing ideology for the colonial project of taking over government from those unfit to govern.

20. See Silverman, *The Subject of Semiotics,* p. 222, for a discussion of suture in classic cinema that describes this relay of gaze and displacement in terms of gender. I think the same dynamic obtains in terms of race.

21. Michel de Certeau, *The Practice of Everyday Life,* trans. Richard Nice (Berkeley: University of California Press, 1988), p. 117.

22. Ibid., p. 120.

23. Edward W. Said has equated this vision with Creighton's Indian Survey. I am making a more explicit reference to the maps the Lama saw early in the narrative. See his introduction in *Kim.*

5

Just When You Thought
It Was Safe to Go
Back in the Water ...

DANIEL L. SELDEN

Hence the inestimable
convenience of AIDS.

—Simon Watney

IT MAKES A GOOD DEAL of difference how we define the field of representation insofar as it relates to AIDS, and I would like to reflect for a moment on that problem by way of a specific text. In the present context, it is only possible to summarize its plot, and this runs more or less as follows:

> *Once upon a time in America, in the heyday of urban consumer culture, a primitive but lethal organism begins to devastate unsuspecting individuals amid their assiduous pursuit of pleasure. Death comes swiftly, and it is particularly gruesome. The first victims are typed as sexually promiscuous and have a history of drug or alcohol abuse. Each is deviant or marginal to the mainstream in some way. The organism also attacks women and, most pathetically, young children, but only in the last instance white, middle-class, heterosexual males who remain monogamous or chaste.*
>
> *Authorities are alerted to the danger early on. However, owing to a combination of political and economic factors, no effective action is taken until the death rate escalates and the threat to society can no longer be ignored. There follow various campaigns of "disinformation," and the allegations of cover-up extend to medical practitioners themselves. Once the media catch on, however, there is a*

> *barrage of irresponsible and exploitative journalism. Anxieties run high and pro-*
> *duce hysterical fears that the peril may spread without limit unless there are con-*
> *certed efforts for precaution and general community surveillance.*
>
> *In the end, three agencies rise up to meet the challenge: law and order, bio-*
> *medical technology, and old-style ingenuity and self-reliance. Together these*
> *three forces join to do combat with the peril, and after much self-sacrifice and*
> *Herculean effort, the deadly organism is isolated, studied, and eventually wiped*
> *out. Many are dead, but American society can now return to normal.*

This is not the story of the eruption of HIV and its proposed eradication as we have witnessed it develop in the 1980s. It is the plot of Steven Spielberg's *Jaws*, a film that went into production nearly ten years before anyone ever heard of AIDS. As all of us who are old enough will remember, the release of *Jaws* galvanized the American imagination as few movies do. The film not only ranks as one of Holly-wood's major achievements of the 1970s but is a document that we now recognize to be central to contemporary mass culture, and it is in this capacity that its paral-lels with the events surrounding AIDS might give us pause for some reflection.

I do not mean to suggest that Spielberg's film is a prophetic allegory of AIDS or that AIDS is the only, or even the most obvious, thing the shark could symbolize. In fact, Fredric Jameson has argued that the very effectiveness of Spielberg's vehi-cle "lies less in any single message or meaning than in its ... capacity to absorb and organize ... quite distinct [historical] anxieties together."[1] I am actually less concerned here with the iconography of the shark per se, though it is depicted in terms that regularly resurface in more recent descriptions of the nature and im-pact of HIV. What interests me is how uncannily *Jaws* outlines the same sequence of reactions and set of solutions with which we are all familiar in the public back-lash unleashed by AIDS. I am thinking here not only of the sociology of the so-called victims or the alleged complicity of government and science with self-serv-ing political and economic ends. The triple partnership between surveillance, technology, and traditional moral fiber is precisely the nexus of forces that has banded together so conspicuously in America's attempt to combat the invisible, though evidently no less primitive and deadly, predator that threatens it today.

I draw two conclusions from this. First, public response to AIDS realizes in a complex but entirely concrete way a scenario that is well attested in popular cul-ture of the immediately preceding years. The forum, to be sure, is different, but the cast of characters and the institutions in the drama are all substantially the same, as are their roles and the general nature of the crisis that has engaged them. One way to explain this recurrence is to attribute it to the "cultivation" of the me-dia, the industry's ability to "mainstream" public values, expectations, and be-liefs,[2] and some effect of this nature should certainly not, I think, be ruled out. More problematically, however, it seems to me that *Jaws* and AIDS as cultural phenomena are both displaced spectacles that rehearse the same deeply entrenched psychosocial narrative and, as admonitory dramas, work to instill—though AIDS is an immeasurably more palpable and violent form—a similar ideological framing of knowledge and power, played out punitively across a lacerated body.

Second, because the two phenomena are similar in this way, the question of AIDS and representation cannot be posed simply at the level of images, perceptions, and metaphors. Studies of the "iconography of AIDS" expose only one factor in a much more complex and insidious syntax of representational drives and forces. *Jaws* is a moving picture and, as such, is not simply a set of situational predicates or propositions but an operator that establishes a series of transformational relationships between terms. "The minimal complete plot," Tzvetan Todorov reminds us, "consists in the *passage* from one equilibrium *to* another."[3] One of the things the script of *Jaws* suggests, then, is that the material *practices* of individuals in response to AIDS, the agitation of different interest groups, and even the agencies that we as a society look to and invest in for a solution live out and thereby reconfirm a motivating narrative scheme. Consequently, a representational critique of AIDS can by no means be simply a matter of "improving" the ways in which the media depict the epidemic or of weeding out "corruptions" in the language of science.[4] However indispensable here an analysis of discourse or iconography may be, it is bound to remain tactically limited unless it goes on to address the larger social syntax that links and hence construes such images in relation to specific patterns of response.

Evidently, this is no less true of the enterprise that we are mutually engaged in here. If you look at Spielberg's film again, you will see that it contains a good deal of self-referential play with the ways in which shark attacks are represented, and there is a significant amount of attention devoted to how these images shape popular perception and affect the making of public policy. Whoever is committed to questioning the representational determinants of AIDS in full will have to go on to ask, then, to what extent that demystificatory gesture itself, however progressively conceived, plays unwittingly into the same public spectacle that it set out to critique.

In the utopian ending of *Jaws,* the police chief and bio–whiz kid triumph over the violence of nature, though significantly the skipper who guides them, linked to an older ethic and an outmoded means of production, is sacrificed along the way. For those of us who reject surveillance as a viable solution to the problems posed by AIDS, science continues to hold out our best hope. If, however, what Simon Watney calls "the miraculous authority of clinical medicine"[5] does succeed in discovering a cure for the disease—as we can only have reason to believe it will—one begins to suspect that this remedy, among other things, will serve to ratify a cultural agenda that effectively organized the entire drama in the first place. If, in our relief, we accept this end uncritically and without resistance, do we not, I wonder, leave ourselves open potentially to the execution of a sequel, most likely in some other form, though equally as violent and where we least expect it—just (as the saying goes) when we thought it was safe to go back in the water?

NOTES

1. F. Jameson, "Reification and Utopia in Mass Culture," *Social Text* 1 (1979), 142.

2. G. Gerbner, L. Gross, M. Morgan, and N. Signorielli, "Living with Television: The Dynamics of the Cultivation Process," in *Perspectives on Media Effects*, ed. J. Bryant and D. Zillman (Hillsdale, N.J.: L. Erlbaum Assocs., 1986).

3. T. Todorov, *The Poetics of Prose*, trans. R. Howard (Ithaca, N.Y.: Cornell University Press, 1977), 111; cf. 218–233.

4. S. Sontag, *AIDS and Its Metaphors* (New York: Farrar, Straus & Giroux, 1988), 94; S. Gilman, *Disease and Representation: Images of Illness from Madness to AIDS* (Ithaca, N.Y.: Cornell University Press, 1988), 16.

5. S. Watney, "The Spectacle of AIDS," in *AIDS: Cultural Analysis/Cultural Activism*, ed. D. Crimp (Cambridge, Mass.: MIT Press, 1988), 78.

6

Versions of the Perverse

CATHERINE GREENBLATT

I FIND MYSELF FOR A MOMENT in the interesting position of not knowing whether what I have to say should be regarded as something long familiar and obvious or as something entirely new and puzzling," writes Sigmund Freud very nearly at the end of his life.[1] Freud's quizzical attitude might describe the modality of much psychoanalytic writing, for the texts that mark the classical period of analysis, say between the 1880s and the 1930s, quite often equivocate between what is commonly and uncommonly known. In this, Freud's statement bears great resemblance to what the Russian formalists called *ostranenie:* rendering the familiar strange, the habitual visible, and the native foreign. Psychoanalysis shares with formalism the task of describing such estrangement in structural metaphors, whether in theories of language, psyche, or sexuality. What formalism is to language and metaphor, psychoanalysis is to sexuality and desire. Perhaps one of the challenges of thinking of sexuality in figures, rather than essences, is to think not of the alienation of sexuality ("that which is most one's own, yet most taken away," writes Catharine MacKinnon)[2] but of the poetics of the perverse.

By asserting the similarity between psychoanalysis and formalism, or rather by attending to the formalist moments of Freud's texts, this essay traces some of the familiar contours of the body's sexuality in psychoanalysis as those shapes change and take other, perhaps unfamiliar and even radical form. That is, rather than positing an essential continuity or "universality" of the psychoanalytic understanding of sex, as many opponents of Freud have long tended to do, I attempt to grasp the morphology of sexuality at several significant junctures of Freud's often obscure, poetic writing. From Freud's fin de siècle case histories of hysteria and the *Three Essays on a Theory of Sexuality* through "Fetishism" and "Splitting of the Ego in the Defensive Process," Freud's depiction of the body's relation to desire is an expression of a distinctly *modernist* sexuality.[3] In other words, sexuality in psychoanalysis is imbricated in the same challenges of form that modernism in the plastic and literary arts undertakes as much as it is articulated in the apparently ahistorical dynamics of desire. Seen in this way, the modernist project of sexuality is a formal conception of desire articulated in the body's morphology. Of course, bodily morphology is precisely the site of sexual difference and sexual politics; and desire is the place where gender and sexuality meet in imperfect and conflictive liaisons: Freud's sexual modernism is a battleground of bodily form. In psychoanalysis, perversion is an inviting place indeed to look for estranged forms of desire and modernist configurations of the sexual.

In 1905, Freud published *Three Essays on the Theory of Sexuality* and Dora's famous case history of hysteria. Both texts turn decisively, emphatically, against the normative history of sexological discourse that understands perversion as pathological. If we grasp that the mania of sexology is to legislate and to classify all the forms of sexual life but especially those of the pervert, then Freud's intervention in the study of sexuality both exploits and incorporates the classification of perversion as an aspect of the "normal," if not routine, practices of adult sexuality. A disruption of order in the reigning encyclopedias of sexology, such as Krafft-Ebing's *Psychopathia Sexualis,* inherits a legacy of normative discourse on perversion; indeed, Freud himself spends a great deal of his life in various attempts to transform the habits and assumptions in these scientific theories of sexual psychology.[4]

The classification of perversion in Krafft-Ebing functions like the head of Medusa on Perseus's shield, a warding off of what sexology cannot acknowledge, namely its own interest in sustaining the masculine subject of sexuality.[5] That is, such sexual encyclopedists as Krafft-Ebing take up what they see as forms of the abnormal as a way of shielding the unquestioned category of the normal from perverse contamination. And yet, Freud's positioning of perversion as an introduction to human sexuality in *Three Essays,* before he claims perversion as something fundamental to well-functioning adult heterosexuality, would seem to repeat this apotropaic gesture. There Freud writes, in what begins as a thoroughly sexological "fact," that "the normal sexual aim is regarded as being the union of the genitals in the act of copulation." In this, he appears to uphold an ideal as normative, as the property-owning, private, and altruistically sexual man at the absent heart of *Psychopathia Sexualis.* However, Freud continues after a time, "But even in the most normal sexual process we may detect rudiments which ... would have led to the deviations described as 'perversions.'"[6]

Thus, there is something in Freud's contribution to the theory of perversions that partakes of what it attempts to displace. Freud repeats the pathologizing of perversions while at the same time locating them within and alongside what is accepted conventionally as "normal" practice. In this apparently equivocal or duplicitous characterization of the perverse, which is in Freud's writing elevated to a textual practice, Freud mimics the initial strategies of sexology's containment in order to claim a different status for perversion later. Moreover, I think that it is quite possible to read in Freud's rhetoric a rather keen generosity, even an identificatory pleasure, in writing about the subjects of perversion. From Freud's texts on perversion, one can assume that Freud is thoroughly versed in the pleasures of the perverse. In this chapter I take up this duplicitous strategy as a tactic of perversity par excellence. The perverse everywhere partakes of the conditions it displaces and reinvests. The figure of the pervert, in this fashion, engages a process of transvaluation of the meanings of the body, forms of desire, and sites of pleasure. Thus a very savvy practice of power and pleasure, the perverse recognizes the law and can perform its practice even bettter than the law's best offices. And yet this figure, in the very mimicry of the tools of the strictest law and order, constructs something else, another embodiment of desire. An exquisite reader, the pervert acknowledges the "proper" reading and then looks to other, fresher regions of the text. As seductive as he is savvy, unfortunately the pervert has one rather formidable strike against him: His desire has hitherto belonged exclusively to the domain of masculine desire.[7]

The desire that animates this essay, no doubt clear to even the most well-adjusted readers, is to reclaim these strategies of the perverse for a feminist possibility of feminine desire: "feminist" because I insist on the capacities of feminism to challenge and reorient normative formations of gender and desire; "feminine" because the pleasures of the perverse may not always comport with good feminist politics. In the following pages, I examine the politics and poetics of two Freudian conceptions of the perverse, both invested fundamentally in the gendered conditions of the body in representation: sadomasochism and fetishism. Both have figured in crucial feminist interventions in the fields of film theory and literary theory, though cast in the negative as manifestations of misogyny and patriarchy, as ideologically gendered relations to and within textuality. It must be said, and probably will be said, that my efforts to reclaim these versions of the perverse for a feminist aesthetics and reading practice risk reconstituting the prevailing shapes of desire in the form of the masculine. This is the risk of the perverse, one well worth taking; for the prevailing metaphors of masculinity continue to shape the conditions of desire for women, and it is precisely the adventure of the perverse to imagine a different body and different subject of desire.

Pleasure and Analysis: The Adventures of Desire

"It is said that analysing pleasure, or beauty, destroys it," writes Laura Mulvey, introducing the critical function of her essay.[8] For Mulvey, theory and pleasure are antithetical; as protagonist and antagonist, the one seeks to defeat the other. Against the exhaustive masculinity of cultural pleasures such as going to a movie or reading a book, for Mulvey only the antidote of analysis can cure the problem of pleasure. Although in my reading of Mulvey I promise neither beauty nor pleasure, I do promise not to find in theory its antagonist.

To give a very brief review of Mulvey's pertinence to my project, Mulvey's object of critical demolition is the pleasure afforded by the spectacle of woman in the gaze of the masculine spectator, and the critical means by which she attempts to destroy this pleasure is "the total negation of the ease and plenitude of the narrative fiction film." The "totally negative" and imperious function of avant-garde, antinarrative cinema and theory is to dismantle pleasure, and nothing seems to fit the bill better than that most "painful" of theories, psychoanalysis. Although Mulvey situates some of the formal innovations of cinema as antithetical to the pleasure of Hollywood, I shall argue that it is precisely those formal techniques and elaborations that allow for the erotics of the perverse subject to emerge. For Mulvey, the inextricable bond of the spectacle of woman to the masculinity of narrative cinematic spectatorship is the only path to pleasure, imbricated in the structures of passivity and activity, masochism and sadism. For Mulvey, the relations between sadism and narrative are intimate, thorough, and exhaustive; sadism saturates narrative, leaves no ambivalent residue, and reclaims every detail; against sadism, narrative can mobilize no resistance, for it is narrative itself that speaks the grammar of sadism.[9] These structural bonds, in the strict sense of the phrase, constitute the central interest of this section of the essay: to examine the ways in which sadomasochism enacts stringent interpretations of the laws of sexual desire as gendered performances. And yet it is within the elaborate configuration of position and performance that a new relation to the sadist and the masochist takes place. That is, through the enactment of narrative sadism, a different voice and modality emerge.

Published in 1975, in the milieu of emergence of the psychoanalytic analysis of film that took place largely, though not exclusively, in the British film journal *Screen*, "Visual Pleasure and Narrative Cinema" still haunts feminist debate on the nature of the cinematic apparatus. In its frequent and varied reproduction and readings, the essay can be said to be a founding text of psychoanalytic feminist film criticism, inaugurating a rich network of debate and theory.[10] Beginning with Mulvey, then, with a totalizing consideration of narrative cinema as an economy of pleasure for men and pain for women, feminist film theory has contended with the rather paradoxically discomforting task of reclaiming pleasure, both in the work of theory, generally accepted as unpleasurable, and in the pleasure of viewing and reading. In the proliferation of binary terms (pleasure and analysis, sadism and masochism, activity and passivity, and so on), one can hear stray lines of dialogue from any one of a number of Hollywood melodramas: Must a feminist in search of pleasure choose between the look of the sadist and the spectacle of the masochist, between the masculine pleasure of looking with guilt and betrayal and the feminine humiliation of passivity and objectification?

Since the publication of "Visual Pleasure," approximately fifteen years of feminist film criticism has reclaimed narrative pleasure, though not in the name of theory. To paraphrase several strains of the feminist film debate at once (at the risk of reduction), since pleasure for women, pleasure in cinema, pleasure in identification, is a rare enough commodity for women as it is, are the stakes in destroying this pleasure more dangerous than in maintaining it? At the center of this consideration of pleasure is the figure of the female spectator, whose subjectivity is distributed ambivalently between at least two spaces of the sadistic apparatus of narrative cinema: between the scopophilic gaze of the spectator, coded as masculine, and the spectacle of woman, subjected to the spectacular and sadistic demands of narrative. In both places at once, the woman who looks, and who takes pleasure in looking, takes on the structuring of desire in an aspect of visual drag, on the one hand, in the scopophilic gaze we have come to know as masculine; on the other hand, embodied in that flesh we call female, the female spectator is identified—however imperfectly—with the screened spectacle of femininity. The woman who looks pleasurably is an expert in oscillation, deploying a savvy ambivalence in a precarious visual economy.

In the embodied contradiction of the female spectator, Mulvey relents slightly in the "Afterthoughts" essay, generalizing both the terrain of narrative and a woman's desire to invest in that terrain in order to include cultural forms other than cinema, such as mass culture and various storytelling traditions, and to underscore the problems of women reading and viewing in a field of masculine investment. Somewhere between the devil and the deep blue sea of masculine sadistic pleasure and feminine masochistic passivity, Mulvey argues, lies the possibility of pleasure in narrative, "an internal oscillation of desire, which lies dormant, waiting to be 'pleasured'" in narrative.[11] Though operating in terms of the mechanisms of fantasy, this formulation recalls the difficult resolution of the Oedipus complex in girls, who must choose painfully between "proper" passive femininity, rebellious and regressive active masculinity, and the denial of sexuality altogether. The masculine identification of the structuring of desire in narrative "reactivates for her a fantasy of 'action' that correct femininity demands should be repressed." Operating through a "metaphor of masculinity," the pleasures of fantasy in narrative are activated by this oscillation of desire in the subjectivity of women.

This metaphor acts as a straitjacket, becoming itself an indicator, a litmus paper, of the problems inevitably activated by any attempt to represent the feminine in patriarchal society. The memory of the "masculine" phase has its own romantic attraction, a last-ditch resistance in which the power of masculinity can be used as a postponement against the power of patriarchy.

"The romantic attraction" of masculinity lying dormant in the psychic life of women viewers and readers subscribes to the rhetoric of melodrama for Mulvey as a heterosexual scenario that plays itself out on the screen of the female spectator's psychic life. In the activation of masculine fantasy in the female spectator's engagement with narrative, Mulvey seems to narrativize, in good Hollywood fashion, the active-masculine and passive-feminine aspects of female pleasure in looking. In other words, if the metaphor of masculinity acts as a strait (and straight) jacket for Mulvey, we should, perhaps, change its rhetorical clothes, sub-scribe to a different fashion of metaphor that dresses fully for an ambivalent occa-sion, one in which the metaphorics of looking might be understood as something more and less than heterosexual "romantic attraction." If we take the metaphor of masculinity as a trope in which "the power of masculinity can be used as a post-ponement against the power of patriarchy," then this trope is useful so long as it provides the ground for pleasure in identification but is useful also for a theory of the functioning of the apparatus as it constitutes gendered relations to narrative and representation in general. So for feminism, let this attraction be romantic rather than fatal, but only as long as the rhetoric of romance and its masculine figures prove to be engaging in the politics and form of pleasure.

In Freud, feminist theory may continue to find useful modes and voices for modifying and elaborating the models of oscillation, identification, and critical transvestism. Feminists have turned to psychoanalysis in the past to reveal the very structures of patriarchal thought, and surely they are to be found in the *Stan-dard Edition*, but a more appositional reading of Freud might reveal more formal uses of psychoanalysis for feminism. Freud's pleasure in the act of deciphering it-self might become a useful way of rethinking the problem of theoretical pleasure, to be sure, but it might also afford a different view of the theory of sadomasoch-ism. For in the construction of these texts, there are traces of pleasure in unex-pected form.

Freud's Adventure

In 1915, Freud published the essay "Instincts and Their Vicissitudes" (Trieb und Triebschicksale)[12] as an introduction to a general project of metapsychology, a network of papers that exemplify the theoretical models of psychoanalysis, distill-ing the mechanisms of psychic functioning that, putatively, underlie all of Freud's writing. The papers on metapsychology are not case histories, nor do they form part of Freud's later project of a psychoanalytic anthropology. They have nothing to do with patients or with cultural artifacts; they constitute nothing less than Freud's critical elaboration of the topographies and economies of psychic life.

"Instincts" is an examination of the ways in which the psyche reacts to stimu-lus, both internal and external to the body, in the form of an economy of pleasure and pain. The paths to the satisfaction of the drives form a troubling and indirect economy for Freud, for a drive must necessarily be impeded by sociality, by taboo and prohibition, and thus the drives are subjected to various vicissitudes, sudden changes, or alterations in their course on the path toward satisfaction. The essay begins with the distinction between "drive" and "stimulus": Drive is what origi-nates from within the organism, whereas stimulus originates from without; the first is neutralized by satisfaction and the second, by flight. The drive in infantile experience gives the unoriented and helpless ego a "first discrimination and a first orientation" between inner and outer experience, and the borders of its body, between that which can be avoided by flight and that which cannot. The task of the nervous system, then, is to master stimuli, avoiding pain. Since instinctual stimuli cannot be gotten rid of by flight, they compel the nervous system to "complicated and interdependent activities, which effect such changes in the outer world" as to enable the satisfaction of the instinct. Therefore, the inner world of the body's drives compels it outward; they propel the embodied subject into the world of social relations, the domain of bodily communication, the realm of infantile semiosis. The extent to which the nervous system is highly efficient is due to this habit of the satisfaction of instinct. With this move, Freud disrupts the facility of mind/body, active/passive, inner/outer distinctions and makes them more complex.

Implicit in these movements of the infantile bodily ego to the domain of social relations is the introduction of the "pleasure principle": An increase in the economy of stimulation generally denotes pain; a decrease generally denotes pleasure. And here Freud claims that the drive appears to us as a "borderland concept" between the mental and the physical, being both "the mental representative of the stimuli emanating from within the organism and penetrating to the mind." The impetus of the drive is its motor element (*Drang*), the amount of force or the measure of the demand upon the energy it represents; its impulsion defines it; it is "its very essence." The aim of the drive (*Ziel*) is always its satisfaction, and abolishing the condition of its source (*Quelle*) is thus invariably its goal. But the aim may have different paths leading to its goal, "various near or intermediate aims, capable of combination or interchange" (as in condensation and displacement in dreams). The object of a drive is the vehicle through which it can achieve its aim; it is the most variable aspect of instincts and "not originally connected to them."

Objects must be invented; in other words, they are constructed artifacts that become attached as a consequence not of original relation but of the construction of the satisfaction of the drive, on account of their "peculiar fitting" to the drive. The construction of satisfaction, clearly a key to the pleasure principle, is considerably more motivated than Freud here elaborates. The "peculiar fitting" of the drive to its object is a cryptic description of the immense task of the Oedipus complex: to construct satisfaction according to the demands of the social and heterosexual contract. The objects of the drive are, therefore, unnatural though utterly naturalized. The narrative of the drive's quest for its object—its conflict with obstacles, its resolution, and its "princesses"—is a story of desire's satisfaction. An episode well known for its repeats, this narrative structure represents the victory of normative desire over inverse and perverse interruptions. This, of course, is the ideal form of the story, the story championed by sexology and functionalism; however, to remember Freud's remarks at the beginning of *Three Essays*, perverse relations of desire thrive within and alongside what is considered conventional, and so too with Freud's metapsychological narrative of the drive's first orientations to the body's demands.

Thus, in a curious admixture of the body and the social, inside and outside, body and mind, Freud describes the paths and orientations of infantile subject and object. The object may be extraneous or part of the subject's body, and it is capable of displacement and condensation: Several objects may satisfy it differentially or one object may serve several instincts. The very structure of the drive is suffused with the structural conditions of representation, for the drive's demand for satiation depends on the "borderland," which retains the orientation to both psyche and soma. Thus, the source of a drive is that part of the body from which stimulus originates, a "somatic process from which there results a stimulus *represented* in mental life by the instinct" (my emphasis). So several paths of mediation open up between a drive and its satisfaction, between the stimulus and its instinctual "representation," between the organic source of the drive and its object. Once again, this is not simply an organic or original relationship but one that must be forged by the subject on its paths through the economy of pleasure and pain, invented though thoroughly inscribed in and by the laws of Oedipus. Freud uses the word "representation" to describe the difficult relation of the drive to its satisfaction, the circuitous paths or adventures that characterize the drive in the economy of pleasure and pain. "Representation" signifies the drive's organic relation not to the object and to its own satisfaction but to the constructedness of this relation.

These paths of mediation are what Freud calls "vicissitudes," the contrived means by which instincts are redirected toward satisfaction as marks of defense against immediate satisfaction of aims, since various censors prevent the "straightforward course" of instinctual satisfaction. Freud names four types, or possible courses, of vicissitudes: reversal into its opposite, turning round upon the subject, repression, and sublimation, the last two of which are treated elsewhere.[13] In the discussion of the first two vicissitudes, Freud describes the reversal and turning of sadism into masochism and scopophilia into exhibitionism. The reversal of a drive into its opposite involves two changes: first, a change in the subject from active to passive with respect to satisfaction, which concerns the aims only—the passive aim turns into an active one. The second change in the reversal of an instinct involves a reversal of its content, which concerns the object of the instinct. In the turning round of the drive upon the subject, masochism is actually sadism turned round upon the subject's own ego, and exhibitionism includes the love of gazing at the subject's own body.

In his discussions of these economies, Freud emphasizes that both types of vicissitudes occur in one process, and it would thus appear that sadism and masochism are forever coupled in the psychic habits of instinctual satisfaction. But there is also more to the story, three more phases of reversal and turning: First, sadism consists in the exercise of violence toward or power over another person as object; second, the object is abandoned and replaced by the subject's own ego. Combined with the turning round of the drive, it denotes a change from active to passive aim. This phase is not yet "properly" masochistic but is narcissistic, a point to which I will return. Third, another person is sought as an object, who because of the second turn takes on the role of sadistic subject, and this phase signifies the proper stance of masochism.

Sadism in this configuration is more complex than the peculiarity of its aim, which is always to satisfy a sexual instinct: To inflict pain is to subject and master its object in the external world. If sadism is a means to instinctual satisfaction, it would seem to take no special aim in inflicting pain; but once the masochistic reversal takes place, the experience of pain is a passive masochistic aim, a pleasurable condition. All of this is then carried back to the sadistic scenario of infliction, which will be enjoyed masochistically through an identification with the victim remembered by its own passage through the masochistic phase.

Reading for Fun

Unlike "Instincts and Their Vicissitudes," "A Child Is Being Beaten" is Freud's examination of sadomasochistic case studies as they pertain to the structuring of fantasy.[14] The title of the essay itself is marked as a quotation, as if the study itself was a citation of something else, an artifact already written. In fact, the fantasies of Freud's patients are revealed to him by a series of utterances, which undergo the very transformation of those vicissitudes described in the metapsychological essay on drives. Freud begins the essay, "It is surprising how frequently people who come to be analyzed for hysteria or neurosis confess to having indulged in the fantasy: 'A Child Is Being Beaten,'" as if the fantasy itself partakes in a genre, is recognizable by the analyst as a piece of classifiable literature. In other words, Freud reads these fantasies as if they are literary artifacts, and like Angela Carter's reader of pornography, in reading plays an analytic "game with his own desire."[15]

The typical subject of the beating fantasy locates the first recollection of the fantasy at school age, and the site of this recollection is so powerful that Freud is tempted to locate the origin of the fantasy at school, when the child sees other children beaten by the teacher and takes pleasure in it. The influence of school is so powerful a memory in the child's psychic life that patients generally associate their beating fantasies as having taken place there, and Freud more than suggests that school may, in fact, be an institutionalization of sadism, if not literally in the fact that teachers beat their students, then in the more sublimated activity of reading.

Though children were no longer beaten in the higher forms at school, the influence of such occasions was replaced and more than replaced by the effects of reading. "The child began to compete with these works of fiction by producing its own fantasies and by constructing a wealth of situations, and even whole institutions in which children were beaten or were punished and disciplined."[16] Freud confines his analysis to the fantasies of girls, "which constitute the greater part of the material" ("the greater part" being four fantasies of girls; there are two of boys) and confines his reading to "the average case," thereby generalizing the feminine to the case of masochism in general in the same way that masochism is characterized as a condition (albeit contestable) of femininity in the film theoretical literature.

The first phase of the fantasy is governed by the utterance "A child is being beaten" and has its origin in very early childhood, so the information regarding the fantasy, due to the force of its repression, is scanty, obscure, and indefinite. What is known is that the child being beaten is never the one producing the fantasy. Rather the fantasizer is often a brother or sister, though this is never constant; neither is the relation of the sex of the child being beaten to the sex of the fantasizer. Therefore, the fantasy is neither strictly masochistic nor sadistic because the identification of the subject in the fantasy is neither in the beater or the beaten, though this first phase begins to acquire a sadistic character. Freud admits that this first phase has not yet acquired the characteristics of fantasy, since the child's desire has not been fully invested in the scenario, but can be termed "recollections of events which have been witnessed, or desires which have arisen on various occasions." Later, the beating subject is discovered not to be a child at all but an adult, and later still in the course of analysis, the beating subject is the father, and the utterance can be reformulated, approaching the second phase, as "My father is beating the child."

The second phase of the fantasy is governed by the utterance "I am being beaten by my father." The child being beaten is now the producer of the fantasy, and it is invariably, "unmistakably masochistic." It is also unmistakably a fantasy, for Freud can discern the mechanism of identification, the basis for the successful constitution of any fantasy. Freud claims this phase is "the most important and momentous of all, but we must say of it in a certain sense that it has never had a real existence. It is never remembered, it has never succeeded in becoming conscious. *It is a construction of analysis, but it is no less a necessity on that account*" (my emphasis).[17] In discerning this phase of the fantasy, Freud does not rely on the reading of symptoms, parapraxes, utterances, displacements of any kind—this phase is entirely a construction of analysis, and the theory here acquires a suspicious degree of fictivity, indeed desire, on the part of analysis to position this feminine perversion as masochistic, not on the basis of the patient's psychic residue but in the force of the desire of analysis itself. This desire is the insistence on the literariness of the scenario, a desire so forceful that it writes the scenario into the case study so that the writer may have the pleasure of reading it. This phase of the fantasy is "accompanied by a high degree of pleasure and has now acquired a significant content." And yet the pleasure cannot be that of the patient, for she remembers nothing, reveals no symptoms of the perversion. The pleasure of "sig-

nificant content," that is, content that signifies to the analyst, is in fact the pleasure of psychoanalysis in constructing the content of the fantasy in the form of an
utterance, in the inscription of literary technique, and in the subsequent legibility
of the utterance—in the onanistic pleasure afforded by psychoanalytic semiosis,
taking as its screen the asignifying space of feminine perversion, which must be
created as a screen by analysis for its own pleasure. But this is too simple. A more
precise model that describes the literary mechanisms of this psychoanalytic desire
is to be found in the "Instincts" essay, to which I will return.

The utterance that governs the third phase resembles the first, "A child is being
beaten"; the beater is never the father, however, but is undetermined or a father
substitute, such as a teacher (or an analyst?). The fantasizer, likewise, is never the
child being beaten but usually several children, usually boys. The third phase is
suffused with unambiguous sexual excitement and is "unmistakably sadistic."
Thus, the three phases correspond roughly to the three movements of reversal
and turning in the "Instincts" essay, yet the precariousness of the second phase is
revealed as psychoanalytic forgery in the sense that the second phases of each
movement do not produce what we have come to expect as "proper" psychoanalytic evidence of the unconscious (slips of the tongue, bodily symptoms) but produce a fiction of necessary connection between the two positions of sadism and
masochism, activity and passivity, masculinity and femininity. Such an intermediate phase is a construction of psychoanalysis, its central fantasy is the intimate
relation of sadism and masochism, its strategy of reading is to produce the feminine screen of masochistic perversity onto which the fantasy of masochism itself
is screened.

If we return to the counterpart of this second, "most momentous phase of all"
in the 1915 metapsychological model of "Instincts and Their Vicissitudes," we read
the following: "It is not superfluous to make the assumption that stage (b) [the
stage of movement between sadism and masochism] is quite clear when we observe the behavior of the sadistic impulse in cases of obsessional neurosis. In
these, we have the turning upon the subject's self, without the attitude of passivity
towards another: the reversal has only reached the second stage. Self-torment and
self-punishment have arisen from the desire to torture, but not masochism. The
active voice is changed, not into the passive, but into the reflexive middle voice."[18]
In this passage, which could easily describe the second phase of either the "Instincts" or the "Child Is Being Beaten" essay, Freud's text performs a discursive
switch, indeed a swerving between two modes of analysis. On the one hand, the
passage begins with the invocation of the psychoanalytic case study ("It ... is
quite clear when we observe the behavior ... in cases of obsessional neurosis"); on
the other hand, it concludes with the introduction of obscure literary or linguistic
categories ("The active voice is changed, not into the passive, but into the reflexive middle voice"). The tropical shift between two disciplines and two modes of
knowledge produces a strange hybrid, stranger still that the "reflexive middle

voice" is not an operative linguistic construct in modern European languages. But Freud does not help us in deciphering the operations of the middle voice; he posits it in the "momentous" position of necessary connection between sadism and masochism, activity and passivity.

The Interests of Analysis

The distinction between active and passive provides an example of a verbal category that seems designed to confuse our usual habits of thought: It appears necessary, and yet many languages do not have it; it is simple, and yet we have great difficulty in interpreting it; it is symmetrical, and yet it abounds in conflicting expressions.[19]

It is not terribly surprising that Freud should inflect such an important moment of his writing with a verbal mode that seems "designed to confuse our usual habits of thought." But I would like to put Freud aside, only momentarily, in order to pay attention to Benveniste's analysis of the middle voice. The opposition between active and passive is spurious for Benveniste, for he establishes that "the passive is a modality of the middle." The Indo-European verb is "thus characterized by an opposition of only two diatheses, active and middle." Such verbs, our verbs, refer only to the subject, not the object; therefore, "voice, which is the fundamental diathesis of the subject in the verb ... denotes a certain attitude of the subject with relation to the process."

It is the subject's "relation to the process" that interests Benveniste centrally in the essay, for it indicates the kind of agency a subject assumes in relation to action. "The principle of a properly linguistic distinction, turning on the relationship between subject and process, is brought out quite clearly by this comparison. In the active, the verbs denote a process that is accomplished outside the subject. In the middle, which is the diathesis to be defined by the opposition, the verb indicates a process centering in the subject, the subject being inside the process."[20] The actively voiced subject is an agent in action external to the subject; the middle-voiced subject is engaged in some self-reflexive process: It is affected by its own effects and actions. Thus, Benveniste rearticulates the active and passive relations as active and middle in a way that complicates a simple subject and object opposition. These two voices constitute two possible diatheses—external and internal—of the subject. This insight affords particular complexity to the middle voice, not simply passive or acted upon, for the subject of the middle voice is in "the seat of the process," both its center and agent. The subject "achieves something which is being achieved in him."

The middle voice can thus articulate a double diathesis, in relation to an external object and to itself. The object of the external diathesis is what Benveniste defines as "interest." That is, the subject's externally diathetical mode takes an "interest" in an object, acts upon it, transforms it verbally. Its internal diathesis thus takes itself as "interest," transforms itself as subject of its own reflexive process. A consideration of the reflexive middle voice might enable a political-theoretical practice, such as a reconsideration of the formal politics of perversion, for it necessarily positions both a negative and critical (and self-critical) verbal mode as well as a positive one. A reflexive middle voice of the perverse might read a normative text and find in it any number of appropriable structures, swerves, and switches that accommodate its drives. Such is the promise of a perverse reading practice for feminism, a complicated voice jointly comprising subject and object, formally savvy as well as interested in the morphology of pleasure.

Freud, writing in the reflexive middle voice, reveals that the second stages of psychoanalytic desire in the "Instincts" and "A Child Is Being Beaten" essays are, to use Benveniste's words, "interesting" and "interested." As transitive stages of the same conversion from sadism to masochism, they describe the movement between the two diathetical structures, between which Freud asserts his own voice in the reflexive middle.[21] If the second phase of the beating fantasy is entirely a "construction of analysis," it is a verbal construction in this linguistic voice, a voice that takes an invested "interest" in imagining that little girls have beating fantasies and that neither sadism nor masochism as pure positions or relations to power can be guaranteed against hybrid contamination, against a formalism that will always exceed content. This invested "interest," moreover, takes pleasure in its own construction of "significant content." The perverse pleasure that Freud takes in "the significant content" of his writing is precisely signification of the meaning of his analysis on the one hand and the matter of his discourse, the shape given to the content by the analysis, on the other hand. In this sense, the middle voice yields a view of perverse textuality that can no longer grasp the simple opposition that theorists like Mulvey deploy in order to describe sexual politics. The discrete separation of subject and object is not possible in the middle voice, nor is the assurance that knowledge written in the middle voice is disinterested.

Freud, again in Benveniste's words, is "inside the process of which he is an agent." It is this inflection of the middle voice that a feminist reading might take up in order to critique cultural objects and sexual politics; in other words, a strategic reading might appropriate this voice, for feminism too has an "interest" in little girls and might acquire significant verbal force by appropriating this complex version of agency. However, the middle voice doesn't readily translate in modern or Western languages. Its effects have to be performed in complex verbal twists, switches, and swerves. That is, the middle voice must be imagined and performed in poetic language, tropes that can disarticulate the distance between subject and object. However, it is important to remember that, at least in the psychoanalytic conception of perverse poetics, the middle voice is only a "moment" in the process of reversal and turning that characterizes the endless circuit linking sadism with masochism. In this way, the perverse troping of the middle voice needs to be sustained as much in theory as in formal practice, though its forms can be invoked within any opposition that masks itself as simple.

The Value of Fetishism

To invoke the perverse implications of the fetish is to raise the question of value. Since Marx—indeed the fetish has a considerable history before him—the fetish represents a problem of value; or better yet, it represents the very structure of value run amok. For Marx, the fetishism of commodities traces a process of valuation from use value to exchange value to the ultimately demystified form of value, the value of labor. In this process, as commodities are exchanged in the market, they are animated not by the labor that has produced them but by the "fantastical" relations that commodities assume in relation to each other. The relations of commodities among themselves thus trace a structure of relations between men. "A social hieroglyph," the commodity thus assumes in the eyes of men "the fantastic form of a relation between things." Men are thus frighteningly static, their commodities magically mobile. It is not my intention to explicate Marx's theory of value or commodity fetishism; I introduce the concept here briefly in order to indicate some of the pre-Freudian history of the fetish. For this history begins well before the mid-nineteenth century. William Pietz traces the history of the idea of the fetish to early Christian doctrine and to the sixteenth-century cross-cultural trade between Europe and West Africa.[22] The history of fetishism is in fact the history of value as the animated and the fantastic as well as the perverse. On the "mystical" character of value, Marx writes: "Value, therefore, does not stalk about with a label describing what it is. It is value, rather, that converts every product into a social hieroglyphic. Later on, we try to decipher the hieroglyphic, to get behind the secret of our own social products; for to stamp an object of utility as a value, is just as much a social product as language." Regrettably crude, this brief history of the fetish serves as introduction to my discussion of the Freudian fetish, itself a hieroglyph that bears the signs of these histories of capitalist and religious conceptions of value. The mystery of value possesses commodities and "converts" them into an opaque language, and the interpretation of this process is nothing less than an act of detection, an investigation of a secret, an unveiling of "the truth" of value. The introduction of labor's products into the market is the original sin of capital's mystique, and the task of Marxism is to demystify the fetishist character of commodities: Metalepsis is its trope, the future anterior its verbal tense, decipherment its hermeneutic desire.[23]

Like Freud, Marx eventually reaches bedrock: For Freud, it is obviously the sexual, more specifically the phallic; for Marx, the economic, specifically the value of labor. But as many have pointed out before me, it is not the bedrock but the decoration, the vicissitudes of form, that make these nineteenth-century modes of interpretation still valuable. In the case of Freud, as in Marx's conception of labor, there is a great deal to be gained politically as well as intellectually by preserving the bedrock of sexual difference. And yet, in the imagination of the fetishist, the value of bedrock takes on rather fantastic forms.

"No other variation of the sexual instinct that borders on the pathological can lay so much claim to our interest as this one," writes Freud on fetishism in the *Three Essays*: "This highly interesting group of aberrations, ... cases which are quite specially remarkable," thus sustain Freud's rather animated attention.[24] It is not difficult to understand why Freud is so fascinated by his fetishists, for they engage some of the more ingenious tactics that characterize his theories of representation. Indeed, fetishism is a perversion that operates on the level of representation, a perversion that understands the representation of value on the body and that grasps the ways that the anatomy of the body comes to represent sexual difference. In fact, fetishism performs a complicated operation of value on the plane of the representation of the body itself; or rather, Freud calls it "overvaluation," what I prefer to call "transvaluation." Overvaluation for Freud is a substitution of the sexual object for another part of the body "in general very inappropriate for sexual purposes." This new object is invested with the significance of "the more appropriate" object, namely that which fulfills the requirements of heterosexual intercourse. The fetish becomes "pathological" when it passes the point of "being merely a necessary condition attached to the sexual object and *takes the place* (Freud's emphasis) of the normal aim, and, further, when the fetish *becomes detached* (my emphasis) from a particular individual." Psychically, "the replacement of the object by the fetish is determined by a symbolic connection of thought."[25] Not only does the fetishist invent a new object, which takes the place of the old one, but the value of the fetish can be detached from the body altogether and projected onto other things. The fetishist, in these ways and by these poetic means, reevaluates the constructions of appropriate sexual objects as well as the conditions of their satisfaction.

Keeping these characteristics of fetishism in mind, I would like to turn to Freud's 1927 essay "Fetishism" in order to examine the fate of Freud's fondness for this perversion. In this later essay, it becomes clear that the value of these "symbolic connections of thought" emerges from the anxious minds of young boys who have recently seen the "horror" of sexual difference. Indeed the "ingenious" operations of value that characterize the fetishist are expressions of "aversion to the real female genitals."[26] The little boy thus denies that what he has seen is the possibility of castration: If, according to his infantile logic, his mother once had a penis and lost it, then his too is at great risk. In order to retain his belief in the maternal penis, denying the "evidence" of castration, he invents the maternal penis in another object, reserves its value in spite of "the truth" of his perception. In this way, the mind of the fetishist has a "double attitude": On the one hand, he admits the value of what he has seen; on the other hand, he displaces that value in the invention of another object. Like Freud, I would like to admire the "artful" psychic agility of the fetishist, for in transforming the bodily sites of value, he also releases the anatomical value of the body from its telos in heterosexuality. Yet it would be an understatement to say that the fetishist's aversion to female anatomy circumscribes his possible access to a female version of fetishism. In order to begin to describe the fetishistic forms that value might take in the imagination of a female fetishist, we must pay attention to the different ways in which the anxious mind of the little girl grasps the significance of sexual difference.

"She makes her judgement and her decision in a flash. She has seen it and knows that she is without it and wants to have it," writes Freud in the 1925 essay "Some Psychological Consequences of the Anatomical Distinction Between the Sexes." With this immediate recognition of sexual difference, the little girl must walk down one of three painful paths of femininity: accepting "proper" feminine passivity, denying sexuality altogether, or "regressing" to a state of masculinity prior to the recognition of her embodied difference. In feminist terms, although the last is preferable, for at least it permits an active relation to desire, none of the three offers a terribly enviable model of female subjectivity. This is precisely where the possibilities of female fetishism emerge as a reevaluation of anatomical difference. If the boy fetishist denies the possibility of his own castration by retaining the belief in the maternal penis, then the girl might also be able to achieve a different operation of value. Indeed, there is no reason why little girls should be more literal minded than little boys. That is, when she sees the penis and recognizes that she is without one, her mind might take hold of a different object. Like the little boy whose head drops at the sight of difference and grasps the overwhelming, lovely, and seductive value of a shoe, the little girl might look elsewhere. Disavowing the power of the penis, which she nonetheless realizes she doesn't have, the female fetishist might effect a displacement of value, adore another object altogether.

The significance of anatomy within psychoanalysis does not reside in some pure indexical relation to the body. Rather, anatomy might be understood as the body's syntagm, an imaginary structure in which the body's order is naturalized and made transparent by what a Foucaultian might call the effects of power. The body's syntagm, moreover, places the value of anatomy in a comprehensible, almost narrative, sequence such that anatomy has the value of the literal, inevitable, and essential: bedrock. Now the artful labor of the female fetishist, in displacing the effect of the value of the penis, is involved in a complicated transvaluation of the body's syntagm. That is, she recognizes the penis, what it means, and how it acquires its significance within the anatomical organization of the body. But she also shifts the locus of phallic value, places that value within an altered narrative sequence, and registers that value elsewhere. Although the female fetishist continues to grasp the significance of the phallus, she locates its value on what has effectively become another body. Although the female fetishist in fact performs this transvaluation of the body within the phallic economy, she places that value along a different axis of meaning. And perversely, she imagines another anatomy altogether.

NOTES

1. Sigmund Freud, "Splitting of the Ego in the Defensive Process," in *Sexuality and the Psychology of Love* (New York: 1963), 220. The essay was written in 1938, though published posthumously in 1940.

2. Catharine A. MacKinnon, "Feminism, Marxism, Method, and the State: An Agenda for Theory," in *The Signs Reader* (Chicago: 1983), 227.

3. I hope to reveal the forms of this discontinuous strand of Freud's writing as more than historical coincidence with aesthetic modernism. Breuer and Sigmund Freud, *Studies in Hysteria* (New York: Basic Books). The case histories and the two theoretical chapters were written 1893–1895, though the analytic encounter of the case histories took place throughout the 1800s. Sigmund Freud, *Three Essays on a Theory of Sexuality* (New York: 1962), was originally published in 1905; "Fetishism," in *Sexuality and the Psychology of Love* (New York: 1963), was originally published in 1927, as was "Splitting of the Ego."

4. "Sexual life no doubt is the one mighty factor in the individual and social relations of man which disclose his powers of activity, of acquiring property, of establishing a home, of awakening altruistic sentiments towards a person of the opposite sex, and towards his own issue as well as towards the whole human race." Such is the normative condition of sex in the discourse of sexology. R. von Krafft-Ebing, *Psychopathia Sexualis: A Medico-Forensic Study* (New York: Stein & Day, 1988), 1.

5. The rhetorical term *apotropaia* is introduced in Freud's fragmentary analysis of the Medusa on the shield of Perseus. It means a warding off of horror by possessing it so that it may also horrify others. The term is useful for my discussion, for its description of turning away or swerving, which is an incisive description of the task of bodily poetics, recurs in the process of fetishism and in the splitting of the ego. Apotropaia is thus one of the metatropes of psychoanalysis. "Medusa's Head," in *Sexuality and the Psychology of Love*, 212–213.

6. Freud, *Three Essays*, 15.

7. Recently, both Teresa de Lauretis, "Perverse Desire: The Lure of the Mannish Lesbian," *Australian Feminist Studies*, no. 13 (Autumn 1991), and Elizabeth Grosz, "Lesbian Fetishism," in the *Queer Theory* issue of *Differences* (Fall 1991, ed. Teresa de Lauretis and Julia Creet) have reconsidered and, to very different ends, resignified the masculine domain of the fetishist.

8. Laura Mulvey, "Visual Pleasure and Narrative Cinema," in *Visual and Other Pleasures* (Bloomington: 1989). I choose to cite this incarnation of Mulvey's highly reprinted text, originally published in *Screen* 16, no. 3 (Autumn 1975), because it is contextualized there in Mulvey's introductory narrative of Western European feminism's history in general as well as in the particular place the essay has in the history of feminist film theory and criticism. "My most influential essay," she writes, "has seemed, over the last decade, to take on a life of its own. This book provides an opportunity to re-place the essay by publishing it within the historical context provided by the chronology of my other writings." I hesitate to con-

tribute to the many reincarnations of the essay, but the spectral character of Mulvey's own description—it seems to have "taken on a life of its own"—fits in well with some of the problems of perverse representation I take up here.

9. My discussion of Mulvey is indebted to Teresa de Lauretis, "Desire in Narrative," in *Alice Doesn't: Feminism, Semiotics, Cinema* (Bloomington: 1985).

10. It is not within the scope of this chapter to survey the literature on the subject of female spectatorship, but I can rather provisionally sketch some of the critical pieces: Laura Mulvey, "Afterthoughts on 'Visual Pleasure and Narrative Cinema,'" in *Visual And Other Pleasures;* Mary Anne Doane, "Film and the Masquerade: Theorising the Female Spectator," *Screen* 23, nos. 3, 4 (October 1982), as well as the first chapter of Doane's *The Desire to Desire* (Bloomington: 1987); and Judith Mayne's survey of the problem of ambivalent identification in "The Ambivalent Terrain," *Signs* (Fall 1985).

11. Mulvey, *Visual and Other Pleasures,* 37.

12. The English translation of *Trieb* in the *Standard Edition* is "instinct"; like others I prefer "drive," for the drive's orientation to the body is not assumed or naturalized as in instinct. Likewise, "vicissitude" is the *Standard Edition's* translation of *Schicksale,* which can also be translated as "adventure," a translation whose narrative orientation is somewhat irresistible. Sigmund Freud, "Instincts and Their Vicissitudes," in *General Psychological Theory* (New York: 1963).

13. "Repression" is a metapsychological essay that can be found in *General Psychological Theory,* and the theory of sublimation does not reappear until *Civilization and Its Discontents.*

14. Sigmund Freud, "A Child Is Being Beaten," in *Sexuality and the Psychology of Love* (New York: 1963).

15. Angela Carter, *The Sadeian Woman: The Ideology of Pornography* (New York: 1978), 14.

16. Freud, "A Child Is Being Beaten," 108.

17. Ibid., 115.

18. Freud, "Instincts," 92.

19. Emile Benveniste, "Active and Middle Voice in the Verb," in *Problems in General Linguistics* (Coral Gables: 1971), 145–152. On the middle voice, see also Roland Barthes, "To Write: An Intransitive Verb?" *The Languages of Criticism and the Sciences of Man: The Structuralist Controversy* (Baltimore: 1970); and Hayden White, "Historical Emplotment and the Problem of Truth," in *Probing the Limits of Representation: Nazism and the Final Solution,* ed. Saul Friedlander (Cambridge: 1992). I would like to thank Hayden White for encouraging me to pursue the intracies of the middle voice in this essay and elsewhere.

20. Benveniste, "Active and Middle Voice," 148.

21. On this point, Lacan writes that Freud situates the reversibility of sadism and masochism for "grammatical reasons, for reasons concerning the inversion of the subject and the object, as if the grammatical object and subject were real functions." "The Deconstruction of the Drive," in *The Four Fundamental Concepts of Psychoanalysis* (New York: 1981), 170. Later, in a related essay, he writes: "Freud now introduces us to the drive by one of the most traditional ways, using at every moment the resources of the language, and not hesitating to base himself on something that belongs only to certain linguistic systems, the three voices, active, passive, and reflexive." "The Partial Drive and Its Circuit," in *Four Fundamental Concepts,* 177. It is not clear to me how Lacan takes issue with Freud's linguistic

description, "as if the grammatical subject and object were real functions." For I understand Lacan's linguistic intervention in psychoanalysis to be precisely a description of the ways in which grammar indeed provides the conditions of subjectivity, what we experience as "real."

22. I quote from Karl Marx, *Capital*, vol. 1 (Moscow: 1954), 76–79. On the pre-Freudian and pre-Marxian history of the fetish, I have learned a great deal from "History of Consciousness," the doctoral dissertation of William Pietz, in *The Origin of Fetishism: A Contribution to the History of Theory* (1988). Pietz locates the origin of the idea of fetishism in two moments of early Christian doctrine: in the prohibition against graven images as an investment of the transcendent in material objects and in the use of objects in witchcraft and magic. He also locates the origin of the fetish in the cross-cultural trade of the sixteenth century, specifically in Portuguese Guinea, as European traders encountered "native" culture in its religious use of objects. Contemporary theorists of fetishism abound, but I would like to point to several discussions here: Luce Irigaray, "Des marchandises entre elles," in *Ce sexe qui n'en est pas un* (Paris: 1977); Jackie Orr, "Theory on the Market: Panic, Inc.," *Social Problems* (November 1990); and Slavoj Zizek, *The Sublime Object of Ideology* (London: 1989).

23. And later in the critique of commodity fetishism: "The characters that stamp products as commodities, and whose establishment is a necessary preliminary to the circulation of commodities, have already acquired the stability of natural, self-understood forms of social life, before man seeks to decipher, not their historical character, for in his eyes they are immutable, but their meaning." Marx, *Capital*, vol. 1, 79.

24. Freud, *Three Essays*, 19.

25. Ibid. 20–21.

26. Freud, "Fetishism," 216.

7

The Politics of Immortality:
Cybernetic Science/Fiction and Death

GABRIEL BRAHM JR.

I N THIS ESSAY I examine a few of the ways in which an ideology of technological progress—progressive subordination of the globe to the will of capitalist consumerism and state administration—reproduces.

Part 1 is an examination of the syntax or plot structure contained in both fictional "warnings" about the dangers of technology and "scientific" reassurances alike. Taking one "dystopic" narrative (William Gibson's *Neuromancer*) and one propagandistic tract (Howard Rheingold's *Virtual Reality*) as examples, I try to expose, or simply note, some important continuities.[1] Part 2 links the desire for technoprogess with the fantasy of immortality as the latter plays out in the contemporary practice of "video eulogy."

Part 1: Syntax of Innovation

We cannot stop VR, even if that is what we discover is the best thing to do.

—Howard Rheingold

Whatever is technically possible must be made available.

—Ivan Illich

Short-Circuiting Fantasy

"Technique enters into every area *of life*," writes Jacques Ellul.[2] We can now see how shortsighted he was as new devices prepare to colonize *death*. Even the boundary between life and death blurs beneath the microscopes of genetic engineers. But this is merely to add to its already being lost in the static of security monitors, the glare of television, the piercing stare of the surveillance camera, and, as I will argue, the practice of video eulogy.[3] All boundaries, landmarks, even the very "keys" to the map, meant to help measure and navigate, are now constantly rearticulated according to logics that defy democratic decisionmaking or even any notion of desirable ends. As Ivan Illich has said, "For those who subscribe to the technocratic ethos, whatever is technically possible must be made available at least to a few whether they want it or not. Neither the privation nor the frustration of the majority counts."[4]

We do not understand well the effects (on animals, on the planet, but especially on people) of the two centuries of runaway technological-industrial "growth" that has produced our postmodern geoculture,[5] but many people seem willing to trumpet what no one can possibly know: the benefits of a new, mostly untried technology—"virtual reality (VR)."[6] This is particularly remarkable in light of the claims being made for its "revolutionary" status. The following is merely one example among many of the glee with which some techno-Jacobins would roll the dice, yet it is characteristic: "There are no limits on virtual reality. … The donning of computer clothing will be as significant for human history as the donning of outer clothing was in the Paleolithic" (Timothy Leary, quoted in Rheingold, 378). The inflated rhetoric of VR enthusiasts/entrepreneurs short-circuits thought about actual (political, material) reality by routing desire through networks of meaning shaped by long-standing narrative structures ("evolution," "natural selection," etc.). As I will argue (using the example of William Gibson's popular as well as critically acclaimed *Neuromancer*), even works that ostensibly contest the desirability of VR fail when they partake of these plot structures too uncritically.

Although virtual reality technology is itself quite actual (it exists in various forms or "stages" of development), whether you are for or against a kaleidoscopic metauniverse of totally simulated worlds in which minds interfaced with computers roam free while bodies either are left behind temporarily or for good, are exchanged at will for better ones, or vibrate in ceaseless waves of enjoyment is irrelevant in terms of the debated goal itself. *It's not going to happen.* "Full virtual reality is impossible," as at least two analysts have usefully stated in no uncertain terms.[7] What matters, then, is whether you uncritically buy into the plot of this technology's future metamorphosis or apocalypse (and how, why, and to what degree and what effect in the present).

Structuring Cyberspeak

The plot had to be something I already felt comfortable with, a familiar structure.

—William Gibson[8]

One of the main functions of the discourse of virtual reality, or "cyberspeak," as I call it, is to make us accustomed to socially constructed reality in the present. Cyberspeak (by which term I designate both "factual" and "fictional" accounts insofar as they partake of the rhetoric to be described)[9] does this in (at least) three ways: (1) by naturalizing the "origins of VR's origins" (that is, by telling stories of an unbroken chain of techno-progress since the dawn of time, culminating with an apparent necessity in the society that makes the leap to the virtual and transferring by association that necessity into the future); (2) by promising to extend and intensify toward the future what already appears as pleasurable under the current reality-performance principle ("leisure" as we know it); and (3) by promising to eliminate the pain, reassuring us that we will all survive—in "comfortable" forms and "familiar structures"—whatever fantastic changes may be in store. In other words, by implying that people could even conceivably survive—and should expect to occupy the same basic subject positions, however gaudy the new decorations—in a world where it is possible, for example, to hop from one body to another at will, cyberspeak displaces real fears about technology onto fantastic scenarios in order to allay fear altogether. More sinister, those real repressed fears inevitably resurface in the form of aggression directed against technology's racial, sexual, and class others. Indeed, the narcissistic rage of the true technophile (demanding a perfectly "functional" world to mirror his or her "needs") has always attacked, perhaps first of all, any part of the *self* that stands in the way of "progress" (read "future perfection"): "Why do these others always keep us back?" On the course pursued by such a paranoid mentality, cyberspeak offers a profound denial of embodiment (earth and the body itself "hold us back" from our future; and the future is thought to hold our essence, as heaven once promised a home to the disembodied soul). Interestingly, in the case of William Gibson's *Neuromancer,* the cunning of cyberspeak even works to deny embodiment while ostensibly affirming the limits of the body. As I argue in more detail further on, the relatively minor consequences that attend Gibson's hero's "trip" into another body are nothing compared to the implicit valorization at work in the very notion of the possibility of being "yourself" in another('s) body. In sum, cyberspeak (even in "dystopic" manifestations) promises on the whole a more pleasant and exciting world in which to consume experience ("Now everything is experience," quips Heidegger); it argues (both thematically and formally) that such a world is not only possible but necessary and inevitable.

Desire circulates—via cyberspeak—among contemporary science fiction, science technology, and consumer and advertising practices—forming a nexus of overlapping discursivities. Ideologies compete to channel the flow, and although opportunities for subversion arise, so do opportunities for continued and intensified domination. Although new technologies mean new chances for subversion and resistance, I think it cannot be stressed enough that "these new goods [do] not spring full-blown from the fevered fantasies of nerds and techno-freaks, but from the competitive imperative of industry, always alert for ways to turn human desires and needs into profitable products."[10] The kind of stratified privation and frustration imagined in *Neuromancer*—cleaving between those who can afford to "jack in" to the new hyperreal territories and those denied access, hence left with a degraded awareness of their bodies as mere "meat" ("virtual immiseration")—is already a "virtual" reality today.[11] As for tomorow, those who venture to predict suggest that "new zones of wealth will exist uneasily alongside vast regions of poverty. Advanced technologies will create a class of products and goods that will empower individuals as never before while shattering traditional bonds to country, community, and family. ... The result will be a kind of nomadic madness."[12]

Repeating the Future

Predicting and preempting the future is, in fact, what it's all about. If the alarming scenarios I am privileging here are themselves open to question, at least I will have written "with the goal that subsequent events would prove me wrong."[13]

Because the future is empty, or open, it must continually be made to signify, to bear contents that are dictated by present struggles, contests designed to "close" it in different ways. In turn, these visions reflect upon the present, valorizing some aspects and not others as being in keeping with "where things are headed." Thus the standard observation, that science fiction is often a displaced commentary on the present, points to something that works both ways. That is to say, projecting contemporary forms of consciousness and social relations—more or less unaltered in their essentials—into a time that is "more advanced," *but merely in a fairly crude technological sense,* serves to domesticate the future to the social relations and psychological forms of the present.

As much as such projections may defamiliarize, "critique," or offer enabling "cognitive maps" of the present, they also, in their formal conservatism, enlist support for maintaining the juggernaut of technoprogress by implicitly promising a livable, or at a minimum survivable, and usually exciting future. In this sense, *the cognitive map precedes the territory.*[14] Paraphrasing Tania Modleski, journeys into the future can indeed present us with the frighteningly familiar because they make the familiar strange.[15] Hence, they warn. But such journeys also tend to make the strange look all too familiar.[16] Hence, they reassure and acclimatize. What, by now, could be more banal, more routine, than innovation?

The "romance" in William Gibson's *Neuromancer*—the readily available artificial body parts and easy "flipping" from one sensorium to another *without major disorientation*—reinforces the comforting notion that the further unfolding of technology will leave us fundamentally intact. Only the titillating possibility of cyberdrag, or occupying the body of another gender, really stands out. "So now you get to find out just how tight those jeans really are, huh?" goes the locker-room talk of the cyberjock (53). Later in the novel cyberdrag means finding out what it feels like to have a broken leg. But the experience of a "virtually broken" leg is apparently no worse or not much different than broken legs here on earth, "in" one's own body (and what would make a body "one's own" if the metaphor of being "in," but not of, a body were literalized?). As the present is implicitly criticized for its likeness to a computerized-simulated universe in which artificial intelligences come to life, the future being sold to us in the present marketplace of new technologies is at the same time valorized as—however dystopic a "place"—a place at least minimally hospitable to life as we know it or imagine it to be in detective novels.

Gibson's "cyberpunk" fiction is allied with the supposed facts of virtual reality technology. Rheingold, the propagandist of the latter, invokes Gibson and *Neuromancer* in at least ten places throughout the pages of a book that is designed to excite interest and placate fears. Rheingold's work begins by suggesting that VR may hold a cure for cancer, then progresses through eroticized descriptions of equipment, goes on to consider "teledildonics," or virtual sex, and contains no serious thought about military applications of VR (14, 15, 345–377). Pious and redundant calls for humans to "be thoughtful" about VR in order to turn it to good uses and never bad are appended to each chapter, where they are always already undercut by the narratives on technologically guaranteed progress that suffuse the book. While comparing some piece of VR hardware to a Harley Davidson motorcycle, for example, Rheingold situates the inventors of the sexy technology within the unbroken and inevitable march from "Leeuwenhoek's microscope" and "Galileo's telescope" (14). Under these rhetorical conditions, the author is correct when he writes that "it's hard not to think of the VR technology of the early 1990's as the Kitty Hawk stage of cyberspace." It certainly is hard for the reader to avoid thinking of new technologies on the model of old as the inevitable "next step" in a benign process of healthy competition when such mythologized entities as the Kitty Hawk frame reception in the form of analogy. Rheingold asks readers both to "imagine ... what the 747 version *will be* like a few years down the road" (22, my emphasis) and to exercise "foresight" in order to make "better decisions, ... our only tool for getting a grip on runaway technologies" (46). Just what is being figured as open to decision and what (fore)closed? It seems someone is running away with the tool itself, envisioning storybook futures that sharply limit visibility: "We still have to wait," he says, "ten or twenty years ... before the full impact of virtual reality technology begins to hit [in order to have] a chance to apply foresight" (46). In the future, apparently, foresight itself will have become so advanced as to be nearly indistinguishable from what was once known as hindsight. Prepare to get "hit."

The term "cyberspace," invoked by "science" author Rheingold, is one coined by "science fiction" author Gibson. Although *no one knows what the physical, psychological or social impact of the stresses of virtual reality/cyberspace* might entail, the closure offered by Gibson's novel is as reassuring, if not seductive, as the closure offered by Rheingold's Easy Rider/Wilbur-and-Orville narrative of technopioneering. One assumes, however, that "virtual work stations," or the use of VR technology in the capitalist work environment, for example, will not be nearly as thrilling as either the "first flight" commemorated on the North Carolina license plate or as fantastic as the retractable claws worn by the seductive Molly in Gibson. "She wore mirrored glasses. Her clothes were black, the heels of black boots deep in the temperfoam. ... She held out her hands, palms up, the white fingers slightly spread, and with a barely audible click, ten double-edged four-centimeter scalpel blades slid from their housings beneath the burgundy nails. She smiled. The blades slowly withdrew" (25). Compare this adolescent vision of a future-world dominatrix (whose work takes her on a trip through the fast-paced and unpredictable world of "the caper,"[17] where the hunt to find clues and solve puzzles is always anything but boring) with that of the exciting quest for the unknown promised by VR: "The metal grip felt like the handlebar of a gargantuan, well-lubricated Harley. I looked up at a million dollars' worth of articulated joints, encoiled by umbilicals of electrical cables. The entire apparatus was suspended from the ceiling a few feet in front of me. I wore lightweight goggles connected by a wire to a computer. ... The task of searching through the universe of possibilities ... has a high degree of difficulty and a high degree of payoff—one of those possibilities in a haystack might encode the shape of a cure for carcinoma" (Rheingold, 15–16). Picture yourself a "console cowboy" (Gibson) or NASA researcher (Rheingold) or even a technologically enhanced cowgirl (Gibson) or a consumer of teledildonics (Rheingold).

Gibson's novel contains one answer to why a mathematized society holds any pockets of excitement or "freedom" at all. "Burgeoning technologies require outlaw zones, not for [the] inhabitants, but as a deliberately unsupervised playground for technology itself" (11). Can we pry critical insights like these from their ideological containers? Can we avoid importing into political thought not only the icons but the very syntax of seductive resolutions to the contradiction between an imaginary technofuture and its real counterparts while affirming the signs of popular anxiety about the effects of future technologies? In order to valorize the dissatisfaction regarding gender roles, manipulated in the previous example, without valorizing the romanticized solutions to dissatisfaction that the containments offer, we might want to be wary of the conflation of the new with the progressive. Texts such as Rheingold's actively work to maintain this conflation; texts such as Gibson's fall prey to it. Will those who do not study the future be doomed to repeat it?

Part 2: On the Dialectics of Virtual Immortality (A Preliminary Report)

How is one to reason with the person who feeds himself into a buzz-saw because the teeth are invisible?

—Marshall McLuhan, *The Gutenberg Galaxy*

It gives you that warm fuzzy feeling.

—Mourner witnessing a video eulogy

Be Kind, Rewind: The New Cure for Cancer

"Television," writes Avital Ronell, "produces corpses that need not be mourned."[18] "We were going to write a eulogy," says a close friend of the departed and, going on to bear out Ronell's remark with amazing literalness, adds, "but now we don't have to." Gazing at the monitor she avers, "This does it better than we ever could." "It gives you that warm fuzzy feeling," offers another mourner. "It makes you want to smile although you're crying. It makes you feel she's still here." *The man consummating his life dies his death triumphantly, surrounded by men filled with hope and making solemn vows.*[19]

The two mourners are watching a videotape. It features in part stock images of landscapes, vistas the promoters of this new commodity promise will inspire in the hearts of one and all a sense of a Greater Continuity at work in the universe—what a spokesperson refers to as a "subconscious" knowledge that "although death has occurred, life goes on." *I commend to you my sort of death, voluntary death that comes to me because I wish it.* The audio sings a popular song, the lyrics of which say, "You're my hero." Most of the time *Dasein* takes for its hero "das Man," the one, the they, explains Heidegger.[20]

The corpse of the slain hero, in this case ordinary citizen Alice George, is in fact right there in the room. But the assembled look past the actual casket at a virtual Alice. They watch a TV monitor display pictures of Alice "alive," during what the National Public Radio (NPR) reporter describes in an understated manner as "happier days" (happier than dead, the listener presumes) as a baby, at her confirmation, at the zoo, and at play with her dog. *Many die too late and some die too early. Still the doctrine sounds strange: "Die at the right time."* Alice knew she was dying. She chose the pictures and the format. It is comforting to realize that this is what she wanted. It was how she wanted to be remembered—not as a victim of cancer, certainly, but as someone who liked to joke and play, a happy person, someone who experienced all the important milestones in life—as a complete person, properly contained in a video narrative of "high points." She was someone who could inspire in others "that warm fuzzy feeling" so well known to television advertisers.

Or is it perhaps rather the video format itself that inspires this feeling (which the mourners "naturally" associate with Alice)? The stock footage is presumably exactly what advertising experts call "warm and fuzzy" because of the ability of its stylized images to call up generalized feelings of comfort and goodwill. And it is surely not Alice, or her story, functioning as hero here; the medium itself provides a model. This soothing, blurring effect has replaced any need to confront, with cold clarity, the corpse (or rather, the fact of death). "Alice," placed beside the monitor, bears the displaced "aura" of advertising. Is this the "cure for carcinoma" of which Rheingold speaks? *I shall show you the consummating death, which shall be a spur and a promise to the living.*

The reporter turns to the director of the funeral home, a man who uses the word "incensed" to describe how he feels about some people who "won't even give it a chance." A little old fashioned, an eighty-year-old woman, for example, walks out without even viewing the tape. (The younger friends of the deceased say that the elderly sister of Alice's grandmother just doesn't understand that "young people prefer something upbeat." On a similar issue, they themselves chose to be "modern" and "upbeat" when they opted for "the nontraditional prayer cards," featuring sunsets.) Everyone has a right to their opinion, admits the proprietor of Dolan's funeral home grudgingly, "to each his own." *That your death may not be a blasphemy against man and the earth, my friends: that is what I beg from the honey of your soul.* But his irritation suggests that there is something fundamentally un-fair about forming an opinion without even trying the product out, a common enough sentiment in a liberal society that privileges above all the individual right (responsibility?) to experience and choose (purchase). If you haven't seen it, expe-rienced it, paid to experience it, don't criticize. What the video merchant's feelings really express, of course, is the idea that every *consumer* has a right either to be satisfied or to petition for a refund. The logic of the money-back guarantee in-forms the entrepreneur's disdain of those who won't even make the initial invest-ment. He would, it seems, feature a trial offer on death, or rather on immortality. If you don't like it, come back to life—which is to say come back to death "the old fashioned way": You stop moving and so do pictures of you.

Unless, of course, you're a "star." Is that the appeal? Another displacement of the visual apparatus?[21] Do video eulogies make us each a star, held forever in the same frame that preserves Marilyn, Elvis, and the rest? *For many a man, life is a failure: a poison-worm eats at his heart. So let him see to it that his death is all the more a success.* That last bit of aura that survives Benjamin's "mechanical repro-duction" (as he says, in the body of the movie star) comes back to haunt us—or do we now haunt it, offering up our own dead bodies in the new ritual sacrifice of everything to the virtual hyperreality of the screen/monitor?

The NPR news report is itself framed with the reporter's reflections on "the eternal quest for immortality," the desire to be remembered that Arendt made such an important part of her understanding of the Greek polis, where great deeds accomplished in public were preserved in the collective memory and passed on through storytelling. Blending this desire and the new practice of video eulogy into an *evolutionary schema*, a quest to be remembered *better* and *more accurately*, the report unsurprisingly notes that videotapes at funerals might be considered (à la Rheingold) as a "next step" progressing from the use of photographs.

Photographs, however, were never felt to replace the need of saying a few words (for Arendt public speech itself was the greatest action, most worthy of being re-called). I would therefore suggest that an important break has occurred with the introduction of a unified presentation of moving pictures and recorded sounds. The break is enhanced insofar as people may plan their own videos, orchestrating ahead of time the content of what is played at their own funerals. Whereas the invention or fact of writing never seemed to imply that people could or should prepare their own eulogies in advance, the video format is repeatedly praised on the basis that individuals "know how they want to be remembered." They know better than those who would do the remembering, but also better than could be conveyed or "remembered" in words alone. "I know how I want to be remembered," says the ostensible inventor of the video eulogy; "I know how I want to be remembered," he repeats for emphasis. *The man consummating his life dies triumphantly, surrounded by men filled with hope and making solemn vows.* Since audiotape, and writing, never seemed to imply this type of control, the attraction must be something about the video format itself, something about being on TV.

Speechmaking at the time of death is thus reduced to an imperfect attempt to gauge how the departed would wish to be "pictured," an inexact attempt to instill the sentiment that video is more precisely able to convey. As Heidegger says, it is the age of the world *picture,* and nothing—or rather not even "nothing"—escapes. The community of mourners—now including the dead person as his or her own proleptic eulogizer (picturer)—has bewitched itself or has been bewitched by the language of technique into forgetting that memory requires a contribution on the part of the one who carries on. No doubt witnesses to video eulogies are "contributing" unconsciously in their reception; but they think they're not. They report having no sense of active participation, and feeling relief at that. A fantasied presence displaces the acknowledgment of absence that is the prerequisite for memory. It seems to remove the need for active participation in the *act* of memorializing.

A spokesperson calls this practice of dictating one's own program, or projecting one's videated personality into the future, "preneed sales." This is the language of the funeral industry taking on new depths of irony in the new medium of death. In cases where the deceased lacked the foresight to plan ahead and the need for some sort of funeral arrangements has set in ahead of any shooting schedule, families are offered not one generic presentation but an array of stock images to choose from. This is post-Fordist death: flexible, small-batch production quickly deployed for well-targeted consumer groups.[22] Although the range of choice is quite limited and homogenized, the effect that consumers report is one of personalization. (Sunsets, in the example previously cited, are modern, for modern people.)

The purchasers of the new technology say they feel relieved of their responsibility to find words. They also express the feeling of being ministered to in the way they themselves would wish as mourners. The video, ostensibly what the dead person wants, fills the survivor's need to feel "okay with things." Death calls up contradictory feelings, but the videos minister only to this postmodern-therapeutic desire to feel comfortable again (immediately).[23] *Everyone treats death as an important matter: but as yet death is not a festival. As yet, men have not learned to consecrate the fairest festivals.* Unlike the challenge of writing a eulogy, unlike groping for words (however much a cliché an elitist observer of language might find some of them), this new process seemingly involves no effort at all, no negotiation, and no room for error. Knowing that this is what *she* would want relieves a certain anxiety, as does the knowledge of the presentation's hyperreal accuracy. The pictures on the screen offer something so self-evidently real and so totally adequate that there is nothing to talk about. *Thus I want to die myself that you friends may love the earth more for my sake; and I want to become earth again that I may have peace in her who bore me.*

The appeal of the new medium for death has the distinct advantage of being an ecumenical one: "Protestant, Catholic, Latter Day Saints, Christian Science, Jewish, Greek Orthodox, Armenian, Lithuanian, Buddhist, Polish, Finnish, Latvian, Ukrainian, you name it, we have all different kinds of people," says the marketer, reeling off the words so fast that it is difficult to separate out any given term from the flow of religions and nationalities that are named interchangeably. It would appear that the global village now extends as high as the heavens. Video Valhalla is for everyone: Jews and Vikings, Buddhists, and people from Poland. In a confused classification, all previous classifications are rendered obsolete. The video ghosts circulate uninhibited by traditional rites or boundaries. But in heaven as on earth, postmodern capital's way of transcending national borders is not necessarily a "blessing," or liberating. "The suppression of national boundaries and the hyper-communicability of the world do not enlarge the space of freedom," writes Paul Virilio. "They are, rather, a sign of its collapse, before the expansion of an all-too-tangible totalitarian power, a technological control over civilized societies that is growing ever more rapid and refined."[24] The totalitarian power embodied in video expands into the realm of death, destroying differences there. There is another parallel between the space of video eulogy and cyberspace: "no nation-state frontiers here to control the flow of information, no public or civil space for individuals to access."[25]

Yet nationalism of course functions in the genesis of its own collapse. Where did the "idea" for this particular manifestation of technopower come from? (A naive question that nevertheless holds some interest.) According to the ostensible inventor (in the scenario of the news broadcast, our Wilbur-and-Orville of the moment), he himself was moved long ago by one of our great national media myths. He claims that the experience of witnessing on tape the death of President John F. Kennedy left him with the feeling that the ordinary person should have the same as "kings and presidents." (Recall the taped music: "You're my hero.") Whatever the status of such a "memory," it certainly seems an appropriate claim, containing the emblematic truth that everyone now "deserves to be famous," hence *ought* to be on TV (everyone needs a good self-*image*). It is also another example of the material circulation of desire from the public to the private through the mass media.[26] The politics and, more generally, the effects of the media presidency extend far beyond what is normally evident. Death is colonized by video at this particular nodal point—not by any single conspiracy but in the overdeterminations of mass-opinion making (turning Kennedy into a "king" in Camelot), plus the vicissitudes of whatever actual conspiracy killed the king-president, the "democratic" sentiments contradicting the king imagery and demanding the same for us all, and, of course, the "long durée" of the nihilistic desire to be free of pain and death altogether. As our iconic sacrificial leader was eulogized in the media, so should you and I be. But "eulogized" is no longer the right word—"immortalized," that's the word. *In your death, your spirit and your virtue should still glow like a sunset glow around the earth: otherwise yours is a bad death.*

The subtext of the remarks proffered by consumers in the NPR report is that the glow of the TV monitor promises immortality. Wanting only to bathe and linger in this warm and fuzzy Imaginary, this matrix of doom, this everlasting narcissism, we are, it seems, a long way from Zarathustra's "voluntary death." Such a death would make of one's life a gift (to be sacrificed). Voluntary death would be chosen out of reverence for life's goal and for those who share goals in common. *And out of reverence for his goal and his heir he will hang up no more withered wreaths in the sanctuary of life. ... Die at the right time: thus Zarathustra teaches.*

Living at the Wrong Time, or "Maybe You're Here"

"Dixie," or "the construct," is the name in Gibson's novel for a simulated person. But Dixie is not, in Baudrillard's word, a "simulacrum," a "copy without any original." Rather, in this case, the original is very important. The original Dixie "had" a body; only the construct does not. Though dead in body, Dixie talks and thinks and functions as a person within the simulated realm of cyberspace, where the "data" of his personality are preserved. In short, he "lives." Or if the death of the body makes of Dixie now indeed a copy with no original, then it is thanks specifically to the *loss* of the original. "The construct" in this case wasn't always "constructed" in quite the same way. This "simulacrum" *remembers* the original. It remembers in the form of a painful absence whose presence is signaled by Dixie's wish to be erased, to "die." There is apparently something unpleasant about being so preserved. But the sense of loss is also itself erased in the novel insofar as Dixie, like Alice George on video, "makes you feel like [he's] still here." The very fact that "he" feels the indignity of his situation so keenly adds to the sense that something very real is "still here," has been reterritorialized—pulled from out of the body and into cyberspace. Gibson's simulacrum remains nostalgic for its ground on more than one level.

In another example, Case meets an old girlfriend in cyberspace (while he is orbiting the earth as well), a woman he saw killed in the flesh, or "meat" as he calls it, back on the planet. She seems rather content as a cybernetic immortal and asks Case to stay with her. He can't, or doesn't, of course; he's the hero and has to pass on through this outerspace-innerspace underworld. In an act of compassion, he hands her his jacket. "Maybe you're here," he says. "Anyway, it gets cold" (Gibson, 244). There is something about the uncertainty as to what is real and what is not that in this instance results in the wager: It is better to be compassionate on the off chance that there might be a "real person" suffering from exposure. The upshot is that we are invited to believe in a new kind of life after death, a living death in cyberspace.

Neuromancer is itself, of course, all about the fantasy of technology surmounting death, and not only with fancy operations, easy prosthetic-limb and optional organ transplants to prolong "biological" life. Neuromancer is the name of a figure who appears near the end of the novel as a player in technology's own struggle to come to self-consciousness as a new life form. The character called Neuromancer explains the etymology of its, and the novel's, name: "Neuro from the nerves, the silver paths. Romancer. Necromancer. I call up the dead. ... I *am* the dead, and their land." The dead, together with the land of the dead, is an entity, an englobing intelligence known as "the matrix" (meaning womb). It is a place where you can have that warm fuzzy feeling forever. "If your woman is a ghost," says Neuromancer, "she doesn't know it. Neither will you" (244). "It makes you feel she's still here," said the mourner in the NPR report. But something is left out, either by design or because it has been repressed. The definition of a "necromancer" is not only someone who contacts the dead but more specifically someone who does so *in order to predict the future*. Gibson's novel, or more accurately the discourses of which the novel forms a part, as I've argued, "predict" the future in more ways than one. The ideology in these discourses would guide us into a future in which we expect to live forever.

Television pervades the imaginary of this un-death toward which we are headed. "The sky above the port was the color of television, tuned to a dead channel," goes the first sentence of *Neuromancer*, as if to clue us that death and television are the real context for the novel. "Imagine a wraparound television," writes Rheingold, in a metaphor for VR (16). In the millennial unfolding of nihilism, from Plato's cave to Disney's Pluto, it would seem that a total substitute for life has finally been found (just another particularly disturbing aspect of Baudrillard's "hyperreality"?). Or rather, another such imagining of a fully adequate substitute finds articulation in/as cyberspeak. Not only exponents of the science fiction subgenre of cyberpunk but proponents of the "science" of virtual reality technology unreflectively situate themselves within a Christian-Platonic discourse, the drive of which is to deny pain and the body in favor of a transcendent realm of value, the "more real" beyond—which, for many, equates with TV. Perhaps this is the deep level at which the virtual-real–hyperreal distinction does indeed break down (see note 6). (But then, at this level so do many others.)

This denial occurs even when authors seem to praise the "erotic" or "bodily" potential of their favored technology. Nietzsche suggests that the essence of weak nihilism is the urge to judge and condemn life or "reality" as a whole. Cyberdiscourse gives voice to this condemnation. "Reality is flawed," say Wendy Kellog, John Carroll, and John Richards in a joint article for the celebratory volume *Cyberspace: First Steps*.[27] According to Michael Benedikt, in the same volume, all attempts to represent reality in previous media have been "somehow less than they reach for," a lack that cyberspace will correct. Michael Heim is correct when he states that "we love the way computers reduce complexity and ambiguity, capturing things in a digital network. ... We are enamored of the possibility of controlling all human knowledge. ... We feel augmented and empowered. ... This," he says, "is eros." But he is incorrect in his evaluation of this drive to capture and control. One might respond that this, if anything, is Thanatos. The desire for rational calculated control of a predictable total environment in digital form surely has more to do with the death drive than with love of life.[28] And if *social* and *political* reality is indeed flawed, this fact is obfuscated or contained in ideological expressions when complaints take the form of condemning the physical world as raw material, as being still inadequately susceptible to manipulation. The desire to seek satisfaction through further trust in technique or the forces of production without any thought for the relations of production is antipolitical. A utopian desire for social change is once again, indeed rather typically, diverted to ideological containment in the nihilistic promise of a purely technical "progress."

Conclusion: The Living End?

As I listen to the NPR report, I think of Dixie and of my own grandfather's recent death. I am glad my cousins and my sisters and I chose to work out a joint statement on the occasion of his funeral, although we all don't know each other that well and the process had its difficulties. In my own way, I suppose, I'm no different from the mourners in the report who choose to let video stand in for oration. For I imagine that oration was what he would have wanted. He was well liked, and it seemed as though he knew everybody in the town of Gloucester, where he lived most of his life and worked as a maintenance engineer, repairing refrigeration machines on the state fish pier. He liked to play the lottery, and he took pride in his grandchildren. I convince myself that this is how he would want to be remembered even if it is not precisely what he would have chosen.[29]

I imagine Alice George's smiling images on the video monitor. But I superstitiously imagine them mutely struggling to scream: "Let me go! Let me out of here!" It occurs to me that that's how this story would end if it were a comic book or a *Twilight Zone* episode. That sort of modern folklore warns that we should not cross certain boundaries, that certain things are off limits, that there may be unanticipated consequences—that if we make pacts with the devil we may find ourselves trapped in a living death, a death worse than fate, a perpetual present shorn of all meaningful transitions.

The latter phrase sounds suspiciously like a stock description of the postmodern moment. If people were not somehow deeply dissatisfied with the present condition of rites concerning death in our secular culture, they would not be so readily swayed by gimmicks (no matter how powerfully evocative new devices may be as a result of their integration with television's channeling of desire). Perhaps this new refusal to deal with physical death has something to do with the death-in-life that most people are condemned to now. Perhaps it is not so different from the mass refusal to vote. What would then be "contained" by the new video eulogy is popular dissatisfaction with the tatters of a nonfunctional sacred realm (as the refusal to vote protests the lack of a public political realm). Likewise, *Neuromancer*, as much as the novel may serve to domesticate the future by encoding it as yet another frontier adventure, would also serve as a barometer of dissatisfaction, manifesting in that very encodation a "resistance to resistance."[30] That is to say, this book, as a machine for reterritorializing utopian desires, offers the "negative" impression of a will to think the future (even that ultimately knowable future of each individual, death) in other than technofetishist-nihilistic terms. Technofetishism, deployed throughout the book, is the container in which people's fears and desires around death are contained. Its continual redeployment serves to resist the resistance to technodomination and meaningless death that people feel and express in the very consumption of fantasy.

The past weighs like a nightmare on the brain of the living (as someone once wrote). But now so does the technocratic future, and in a sense more literal than any nineteenth-century prophet could have imagined. Many have sought to repudiate the legacies of an unjust past. Can we repudiate an unjust future? Can we reconfigure elements of the past and hope to ward off the intensified colonization of experience promised by the twenty-first century? What are the radical-marginal practices of remembrance, of rituals surrounding death, devalued as unreal in a postsacred culture, which an interpretive analytics might pose alongside the "new" options being sold by technocapital?[31] "We cannot stop VR, even if that is what we discover is the best thing to do," we are told by the likes of whom Rheingold is merely a momentary incarnation. Perhaps not. Perhaps cyborgs shouldn't even dream of it. But can we not encourage these alternatives to the virtual reality of living death in cyberspace, if—*pace* Rheingold—"we discover [it] is the best thing to do"?

NOTES

An earlier version of this essay was presented on a panel arranged by the Marxist Literary Group at a conference sponsored by *Rethinking Marxism,* "Marxism in the New World Order: Crisis and Possibilities." Thanks to the *RM* and MLG organizers. Thanks to Pamela Bailey, Laura Brahm, Rich Clayton, Douglas Fogle, Patrick Durkee, Beth Pittenger, and Jack Schaar for helping me with the essay (and much else).

1. William Gibson, *Neuromancer* (New York: Ace Books, 1984); Howard Rheingold, *Virtual Reality* (New York: Simon and Schuster, 1991). All references to these editions appear in the text.

2. Jacques Ellul, *The Technological Society* (New York: Knopf, 1964), 6. Subsequent references to this edition appear in the text.

3. "Where will we find death? In the destruction of the last clone of oneself, or in the forgetfulness of others? And will we still be able to speak of life when man is thought of as only a product and an object?" Jacques Attali, *Millennium* (New York: Random House, 1991), 113. On the significance of "monitoring" the world (for security and entertainment and as this relates to confusing life and death), see Mike Davis, "Fortress L.A.," chapter 4 in *City of Quartz* (London: Verso, 1990); Stanley Cavell, "The Fact of Television," in *Themes out of School* (Chicago: University of Chicago Press, 1984); Jay Cantor, "Death and the Image," in *On Giving Birth to One's Own Mother* (New York: Knopf, 1991); Thomas Pynchon, *Vineland* (Boston: Little, Brown, 1990).

4. Ivan Illich, *Toward a History of Needs* (Berkeley: Heyday Books, 1977).

5. See Ellul, *The Technological Society;* and Martin Heidegger, "The Question Concerning Technology," in *The Question Concerning Technology and Other Essays*, trans. William Lovitt (New York: Harper and Row, 1977).

6. Although some VR aficionados like to subsume all visual representation under the new rubric, the entrance of the term itself into widespread use depends on developments a good deal more recent than cave paintings. See, for example, Rheingold's violently anachronistic assertion that the caves at Lascaux constitute "the first virtual reality," *Virtual Reality,* 379.

7. Chris Hables Grey and Mark Driscoll, "What's Real About Virtual Reality?" *Visual Anthropology Review* 8, no. 2 (Fall 1992): 41. Upon review of the data, they conclude, "Virtual reality technologies, for play or war or business, seem [unlikely] to cause ... sweeping ruptures for many years to come, if ever." Nonetheless, they alert us to some of the less than sweeping but significant threats and benefits posed by advancing technology while seeking for their part to dispel "apocalyptic claims" (47).

8. Larry McCaffery, "An Interview with William Gibson," *Mississippi Review* 47–48 (1988): 225. Thanks to Diane Nelson for this reference. Though a consideration of the gendered, deeply Oedipal nature of the "familiar structure" about to be examined exceeds my purposes here, I wish to note that Teresa de Lauretis's "Desire in Narrative" can be applied effectively to all that follows (*Alice Doesn't: Feminism, Semiotics, Cinema* [Bloomington: Indiana University Press, 1984]).

9. Though I think it crucial to distinguish between the overblown ideology of virtual reality and the underlying (relatively meager) actuality of VR in most contexts, the term "cyberspeak" does not do so because it is exclusively concerned with the ways we talk about VR and cyberspace whether we are talking "fact" or "fiction."

10. Attali, *Millennium*, 89.

11. "The ragged edges of the Real, of *Necessity,* not to be able to eat, not to have shelter, not to have health care, all this is something that one cannot not know. The black condition acknowledges that. It is much more acutely felt because this is a society where a lot of people live a teflon existence, where a lot of people have no sense of the ragged edges of necessity, of what it means to be impinged upon by structures of oppression. To be upper-middle class American is actually to live a life of unimaginable comfort, convenience, and luxury. Half of the black population is denied this, which is why they have a strong sense of reality." Cornell West, interview, in *Art and Philosophy* (Milan, Italy: Flash Art Books, 1991), 161.

12. "Nomadic madness! Hey, sounds good to me!" you say (all except for that awkward bit about "regions of poverty"). But this is not necessarily the nomadism of Deleuze and Guattari. As Wendy Brown points out, "When we can no longer declare what is True in the registers of morality, cosmology, or politics, the spaces evacuated by such Truths do not remain empty but, to the contrary, grow crowded with technical truths—instrumentalist discourses dangerously cut loose from regulating values and substantive, accountable aims" ("Feminist Hesitations, Postmodern Exposures," in this volume). While technology contributes to the "shattering" of the bourgeois family (as other traditional associations)—which is arguably good news taken in itself—it at the same time tries effectively, powerfully, to "reterritorialize" the fragments in keeping with its own designs. See Michele Barret and Mary McIntosh, *The Anti-Social Family* (London: Verso, 1982); and Christopher Lasch, *Haven in a Heartless World* (New York: Basic Books, 1977).

13. Jacques Ellul, *In Season, Out of Season* (New York: Harper and Row, 1981), 74. "Being right was only evidence to me that I had failed." If science fiction also intends to warn, then the advantage the social philosophers have over the cyberpunks, as I see it, is that the former are willing to predict an unrecognizable future; the conservative power of fiction makes itself felt in any representation of what can then only be imagined as "representable." To my way of thinking, Thomas Pynchon's *Gravity's Rainbow* is the sort of thing you need formally if you really want to scare people.

14. A good argument for the uses of *Neuromancer* as, in Jameson's usage, a "cognitive mapping" of late-capitalist transnational space is offered by Peter Fitting. See "The Lessons of Cyberpunk," in *Technoculture*, ed. Constance Penley and Andrew Ross (Minneapolis: University of Minnesota Press, 1991), 295–316. Though he disagrees, arguing against "fashionable despair" in favor of "SF's role [being] to wake us up," Fitting points out that "for some cyberpunks ... the idea of science fiction is to 'acclimatize' us to the future" (307).

15. Tania Modleski, *Loving with a Vengeance: Mass-Produced Fantasies for Women* (New York: Methuen, 1982), 20.

16. See Andrew Ross, "Boystown," in *Strange Weather* (London: Verso, 1991). "Sociologically dense description[s] of ... technoculture [set in the future] ... help to naturalize the image of survival under adversity." Science fiction "construct[s] the look and feel of inevitable futures." See also Pam Rosenthal, "Jacked In: Fordism, Cyberpunk, Marxism," *Socialist Review* 21, no. 1 (1991): 21.

17. "*Neuromancer* is a classic noir caper narrative." Fitting, "The Lessons of Cyberpunk," 297.

18. Avital Ronell, *Differences* 4, no. 2 (1992): 5.

19. These and subsequent quotations are from a report broadcast on the *All Things Considered* program, National Public Radio, September 1992. The italicized text in this section is from Friedrich Nietzsche, "Of Voluntary Death," in *Thus Spoke Zarathustra*, trans. R. J. Hollingdale (New York: Penguin, 1961), 97–99. Lest the contrast between the ordinary "bourgeoisie" and Nietzsche's bridge to the *Ubermensch* seem altogether too snotty, let me acknowledge that when these are the alternatives, I can hardly fail to include myself on the former side of the bridge with the other slackers.

20. Martin Heidegger, "Division II," *Being and Time*, trans. John Macquarrie and Edward Robinson (New York: Harper and Row, 1962).

21. My loose use of the term "apparatus" here blurs all the important distinctions between film and video. But I think the "warm and fuzzy" logic that I am tracing is one thing

that can overlap such distinctions in the very circulation I mean to show. Indeed, for "circulation" to be a valid metaphor, it must be so. (The news report I am drawing my examples from was a *radio* report, which I am transcribing into a *computer* screen, which you are now reading in *print*. I take this, too, as emblematic of technology's deterritorializing power to channel us across various media.)

22. On "post-Fordism" see *Socialist Review* 21, no. 1 (1991), which contains an "Introduction" to the topic, as well as a "Reader's Guide to Post-Fordism."

23. On "therapeutic individualism" and the ideology of "therapy," see Robert Bellah et al., *Habits of the Heart* (New York: Harper & Row, 1985).

24. Paul Virilio, *Popular Defense and Ecological Struggles* (New York: Semiotext[e], 1990), 64.

25. Andrew Ross, "Boystown."

26. On the " 'material circuits,' " or "the real concrete linkages that conduct ideas, issues, and meanings, as well as fears, tensions, and desires, from society to film," and presumably (despite other very important differences) video, see Michael Ryan, "The Politics of Film: Discourse, Psychoanalysis, Ideology," *Marxism and the Interpretation of Culture*, ed. Cary Nelson and Lawrence Grossberg (Urbana: University of Illinois Press, 1988), 477–486.

27. Michael Benedikt, ed., *Cyberspace: First Steps* (Cambridge: MIT Press, 1991). The subtitle itself tells us nearly all we need to know about how to receive cybertechnology: as another giant leap for mankind. All citations are to this edition.

28. "This would suggest that progress remains committed to a regressive trend in the instinctual structure (in the last analysis, to the death instinct), that the growth of civilization is counteracted by the persistent (though repressed) impulse to come to rest in final gratification." Herbert Marcuse, *Eros and Civilization* (Boston: Beacon, 1955), 108. The "death instinct" (posited by Freud in *Beyond the Pleasure Principle*), Marcuse reminds us, originates as "the impulse to return to the Nirvana of the womb," or matrix (55).

29. George E. Walters (1912–1992). I dedicate this essay to him.

30. The phrase "resistance to resistance" is Michael Ryan's ("The Politics of Film") and is a formulation designed to grant the priority of popular desires over the ideologies that contain them ("Forces and structural differences in white patriarchal capitalist society … make ideology necessary" [485]).

31. "Interpretive analytics" is the term Hubert Dreyfus and Paul Rabinow give to that method (which they derive from Foucault) of searching the genealogical record for the undervalued elements within a culture that are swept along in the course of things and that, if reconfigured actively in the present, may offer materials for effective resistance and renewal. The Berkeley philosophers are like Thomas Pynchon's heroine, Oedipa Maas, in *The Crying of Lot 49*, when she wonders if the last will and testament of a certain real estate mogul (the "will" of the dominant patriarchal capitalist tradition) might not contain something worthwhile for her to inherit, without the patriarch having intended it that way. "Had that been in the will, in code, perhaps without [him] really knowing, having been seized by some headlong expansion of himself, some visit, some lucid instruction?" (New York: Harper & Row, 1966), 173. One of Foucault's own examples of counterinheritance is friendship. "Friendship as a Way of Life" is the title given to an interview in which Foucault makes the idea behind interpretive analytics particularly clear. *Foucault Live* (New York: Semiotext[e], 1989), 203–210. Perhaps it is Thoreau, however, who says it best, also speaking in praise of friendship and interpretive analytics at once: "There is on the earth no in-

stitution which Friendship has established; it is not taught by any religion; no scripture contains its maxims. It has no temple, nor even a solitary column. There goes a rumor that the earth is inhabited, but the shipwrecked mariner has not seen a foot-print on the shore. The hunter has found only fragments of pottery and the monuments of inhabitants." "Friendship," *Great Short Works of Henry David Thoreau,* ed. Wendell Glick (New York: Harper & Row, 1982), 159.

8

Feminist Hesitations, Postmodern Exposures

WENDY BROWN

THAT WE LIVE in postmodern times is nearly inarguable, but like all things postmodern, there is no consensus even among North Atlantic post-Marxist, postmodernist feminists about the configuration of this condition, its most striking markers, implications, and portents. Nor is there agreement about postmodernity's sites and sources of origin, current geodemographic headquarters, or dynamic of production: Is postmodernity the issue of "advanced" capitalism; of late-twentieth-century technology, art, or architecture; of Europe's self-decentering, or a global intifada of the margins against the center; of post-philosophy's murder of truth, the subject, the solidity of the earth, and the promise of the heavens? Ambiguity on these issues itself accords with postmodern dissembling of origins, headquarters, engines of development, and of reason, coherence, or continuity in history. Refusal to self-define or write a single-origins story similarly reflects postmodern consciousness of the exclusions and violations accomplished by master narratives, the oppressiveness of closure on identity, the vulnerability to co-optation, colonization, and regulation posed by definitive naming.

We may respect this impulse toward elusiveness and subterfuge, this refusal to speak authoritatively or consistently, even as we seek partially to overcome it. Postmodern epistemological and ontological insights commission political claims of a partial, situated, and local character; yet the development of an oppositional politics within postmodern political conditions requires relentless theorization of these conditions and at times at least, a global view of their movement. To do less, to abandon theory and global accounting at this juncture, leaves us rudderless in postmodernity rather than appropriating and navigating for radical political projects its peculiar (dis)organization of social, political, and economic life. Of course, theory and global accounts today are striving to develop their own (defensively) postmodernist parlance: self-consciously perspectival rather than Archimedean, temporally situated rather than floating above history, framed by and within a particular idiom rather than pretending to universal voice. However, within the false purity of its etymological life, theory bears no inherent relation to the universalizing, colonizing, ahistorical, or ethnocentric tendencies against which it is now defending itself. The Greek *theoria,* from which our term descends, promises only the vision or perspective achieved by corporeal, cognitive, or spiritual traveling. Insofar as postmodernity's more treacherous attributes include disorientation resulting from boundary breakdowns, collapsed narratives, high object density, excessive speeds, and sensory bombardment, we are in no little need of the perspective theory promises. Confounded as well by the decertification of god, science, philosophy, and intuition as epistemological and normative authorities, theory's promise of vision, and especially of developing a postfoundational angle of (in)sight, also carries unparalleled political importance in our time.

ᔕ   ᔕ   ᔕ

With its affiliates—postindustrialism, postphilosophy, poststructuralism, post-Marxism, and *posthistoire*—postmodernity signifies a pervasive condition and experience of "being after."[1] In political theory and practice, postmodernity is after Platonic forms, Hobbesian sovereignty, Hegelian totality, Millian liberty, Marxian dialectics, and redemptive politics. In history, it is after Hegelian and Marxian discernments of reason, purpose, and progress in time, human affairs, and human nature; it is also after periodicity, teleology, and facticity detached from discourse. In social life and sociology, postmodernity is marked by fragmentation without corresponding wholes, heterogeneity without the unity that converts difference to diversity, deterritorialization of production and peoples, social surfaces without depths. In political economy, postmodernity registers postindustrial capitalist production as well as capitalism's triumphant global reach in heretofore unimagined combination with substantial variety among regional capitalist cultures. Postmodern capitalism also features the reversal of a centuries-old process of economic concentration, although the shift from consolidated and hierarchical to dispersed and networked production is accompanied by increased privatization and monopoly of ownership. Postmodern capitalist power, like postmodern state power, is monopolized without being concentrated or centered: It is tentacular, roving, and penetrating, paradoxically advanced by diffusing and decentralizing itself.[2]

To speak of postmodernity as specific configurations and representations of social, economic, and political life is not (yet) to take a political position on it or within it or even to adopt, in Lyotard's intonation, a particular "sensibility."[3] It is simply to draw, in necessarily partial and contestable ways, some of the contours of the contemporary world, within which there are as many political possibilities as there are political locations, attachments, and imaginations. Nietzsche, Rousseau, Hegel, and Marx were all theorists of modernity, were specifically produced by and preoccupied with modernity, but also adopted different positions *on* and *within* modernity. Similarly, postmodern conditions produce certain historical, epistemological, and ontological ruptures in terms of which we are challenged to develop new political understandings and projects, but these ruptures do not by themselves produce a particular politics; they have no necessary or inevitable political entailments.

From feminists who array themselves "against postmodernism," the rare acknowledgment of a distinction between postmodern conditions and theory, between epoch and politics, is a political move. The conflation of such elements by those steeped in materialist analysis and practiced at attending to fine gradations of *modernist* feminisms suggests a stubborn determination to vanquish evidence of historical developments that its antagonists blame on *thinking*—often portrayed as dangerously relativist, irresponsible, unpolitical, or unfeminist. In other words, the move to blur or collapse these critical distinctions bespeaks a desire to kill the messenger, and what I want to explore in this essay is the nature of this desire. If the "postmodern turn" in political feminist theory is, at its best, an attempt to articulate and engage the characteristic powers of our age, what frightens feminism about this age and about developing a politics appropriate to it?

In casting postmodernity as a time, circumstance, and configuration rather than as an intellectual tendency or political position, I do not mean to underestimate the troubling nature of some of its constituent qualities. For those desirous of alternatives to existing dominations, exploitations, and inequalities, postmodernity carries abundant political perils, many of which are heightened by inadequate apprehension of specifically postmodern modes of power. Indeed, it is quite possible that our greatest impediments to developing cogent oppositional politics today arise not from the academically crumbled foundations of Truth, facticity, or the modernist subject, as those who array themselves against postmodern theory ordinarily contend, but rather from certain "material" features of our age: the expanding hegemony of technical reason, cultural-spatial disorientation, and a political tendency produced by this disorientation—"reactionary foundationalism."

Technical Reason

Marcuse before Habermas, and Weber before Marcuse, identified as the most ominous feature of a fully "disenchanted age" not an immaculate nihilism but a form of nihilism in which "technical reason" (Marcuse), "means-end rationality" (Habermas), or "instrumental rationality" (Weber) becomes the dominant and unchallengeable discourse framing and ultimately suffusing all social practices.

The growing predominance of instrumental rationality is one of the strongest contemporary forces erasing both the standing and significance of the subject; it is far more potent than the ostensibly subject-disintegrating effects of postmodern theory. As Foucault makes clear in his analysis of the achieved partnership between jurisprudential and disciplinary discourse—the latter may be seen as one social face of the modernist hegemony of instrumental rationality—disciplinary or instrumental rationality easily absorbs both the modern subject and opposition from within liberal discourse.[4] Moreover, as even the most casual ethnographer of contemporary North American and European cultures may discern, technical reason extends its hegemony as other legitimating discourses of a culture—political, religious, or scientific—are fractured or discredited, a process that is a defining feature of postmodernity. When we can no longer declare what is True in the registers of morality, cosmology, or politics, the spaces evacuated by such Truths do not remain empty but, to the contrary, grow crowded with technical truths—instrumentalist discourses dangerously cut loose from regulating values and substantive, accountable aims.

Technical reason conjoins with postmodern fragmentations of political and social power to make the critical articulation of domination extraordinarily difficult, especially if this articulation is attempted in a modernist idiom. Postmodernity decenters, diffuses, and splays power and politics. Postmodern power incessantly violates, transgresses, and resituates social boundaries;[5] it flows on surfaces and irrigates through networks rather than consolidating in bosses and kings (Foucault, *Power* 98); it is ubiquitous, liminal, highly toxic in small and fluid doses.[6] In the absence of a critical discourse attuned to such configurations and conduits of power, we risk becoming unresisting vehicles of its objectionable contemporary functions, more eviscerated of soul than simulacra, more oblivious to our unfreedom than one-dimensional man. Here lies the serious threat of a thoroughly disintegrated subject, of false consciousness beyond what either Marx or radical feminism ever dreamed, of a total "system" that no longer requires a systematic form to operate as containment.[7]

Disorientation

Another consequence of postmodernity's decentering and diffusion of power—its *centrifugation* of power—is that we are today very susceptible simply to getting lost. In Fredric Jameson's reading, insofar as being lost means being without (fixed) means of orientation, postmodernity renders this condition a normal feature of our world: "What is striking about the new urban ensembles around Paris ... is that there is *absolutely no perspective at all*. Not only has the street disappeared (that was already the task of modernism) but all profiles have disappeared as well. This is bewildering, and I use existential bewilderment in this new postmodern space to make a final diagnosis of the loss of our ability to *position our-*

selves within this space and cognitively map it. This is then projected back on the emergence of a global, multinational culture that is decentered and cannot be visualized, a culture in which one cannot position oneself."[8]

Stanley Aronowitz offers a similar reading of the effect of deterritorialization of production on the "patterns of everyday life. It means ... that we have lost a sense of place."[9] In the absence of orienting instruments, to avert "existential bewilderment," and substituting (poorly) for more comprehensive political analysis, inhabitants of postmodernity resort to fierce assertions of "identities" in order to know or invent who, where, and what they are. Drawing upon the historically eclipsed meaning of disrupted and fragmented narratives of ethnicity, race, gender, sexuality, region, continent, or nation, identity politics permits a sense of situation—and often a sense of filiation or community—without requiring profound comprehension of the world in which one is situated. Identity politics permits positioning without mapping, a feature that sharply distinguishes it from (Marxian) class analysis and reveals its proximity to (liberal) interest-group politics. In this respect, identity politics—with its fierce assertion and production of subjects—appears less a radical political response to postmodernity than a symptom of its ruptures and disorienting effects.[10] As much a signifier of powerlessness as a redress of it, identity politics may also be read as a reaction to postmodernity's cross-cultural meldings and appropriations, as well as to its boundless commodification of cultural practices and icons. Identity politics emerges as a reaction, in other words, to an ensemble of distinctly postmodern assaults upon the integrity of communities producing identity.

Reactionary Foundationalism

Along with identity politics, there has arisen a second strategy for coping with our "lost" condition in postmodernity, one equally familiar to even the most casual reader of postmodern culture or the subset of it that is the knowledge industry. This is the strategy of political, religious, or epistemological fundamentalism, "foundationalism without a grand narrative," or reactionary foundationalism (Feher and Heller, 7–8). What constitutes this strategy as reactionary rather than merely conservative is its truncated, instrumental link to a foundational narrative; it is rooted not in a coherent tradition but in a fetishized, decontextualized fragment or icon of such a narrative—"the American flag," "the great books," "the traditional family." Thus, "fundamentalists select one aspect of the dogma, one 'text of foundation' with regard to which they declare all attempts at hermeneutics politically subversive" (p. 7).[11] Importantly for our purposes, reactionary foundationalism is not limited to the political and intellectual Right but emerges across the political spectrum from those hostile to what they take to be postmodern political decay and intellectual disarray. Like identity politics, it is both a symptom of and act of resistance against the epistemological, political, and social terrain postmodernity forces us to inhabit. Reactionary foundationalism, unlike its more coherent and dignified ancestor, rarely and barely postures as Truth. More often, it presents and legitimates itself as the indispensable threads preserving some indisputable good, for example, Western civilization, the American way of life, feminism, or Left politics.

Both the mien and the reasoning constitutive of Nancy Hartsock's principles for "revised and reconstructed [feminist] theory" exemplify the anxieties and strategies of reactionary foundationalism. In "Foucault on Power: A Theory for Women?" Hartsock writes: "We need to be assured that some systematic knowledge about our world and ourselves is possible. ... We need to constitute ourselves as subjects as well as objects of history. ... We need a theory of power that recognizes that our practical daily activity contains an understanding of the world."[12] In Hartsock's insistence that "we" need these (articles of faith? ontological assumptions? political principles?) if "we" are to have feminist politics at all—as other fundamentalists claim "we" need the family or taboos against homosexuality for cultural survival—Hartsock does not concern herself with the defensibility or persuasiveness of the narrative out of which these items are torn. She is concerned only with rescuing them from the discredited narratives, a rescue waged in order to "preserve" feminism from what she takes to be the disorienting, debilitating, and depoliticizing characteristics of postmodern intellectual maneuvers.

When these precepts "without which we cannot survive" issue from the intellectual or political Right, they are easy enough to identify as both reactionary and fundamentalist. It is fairly clear what they oppose and seek to foreclose: inter alia, democratic conversation about our collective condition and future. But when they issue from feminists or others on the Left, they are more slippery, especially insofar as they are posed in the name of caring about political things, caring about "actual women" or about women's "actual condition in the world," and are set out against those who presumably do not or cannot care given their postmodern entanglements. The remainder of this essay is concerned with turning this argument on its head. I will suggest that feminist wariness about postmodernism may ultimately be coterminous with a wariness about politics when politics is grasped as a terrain of struggle without fixed or metaphysical referents and of power's irreducible and pervasive presence in human affairs. Contrary to its insistence that it speaks in the name of the political, much feminist anti-postmodernism betrays a preference for extrapolitical terms and practices: for truth (unchanging, uncontestable) over politics (flux, contest, instability); for certainty and security (safety, immutability, privacy) over freedom (vulnerability, publicity); for discoveries (science) over decisions (judgments); for separable subjects armed with established rights and identities over unwieldy and shifting pluralities adjudicating for themselves and their future on the basis of nothing more than their own habits and arguments. This particular modernist reaction to postmodernism makes sense if we recall that the promise of the Enlightenment was a revision of the old Platonic promise to put an end to politics by supplanting it with

Truth. In its modern variant, this promise was tendered through the multiple technologies of nature's rationality in human affairs (Adam Smith); science, including the science of administration (Hobbes); and universal reason (Hegel, Marx). Modernity could not make good on this promise, of course, but modernists do not surrender the dream it instilled of a world governed by reason divested of power.[13] Avowed ambivalence about Western reason and rationality notwithstanding, feminist modernists are no exception, but the nature of our attachment to this ironically antipolitical vision is distinctively colored by feminist projects. To the particulars of this attachment I now turn.

∽   ∽   ∽

Contemporary Western nomenclature for politics emerges not only from *polis* but also from *politeia,* an ancient Greek term marking the singularly human practice of *constituting* a particular mode of collective life through the generation of multiple associations, institutions, boundaries, mores, habits, and laws. The rich connotative content of *politeia* suggests that politics refers always to a condition of plurality and difference, to the human capacity for *producing* a world of meanings, practices, and institutions, and to the constant implication of power among us—its generation, distribution, circulation, and effects.

The constitutive elements of politics suggested by *politeia* do not disappear in postmodernity but are starkly featured within it, at times exaggerated in topographical articulation and complexity. In the regional cultural diversification accompanying the relentless process of global integration, and in the discovery of difference's infinitude, the dimensions of human plurality productive of politics now appear as permanent and irresolvable, no longer reducible to class society or interest-based politics but also never innocent of power and stratification. The measure of our world-making capacity is paradoxically both amplified and diminished by postmodernity's disenchanting effects: Without the assistance of progress, essences, god, teleologies, iron laws of development, or any other reasons in history, humans appear as the only fabricators of culture but simultaneously as so completely fabricated, so void of being of our own, that we do not exist, *we* create nothing. The subject is dissolved at the same time that postmodernity reveals us as all there is; there is no "maker" anywhere, only the constant effects of what has already been made, including ourselves. Postmodernity produces a similar accentuation and diffusion of the political problematic of power. Bursting modernist containment by the formal categories and boundaries of sovereignty and the public, power reveals itself everywhere: in gender, class, race, ethnicity, and sexuality; in speech, writing, discourse, representation, and reason; in families, curricula, bodies, and the arts. This ubiquity of power's appearance through postmodernity's incessant secularizations and boundary erosions both spurs and frustrates feminist epistemological and political work: On one hand, it animates and legitimizes feminism's impulse to politicize all ideologically naturalized arrangements and practices; on the other, it threatens to dissipate us *and* our projects as it dissolves a relatively bounded realm of the political and disintegrates the coherence of women as a collective subject.

Whereas human plurality, human agency, and the problem of power are in these ways transmogrified in and by postmodernity, these elements of political life continue to constitute rich resources for feminist political imaginations. Yet it is significant that in the course of this brief itinerary of elements of *politeia* in postmodernity, there has been little mention of the subject, truth, or normativity, those terms and practices without which some have argued that (feminist) politics cannot survive.[14] We may thus begin to wonder if it is not politics as such but politics of a particular, peculiarly modern, and possibly problematic sort that depends so heavily upon this triad.

Despite Luce Irigaray's formulation of "the subject [as] always masculine," Judith Butler's exposure of the gendered subject as a "regulatory fiction," Denise Riley's account of the category *women* as "historically, discursively constructed, and always relative," and extensive feminist critiques of masculinist models and practices of the subject, postmodern deconstruction of the subject incites palpable feminist panic.[15] Insofar as the subject as self is a specific creation of modernity, and even more of liberalism, this panic would seem to rest in feminism's genealogically intelligible (albeit politically questionable) attachment to these overlapping political and cultural modalities.[16] However, few feminist objections to postmodernism have been explicitly grounded in a valorization of liberalism, and few concerned with sustaining a strong notion of the subject express affection for the (masculine) liberal subject. Moreover, modes of political life transpiring prior to or beyond the boundaries of modern, Western cultures of liberalism have not been without promising feminist political formations. Indeed, insofar as the condition of politics as a problem of collective life is plurality rather than individuality, a politics devoid of the rational, willing, autonomous, and self-determining subject of modernity is not that difficult to conceive. Why, then, is putting the subject in question—decentering its constitution, deconstructing its unity, denaturing its origins and components—such a lightning rod for feminist hostility to postmodernity? Seyla Benhabib answers this way: "Carried to its logical consequences, poststructuralism leads to a theory without addressees, to a self without a center. ... Is not a feminist theory that allies itself with poststructuralism in danger of losing its very reason for being?"[17] Albeit rhetorically compelling, there is something slightly disingenuous about this worry. After all, the most ardent feminist poststructuralists do not claim that women's pervasive economic subordination, lack of reproductive freedoms, and vulnerability to endemic sexual violence simply evaporate because we cannot fix or circumscribe who or what woman is.

In fact, postmodern decentering, disunifying, and denaturalizing of the subject are far more threatening to the status of feminism's well of truth than to feminism's raison d'être. While often cast as concern with retaining an object of political struggle, feminist attachment to the subject is more critically bound to retaining women's experiences, feelings, and voices as sources and certifications of postfoundational political truth. When the notion of a unified and coherent subject is abandoned, we not only cease to be able to speak of woman or of women in an unproblematic way, we forsake the willing, deliberate, and consenting "I" that liberalism's rational actor model of the human being proffers, and we surrender the autonomous, rights-bearing fictional unity that liberalism promises to secure. Yet each of these terms and practices—woman, willing, deliberate, consenting, an "I," rational actors, autonomy, and rights—has been challenged by various *modernist* feminisms as masculinist, racist, ethnocentric, heterosexist, culturally imperialist, or all of the above. Moreover, dispensing with the unified subject does not mean ceasing to be able to speak about our experiences as women, only that our words cannot be legitimately deployed or construed as larger or longer than the moments of the lives they speak from; they cannot be anointed as Authentic or True, since the experience they announce is linguistically contained, socially constructed, discursively mediated, and never just individually "had." But this is precisely the point at which many contemporary North Atlantic feminists hesitate and equivocate: While insisting on the constructed character of gender, most also seek to preserve some variant of consciousness-raising as a mode of discerning and delivering the "truth" about women. Consider Catharine MacKinnon's insistence that women are wholly the products of men's construction and her concomitant but ontologically contradictory project of developing a jurisprudence based on "an account of the world from women's point of view."[18] Consider the similar problematic in other theories of "the feminist standpoint," the sharp but frequently elided tensions between adhering to social construction theory on the one hand and epistemologically privileging women's accounts of social life on the other. "The world from women's point of view" and "the feminist standpoint" attempt resolution of the postfoundational epistemology problem by deriving from within women's experience the grounding for women's accounts. But this resolution requires suspending recognition that women's "experience" is both thoroughly constructed and interpreted without end. Within feminist-standpoint theory as well as much other modernist feminist theory, then, consciousness-raising operates as feminism's epistemologically positivist moment. The material excavated there, like the material uncovered in psychoanalysis or delivered in confession, is valued as the hidden truth of women's existence—true because it is hidden, and hidden because women are oppressed, silenced, and privatized.

Those familiar with Foucault's genealogy of confession will have discerned in this argument an inferred homology between the epistemological-political operations of consciousness-raising and those of confessional discourse. In Foucault's account of modern sexuality as structured by such discourse, he argues that confession—inaugurated by the Church as a technique of power that works by exposure and individuation—produces truth as a secret contained within.[19] Revelation through confession is thus construed as liberation from repression or secrecy, and truth-telling about our desires or experiences is construed as deliverance from the power that silences and represses them. What Foucault terms the "internal ruse of confession" is reducible to this precept: "Confession frees, but power reduces one to silence; truth does not belong to the order of power, but shares an original affinity with freedom" (*History* 60).

Since women's subordination is partly achieved through the construction and positioning of us as private—sexual, familial, emotional—and is produced and inscribed in the domain of both domestic and psychic interiors, then within modernity, the voicing of women's experience acquires an inherently confessional cast. Indeed, "breaking silence" is a standard feminist metaphor for what occurs in consciousness-raising sessions, speak-outs, and other forums for feminist truth-telling. Consciousness-raising, as/like confession, delivers the "hidden truth" of women and women's experience, which accounts for those symptomatically modernist paradoxes represented in MacKinnon's work: Although women are socially constructed to the core, women's words about their experience, because they issue from an interior space and against an injunction to silence, are anointed as True and constitute the foundations of feminist knowledge. Within the confessional frame, even when social construction is adopted as a method for explaining the making of gender, "feelings" and "experiences" acquire a status that is politically, if not ontologically, essentialist—beyond hermeneutics. This strand of feminist foundationalism transports the domain of Truth from Reason to subjectivity, from *Geist* to inner voice, even while femininity itself is submitted to a methodology elaborating its fully fabricated nature.

As a source of truth, the subjectivity of the subject constitutes feminism's alternative to aperspectival and, presumably, masculinist reason and science. Through articulations of "standpoint" or women's "point of view," this alternative seeks legitimacy as a form of knowledge about the world that, while admitting to being "situated," cannot admit to partiality or contestability and above all cannot be subjected to hermeneutics without giving up its truth value. If feminist anxieties about deconstructing the subject are in this way linked to feminist anxieties about a postfoundational knowledge universe, we may proceed to this problem directly: What is it about feminist politics that cannot survive, or worries that it cannot survive, the radically disenchanted postmodern world? What is it about feminism that fears the replacement of truth with politics, philosophy with struggle, privileged knowledge with a cacophony of unequal voices clamoring for position?

℘   ℘   ℘

Feminism's complex relationship to Truth—its rejection of Truth's masculine Western modes and its need for grounded knowledges of its own that are equal in potency to those it rejects—has been productively explored by feminist philosophers and historians as an ensemble of epistemological and political conundrums.[20] But in order to fathom our anxiety about a politics unarmed with Truth, I want to explore the problem in Nietzschean terms—the terms of cultural dreads, displacements, ailments, and diagnoses. In this endeavor, it is necessary to retell a portion of a story Nietzsche tells, for Nietzschean "conclusions" have little nonnihilistic force in the absence of Nietzschean genealogies.

In *On the Genealogy of Morals,* Nietzsche inaugurates his deconstruction of morality with a disarming query: What if moral goodness were not the telos of the human capacity for splendor and accomplishment but rather its nemesis? "What if a symptom of regression were inherent in the 'good,' likewise a danger, a seduction, a poison, a narcotic, through which the present was possibly living *at the expense of the future?*"[21] In short, what if morality is not a spur to human cultural achievements but a strangulation of them? Nietzsche traces these possibilities by hypothesizing morality "as consequence, as symptom, as mask, as tartufferie, as illness, as misunderstanding, but also morality as cause, as remedy, as stimulant, as restraint, as poison" (20). Through a weave of etymological, demographic, literary, and historical fragments, Nietzsche conjures a genealogy of morality that begins with the historical inversion of an "aristocratic equation of power with truth, goodness, beauty, happiness and piety" (32–34). This ancient equation Nietzsche endorses for its homage to "the noble instincts of man," but it is opposed by "the slave revolt in morality," a 2,000-year-old-and-long revolt accompanying the birth of Western civilization and one "we no longer see because it—has been victorious" (34). "The slave revolt in morality begins when *ressentiment* itself becomes creative and gives birth to values: the *ressentiment* of natures that are denied the true reaction, that of deeds, and compensate themselves with an imaginary revenge" (36).

In his insistence that morality springs from and compensates powerlessness, Nietzsche challenges the Marxian thesis that all ideology, including ethical and moral codes, issues from class divisions to legitimate the power of the privileged. In Nietzsche's reversal of this thesis, morality emerges from the powerless to avenge their station; it enacts their resentment of strengths that they cannot match or overthrow. Rather than a codification of domination, moral ideas are a critique of a certain kind of power, a complaint against strength, an effort to shame and discredit domination by securing the ground of the true *and* the good from which to (negatively) judge it. In this way, of course, morality itself becomes a power, a weapon (which is how it eventually triumphs), although this expression of the "will to power" is far from the sort Nietzsche savors or respects: Power born of weakness and resentment fashions a culture whose values and ambitions mirror the pettiness of its motivating force. Moreover, *ressentiment*'s acquisition of power is facilitated by what Nietzsche terms the overdeveloped quality of its cleverness; it ascends to power through its cultivation of reason—an "imaginary revenge" taken in lieu of "the true reaction, that of deeds." Because *ressentiment* reacts, needs a hostile external world in order to exist at all (37), and is preoccupied with discerning and discrediting the nature of what it seeks to undercut, "a race of such men of *ressentiment* is bound to become eventually cleverer than any noble race; it will also honor cleverness to a far greater degree: namely as a condition of existence of the first importance" (38).[22]

Nietzsche means to be telling a generic story about the West and especially about modernity, a story in which "slave morality" has triumphed so completely that "we have lost our love for man," "we are weary of man"—this, and not Nietzsche's analysis, betokens "the true nihilism of our age" (44). I want to suggest that much North Atlantic feminism partakes deeply of both the epistemological spirit and political structure of *ressentiment* and that this constitutes a good deal of our nervousness about moving toward an analysis as thoroughly Nietzschean in its wariness about truth as postmodern political theory must be. Surrendering epistemological foundations means giving up the ground of specifically *moral* claims against domination—the avenging of strength through moral critique of it—and moving instead into the domain of the sheerly political: "wars of position" and amoral contests about the just and the good in which truth is always grasped as coterminous with power, as "already power," as the voice of power (Foucault, *Power* 133). Apparently lacking confidence in our ability to prosper in such a domain, feminism appears extremely hesitant about such a move.

This hesitation is evident first in the feminist worry that postmodern theories of discourse, particularly that proffered by Foucault, "reduce all discourse to rhetoric ... allow[ing] no distinction between reason and power."[23] Presumably, the objection here lies not in the discernment of power, even violence, in discourse—feminists work assiduously at just such discernments—but to the "reduction of *all* discourse to rhetoric," to the insistence on the will to power in *all* of reason's purveyors, ourselves included. Consider Hartsock's "need to be assured that some systematic [undistorted or power-free] knowledge about our world and ourselves is possible" ("Foucault" 171). For the moralism issuing from *ressentiment* to "work," reason must drape itself in powerlessness or dispossession: It attacks by differentiating itself from the political-ontological *nature* of what it criticizes, by adopting the stance of reason against power. This desire for knowledge accounts that are innocent of power, that position us outside power, is rooted in the need to make power *answer* to reason/morality and to prohibit demands for accountability in the opposite direction. In Nietzsche's telling, the supreme strategy of morality based in *ressentiment*, the source of its triumph over 2,000 years, is its denial that it has an involvement with power, that it contains a will to power or seeks to (pre)dominate.

There is no more vivid historical illustration of morality's dependence upon a discursive boundary between truth and power than Plato's attempt to distinguish Socrates from his rivals, the Sophists, by contrasting Socrates' ostensible devotion to truth for its own sake with the Sophists' practice of open consortion with political interests. In this picture, the impoverished, purely philosophical, and formally powerless Socrates is presented as uncontaminated by power interests or power desires; his life and utterances are cast as "moral" and "true" because they are not directly hinged to political power, indeed, because philosophy is "out of power." Unsurprisingly, Socrates is Nietzsche's prime example of (plebeian) *ressentiment*—"One chooses dialectic only when one has no other means. ... Is dialectic only a form of *revenge* in Socrates?"[24]

A contemporary feminist instance of the Platonic strategy for legitimizing "our truth" through its relation to worldly powerlessness, and discrediting "theirs" through its connection to power, is again provided by Hartsock. Arguing that there can or must be an "epistemological base" in which knowledge of "how the world really works" is possible, she declares: "Those (simply) critical of modernity can call into question whether we ever really knew the world (and a good case can be made that "they" at least did not). They are in fact right that they have not known the world as it is rather than as they wished and needed it to be; they created their world not only in their own image but in the image of their fantasies" ("Foucault" 171). In this account, powerlessness is truthful (moral), and power inherently distorts. Truth is always on the side of the damned or the excluded, hence truth is always clean of power, always reproaches power. "The vision available to the rulers will be both partial and will reverse the *real* order of things" (172, emphasis added). In deconstructing the fixity of the real, the easy opposition between rulers and ruled, and the ascription of universal vision to the oppressed, postmodernity exposes these ontological and epistemological shortcuts for what they are, but it does not resolve what it so thoroughly problematizes: What would be required for us to live and work politically without such myths, without claiming that our knowledge is uncorrupted by a will to power, without insisting that our truths are less partial and more moral than "theirs"? Could we learn to contest domination with strength and an alternative vision of collective life, rather than through moral reproach? In a word, could we develop a feminist politics *sans ressentiment?*

Thus far, I have situated feminist anxieties about postmodernity in its disruption and deauthorization of our moral ground—the feminist subject that harbors truth, and the feminist truth that opposes power. But preference for moral reasoning over open political contest is not the only legacy of the modernist feminist story: Modernity also bequeaths to us a preference for *deriving* norms epistemologically over *deciding* on them politically. From Plato to Marx, from natural law theory to Christian idealism and historical materialism, Western political theory has derived (and legitimized) the Good from the True, and feminist theory is no exception, notwithstanding the sharply competing conceptions of "truth" harbored under its auspices. Feminist-standpoint theory takes this effort furthest in its imitation of the Marxian effort to vest the class that is "in but not of civil society" with the capacity for a situated knowledge capable of achieving universal vision and producing universal norms. In this account truth is apprehended by, because produced by, the daily experience of society's most exploited and excluded. With their special capacity for seeing truth and their standing as the new universal class (the class that represents universal interests because its interests lie with the complete abolition of class), this population also has a unique purchase on "the good" (Hartsock, "Foucault" 290–300).

The postmodern exposure of the imposed and created rather than discovered character of all knowledges—of the power-suffused, struggle-produced quality of all truths including reigning political and scientific ones—simultaneously exposes the groundlessness of discovered norms or visions. Our alternative to reliance upon such normative claims would seem to be engagement in political struggles in which there are no trump cards like morality or Truth. Our alternative, in short, is to struggle within an amoral political habitat for temporally bound and fully contestable visions of who we are and how we ought to live. Put another way, postmodernity unnerves feminist theory not merely because it deprives us of uncomplicated subject standing, as Di Stefano suggests, or of settled ground for knowledge and norms, as Hartsock argues, or of "centered selves" and "emancipatory knowledge," as Benhabib avers. Postmodernity unsettles feminism because it deprives us of the *moral* force that the subject, truth, and normativity coproduce in modernity. When contemporary feminist political theorists or analysts complain about the antipolitical or unpolitical nature of postmodernism, they are protesting, inter alia, a Nietzschean analysis of truth and morality as fully implicated in and by power, and thereby delegitimated *qua* truth and morality. Politics, including politics with passionate purpose and vision, can thrive without a strong theory of the subject, without Truth, and without scientifically derived norms—one only need reread Machiavelli, Gramsci, or Emma Goldman to see politics flourish without these things. Our question is whether *feminist* politics can prosper without a moral apparatus, whether feminist theorists and activists will give up substituting Truth and morality for politics. Are we willing to engage in overt struggle for position rather than recrimination, to develop our faculties rather than avenge our weakness with moral and epistemological gestures, to fight for a world rather than conduct process on the existing one? Nietzsche insisted that extraordinary strengths of character and mind would be necessary to operate in the domain of epistemological and religious nakedness he heralded. But in this he excessively individualized a challenge that more importantly requires the deliberate development of postmoral and antirelativist political spaces, practices of deliberation, and modes of adjudication.

❧   ❧   ❧

"The only way through a crisis of space is to invent a new space" (Jameson, 18). Postmodernity poses the opportunity to radically sever the problem of the good from the problem of the true, to decide what we want (to be) rather than derive it from assumptions or arguments about who we are. Our capacity to positively exploit this opportunity will be hinged to our success in developing postontological but also noninstrumental modes and criteria for political judgment. It will depend as well upon our willingness to break certain modernist radical attachments: However failed the promise, what Marxism tendered was meticulously articulated connections between a comprehensive critique of the present and norms for a transformed future—a science of revolution rather than a politics of one.

Resistance, the practice most widely associated with postmodern political discourse, responds to, without fully meeting, the normativity challenge of postmodernity. A vital *tactic* in much political work as well as for mere survival, resistance by itself does not contain a critique, a vision, or grounds for organized collective efforts to enact. Contemporary affection for the politics of resistance issues from postmodern criticism's perennial authority problem: heightened consciousness of the will to power in all political "positions" and wariness about totalizing analyses and visions. Insofar as it eschews rather than revises these problematic practices, resistance as politics does not raise the dilemmas of responsibility and justification entailed in "affirming" political projects and norms. In this respect, like identity politics, indeed sharing its tendency toward positioning without mapping, the contemporary vogue of resistance is more a symptom of postmodernity's crisis of political space than a coherent response to it. Resistance goes nowhere in particular, has no particular attachments, and hails no particular vision; as Foucault makes clear, resistance is a product of and reaction to power, not an arrogation of it.

What postmodernity disperses and postmodern feminist politics requires is cultivated political *spaces* for posing and arguing about feminist political norms, for discussing the nature of "the good" for women. Democratic political space is quite undertheorized in contemporary feminist thinking, as it is everywhere in late-twentieth-century political theory, primarily because it is so little in evidence. Dissipated by the increasing technocratization of would-be political conversations and processes, by the erosion of boundaries around specifically political domains and activities, and by the decline of movement politics, political spaces are scarcer and thinner today than even in most immediately prior epochs of Western history. In this regard, their condition mirrors the splayed and centrifugated characteristics of postmodern political power. Yet precisely because of postmodernity's disarming tendencies toward disorientation, fragmentation, and technocratization, the creation of spaces where political analyses and norms can be proffered and contested is supremely important.

Political space is an old theme in Western political theory, incarnated by the polis practices of Socrates, harshly opposed by Plato in the *Republic,* redeemed and elaborated as metaphysics by Aristotle, resuscitated as salvation for modernity by Hannah Arendt, and given contemporary spin in Jürgen Habermas's theories of ideal speech situations and communicative rationality (*The Theory of Com-*

municative Action I). The project of developing feminist postmodern political spaces, although enriched by pieces of this tradition, necessarily also departs from it. In contrast with Aristotle's formulation, feminist political spaces cannot define themselves against the private sphere, bodies, reproduction and production, mortality, and all the populations and issues implicated in these categories. Unlike Arendt's, these spaces cannot be pristine, rarified, and policed at their boundaries but are necessarily cluttered, attuned to earthly concerns and visions, incessantly disrupted, invaded, and reconfigured. Unlike Habermas, we can harbor no dreams of perfect communication, or even of a "common language," but confront as a permanent political condition partiality of understanding and expression, cultural chasms vigilantly identified but rarely "resolved," and the powers of words and images that evoke, suggest, and connote rather than *transmit* meanings.[25] Our spaces, while requiring elements of definition and protection, cannot be clean, sharply bounded, disembodied, or permanent: To engage postmodern modes of power *and* honor specifically feminist knowledges, they would be heterogeneous, roving, noninstitutionalized, and democratic to the point of exhaustion.

Such spaces are crucial for developing the skills and practices of postmodern *judgment*, for addressing the problem of "how to produce a discourse on justice ... when one no longer relies on ontology or epistemology."[26] Postmodernity's dismantling of metaphysical foundations for justice renders us quite vulnerable to domination by technical reason unless we seize this opening to develop democratic processes for formulating collective postepistemological and postontological judgments. Such judgments require learning how to have *public* conversations with each other, arguing from a vision about the common ("what I want for us") rather than from identity ("who I am") and from explicitly postulated norms and potential common values rather than from false essentialism or unreconstructed private interest.[27] Paradoxically, such public and comparatively impersonal arguments carry potential for much greater accountability than arguments from identity or interest. The former may be interrogated to the ground by others; the latter are insulated from such inquiry with the mantle of "truth" worn by identity-based speech. Postidentity political positions and conversations also potentially replace a politics of difference with a politics of diversity—differences *regarded* from a perspective larger than one point in an ensemble. Postidentity public positioning requires an outlook that discerns structures of dominance within diffused and disorienting orders of power, thereby stretching toward a more politically potent analysis than that which our individuated and fragmented existences can generate. In exact counterpoint to Di Stefano's insistence that "shared identity" is the only "psychologically and politically reliable basis for attachment and motivation on the part of potential activists" (76), I am suggesting that only political conversation oriented toward diversity and the common, toward world rather than self, and involving conversion of one's knowledge of the world from a situated (subject) position into a public idiom offers us the possibility of countering postmodern social fragmentations and political disintegrations.

We have learned well to identify and articulate our "subject positions"—we have become experts at *politicizing* the "I" that is produced through multiple vectors of power and subordination. But the very practice so crucial to making these elements of power visible and subjectivity political may be partly at odds with the requisites for developing political conversation among a complex and diverse "we." For the political making of a feminist future, we may need to loosen our historically feminized attachments to subjectivity and morality and redress our historically underdeveloped taste for political argument. We may need to learn public speaking and the pleasures of public argument, not to overcome our situatedness but to assume responsibility for our situations as well as to acquire perspective and aspire to possibilities that expand them.

NOTES

1. Ferenc Feher and Agnes Heller, *The Postmodern Political Condition* (Oxford: Polity Press, 1988), 4. Subsequent references to this edition appear in the text.

2. Sheldon Wolin, *The Presence of the Past: Essays on the State and the Constitution* (Baltimore: Johns Hopkins University Press, 1989), 173–179. Wendy Brown, "Deregulating Women: The Trials of Freedom Under a Thousand Points of Light," *Sub/versions* 1 (1990): 4. Scott Lasch and John Urry, *The End of Organized Capitalism* (Madison: Wisconsin University Press, 1987), 5–16.

3. Jean-François Lyotard, "Rules and Paradoxes and Svelte Appendix," *Cultural Critique* 5 (1986–1987): 209.

4. Michel Foucault, *Power/Knowledge: Selected Interviews and Other Writings 1972–1977,* trans. Colin Gordon, et al., ed. Colin Gordon (New York: Pantheon, 1980), 105–108. Subsequent references to this edition appear in the text.

5. One clear example of this in the policy domain appears in the vicissitudes of welfare state policy since 1980: The boundaries and relations between family, state, society, economy, workplace, and individual have been incessantly and contradictorily reworked. See Brown, "Deregulating Women"; Wolin, *The Presence of the Past;* and Nancy Fraser, *Unruly Practices: Power, Discourse and Gender in Contemporary Social Theory* (Minneapolis: University of Minnesota Press, 1989), chs. 7–8.

6. Donna Haraway, "A Manifesto for Cyborgs: Science, Technology, and Socialist Feminism in the 1980s," in *Feminism/Postmodernism,* ed. Linda Nicholson (New York: Routledge, 1990), 195.

7. Arguing that a good deal of this nightmare is already upon us, Wolin names its expressly political face "democracy without the demos" or "managed democracies" that "make only rhetorical gestures toward egalitarianism [or] widespread participation in power." He also insists that postmodern theory, or the strand of it incarnated by Richard Rorty, accelerates and assists this phenomenon through celebration of the severance of truth from politics, adulation of "difference" that is actually recycled liberal/repressive tol-

erance, and cultivation of language games—"stories"—that mock the value of reportable, discussable, political reality. Sheldon Wolin, "Democracy in the Discourse of Postmodernism," *Social Research* 57, no. 1 (1990): 26–29.

8. Fredric Jameson, "Regarding Postmodernism—A Conversation with Fredric Jameson," *Universal Abandon? The Politics of Postmodernism,* ed. Andrew Ross (Minneapolis: University of Minnesota Press, 1988), 7. Subsequent references to this edition appear in the text.

9. Stanley Aronowitz, "Postmodernism and Politics," in *Universal Abandon?* ed. Andrew Ross.

10. See Ernesto Laclau and Chantal Mouffe, *Hegemony and Socialist Strategy: Towards a Radical Democratic Politics* (London: Verso, 1985), for a sharply contrasting account of identity politics as a response to postmodernity.

11. If one compares Allen Bloom's *The Closing of the American Mind* (New York: Simon and Schuster, 1987) with the older Straussian tradition of interpreting political theory, from which Bloom hails, one can see quite clearly the postmodern quality: The former operates as overt fundamentalism, is littered with icons of "truth," and opposes itself to relativism and hedonism; the latter, however conservative, is foundationalism self-conscious of the indispensability of hermeneutics for its existence, intentionally and provocatively opening itself to other interpretations in the political theory canon.

12. Nancy Hartsock, "Foucault on Power: A Theory for Women?" in *Feminism/Postmodernism,* ed. Linda Nicholson, pp. 171–172. Subsequent references to this Hartsock essay appear in the text.

13. Jürgen Habermas remains the exemplar of this modernist impulse. See *Knowledge and Human Interests* (Boston: Beacon, 1971); "Modernity vs. Postmodernity," *New German Critique* 22 (1981): 3–14; "A Reply to My Critics," in *Habermas: Critical Debates,* ed. J. Thompson and David Held (London: Macmillan, 1982), 219–283; *The Theory of Communicative Action I: Reason and the Rationalization of Society,* trans. Thomas McCarthy (Boston: Beacon, 1984).

14. In "Dilemmas of Difference: Feminism, Modernity, and Postmodernism" (in Nicholson, *Feminism/Postmodernism*) Christine Di Stefano argues: "The postmodernist project, if seriously adopted by feminists, would make any semblance of a feminist politics impossible. To the extent that feminist politics is bound up with a specific constituency or subject, namely, women, the postmodernist prohibition against subject-centered inquiry and theory undermines the legitimacy of a broad-based organized movement dedicated to articulating and implementing the goals of such a constituency" (76). Subsequent references are in the text.

15. Luce Irigaray, "Any Theory of the Subject Has Already Been Appropriated by the Masculine," *Speculum of the Other Woman,* trans. G. Gill (Ithaca, N.Y.: Cornell University Press, 1985), p. 133; Judith Butler, *Gender Trouble: Feminism and the Subversion of Identity* (New York: Routledge, 1989), p. 141; and Denise Riley, *"Am I That Name?": Feminism and the Category of "Women" in History* (Minneapolis: University of Minnesota Press, 1988), p. 1.

16. According to Di Stefano, "Contemporary Western feminism is firmly, if ambivalently, located in the modernist ethos, which made possible the feminist identification and critique of gender" (Ibid., 64).

17. Seyla Benhabib, "On Contemporary Feminist Theory," *Dissent* 36 (1989): 369.

18. Catharine MacKinnon, *Feminism Unmodified: Discourses on Life and Law* (Cambridge: Harvard University Press, 1987), 48–50.

19. Michel Foucault, *The History of Sexuality, Volume 1: An Introduction,* trans. Robert Hurley (New York: Pantheon, 1980), 58–63. Subsequent references to this edition appear in the text.

20. In Haraway's words: "My problem, and 'our' problem, is how to have *simultaneously* an account of radical historical contingency for all knowledge claims and knowing subjects, a critical practice of recognizing our own 'semiotic technologies' for making meanings, *and* a no-nonsense commitment to faithful accounts of a 'real' world" ("Situated Knowledges: The Science Question in Feminism and the Privilege of Partial Perspective," *Feminist Studies* 14 [1988]: 579). See also Sandra Harding, *The Science Question in Feminism* (Ithaca: Cornell University Press, 1986); Nancy Hartsock, "The Feminist Standpoint," in *Discovering Reality,* Sandra Harding and Merrill Hintikka, eds.; Evelyn Fox Keller, *Reflections on Gender and Science* (New Haven: Yale University Press, 1984); and MacKinnon, *Feminism Unmodified.*

21. Friedrich Nietzsche, *On the Genealogy of Morals,* trans. Walter Kaufmann (New York: Vintage, 1967), 20. Subsequent references to this edition appear in the text.

22. Nietzsche elaborates: "While the noble man lives in trust and openness with himself, the man of *ressentiment* is neither upright nor naive nor honest and straightforward with himself. His soul *squints;* his spirit loves hiding places, secret paths and back doors, everything covert entices him as *his* world, *his* security, *his* refreshment; he understands how to keep silent, how not to forget, how to wait, how to be provisionally self-deprecating and humble" (*On the Genealogy of Morals,* 38).

23. Nicholson, *Feminism/Postmodernism,* 11.

24. Friedrich Nietzsche, "Twilight of the Idols," *The Portable Nietzsche,* trans. and ed. Walter Kaufmann (New York: Viking, 1954), 476.

25. In Haraway's words, "Feminism loves another science: the sciences and politics of interpretation, translations, stuttering and the partly understood" ("Situated Knowledges," 589).

26. Emelia Steurman, "Habermas vs. Lyotard: Modernity vs. Postmodernity?" *New Formations* 7 (1989): 61.

27. Haraway makes a similar argument ("Situated Knowledges," 586–587).

PART TWO

PROSTHETICS: CYBORGS, ANDROIDS, & ALIENS

9

Autotopographies

JENNIFER A. GONZÁLEZ

IN 1973 CHRISTIAN BOLTANSKI wrote the following letter, copies of which he then sent to the conservators of 62 museums: 'I should like you to exhibit in one room of your museum all the objects that surrounded a person during his lifetime and which, after his death, remain as witnesses of his existence. These objects ranging for example from the handkerchiefs used by the person to the wardrobe which stood in his room, should all be displayed in show-cases and carefully labeled.' He received 35 replies, and four museums implemented his plan."[1]

Clothing and cloth with all of its scents and residues; furniture with all of its bodily imprints, shapes, and sags from years of use; worn silverware and shoes: All of these serviceable objects receive the imprint of a human trace as the autonomy of their purely functional status is worn away by time. Used initially as prostheses (to cover and protect, to extend and support the body), such objects often become, after years of use, integrated so inextricably with one's *psychic body* that they cannot be replaced or removed without a subversion of the physical body itself. The same holds true for objects that function as prostheses of the mind. No less integral to the subject, such physical extensions of the psyche—trophies, photographs, travel souvenirs, heirlooms, religious icons, gifts—take the form of autobiographical objects. These personal objects can be seen to form a syntagmatic array of physical signs in a spatial representation of identity—what I call an *autotopography*. Its own form of prosthetic territory, this private-yet-material memory landscape is made up of the more intimate expressions of values and beliefs, emotions and desires, that are found in the domestic collection and arrangement of objects. Such private collections can range from a formal home altar—complete with statues of saints, family photographs, and offerings of food—to the informal arrangement and display of memorabilia.

Although some of my recent writing includes a study of home altars and installation art,[2] the present text takes as its focus more secular forms of autotopographies that can also be described as "museums of the self."[3] Existing along the continuum of monument and microcosm, this collection, arrangement, or storage of symbolically significant objects represents a personal identity in relation to a larger social network of meaning and functions to anchor the self-reflective image of the subject within a local, earthly cosmos. In the creation of an autotopography—which does not include all personal property but only those objects seen to signify an "individual" identity—the material world is called upon to present a physical map of memory, history, and belief. The autobiographical object thus becomes a prosthetic device: an addition, a trace, and a replacement for the intangible aspects of desire, identification, and social relations.

Space and time define the domain of "things"—a domain penetrated by human language in search of concrete and immortal signification. Taking a moment to name an object, one claims its power of presence; but the object always defies this claim by becoming lost, turning to dust, or, more often than not, "outliving" those who own it. As Grasskamp notes, "All the paraphernalia of furniture, tools, clothes, bags and cases, books, pictures, etcetera, etcetera which we drag around with us throughout our lives because we seem to need them, look like banal collections without the person for whom they possess some degree of utility. These demonstrations of the estates of deceased persons are not studies in sociology or archeology. In their concentration on individuals they rather touch upon the question as to what contribution *things* make to the *identity* of the person who possesses them, the question of the *biographical role of property*" (italics in original).[4] Despite the fact that, at death, each individual will leave behind traces of his or her own autotopological path, comprising an array of very personal objects within a domestic landscape, such objects also are part of an important living practice.

Whether consciously or unconsciously, the creation of an autotopography is, in each case, a form of self-representation. Just as a written autobiography is a series of narrated events, fantasies, and identifications, so too an autotopography forms a spatial representation of important relations, emotional ties, and past events. Within both modes of expression there are a multitude of forms. In the case of the autotopography, for example, a careful, visual arrangement of mementos and heirlooms, on the one hand, and a jumbled, hidden assembly of dusty and unkempt objects, on the other, can *both* constitute a material memory landscape. Each space preserves or gathers together objects that, whether they reflect pleasant memories or repress unhappy ones, ultimately form a visible and tactile map of the subjectivity. Found in boxes and drawers, on table tops, mantelpieces, and shelves, such collections most often include mementos and other indexical or symbolic traces used to create a metonymic link with past events and absent persons.

For the purposes of this chapter I have chosen the following example to illustrate the working of one such autotopography. In describing a piece of bone that had been removed during an "extrapleural pneumothorax" operation, Roland Barthes writes,

> For a long time I kept this fragment of myself in a drawer, a kind of body penis analo-
> gous to the end of a rib chop, not knowing quite what to do with it, not daring to get
> rid of it lest I do some harm to my person, though it was utterly useless to me shut up
> in a desk among such "precious" objects as old keys, a schoolboy report card, my
> grandmother B.'s mother-of-pearl dance program and pink taffeta card case. And
> then, one day, realizing that the function of any drawer is to ease, to acclimate the
> death of objects by causing them to pass through a sort of pious site, a dusty chapel
> where, in the guise of keeping them alive, we allow them a decent interval of dim ag-
> ony, but not going so far as to dare cast this bit of myself into the common refuse bin
> of my building, I flung the rib chop and its gauze from my balcony, as if I were ro-
> mantically scattering my own ashes, into the rue Servandoni, where some dog would
> come and sniff them out.[5]

Here the death of the object comes at the moment of its release from the confines of the autotopographical space of the drawer. Prepared to scatter his bodily remains and the memories associated with this corporeal sign, Barthes nevertheless clings to the other talismans of his past as though they were more integral to his life than his own bones. Those once "precious" items that continue to haunt the sacred reliquary of his desk—the schoolboy report card, the mother-of-pearl dance program—take on a meaning that lies far deeper than the layer of language that names them. Lingering on after the expulsion of the rib chop, their mere presence signifies a desire not to part with the past. Apparently used as mnemonic devices, these objects may also, however, act as a screen to veil a hidden memory or desire.

Memory, Nostalgia, Souvenir

Memory, like identity, is a process of situating not unlike placing within an architectural model for our perusal those rooms, objects, events, and landscapes that we have encountered again and again in pacing through time. Umberto Eco remarks that "remembering is like constructing and then traveling again through a space. We are already talking about architecture. Memories are built as a city is built."[6] With each remembrance we adjust the space of the past, now adding, now removing images and events to suit our purpose. In this sense memory must be seen as constitutive rather than merely reflective. We use props to maintain the structure of this mental architecture. In his article "Prosthetic Theory: The Disciplining of Architecture," Mark Wigley writes of prosthesis that "it is a foreign element that reconstructs that which cannot stand up on its own, at once propping up and extending its host. The prosthesis is always structural, establishing the place it appears to be added to."[7] Similarly, the mnemonic devices that make up an autotopography can thus be seen to *create a space* for the memory they repre-

sent. The past is reconstructed from a moment in the present to convince ourselves of something we wish to be or have been. The objects of memory, then, become a *spatial annex* to the mental images that, voluntarily or involuntarily, are
projected into consciousness.

In *Remembrance of Things Past,* Marcel Proust distinguishes between *intellectual* and *involuntary* memory—or *mémoire involontaire.*[8] The former is the type
of mental recall characterized by Proust as "an exercise of the will," those memories that are built not so much from personal experience as from social knowledge
and reasoning. In contrast, the *mémoire involontaire,* as its name suggests, extends
beyond the control of the subject to either solicit or reject its influence. Such
memory, arising from a preconscious or previously unconscious state, is most often activated by an external force—an object. "The past is hidden somewhere
outside the realm, beyond the reach of the intellect, in some material object (in
the sensation which that material object will give us) which we do not suspect."[9]
Here the intangible aspect of memory becomes concretized in a bodily sensation
triggered by an object. Of course both voluntary and involuntary memory may be
at work in the construction of a single representation of the past. It is possible, for
example, to think of two different movements that make up the work of reviewing
the past: *memory,* which is an intrusion of the past into the present, and *remembering,* which is a retrogressive movement from the present into a reconstruction
of the past—not unlike the "secondary revision" that takes place in Freud's
dreamwork. And just as in a dream, the material object may be the site of conden-
sations and displacements of meaning.

The possible ambivalences and complexities that must underlie the selection
and care of autobiographical objects can be described in part by Freud's theory of
the *screen memory.* Functioning to hide rather than reveal a traumatic moment,
screen memories protect the individual from his or her own unconscious. Screen
memory thus "owes its value as a memory not to its own content but to the relation existing between that content and some other, that has been suppressed."[10]
This relation is usually one of metonymy: "It is a case of displacement on to
something associated by continuity; or, looking at the process as a whole, a case of
repression accompanied by the substitution of something in the neighborhood
(whether in space or time)."[11] Such displacement may, as in the case of the fetish,
create the need for what might be called a "screen object."[12] Just as there are voluntary and involuntary memories, there are also intentional and unintentional
devices of memory. The autotopography may, in other words, comprise artifacts
that are designed to promote forgetting as well as remembering. As either catalyst
or mask, herald or code, such objects will always provoke the subject to decipher
them. In the process they act to tether desires and memories like a quilted loop on
the surface of past experiences. The subject chooses (or is chosen by) a sign from
the field of concrete signification and refashions this "objective object" into a

"subjective object."[13] By this act, the free fall of memory is anchored to significant moments that will be relived again and again.

Nostalgia is often the path to these frequented "sites." An emotional state pejoratively marked as excessive, nostalgia names one way in which the past is produced from a present yearning. It therefore may provide a clue to the nature and use of objects in the process of re-membering the self. In her article "Freud's Mnemonic: Women, Screen Memories and Feminist Nostalgia," Mary Jacobus suggests that nostalgia is a memory of that which never was. Just as for Freud certain forms of screen memory create the past from fears and desires of the present, for Jacobus the past represents a reworking of leftover materials, patiently turning over the personal detritus of memory that compose a woman's life ("bits of yarn, calico and velvet scraps," shells, skeins of milkweed, petunia petals, seaweed, cats' whiskers, bird feathers). These are "the finest findings"—the mnemonics or *objets trouvés*—in which a woman "finds herself" where she is not. Memory is less "found" than fabricated. Consciousness is a patchwork rather than a seamless web. "Such a composition has nothing to do with eternity" or wholeness; it has to do with temporality and fragmentation.[14]

The same observation has been made by Susan Stewart. In her book *On Longing* she writes, "Nostalgia, like any form of narrative is always ideological: the past it seeks has never existed except as narrative, and hence always absent, that past continually threatens to reproduce itself as a felt lack."[15] Like the Lacanian notion of desire, nostalgia is always a desire for desire itself. An internally structured lack, nostalgia is the longing for an imaginary place, time, or event that, by definition, cannot be satisfied because it is the longing itself that structures this desire. An autotopography might thus comprise such material representations of longing. Robinson Crusoe marked time with objects he had constructed. The objects provided the truth of time; they were the source of the narrative of existence. And yet narrative is itself constitutive of the object's history. It is that which "bridges" the gap between past and present, memory and identity. Nostalgia is therefore that subjective state that arises in the recognition that this gap between signifier and signified, between the construction of a narrative and its referent, can never really be crossed. The belief in narrative as transparent and "unmotivated" allows for the belief in a "reality" that has, in fact, been ideologically constructed.

Kathleen Stewart, in her article "Nostalgia—A Polemic," traces the regional uses of nostalgia in the changing cultural landscape of the contemporary United States.[16] Contrasting the "mirage" of "artificial" environments (overbuilt architectural structures such as hotel and commercial complexes and reconstructed tourist towns) and the smaller scale spaces of "marginal" communities, Stewart outlines a theory of cultural decay and reconstitution that is based upon sites of narrative and objects of memory. She writes, "In positing a 'once was' in relation to a 'now' [nostalgia] creates a frame for meaning, a means of dramatizing aspects of an increasingly fluid and unnamed social life. ... By resurrecting time and place, and a subject *in* time and place, it shatters the surface of an atemporal order and a prefab cultural landscape."[17] In this "prefab" landscape, which seems to leave little room for local community memories that once held such importance for personal identity "and where the self is a pastiche of styles glued to a surface, nostalgia becomes the very lighthouse waving us back to shore—the point on the landscape that gives hope of direction."[18] Here the activity of nostalgia is a looking back upon the past with the hope of finding an identity that, never having really existed, is still the only source of support for a present subjectivity. Without romanticizing the term, Stewart points to the various uses of nostalgia within "exiled" communities struggling for a sense of identity and place. Her anthropological analyses of "marginal" cultures in West Virginia reveal that such groups construct highly developed systems of material memory that serve to maintain local notions of self and place. For them, having a culture is a matter of people leaving their mark on the place; in turn, the place and its history leave "marks" on the people, even as bodily scars. The interiors of the houses, like the hills outside, are crowded with signs of the past. Rooms are filled to overflowing with "whatnots," and every inch of the walls is covered with nostalgic pictures of the dead and souvenirs of lost moments. The inhabitants seek a continuity in life by always piecing together what is always falling apart. Women piece together quilts from scraps of clothing, and in every scrap exists a memory and so a story.[19]

There are many communities that pursue this kind of activity. But it is most often those people in exile, from their native land or *within their own country,* who are in need of a locally produced representation of the past. Mainstream representations of cultural history do not include the nostalgic memories of "deterritorialized" groups. As a result, the autotopographies of immigrants, exiles, and minorities often form strong testimony, at the local or even personal level, of an ambivalent representation of identity in crisis. Objects that symbolically or indexically represent a "homeland," whether actual or ideological, in this case serve to support a communal notion of "self." Memories are made manifest in a material form. They obey the logic of decay but also are carefully preserved and located in a semiotic system of placement and display. In this context one could say that memories *take place* in a way that history does not.

Pierre Nora in "Between Memory and History: Les Lieux de Mémoire"[20] describes a need for private stories and local memories in the face of a cultural system that increasingly favors public histories. In so doing he suggests that memory is a dying practice; and because of its decline, with the subsequent rise of history, the sites of memory, or the *lieux de mémoire,* have become more poignant in their demand to be recognized. "These *lieux de mémoire* are fundamentally remains, the ultimate embodiments of a memorial consciousness that has barely survived in a historical age that calls out for memory because it has been abandoned."[21] Although it is possible to see that memory—as well as amnesia—informs the social construction of history, history cannot be read simply as a collection of memories. Memory and history do not exist on a continuum in which the former is a more personal and local version of the latter. Rather, each has a unique power over the experience of time; each produces a qualitatively different representation and organization of past events. It is therefore crucial to make distinctions among the ways in which material culture is called upon to serve each of these concerns. Nora writes,

> Memory is life, borne by living societies founded in its name. It remains in permanent evolution open to the dialectic of remembering and forgetting, unconscious of its successive deformations, vulnerable to manipulation and appropriation, susceptible to being long dormant and periodically revived. History, on the other hand, is the reconstruction, always problematic and incomplete, of what is no longer. Memory is a perpetually actual phenomenon, a bond tying us to the eternal present; history is a representation of the past. Memory, in so far as it is affective and magical, only accommodates those facts that suit it; it nourishes recollections that may be out of focus or telescopic, global or detached, particular or symbolic—responsive to each avenue of conveyance or phenomenal screen, to every censorship or projection. ... Memory installs remembrance within the sacred; history, always prosaic, releases it again.[22]

Memory, then, is necessarily in a state of constant change. The dialectic of remembering and forgetting maps the path of internal revisions and debate. Memory is never fixed. In a culture heavily invested in factual histories, however, memory is relegated to specific locations and practices. History announces the immortal, monumental nature of its representations and—despite its practice— is *not* built on a paradigm of flexibility and reinterpretation. The mediation of history has made it impossible to conceive of the present in relation to a mutable memory. Instead, all activity becomes directed toward its own representation in the future. The present becomes conceived as "historical moment." Art and artifacts are created for the sole purpose of claiming a place in a future history of the present.[23] In a culture where the present is "produced" primarily in the interest of its preservation for the future, history has eclipsed memory. It is out of this historicizing environment that *lieux de mémoire* are constructed. For, Nora claims, "There are *lieux de mémoire*, sites of memory, because there are no longer *milieux de mémoire*, real environments of memory."[24] In the activity of contemporary Western cultures, history proclaims its authority over memory. To resist erasure, sites of memory undermine history's seamless narratives by providing the material traces of a shifting symbolic and sacred relationship to things. More important, memory implies, as against history, that there are *multiple* stories to be told in an overlapping layering of signification that does not take place in a linear, linguistic, or necessarily coherent manner. On a microcosmic scale, then, an autotopography may be a *lieu de mémoire* that provides a personal revision of the totalizing narratives of history.

"Memory takes root in the concrete, in spaces, gesture, images and objects; history binds itself strictly to temporal continuities, to progressions and to relations between things."[25] It is in the tension *between* memory and history that *les lieux de mémoire* are created. Nora suggests that an object, archive, museum, monument, or even an individual can be considered a *lieu de mémoire.* This site of memory implies "a decisive shift from the historical to the psychological, from the social to the individual, from the objective message to its subjective reception, from repetition to rememoration. The total psychologization of contemporary memory entails a completely new economy of the identity of the self, the mechanics of memory, and the relevance of the past."[26] I would like to suggest that the economy of this identity rests, in many cases, with the very gathering and collecting of material artifacts of an individual past that constitutes the autotopography. Pierre Nora and Kathleen Stewart provide an initial view into the need for this collecting and storing up of objects of memory and identity. Nora points out that "the defense, by certain minorities, of a privileged memory that has retreated to jealously protected enclaves in this sense intensely illuminates the truth of *lieux de mémoire*—that without commemorative vigilance, history would soon sweep them away. We buttress our identities upon such bastions, but if what they defended were not threatened, there would be no need to build them."[27]

One forms models of self-representation—in this case autotopographies—not only to reflect memories and desires but also to protect a threatened identity. Objects themselves function as *lieux de mémoire,* as material support to claims of specific and contingent identities that rely upon an open, flexible, and changing narrative. Memory cannot become fixed by the object, rather the object serves the purposes of memory by providing that necessary trace of something specific, individual, and redefinable. As Kathleen Stewart notes, "From here, resistance takes the form of making further inscriptions on the landscape of encoded things—inlays on the existing inscriptions—in an effort to fragment the enclosing, already finished order and reopen cultural forms to history."[28] A general lack of cultural memory within the public sphere of contemporary Western societies is felt and expressed through the individual interventions of memory as against history. "It gives everyone the necessity to remember and to protect the trappings of identity; when memory is no longer everywhere, it will not be anywhere unless one takes the responsibility to recapture it through individual means."[29]

One of the more common traps of memory is the object made or chosen specifically for this purpose—the souvenir. As the material site of memory, it creates a bond between the concrete particularity of the present and the seemingly intangible past. It does not, however, *unexpectedly* trigger memories from the depth of the past or the unconscious. Rather, it is intended from its very conception, and in some cases fabrication, to become the token for a particular individual or group. Indeed, it functions much like the Freudian fetish in its recreation of satisfaction, with an important difference. Unlike an heirloom, screen object, or fetish, a souvenir is acquired or kept by choice. The fetish is used to mask the event for which it is the representative; the souvenir is kept for the purposes of more clearly remembering the event. The fetish creates a *screen memory;* the souvenir is used to create a nostalgic memory.

In "The Refuges of Intimacy" Orest Ranum writes of the souvenir in early-modern France:

> The souvenir-space (walled garden, bedroom, ruelle, study or oratory) and the souvenir-object (book, flower, clothing, ring, ribbon, portrait, or letter) were quite private, having been possessed by an individual unique in time and space. Nevertheless, the significance of such spaces and objects was encoded and perfectly comprehensible to others.
>
> In the vocabulary of intimacy, the word souvenir, though not limited to memories of the passions, became the preferred word for them in the eighteenth century. It even acquired a double meaning, denoting both a memory and/or a common object such as a ribbon or combe that belonged to a loved one or a gift that expressed the identity of the giver or recipient. Through the exchange of souvenirs, the self became other and the other, the self.[30]

In this case the souvenir is located within a larger discourse of material communication. Because souvenirs were so easily recognizable as intimate objects, it was necessary to keep them hidden in such spaces as the ruelle (a concealed closet behind or beside the bed). Such an object might otherwise implicate its bearer in a network of passionate relations.

In the contemporary United States, mnemonic devices are more often used within the context of a personal historical narrative that has its own system or code of signification. It is for this reason that one person's well-loved and well-worn souvenirs will appear as so much junk to anyone else. This discrepancy reveals that the souvenir functions as one sign within a personally constructed code of signification. In each case, for each subject, the semantic or semiotic component of the sign is unique even if its form has, in addition, a socially recognizable meaning. Thus, the souvenir operates as part of a relatively solipsistic *system* of communication. As Susan Stewart notes, "Such souvenirs are rarely kept singly; instead they form a compendium which is an autobiography."[31] These autobiographical material artifacts that assert a presence of the past also locate individuals in that past—individuals who turn to these objects for the reassurance, indeed material proof, of having been a particular person in a particular place, time, and community.

The object thus also represents the imaginary body, a body that is both incomplete (because always changing) and overabundant (because it signifies all possible desires). It is only because of our own bodily existence, and our relation to the materiality of this body, that we are able to become emotionally invested in external objects that represent an important aspect of identity. But the relation to this prosthetic extension might be ambivalent. One writer has remarked, "I remember how my familiar objects tortured me. They would transform overnight from cherished, adored figurines to nightmarish ghouls haunting me with familiarity. Once when I was eight I packed them desperately away, each in tissue into a box. I resisted the desire to destroy them all, to smash the china and plastic and wood figures into raging tiny, controllable pieces. I hid the boxes far underneath the bed and then sat on the edge of the mattress, looking at the absences, the holes in the familiar universe. I was terrified by their still presence under the bed, not sure how to escape them."[32] In this case, the autotopographical landscape, having become a haunting presence or witness of unbearable meanings, cannot be left to stand but must be transformed or destroyed to remove its reflective gaze.

Narrative Traces

If recollection is "a process of emplotting the landmarks of one's life history as it is presently perceived,"[33] then this "emplotting" takes place both by marking out a physical, temporal map with objects and by creating a narrative plot that organizes these scattered pieces. The autobiographical nature of the souvenir is not often to be found in the object alone. It emanates equally from an accompanying narrative, an individual story line that is usually the result of a changing pattern of memories and identifications. Such a story line might be identified as what Hayden White has called a "mythic narrative," which "is under no obligation to keep the two orders of events, real and imaginary, distinct from one another."[34] The "mythic narrative" is contrasted by White with "historical representation," which "belongs to the category of what might be called 'the discourse of the real,' as against the 'discourse of the imaginary' or 'the discourse of desire.'"[35] Yet the discourses of the "real," the "imaginary," and "desire" become entangled in individual memory. As is the case with Nora's *lieux de mémoire,* a struggle between the desiring imaginary of memory and the concrete manifestations of "history" constitute the narrative of the "self." Time marks the struggle between the imaginary and the real with physical as well as narrative traces, traces that are not necessarily semantically anchored. Autobiography thus becomes an act of collection, arrangement, and authentication of objects as much as the construction of narrative that accompanies these activities. In this case, there is an equally strong demand upon an object to both provide historical "proof" of a particular occurrence and to allow for an imaginary development of narrative. The flexibility of the second is as important to the story as the rigidity of the first. It is in the interplay of these two types of recounting that the object finds its most powerful narrative force.

In *Time and Narrative,* Paul Ricoeur links this notion of the autobiographical object to the narrative construction of individual identity through his theory of "traces": "People from the past left these vestiges. However they are also the products of their activities and their work, hence they are those things Heidegger speaks of as subsisting and at hand (tools, dwellings, temples, tombs, writings) that have left a mark. In this sense to have passed this way and to have made a mark are equivalent."[36] The "mark" is testimony to the *having happened* of the past. In this sense it is not unlike the Peircian index. Ricoeur, however, reminds us to be aware of the problematic of time that makes up this relation. "In the first place, to follow a trace is one way of 'reckoning with time.' How could the trace left in space refer back to the passage of the sought-for object without our calculations concerning the time that passed between them, that is, between the passage and the trace I left? Immediately then, datability with its 'now,' 'then,' and 'earlier,' and so on, is brought into play."[37]

Although the trace remains, the world from which it came is absent. The trace thus has the unique ability to represent time as neither past nor present but as both simultaneously. "The act of following or retracing a trace, can only be carried out within the framework of a historical time that is neither a fragment of stellar time nor a simple aggrandizement of the communal dimensions of the time of personal memory; this is a hybrid time, issuing from the confluence of two perspectives on time."[38] It is as an embodiment of this "hybrid" time that the trace becomes interesting. In this sense any "trace" works like a photograph: It is a material representation of the disappearance of time. It is a spatial triumph over time. Thus the trace also functions much like bodily experience: materially present and enduring yet having had an existence in the past. The subject, like the object, is a material hybrid of time and, like the object, inhabits certain historical as well as imaginary narratives.

This process finds its culmination in what Ricoeur calls "narrative identity": "The fragile offshoot issuing from the union of history and fiction is the assignment to an individual or a community of a specific identity that we can call their narrative identity. Here "identity" is taken in the sense of a practical category. To state the identity of an individual or a community is to answer the question, 'who did this?' ... Unlike the abstract identity of the Same, this narrative identity, constitutive of self-constancy, can include change, mutability, within the cohesion of one lifetime. The subject then appears both as a reader and the writer of its own life."[39] History and fiction are thus mutually constitutive of an individual identity that exists in a "third-time" of present and past.[40] Stuart Hall, in his essay "Cultural Identity and Diaspora," outlines a similar notion of identity that is both importantly historical and simultaneously constructed through imaginative narration. He says of "cultural identity" that "It is *something*—not a mere trick of the imagination. It has its histories—and histories have their real, material and symbolic effects. The past continues to speak to us. But it no longer addresses us as a simple, factual 'past,' since our relation to it, like the child's relation to the mother, is always-already 'after the break.' It is always constructed through memory, fantasy, narrative and myth."[41] In Hall's view there is also a tension between the "real, material" effects of history and the construction of "fantasy, narrative and myth."

The subject, like the material trace, "stands-for" a particular past insofar as that past can be read on or in the body and is reconstructed through a narrative that can only be told after the "fact" of the body. Race, ethnicity, and class are not originally chosen "traits," nor is biological sex. Moreover, these categorical distinctions form a material ground that resists individual and social redefinition. Thus myth and concrete existence mesh to produce a system of signification that must include both linguistic *and* material sign systems by recognizing their necessary overlap and *mutual constitution*. The object that serves as the narrative nodal point of an "individual" identity functions in the same manner. Each is a material trace that holds a particular historical status and yet can be understood only within the context of contemporary narrative. It is perhaps this similarity in ontological status that makes the material sign (souvenir, heirloom, photograph) a popular representative of personal history. Eugen Bär, in his article "Things Are Stories," writes, "Any mapping of the world into things is always relative to the subject doing the mapping (in German the phrase is "die Welt ist subjektiv bedingt") and that means in this context that things tell, among other stories, also and maybe primarily the story of the subjects for whom they are things."[42] But the "story" of personal objects need not follow a tidy linear construction. Rather, it might be a series of unconnected associations that follow one from another, each aspect forming an image or meaning that rests in the mind without a plot—a narrative fragment, a piece of signification that might make up a narrative were it connected with other bits and pieces. Narrative is that which allows one to make sense of time in a fictional and historical sense. The object functions as the material site for an already developed narrative to be grounded or condensed, or as a fragment of a larger narrative for which it serves as one trace among others. This notion of associative relations is in agreement with Barthes's claim that "the object is polysemous, i.e., it readily offers itself to several readings of meaning; in the presence of an object, there are almost always several readings possible, and this not only between one reader and the next, but also, sometimes, within one and the same reader."[43]

Associative meanings that are attached to objects are thus as free and flexible as those attached to words; but the object itself, in its materiality, provides a resistance that seems, just as does the human body, to anchor more firmly, though not absolutely, its range of signification.

The Collection of Identification

The autotopography as a whole is often seen as a coherent series of relations. Interviews conducted with several individuals have suggested that the collection and arrangement of objects, especially souvenirs and gifts, into a visible space creates a representative reconstruction of personal memory. In addition, however, these collections almost invariably contain images of respected or admired individuals, as well as ancestors directly or indirectly connected to the life history of the individual. The microcosmic space of the autotopography is a phantasmal space where the subject can "keep company" with others by the juxtaposition of representative tokens and images. Roland Barthes's dusty but "precious" collection reveals the influence of his relationship with "Grandmother B." Placed in proximity with his schoolboy report card, the mother-of-pearl dance program and pink taffeta card case are associated with memories of his youth. They may be the traces of a cross-gendered identification with the grandmother herself. In this case, to "acclimate the death of the object" is also to acclimate the death or aging of the subject, who may be passing through his or her own "decent interval of dim agony."

Conversely, the autotopography is frequently a space of *utopian* identification and mythic histories—an idealized recreation of subjectivity that uses carefully selected artifacts as concrete evidence. During interviews I conducted with people who had purposely constructed an autotopography in the form of a home altar, it became clear that the juxtaposition of objects was a recreation of an idealized "self" in relation to a larger social community. In speaking of this more formal collection of objects one interviewee said:

> These various objects either represent where I've been or where I would like to go. They either represent literal travels, of my self or people that have been close to me or they represent past relationships and what those relationships have meant. This is a way ... that I keep those memories alive and the way those people have touched me and formed me. And it is also about pushing myself to rethink certain concepts of myself; this is the place I can come to think about what my next move will be ... a move to the future. ... But these images, these are particularly images [that] in some way reflect who I am more than others. And there's a way that I want *that* to be a presence in my life ... having images around me that reflect who I am, rather than not, or how I envision what I am.[44]

In this case the autotopography creates not only a microcosmic representation of relations to a larger community of people but also a concrete mapping of a future vision. In this sense, the objects and images are used for the purposes of identification with others and with an ideal "self."

It is also possible to think of the autotopography as a space of adult "transitional objects." Not unlike in D. W. Winnicott's definition of the term, this possession becomes both an extension of the subject (a prosthesis of sorts) and a kind of soothing presence external to the subject.[45] One interviewee remarked:

> Whenever I move—and I've moved a lot—whenever I move I know that everything is okay if I can find a spot to put my little things. It gives a sense of being able to settle and a sense of purpose there, a feeling of ground and a sense of home. ... So to me they are a way of grounding me. Since I seem to have traveling, wandering, in my stars, I've very rarely had a home. ... For me [these objects] have always been my roots—giving a sense of home and place and stability and that kind of thing. And be-

cause I have been so many places and had to make these little homes, I have always been very aware of those things that I trip over. To pick them up provides continuity and stability at the same time.[46]

The moment of personal or cultural transition, the movement from one place to another, from one role to another, can create the felt need to have certain objects that form a continuity between a previous life and a new life, a previous identity and a new identity. Certain books, articles of clothing, tokens, and symbols of the past—these become "transitional objects" that ease the passage from one psychic or physical state to another.

Thus, whether a conscious or unconscious process, the act of collecting a material representation of identity is highly motivated. Making a similar point in *The Predicament of Culture*, James Clifford points out that collection and preservation are always informed by politics and desire. He suggests that even private collections of objects eventually will be expected to conform to rule-governed, traditional categories of collecting.[47] And this expectation may indeed be pervasive. However, the autotopographies discussed here remain for the most part outside the domain of systematic collection and economic values of objects determined by the marketplace.[48] So unique are autobiographical objects that they cannot be readily sold, nor can they necessarily conform to the characteristics of a "good" collection. This does not preclude the possibility—or likelihood—that systematic and formal collections are also autotopographical. Books, coins, artwork, and all the other possible objects that form traditional, categorical collections quite often reflect the personal history and identity of the individual. The relation between the collector and the collected, in other words, is always to some degree autobiographical.

Why "Autotopography"?

The notion of an autotopography, like Michel Foucault's concept of *heterotopia*, marks the "countersites" that construct a "simultaneously mythic and real contestation of the space in which we live."[49] A representation of memory and identity takes place in the physical sites of domestic and other private spaces where the gathering of artifacts becomes a reconstitution of personal and social history. Countering and conversing with the images available in the powerful realm of mass media, as well as drawing from the resources of life events and cultural identity, the autotopography lays out the reflection of private identifications and projected desires.

Each of the texts previously discussed elaborates one or more important aspect of the concept of material self-representation; taken together they begin to form an associational compendium of characteristics. Beginning with the architecture of prosthesis as the material annex of mental as well as physical phenomena, they show that the spaces of the autotopography (the private corners of rooms, boxes, desks, drawers, and shelves) include the metaphorical architecture of memory as well. The representation of the past, it is suggested, evolves out of the mnemonic devices of both voluntary and involuntary memory: Both the nostalgic souvenir and the "screen object" make use of memory as the framework upon which to locate a material identity. Such objects taken from a larger social scheme of meaning are redefined in a private or local system of signification, causing the artifact to pass through a process of "subjectification." But the desire to remember, alone, is not enough to explain the need for an autotopographical space. Nostalgia, born from the sense of longing and lack that accompanies the loss of some cherished moment, person, or identity, is often the impetus behind the individual need for a mythic construction of the past based upon the desire for a different, idealized memory. The disavowal that defines nostalgia is thus allowed to contribute to the construction of memory, but not to that of history. Memory and history are observed to make equal demands upon the evidence of material culture while simultaneously making very *different* claims about the *status* of this evidence. Memory allows the object to have changing and multiple meanings, whereas history demands of the object a specific and single identity. Both discourses are present in the autotopography—and the narrative that accompanies this process is no less powerful for its being "mythic." The concept of the trace, as developed by Ricoeur, helps to support the thesis that an autotopography is a combination of "fictional" memory and "factual" history embedded in a material object. But more important, it is the representation of an identity that is also between fiction and history and between past and present that makes the autotopography a powerful tool of "evidence"—linking time, space, and event in a material manifestation of "self." This hybridity of time, which characterizes the ontological resemblance between body and object, also appears in the autotopography. The past and present of a personal or cultural identity can thus be relocated in a tangible space of icons, souvenirs, and other collected objects, each referring to specific sites and moments, psychic states and symbolic relations.

Within a growing number of academic disciplines, a focus upon material culture and representation (studies of museums, of collections, of property) reveals a renewed and continuing fascination with the physical world of the object (fetish, relic, historical artifact, and industrial product). Yet none of these studies have adequately accounted for the tactical act of self-representation at the level of intimate objects. The texts used here to elaborate the theory of the autotopography touch upon important aspects of this concept, but none see it as a total phenomenon—as a common yet subjective practice of making identity materially manifest. It is from the need to name this phenomenon, and by so doing to allow for a more detailed study of its forms and effects, that I have here introduced the concept of the *autotopography*.

NOTES

1. Walter Grasskamp, "Artists and Other Collectors," in *Museums by Artists,* ed. A. A. Bronson and Peggy Gale (Toronto: Art Metropole, 1983), p. 129.

2. Jennifer A. González, "Rhetoric of the Object: Material Memory and the Artwork of Amalia Mesa-Bains," *Visual Anthropology Review* (Spring 1993).

3. The "self" is a problematic term because if its multiple implications in the vocabularies of both humanism and ego psychology. However, the "self" for the purposes of this chapter can be thought of as an idea and an emotional matrix that is held in the mind of one person in relation to all the other institutional, linguistic, and cultural contexts of definition that make that person identifiable. The "self" is therefore hardly singular, for it is defined only in the context of multiply situated relations with other "selves" and communities. Yet it has a kind of *local position,* a point from which it radiates outward. This local position provides the ground of agency that is neither entirely singular nor evenly distributed within the political environment. Thus, to represent the "self" is a process that entails recognizing the complexity of this human matrix.

4. Grasskamp, "Artists and Other Collectors," pp. 129–130.

5. Roland Barthes, *Roland Barthes,* trans. Richard Howard (New York: Noonday Press, 1977), p. 61.

6. Umberto Eco, "Architecture and Memory," *Via* 8 (1986), pp. 88–94.

7. Mark Wigley, "Prosthetic Theory: The Disciplining of Architecture," *Assemblage,* no. 15, (1991), p. 9. Wigley also points out that in the teaching of both building and architecture, the concept of the collection was central. The clear and rational arrangement of diverse objects would legitimize their use as models of the external world for students of architecture. See p. 13.

8. Marcel Proust, *Remembrance of Things Past: Swan's Way,* vol. 1, trans. C. K. Scott Moncrieff (New York: Random House, 1934).

9. Ibid., p. 34.

10. Sigmund Freud, *The Standard Edition of the Complete Psychological Works of Sigmund Freud,* vol. 3 (London: Hogarth Press, 1960), p. 320.

11. Ibid., p. 308.

12. The word "object" comes via Middle English from the Latin *objectus,* "something thrown before or presented to (the mind)" from the past participle of *obicere,* to throw before or against. The object is located in the presence of, but in opposition to, the subject. As mask or screen, the object is, in this sense, thrown in the path of the mind and can be seen either as an obstacle that hinders or as a sign that directs.

13. It might be interesting to think of this movement as similar to Lacan's notion of "quilting," which Zizek discusses in *The Sublime Object of Ideology.* An object becomes the *point de capiton* within the chain of possible material signifiers; it becomes that which is the site of the passage of the Real to the Symbolic. Zizek writes, "The *point de capiton* is the point through with the subject is 'sewn' to the signifier, and at the same time the point which interpellates individual into subject by addressing it with the call of a certain master-signifier ('Communism,' 'God,' 'Freedom,' 'America')—in a word, it is the point of the *subjectivation of the signifier's chain*" (italics mine), p. 101.

14. Mary Jacobus, "Freud's Mnemonic: Women, Screen Memories and Feminist Nostalgia," "Women and Memory," special issue. *Michigan Quarterly Review* 26, no. 1 (Winter 1987), p. 138.

15. Susan Stewart, *On Longing: Narratives of the Miniature, the Gigantic, the Souvenir, the Collection* (Baltimore: Johns Hopkins University Press, 1984), p. 23.

16. Kathleen Stewart. "Nostalgia—A Polemic," *Cultural Anthropology* 3, no. 3 (August 1988), p. 227–241.

17. Ibid., p. 227.

18. Ibid., p. 229.

19. Ibid., p. 235–236.

20. Pierre Nora, "Between Memory and History: Les Lieux de Mémoire," *Representations*, no. 26 (Spring 1989), pp. 7–25.

21. Ibid., p. 12.

22. Ibid., pp. 8–9.

23. See Philip Fisher's *Making and Effacing Art: Modern American Art in a Culture of Museums* (New York: Oxford University Press, 1991).

24. Nora, "Between Memory and History," p. 7.

25. Ibid., p. 9.

26. Ibid., p. 15.

27. Ibid., p. 12.

28. Stewart, "Nostalgia," p. 232.

29. Nora, "Between Memory and History," p. 16.

30. Orest Ranum, "The Refuges of Intimacy," in *A History of Private Life,* vol. 3, *Passions of the Renaissance,* ed. Roger Chartier, trans. Arthur Goldhammer (Cambridge, Mass.: Belknap Press of Harvard University Press, 1989), p. 207 and p. 232.

31. Stewart, *On Longing,* p. 139.

32. Megan Boler, *Sistered Angels,* work in progress, 1992. This example contrasts with the observation made by Csikszentmihalyi and Rochberg-Halton in *The Meaning of Things* that usually, "for children [the bedroom] is a private area that gives a greater feeling of control over the activities and objects than other rooms and thus is a place where autonomy itself can be cultivated through 'dialogues' with the self, mediated by cherished possessions" (p. 137).

33. Patrick H. Hutton, "The Art of Memory Reconceived: From Rhetoric to Psychoanalysis," *Journal of the History of Ideas* 48, no. 3 (July-September 1987), p. 384.

34. Hayden White, *The Content of the Form* (Baltimore: Johns Hopkins University Press, 1987), p. 3–4.

35. Ibid., p. 20.

36. Paul Ricoeur, *Time and Narrative,* trans. Kathleen Blamey and David Pellauer (Chicago: University of Chicago Press, 1988), pp. 119–120.

37. Ibid., p. 124.

38. Ibid., p. 122.

39. Ibid., p. 246.

40. Ibid.

41. Stuart Hall, "Cultural Identity and Diaspora," in *Identity: Community, Cultural, Difference,* ed. Jonathan Rutherford (London: Lawrence and Wishart, 1990).

42. Eugen Bär, "Things Are Stories: A Manifesto for a Reflexive Semiotics," *Semiotica* 25, no. 3–4 (1979), p. 198.

43. Roland Barthes, *The Semiotic Challenge,* trans. Richard Howard (New York: Hill and Wang), 1988, p. 188.

44. Excerpt from an interview conducted in Santa Cruz, California, 1992.

45. See D. W. Winnicott, *Playing and Reality* (London: Tavistock Publications, 1971), p. 2.

46. Excerpt from an interview conducted in Santa Cruz, California, 1992.

47. James Clifford, *The Predicament of Culture* (Cambridge, Mass.: Harvard University Press, 1988), p. 218.

48. It is possible to think of such objects as functioning "allegorically"—within a loose etymological definition of that term. The two roots of allegory are highly suggestive: al- , the other of two, alias, alibi; Greek *allos*, other; ger- , to gather; Greek *agora*, the marketplace, or to speak publicly. From this, the "real" meaning of an object can be seen as *other than* its market value (its publicly advertised value). It is outside the market. Conversely the object can be seen as the *other of* the market—its alias or alibi. The market value (the exchange and use value) of an object is either *other than* the "true" meaning of the object, or it is intimately related to it *as its other* (as is the case with museum acquisitions). The allegorical is a structure that allows those things *gathered* in a place to have a meaning that expands beyond that place and yet is intimately tied to this placement or gathering itself.

49. Michel Foucault, "Of Other Places," *Diacritics* (Spring 1986).

10

Video Production, Liberation Aesthetics, and U.S. Third World Feminist Criticism

CHÉLA SANDOVAL

IN THIS CHAPTER I examine the forms of video production, historical consciousness, and oppositional politics generated during the 1970s social movement known as "women's liberation." The issues considered here range across problematics of video representation and liberation aesthetics by asking questions such as, What kinds of video forms were imagined and constructed by radical oppositional agents during the 1970s as they sought to change their positions of subordination in relation to the dominant social order? How were questions of identity and politics bound up with the generation of "alternative" video programming? What were the varying technical approaches utilized by the women's media movement, and what was the relationship of those approaches to the movement's conceptions of "truth?"[1] How was U.S. third world feminism responded to, and expressed, in the development of feminist video production? And finally, does a specifically U.S. third world form of criticism or aesthetics exist; if so, what is its relationship to truth, reality, or aesthetic representation? My focus here is on the media component of the women's liberation movement understood as a template for identifying representations imaged not only within the seventies women's movement but throughout the diverse social movements of the seventies as they sought to construct liberatory forms of identity, politics, and community.

Here, the term "community" is understood in a Foucaultian sense, as an inventive discursive formation within which oppositional agents must find creative means of exchange or be relegated to silence. In the example of the 1970s women's media movement, we will see how one subordinated group attempted to imagine and generate new kinds of communities for itself, new territories of being and speech, through the production of varying forms of reality-in-video. The social movement that was women's liberation of the 1970s was for the most part an insurgent project of consolidation, formation, and separation from what was considered a dominant patriarchal order. In what follows we trace the lines and forms of feminist insurgency in its attempts to construct a new order of "truthful" reality through the production of women's documentary videos.

In the search for a liberatory collective political identity that could be imaged in video or film, feminist media activists experimented with a range of counter-hegemonic aesthetics. Yet throughout its most activist years the women's media movement was not able to bind the specificities of U.S. third world feminism to its politics or to its representations. Meanwhile U.S. third world feminism was itself demanding its own forms of authority, community, and nation, indeed its own modes of aesthetic representation, which have since been gathered under many names, including "womanism," "la consciencia de la mestiza," "world traveling," or "inappropriate/d-otherness."[2] It is here, in the borders between aesthetic forms, in the limits that stretch between gender and race and sex and class, that we find an "other" aesthetics, what I have called a "differential" form of aesthetics and resistance.[3] The differential mode of oppositional consciousness permits new kinds of translations that link the women's media movement of the 1970s not only with the aesthetics of U.S third world feminism but more broadly with questions of a revolutionary "third cinema" conceptualized as an oppositional aesthetic capable of negotiating and reconfiguring the process of transnationalization.[4] The following survey of consciousness and aesthetics outlines the five forms of video production generated by movement activists in order to further clarify and incite the differential and postmodern aesthetics-in-opposition of U.S. third world feminism.

Alternative Video Truths

When video became affordable and portable enough to be accessible to the public in the late 1960s, women's liberationists believed that its control would provide the women's movement the opportunity to expose, affirm, and clarify what had been ignored for so long by the dominant media—the "truth" of women's experience.[5] In these early moments, truth was understood as the essence underlying all representations of reality, and it was feminism, the social movement committed to honesty, to openness, to the outspoken demonstration of what is, that would release that truth from the strictures of falsehood that bound and deceived the world of culture. In resistance to what were viewed as the damaging misrepresentations of the powers available to women, which were created by the dominant media, the movement regrouped to organize its own women's media collectives. In 1970 the following call to action was published as an editorial statement of objectives in the first nationally distributed newspaper of the women's liberation movement, *Off Our Backs:*

> The mass media are our enemy: no matter how seriously they may approach, no matter how enlightened they may seem, women's liberation threatens the power base of the mass media. Each time we respond to them we legitimize them and the reality they are defending, and we risk sacrificing all that we are working for. It is time to call a halt to all dealings with the mass media—no more interviews, no more documentaries, no more special coverage. We don't need them and we don't want them. In the interests of self-defense and honest communication our energies must turn now to the strengthening and expansion of our own media.[6]

By 1972 community-based women's media collectives had formed throughout the United States, creating a full-fledged women's media movement, an underground network of alternative "media women." With the aid of the tools and techniques of the dominant media, feminist activists believed that the empirical and "honest" reality of women's experience, conceived as shared and thereby unitary, could now at long last be revealed. Thus, the media component of the women's liberation movement was mandated a central role: that of beacon-runner, the arm of the movement that would carry the light of truth for all to see. Inspired by a kind of heroic resolve, feminist media activists regeared their lives to the accomplishment of the difficult yet noble tasks before them. Between 1970 and 1980, varying video forms and contents were proposed for representing the reality of women's experience, from the traditional documentary to surrealistically fashioned video experimentations that claimed to reveal the essence of female existence. But every aesthetic form proposed was motivated by the same intent: to dispel the illusions keeping women subordinate. The video camera, capable of rendering a point-by-point representation of reality, was understood as the instrument that would, in the right hands, expose the lies on the one side while uncovering the truth on the other. It was the verisimilitude of truth, then, that would dissolve all barriers blocking the realization of women's power.

Retrospectively, however, we now know that the women's movement became filled with many kinds of truths and, moreover, that those truths became the ideological differences that divided the movement from within. In what follows, the seventies are traced as the decade in which a feminist social practice in relation to video technology developed and then expanded beyond the imaginations of those involved. For the history of this decade shatters into often antagonistic ideological, technological, and aesthetic moments, and it is these varying moments that speak to us today about the multiformity that consciousness in opposition can take. In the following preliminary mapping of feminist representation-in-video, I have traced six of these modes of oppositional consciousness and their corresponding aesthetic forms, which I identify as (1) the traditional documentary, (2) cinema verité, or truth-video, (3) fictional truth video, (4) separatist video, (5) self-reflexive video, and (6) the differential form of oppositional aesthetics.

Traditional Documentary

In 1970 the traditional documentary mode was utilized by the dominant media as the aesthetic form most capable of capturing "the real."[7] Formulated explicitly to represent "nonfiction" reality, its techniques were seen as conjuring the most objective, point-by-point representation possible. Media studies have since demonstrated, however, that the traditional documentary form generates a highly mediated *construction* of what is, through dependence upon edited segments, arranged interviews, music, voice-over visuals, and so on. Today we speak of the "narrative structure" of this form revolving around orthodox relations between beginning, middle, and end. Moreover the gendered-male voice of authority is no longer "inaudible," heard as the sign of objectivity itself, rather we hear it working to guide the spectator's perceptions through what are understood to be instrumentally displayed forms of knowledge and power.

Insofar as the women's media movement of the early seventies recognized the importance of the power to speak, and thus to define reality, the traditional documentary form was grasped as the most direct route by which to convey to a broad mass audience the truth of women's oppression. By 1974, for example, the Santa Cruz Women's Media Collective alone had produced thirteen videos in the traditional documentary style ranging from *Women Cannery Workers* to *Women and Health Care, Women and Sex, Women and Child Care, Women and Music,* and so on.[8] For them, as well as for women's media collectives across the country, the traditional documentary conveyed in its very principles and practices all the legitimacy and power of the social order, a legitimacy activists wanted to appropriate in order to further the movement's goals. Feminist media activists were eager to shoulder the discipline of purpose necessitated by the demanding technical construction of the form. Moreover, activists felt that the reliance of traditional documentary upon a powerful narrative voice of authority to guide perception through the programming was a tactic that could be appropriated not just to add credibility to the program's content; but even more important, perhaps, women could now demonstrate through its use that they had the right and responsibility to call up, guide, and define reality themselves. Under women's liberation, however, this narrative voice of authority was changed, transferred out of its patriarchal mode. Authority now came in the voice of woman. This appropriation and reproduction of the dominant culture's style of speaking prompted new challenges and questions from within the movement itself, however, especially from U.S. feminists of color, who charged media activists with reproducing the same kinds of dominations that belonged to the white, patriarchal order, only now under a white and matriarchal rule. The questions that moved the women's media movement to its new phase were, Does an antiauthoritarian, and thus uniquely *women's,* form and content exist? And if it does, what does it look like, sound like?

Cinema Verité

The earliest technical answer to these questions became the "cinema verité" form claimed as a particularly *woman's* aesthetic practice, the "real" form of truth itself.[9] This "truth form" meant using the camera as a tool that should only capture honestly what comes before it: Video programs contained little or no editing; images and sound track always coincided; programs consisted of sequences of long takes in "real" time; and the guiding, narrative female voice of authority disappeared altogether. Verité video represented the form of truth that required little, if any, intervention in reality by its producers. A "woman's" form and content in video representation, then, was to be composed of truth in all its unadorned and unedited specificity.

A famous example of this early cinema verité programming is the 1974 documentary *Three Lives* by Kate Millet, which is organized around three white women who speak directly to the camera about their experiences. Millet wrote that her impetus for making the film was that she "didn't want to analyze anymore" but wanted only "to express" what is simply "already" there.[10] Millet's conception of expression here means entry into a kind of utopian freedom of being that she and many others at the time saw as the mark, in its unmanipulated honesty, of a particularly woman's aesthetic. For a while the movement appeared one step closer to constituting an effective, and particularly female, counterhegemonic programming.

Using video verité as a formal strategy for the creation of woman's truth, however, resulted in escalating challenges and questions about the shared nature of that truth. Productions created and presented to be specifically "by and for women" were accused of betraying that very precept when cinema verité productions like Millet's *Three Lives* called up whole new communities of marginalized populations within the women's movement by recognizing only the truths of white or middle-class women while at the same time claiming to represent the essence of "all women's experience." The challenges by feminists of color and working-class feminists forced video activists to recognize that the liberatory video-truth form worked to reinforce the same relations of exclusion, especially by race or class, that already existed in the dominant culture. What feminist media activists had not taken into account was that "reality" on the spectator's side of the camera, what truth video sought to capture, was just as constructed as the versions of reality that get constructed in any traditional and white male approach to documentary video production. The media movement was forced to recognize that reality itself must already be encoded like a film.

What had seemed a fairly clear task for media women at the beginning of the movement, that is, to represent the truth of women's experience on video, turned out in practice to be a much more complicated endeavor. Indeed, the desire of the movement to confront the world, name it correctly, and dispel all illusion began to wane as the marginalized within the movement continually pushed back to question whatever images of the world that were being produced in the name of all women. The hope that women's truth, understood as singular, would some-how be made clear before an unediting camera if only the technology were used to capture reality faded, along with the status of video truth as the unique form for representing woman's style and content. In its place a whole barrage of experi-mental, surreal, documentary, and fiction productions emerged. But feminist video producers, though offering new kinds of video and film images, stubbornly continued to seek if not the form, then at least the content of a reality that would be uniquely woman's.

Fictional Truth Video

Out of this third "fictional truth" phase emerged video productions notable for their experimental techniques in sound, visuals, editing, mise-en-scène, genre, and narrative structure. Science fiction, personal autobiographical statements, experimental avant-garde journeys through female consciousness and surreal combinations of forms, styles, and genres emerged as permissible and useful ar-tistic routes to finding and expressing woman's truth. Every style, form, and con-tent were experimented with, from Barbara Hammer's 1975 Goddess films, which transformed dancing women's bodies into surreal figures moving toward connec-tions, to Nancy Angelo's self-revealing internal journeys that featured sound track over visuals of a single red rose to the self-parodying video theater of the Santa Cruz Women's Media Collective; the hope that underlay this multifaceted effort was that fictionalized productions of the women's media movement, when con-sidered all together, would finally reveal truth in the form of an essence of being that belonged to women alone.[11]

As long as feminist video productions continued to claim the truth of woman's essence, however, no fictionalized approach appeared quite able to capture the imaginative requirements for audiences composed of feminists of color and other marginalized feminist constituencies. With the continuation and proliferating articulation of ideological perspectives within the woman's movement, with the categories of "woman" itself breaking apart at the seams and proliferating, the women's media movement could no longer retain its original role, that of beacon-runner, the arm of the women's movement that would carry the light of truth for all to see. By the end of the seventies, the heroic resolve motivating the women's media movement had dissipated under the force of disillusionment.

I have presented this schematic of video aesthetics in order to suggest how the history of social movement over the past thirty years in this country can be said to have shattered into a series of ideological and technological moments. These moments speak to us about the various modes that consciousness in opposition can take, and the ways in which these modes came to be represented in the alternative video forms of the women's liberation movement. I summarize these modes as follows:

1. The marginalized desired equality with the dominant definers of reality; their mode of filmic and video representation became the traditional documentary form.

2. The marginalized desired a video or filmic representation that focused on their unique differences from those in power; they believed that the cinema verité form would allow this unique dissimilarity to manifest and would encourage the social changes necessary to accommodate it. But cinema verité captures both too many and too few realities. It is at least as structured by the social order it is capturing as by any of its technological freedoms.

3. The third form resulted in a proliferation of "fictionalized" pieces when the women's media movement turned toward creating accounts of woman's emotional life—of the forms her domination took or of her various fantasies and hopeful utopian imaginings—yet all these fictionalized pieces continued to reflect the desire of the marginalized to revel in an essence that is particularly their own. This essence is viewed as superior to that of the most legitimized form of the human insofar as it believed to provide the subordinated with insights capable of leading the social order to a higher evolutionary plane. This mode of oppositional consciousness, however, like the others, became decentered because no agreement could be reached as to what images might represent a true picture of woman's essence.

4. And finally, many videos and films, especially of the previous type, were made by women and for women's eyes alone. This fourth political and aesthetic position was not based upon a desire for recognition or exchange with the dominant culture, for its radical re-formation, or for its leadership. What was desired was a formal secession and re-formation of a new psychic territory for women alone—the architectonics of a new "Amazon" nation that would not rely upon a world previously "man" constructed.

Each of the previous four modes of liberation aesthetics and oppositional politics, from the traditional documentary form to verité video, from fictional truth video to separatist video, were organized around representing the truth of the oppressed class. But defiant, if minority, feminist differences over what that truth should look and sound like pushed each phase into another incarnation. It was the political practice of U.S. third world feminism that insisted upon this theory of stages insofar as it was primarily the challenges and critiques of feminists of color that summoned fundamentally different representations of woman's truth other than those being discovered and displayed. These ongoing challenges called up another and final form of video production for the women's media movement.

5. The "self-reflexive" phase represented the last attempt to sustain the mission of the 1970s women's media movement. In this phase activists gave up the attempt to represent the truth of the oppressed class. In response to feminist criticisms by women of color, the self-reflexive video form was constituted to draw attention to itself as just one other constructed version of a reality that is itself also constructed, in a kind of Möbius-like effect. This video form represents an oppositional consciousness no longer hungry to reveal an ultimate truth of gender, identity, politics, community, or aesthetics. The emergence of the self-reflexive mode of production reflected the movement's inability to find any single, "most correct" response to oppression; rather, this mode of production drew attention to each video form considered as only another style or rhetorical tactic that might or might not be convincing to its viewers. As the Santa Cruz Women's Media Collective claimed in 1975 in one of its last videotapes, *The Amazon Music Festival,* any video produced, no matter how persuasive its rhetoric, "must be responsible" for demonstrating, in the form of self-reflexivity, "the producer's final responsibility for the content of the video." But even this strategy of feminist self-reflexivity could not tame the disorderly ideological differences that continued to insist on their own feminist imaginaries.

By 1980 it was clear that no single technique, aesthetic, or politics could guarantee a feminist, women's, or revolutionary aesthetic. That year, women's media collectives across the country disbanded, their mission now outmoded by the new challenges of difference itself that would determine the shape of the eighties. But if we can recognize U.S. third world feminism as a useful theoretical grounding, we can say not only that these five collective modes constitute differently interested tactics in the representation of truth, reality, or female identity itself but that it is in the recognition of their equally useful but differing possibilities that another aesthetic mode for the generation of a different kind of "true" alternative video production, or "third cinema," can be articulated. This aesthetic form was already represented in the sublimated oppositional politics of U.S. third world feminism throughout what was renamed by feminists of color (in order to turn the liberation movement for women toward a new logic) the white women's movement.[12]

I am (re-)insisting on what feminists of color throughout the seventies demanded: that U.S. third world feminism be recognized as a theory, a method, a criticism, and an aesthetics that permit a particular kind of access to history, representation, feminism, and the nature of truth itself. It is no accident that third world decolonial formations on a global level are today suggesting oppositional geopolitical coalitions among resistant subjects that are equivalent to the global linkages developing among dominant transnational powers. These theories, methods, and practices must be recognized, legitimized, and utilized. I emphasize here what is generally unattended within the academy, that the theories and methods of difference articulated by U.S. feminists of color throughout the 1970s and 1980s, and signaled through the names of major theorists of color from Audre Lorde to Gloria Anzaldua, from Janice Mirikitani to Trinh T. Minh-ha, and from Paula Gunn Allen to Mary Crow Dog are those, however sublimated they may be, that will provide the forms of consciousness and aesthetics necessary for resistance under contemporary first world cultural conditions.

U.S. Third World Feminism

I have pointed out that the U.S. women's liberation movement produced five forms of video representation during the 1970s, the traditional documentary form, verité video, fictional truth video, separatist video, and self-reflexive video, and I have argued that these representations were directly linked to the political modes of oppositional consciousness motivating the movement. Video and film were thus used as tools that had the power to make manifest forms of consciousness in opposition. But this effort then made possible the imagination of another kind of space, one that takes into account all of the others and yet goes beyond them. I have argued that this form of consciousness has been clearly articulated throughout the 1970s in the cultural expressions of U.S. feminists of color: Its articulation worked to supplant all attempts to produce a "most revolutionary" video or cinematic mode. I call it the "differential form of oppositional aesthetics."

During the mid-1970s, the U.S. women's liberation movement experienced a major tremor when U.S. feminists of color insisted on recognizing and naming the hierarchical nature of the movement—based upon the distances they had been forced to experience from the heretofore naturalized category of "women"— by demanding that the movement be renamed the *white* women's movement.[13] By the end of that decade, feminists of color had begun to form a new kind of political unity in their name. But what about the profusion of differences in physiological capacities, sexual preferences, race, culture, or class that a single naming such as U.S. third world feminism brings together? First, these differences were neither made invisible nor denied in the name of all women or of humanity in general, for these variances were painfully manifest in any gathering of them; power-charged; unfairly, socially constructed; materially marked upon the body, these differences continually confronted U.S. feminists of color with the power of their undeniability. By 1980, it was these constant variances that stood at the crux of the unity they were newly constructing. And it was through the complexity of these differences that contemporary U.S. third world feminists constructed a new meaning for the word "unity" itself.

Outside the law of the social order, many U.S. third world feminists claim to be representative of no country, without origin or destination; yet they seek in their

political project to self-consciously create a presence whose function is the subversion of every realm. To reside neither within the dominant symbology nor
completely outside of it is to reside within an invisible zone, the one that makes
binary oppositions possible.[14] The first step in the decolonization of this zone is
to claim the force of the affinities that exist with other citizens of its borders. U.S.
feminists of color have claimed this force and the polymorphous unity it creates
among them. This is not a collaboration, as in alliances made with enemies that
occupy one's own country, nor is it alliance by treaty. It is an act of mutual and
self-conscious influence, affection, and movement—indeed, differential movement. The emergence of this affinity reaches beyond itself, for it claims in its con-
junctions to represent the political presence and desires of the marginalized.
These emergences challenge the powers that limit insofar as they call up the presence of new social beings, movements, and aesthetic forms capable of referring
beyond their own captivity.

The category of U.S. third world feminism is presently the central locus of possibility for the enactment of the differential and oppositional form of consciousness and aesthetics. This category represents an insurgent movement that shatters
the construction of any one mode of aesthetic or political representation as the
single "most correct" site of truth. Without making this metamove outside of any
one of the five modes of consciousness and revolutionary aesthetics examined
earlier, any oppositional movement will be destined to repeat the oppressive au-
thoritarianism from which it is attempting to free itself and will become trapped
inside a drive for truth that only ends in constructing its own brand of dominations. By 1981, U.S. third world feminists were organized to speak against the existence of any final essences or realities.[15] More than any other group, feminists of
color had been forced to renounce belief in any single ideological positioning, for
their grounds of speaking were undercut at the moment they were claimed: The
moment a feminist of color spoke authoritatively from a secure ideological position, she was sabotaged by male chauvinism within ethnic liberation groups or by
Anglo-chauvinism within the women's liberation movement.[16] And so these
women have come to speak of the silenced protests and desires, the theories and
the methods that have permeated the world of the oppressed over time both
within and outside of liberation movements.

U.S. third world feminism relies upon an enactment of the theory and methodology of the oppressed, a set of practices, principles, and techniques developed by
people who have been born into, forced into, or voluntarily but irrevocably
moved into the semiperipheries or peripheries of the dominant society, culture,
and economy. The ability to see dynamics as they occur beneath the manifest reality, to be sensitive to the many levels of power at work, and to detect varying
processes in action has been understood as a skill that allows one to interpret and
gauge the subtle weave of power and its complicated web.[17] Usually, those who are
the most adept at this kind of decipherment, or "deep reading," are those forced

to develop the capacity in order to survive, but it is a survival skill that can be taught. Oftentimes, its cultivation allows its practitioner the facility of moving from the margins of society to its centers—and back again—experientially crossing the many thresholds of meaning. This kind of perceptiveness, intuition, or consciousness, if you will, is not determined by race, sex, or any other genetic status. It is a kind of perceptive and semiotic skill utilized by the powerless. Its cultivation creates the opportunity for a particularly effective form of resistance to the dominant culture within which it is formed insofar as it focuses on reading the signs of power and then differentially moving among them in order to ensure survival. These skills have been depended upon by the powerless who have never had the luxury of constructing a solid sense of self in a society that constantly shatters it. For them, the form of oppositional consciousness suggested here was first a survival skill that required the ability to do deep readings of the situation at hand, and then as a form of resistance, it meant tactically choosing the best response suited to ensure survival: It is a semiotic and differential form of oppositional consciousness.

U.S. third world feminism systematically recognizes and organizes such skills as the principles, practices, and procedures composing the methodology of the oppressed, whether conceived under rubrics as different as "womanism," "*la facultad*," "the house of difference," "strategic essentialism," or "world traveling."[18] The methodology of the oppressed offers new grounds for making political affinities across differences, for welding new postmodern coalitions. The five modes of video representation and their associated forms of political consciousness outlined earlier are all oppositional. But it is only in a mobile and *differential* usage of them as tactical weaponry against mobile, transnational powers that political actors can free themselves from aesthetics lived as stubborn, frozen ideologies and thus open the way for the construction of new affinities, new lines of force in the generation of oppositional social movement.

Differential Oppositional Aesthetics

I have referred to the differential process of consciousness or aesthetics as "oppositional," but this term refers only to the ideological effects it can have. Differential consciousness represents a mobile, perceptual, and intellectual process that must not become frozen, static, or claimed as biologically or culturally determined. Binary thinking does not pertain to its activity; it functions somewhere in between, and this is one reason that thinking about it or practicing it is difficult for those who have been privileged enough to comfortably rely upon binary modes of thinking, as if such divisions as right/wrong, clean/dirty, black/white, same/different, can represent unproblematic or ethical divisions of reality. The grounds of what I call the differential mode of oppositional consciousness shift, even as they are identified, so that perhaps this mode of consciousness should bear no single name, but rather "U.S. third world feminism," "womanism," "world traveling," "inappropriated otherness," "strategic essentialism," "the outsider within," "sister outsiders," "hybridity," "*la consciencia de la mestiza*," "différence," or "nomad thought." Thus we can constantly be reminded that a differential consciousness is always the disparity, the variant; once identified it becomes something else, yet it always refers to a realm with constantly shifting boundaries, the purpose of which is to de-limit. The differential consciousness of U.S. third world feminism occurs in another countryside, the features of which testify to the very dominant order that, ironically, subordinated people once made possible through the function of their repression. The descending powers of differential consciousness, and the rising methods of oppressed peoples, summon into being a new realm not theologically governed by any transcendent truth outside of differential movement itself. Entrance to this realm requires a *psychic* commitment within which one experiences a disorder of being that is trans-formational.[19] U.S. third world feminism is a processual and morphing state of consciousness wherein everything is a matter of strategy, tactics, and risk: Its politics call up the creation of new ethics, affinities, aesthetics, people.

In the previous example of the seventies women's media movement, we have seen that feminist agency itself changes, depending upon the forces to be confronted, indeed just as dominant powers are themselves constantly trans-forming. So too, the agency of seventies U.S. third world feminism, its authority to act, was not based on any previous dominating authority but on the possibilities of differential movement itself as guided by the methodology of the oppressed, the visions of the "marginal eyes." The question we must now ask is, Can the differential form of oppositional consciousness itself be viewed, or is it only a method for viewing? Can it be imaged other than through the kaleidoscopic political use of all previous video forms outlined earlier? Let me propose the following formulation for thinking about the production of liberation aesthetics: Video techniques such as cuts, edits, sequences, mise-en-scène, voice-over, and so on, can be understood as representing only the outer, manifest form of a video representation; when taken together, these techniques result in a generic classification such as "documentary," "fiction," "surrealism," "cinema verité," and so on. Underlying this work of the video is the question that the video posits and seeks to answer (for example, Is there an essence of woman's reality?). The ways in which this question is answered reveal the ideology—the ultimate and particular messages, or levels—of the video. Each of these levels works to structure the meanings available to the other levels.[20]

In the production of a differential oppositional aesthetic these ideological messages must be produced and encoded through the grid of what I have described as the methodology of the oppressed. Briefly summarized, this method requires that readings of signs are provided at each level with the aim of challenging or transforming perception; signs and images are deconstructed, emptied of their

previous meanings, again and again; ideologies are "metaideologized," that is, de-naturalized by the addition of other, higher levels of meaning. All of these transformations are occurring, meanwhile, with the overriding purpose of bringing about egalitarian redistributions of power for all the figures concerned, whether those figures are inside or outside the camera frame. Finally, none of these techniques are possible without a mobility that can occur only differentially through signifying bodies of every kind. What kinds of image examples can we find to populate this differential aesthetic, which is endemic yet oppositional to late capitalist cultures? The differential mode of oppositional politics should generate what Laura Mulvey calls a "phantasmagoric" space (originally the description for an early nineteenth-century magic-lantern show that produced optical illusions, specters, apparitions).[21] In this "space" it must be understood that *any* aesthetic form can be implemented as long as it serves to generate a "disturbance" in dominant images of and for the human. We have seen such disturbances occur in recent films with varying aesthetic approaches, from *Daughters of the Dust* to *Jumpin' Jack Flash,* from *Total Recall* to *Silence of the Lambs.* Liberation aesthetics, then, in the view of U.S. third world feminist criticism, is not only the possibility of the singular or combined use of the traditional documentary, cinema verité, fictional, separatist, or self-reflexive forms to organize their various possibilities according to power relations and the kinds of subjectivities to be called up or intervened upon. It must also be imagined as the production of the video or film experience as poetic intervention in the narrative social systems of meaning: The differential is conceived here as a rupture, a third meaning, that which punctures through the same with the truth of difference, yet this form of liberation aesthetics can at the same time satisfy with narrative pleasure and closure. *Terminator I* and *II, Scent of a Woman, Falling Down, El Mariachi,* all imagine women and men differently while combining fiction and documentary, personal or self-reflexive styles, cinema verité and any number of their permutations, which together produce an MTV experience—the experience of everyday life under postmodern conditions. Differential aesthetics is that and much more: It is what lives on the limits, the peripheries of vision, disappearing when looked at too long; it is a real sight only through the marginal eyes of the marginalized. We need to be able to image the existence of this differential mode of opposition as a possibility of being insofar as it represents, after all and at least, the consciousness of U.S. third world feminism. Then this form of differential resistance can be imaged both as content and as *a possible form* in video aesthetics-of-resistance: It can emerge in a "gap" left open between the contents and what displays them or as any "disturbance" in visual, audio, narrative, or aesthetic meanings.

How our everyday experiences can be remade, -appropriated, -sequenced, -dreamed, or otherwise called upon in order to make effective oppositional interventions in material and psychic powers we are beginning to know how to imagine. Our techniques for reading social power and its movements through our bodies and psyches are being developed and honed, our skills in utilizing resistance as a form are being refined and tooled. These are the very techniques demanded through enactment of the methodology of the oppressed and the political practice of U.S. third world feminism. I have traced a particular form of social movement in its relationship to liberation aesthetics, U.S. third world feminism, and video production. It is a differential form of consciousness and aesthetics that represents the philosophy of the disenfranchised: Its content relies upon the methodology of the oppressed, and its effects map the routes of an oppositional consciousness through culture. Through the prism of a particular form of U.S. third world feminism developed since the early fifties, the sounds and images of what is differential have been conjured and made to signify new imaginations, other passages, people under revision.

But none of this is new to activists and theorists of the postmodern of whatever stripe. What is new is the notion that oppositional video forms produced during the seventies and understood as the liberal (or traditional), revolutionary (or video-truth), supremacist (or fictional truth), separatist, and self-reflexive forms of construction can be reaestheticized, politicized, and apprehended through U.S. third world feminism understood not only as an alternative oppositional politics present during the seventies but as an alternative form of aesthetic representation for video producers. It is this methodology and presence that must not be erased from our collective memory.

NOTES

An earlier version of this essay was presented as "The Construction of Subjectivity and Oppositional Consciousness in Feminist Film and Video: A Third World Feminist Critique" at the 1984 American Studies Association Conference "Poetic Tools and Political Bodies: Feminist Approaches to High Technology Culture (Technology in Culture, Culture in Technology)" with panelists Donna Haraway, Katie King, and Zoe Soufoulis; and at the 1976 MLA conference with Judith Mayne. The videotaped version of this talk and associated research are available as part of my 1984 qualifying essay, "Dis-illusionment and the Poetry of the Future: The Making of Oppositional Consciousness," available from the University of California Santa Cruz, History of Consciousness archives. Thanks to media activists Pam Springer, Anne Irving, David Castro, and Sarah Nelson and to the 1973 Santa Cruz Women's Media Collective.

1. An excellent contribution to debates on the nature of truth and its aesthetic representation is the recent collection entitled *Probing the Limits of Representation: Nazism and the "Final Solution,"* ed. Saul Friedlander (Cambridge: Harvard University Press, 1993).

2. Alice Walker, *In Search of Our Mother's Gardens: Womanist Prose* (New York: Harcourt Brace Jovanovich, 1983); Gloria Anzaldua, *Borderlands/La Nueva Frontera: The New Mestiza* (San Francisco: Spinsters/Aunt Lute Press, 1987); Maria Lugones, "Playfulness, 'World'-Traveling, and Loving Perception," *Hypatia: A Journal of Feminist Philosophy,* vol.

2, no. 2, 1987; Trinh T. Minh-ha, ed., "She, the Inappropriate/Other," *Discourse*, vol. 8, (1986–1987).

3. In "US Third World Feminism: The Theory and Method of Oppositional Consciousness in the Postmodern World," *Genders* (Spring 1991), 1–24.

4. See on this the excellent collection edited by Jim Pines and Paul Willeman, *Questions of Third Cinema* (London: BFI, 1989).

5. See Maurine Beasley and Sheila Silver's *Women in Media: A Documentary Source Book* (Washington, D.C.: Women's Institute for Freedom of the Press, 1977).

6. Nancy Ferro, Coletta Reid Holcomb, and Marilyn Saltzman-Webb, *Off Our Backs* (March 1970).

7. See Erik Barnouw, *Documentary: A History of the Non-Fiction Film* (New York: Oxford Press, 1977); and Richard Barsam, *Nonfiction Film Theory and Criticism* (New York: Dutton, 1976).

8. Collected by the Whitney Museum of Modern Art, Washington D.C., and by the University of California at Santa Cruz Media Archives.

9. Alan Rosenthal, *The New Documentary in Action: A Casebook in Film Making* (Berkeley: University of California Press, 1971); Stephen Mamber, *Cinema Verite in America: Studies in Uncontrolled Documentary* (Cambridge, Mass.: MIT Press, 1974); Lesley Stern, "Feminism and Cinema: Exchanges," *Screen*, vol. 20, nos. 3–4, pp. 89–105, 1979–1980.

10. Claire Johnson, "Notes on Women's Cinema," *Screen Pamphlet*, no.2 (1975) pp. 1–8; and "Dorothy Arzner: Critical Strategies," in *The Work of Dorothy Arzner: Towards a Feminist Cinema*, ed. C. Johnson (London: BFI, 1975).

11. See *Jump Cut* double issue 24–25, 1980, on the films of Jan Oxenberg and Barbara Hammer; the Feminist Video Collection at the Whitney Museum of Modern Art, Washington, D.C.; Claire Johnston, "Feminist Politics and Film History," *Screen*, vol. 6, no. 3, (1975), pp 115–124; Annette Kuhn, "Women's Cinema and Feminist Film Criticism," *Screen*, vol. 16, no. 3 (1975), pp. 107–112; Julia Lesage, "The Political Aesthetics of the Feminist Documentary," *Quarterly Review of Film Studies*, vol. 3, no. 4 (1975), pp. 507, 523; Lucy Lippard, "Yvonne Rainer on Feminism and Her Film," in *From the Center: Feminist Essays on Women's Art* (New York: Dutton, 1976); Janey Place and Jullianne Burton, "Feminist Film Criticism," *Movie*, no. 22 (1976), pp. 53, 62; B. Ruby Rich, "The Crisis of Naming in Feminist Film Criticism," *Jump Cut*, no. 19, (1978), pp. 9–12; and Annette Kuhn, *Women's Pictures: Feminism and Cinema* (London: Routledge and Kegan Paul, 1982).

12. This renaming began as early as 1969, as indicated by Frances Beal's warning in her essay "Double Jeopardy: To Be Black and Female." Beal's essay warns that "any white women's group that does not have an anti-imperialist and antiracist ideology had absolutely nothing in common with the black woman's struggle. In fact, some groups come to the incorrect conclusion that their oppression is due simply to male chauvinism." If white women's groups "do not realize that they are in fact fighting capitalism and racism, we do not have common bonds." By 1978 this warning had escalated to the point where U.S. feminists of color were renaming an uncompromising "women's movement" the white women's movement. See *Sisterhood Is Powerful*, ed. Robin Morgan (New York: Random House, 1970) , pp. 350–351.

13. For an excellent bibliography that collects the seventies writings of U.S. feminists of color, see Cherrie Moraga, "Third World Women in the United States—By and About Us: A Selected Bibliography," in *This Bridge Called My Back, A Collection of Writings by Radical*

Women of Color, ed. Cherrie Moraga and Gloria Anzaldua (Mass.: Persephone Press, 1981). Indeed, *This Bridge* must be understood as the result and the explosion of the political energies of U.S. feminists of color active during the seventies. Unfortunately, an anthology has never been produced that collects essential writings by feminists of color that emerged in relation to the seventies women's movement; these essays, however, can be found scattered throughout alternative feminist and ethnic journals of that decade. A few sources where these seventies publications can be found are *Conditions, A Magazine of Writing by Women; Frontiers: A Journal of Women's Studies; The Third Woman; Plexus; Off Our Backs: A Women's News Journal;* and *Sinister Wisdom: A Journal of Words and Pictures for the Lesbian Imagination in All Women.*

14. U.S. third world feminists are by definition inside/outsiders, a presence that serves to grease the laws of the dominant social order by providing its emotional hinge between binary oppositions, its steam valve, and its transitional structure, as reflected in the titles of books by women of color ranging from *All the Blacks Are Men, All the Women Are White, But Some of Us Are Brave* to *This Bridge* (between terms) *Called My Back* to *Ain't I a Woman?* to *The Third Woman.* It should not be surprising, therefore, that U.S. feminists of color developed different conceptual, aesthetic, and political schemas than those that drove their white sisters during the 1970s white women's liberation movement. This "difference" was variously construed as "betrayal" to the movement, "uninvolvement," and worse; as time went by, white feminists then claimed that feminists of color were "altogether absent" from the social movement by and for women of the 1970s. Today, this claim can be seen as being especially ironic given that it was feminists of color who shocked white feminist activists in the 1970s by renaming the women's movement "the *white* women's movement" in order to draw their attention to the idea that white women ran the movement as if they owned it. The irony intensifies when we find certain white feminist scholars, almost twenty years later, who have proudly appropriated this renaming of the seventies "white women's movement" literally, announcing that "there must have been very few women of color involved in the women's movement of the seventies, as the name 'white women's movement' testifies." In the 1990s, the original irony around the term "white women's movement" has disappeared and another appropriation has taken place. This second making-invisible of U.S. third world feminism, however, is one that history, understood as a *constructed* system of meaningful signs, will not support.

15. "We are the queer groups, the people who don't belong anywhere, not in the dominant world nor within our own respective cultures. Combined we cover so many oppressions. But the overwhelming oppression is the fact that we do not fit, and because we do not fit *we are a threat.*" Anzaldua, *This Bridge,* p. 209.

16. See for example, Angela Davis, *With My Mind on Freedom: An Autobiography* (New York: Bantam, 1974); and *Women, Race and Class* (New York: Random House, 1981).

17. See Audre Lorde, "There was a whole powerful world of non-verbal communication and contact between people that was absolutely essential and that was what you had to learn to decipher and use. ... You have to get it for yourself, whatever it is that you need in order to survive." From an interview held in 1979 and published in *Sister Outsider* (New York: Crossing Press, 1984); Henry Louis Gates Jr., "The Blackness of Blackness: A Critique of the Sign and the Signifying Monkey," in *Black Literature and Literary Theory,* ed. Henry Louis Gates Jr. (New York: Methuen, 1984); Gloria Anzaldua, *Borderlands,* on "*la facultad*" as a survival skill, p. 38.

18. Audre Lorde, *Zami: A New Spelling of My Name* (Freedom, Calif.: Crossing Press, 1982), p. 226; Gayatri Spivak, "In a Word, Interview," *Differences: A Journal of Feminist Cultural Studies,* "Essentialism" issue (Summer 1989), pp. 124–156.

19. Calls for the activation of this "painful" but "transformational" form of consciousness appear to be endemic in writings by U.S. third world feminists over the past thirty years. A small sampling of these include Bernice Reagon, "Coalition Politics: Turning the Century," in *Home Girls—A Black Feminist Anthology,* ed. Barbara Smith (New York: Kitchen Table Press, 1983) pp. 356–368; Patricia Hill Collins, "Learning from the Outsider Within: The Sociological Significance of Black Feminist Thought," *Social Problems,* vol. 33 (1969), pp. 14–32; Paula Gunn Allen, "Some like Indians Endure," in *Living the Spirit: A Gay American Indian Anthology,* ed. Will Roscoe (New York: St Martin's Press, 1988).

20. See Hayden White's explication of the method utilized by Fredric Jameson, who follows Louis Hjelmslev's suggestion that every text can be read through four levels, which White describes as the literal, figurative, moral, and mystical meanings. Hayden White, "Jameson's Redemption of Narrative," in *The Content of the Form* (London: Johns Hopkins University Press, 1987), pp. 152, 153.

21. Laura Mulvey, "Pandora: Topographies of the Mask and Curiosity," in *Sexuality and Space,* ed. Beatriz Colomina (Princeton Papers on Architecture), p. 57.

11

Re/Sounding Race, Re/Signifying Ethnography: Sampling Oaktown Rap

JACKIE ORR

The ethnographer is one of those rare creatures who devotes his time to working for the losing side. He "has introduced law and order into what seemed chaotic and freakish. [He] has transformed for us the sensational, wild and unaccountable world of 'savages' into a number of well-ordered communities governed by law, behaving and thinking according to consistent principles." Any investigator who claims to be merely "recording facts" thereby deludes himself, for the Great Master has said it: "Only laws and generalizations are scientific facts, and field work consists only and exclusively in the preparation of the chaotic reality, in subordinating it to general rules." "Discourse," "law," "order," "generalizations," "consistency"—what he values and looks for is, fortunately, what he always only finds.

—Trinh Minh-ha

De buckruh hab scheme, en de nigger has trick, en ebry time de buckruh scheme once, de nigger trick twice.

—African American slave saying

Bring the noise!

—Chuck D., *Public Enemy*

Track 1

Everything begins with the sound of a police siren rising, falling. Or maybe it's a firetruck. I still can't tell the difference, my ears trained for years on the single, sonorous wail of the civil defense siren—a thirty-foot tower next to the neighborhood swimming pool—systematically tested the first Wednesday of every month of my whitesuburban childhood. Repeat. The sound of a police siren. Or a firetruck. Now an arhythmic mix of background sound, interference, and the recorded humanvoice message left on my answering machine says—*I'm watching Los Angeles burn on my TV screen. Do you know what's happening? Call me.* Click. Dial tone. White noise. Black, black sky. Cut with sirens and flame. It's Wednesday, April 29, 1992, and Los Angeles is on fire. Click. White noise. *Do you know what's happening?*

Track 2

Hot pursuit / Adrenalin / Rush / A license to kill / Another brother with a bone crush ... 25 on one / Makes a white eye sore / But it makes Premo hate to the core / So if you / Black in the night / A target you are / To be beat with a / Night stick / A boot / And a crow bar ... each boot to your side / I felt in my body / It made me sick to see / A triple K frat party —Premo (Oakland, 1992).[1]

Track 3

The second message on my answering machine announces the time and place to meet the next day, in San Francisco, for a mass public demonstration to protest the not-guilty verdict of four white cops charged with the beating of Rodney King, a black man from Los Angeles. The trial was conducted in Simi Valley, where the suburban stretches of L.A. expand into green lawns and white people, including an unusually large population of active and retired police officers. The not-guilty verdict stuns a national audience of TV viewers, who have seen an eighty-one-second videotape of the March 1991 police beating of King. But thirteen months later, TV viewers absorb another horrific spectacle as entire neighborhoods in Los Angeles erupt in a contradictory carnival of rebellion and rage at the jury's verdict, at this whitewash of brutality against a black man.

I telephone Jamal to cancel my plans to attend a rehearsal the next day for his rap group, Shot 'O Soul. "Fine—you have other plans?" I hear Jamal ask across the wires. "Well, I need to go to this protest about the Rodney King thing," I say, feeling the complexity, the density of color in this space of sound. His words are marked by an African American accent I cannot locate; I cannot hear its geographic genealogy or assign its specificity. My words are accented by awkwardness, buzzing for me against a background of white noise that hasn't gone away, that troubles my listening ever since I entered this field of blackurban[2] rap. Trouble amplified tenfold by the sounds of Los Angeles burning in the background. Click. White noise. I don't know what's happening.

My fieldwork on rap music in Oakland continues to explode with the impossibility of constructing stable, certain boundaries around my "object" of research. The desire to study rap has led me over and over again to experience the insistent, sometimes violent undecidability of the psychogeography of my field, charged as it is by racism and race and loaded with the explosive complexities of rap's positioning within the minefields of contemporary race, gender, class, and cultural relations. Moving between the methodological commitment to listen to the field and the epistemological terror of hearing nothing that sounds like well-ordered knowledge, I open my ethnographic ear to a range of frequencies. The proliferating fragmentation and frenzy of connections I tune into as I encounter rap on the local radio airwaves, in the technoprivacy of the Walkman and the temporary public of live performance, in the Oakland shopping malls and streets, over the pulsing car stereos, and in interviews with rap musicians, music critics, promoters, or radio DJs, seem to me a significant property of the field itself. "Indeed, one of the general properties of fields is that *they encompass struggles over their very boundaries.*"[3]

I watch live news footage of the riots on anxious, excited midnight TV. Los Angeles is awake and burning, huge billows of gray-black smoke cover the city, darken the screen. Before I go to bed, I change the message on my answering machine to a ten-second fragment from Public Enemy's "Burn Hollywood, Burn."

Track 4

"In traditional African cultures, the surfaces, depths, and beyonds were barely distinguishable from each other. Oscillating the demarcations with his own movements, man was simultaneously located in every dimension. *Imprecision, fuzziness,* and *incomprehension* were the very conditions which made it possible to develop a viable knowledge of social relations. *Instead of these conditions being a problem to be solved by a resolute knowledge, they were viewed as the necessary limits to knowledge itself,* determined the value with which such knowledge was held, and the attitudes taken toward it."[4]

Track 5

Flash. Back. My body moving late night through the glass doors twanging deep sound as I hit palms out and push through like a—flash—back—two black men out of nowhere noisy crazy late night caught between the glass doors banging. Deep and twanging. His hand holds open the glass door and I think to smash that hand black to blue in the noisy door crazy late night niggers following close behind. Catch me between the glass doors and I flash—black—as he holds the door with one hand and pulls a gun with—flash—I go black—he pulls a gun and flash—back—I bang quiet, deep and twanging, flash—a gun at my back and I go black and walk back I flash—back and caught between glass doors and two crazy niggers I flash—back and go black—flash back—I turn my back and go black I turn back I go black I go black but I still ain't no nigger—I stand back and let the two black men pass through the glass doors. They shut with a deep sound banging.

Track 6

Baby was a black sheep— Second grade, Southern Pennsylvania, 1968, it was recess. We were playing court ball and somebody whiteboy got me out with a flashy shot and I shot back, "Nigger!" *Baby was a whore*— He reported me to the blonde teacher who made me stay after school for using dirty words didn't I know better? I was ashamed and didn't know why I shot back "Nigger!" I couldn't remember where I learned that word "nigger." Not from my parents who I knew would wash out my mouth with Ivory soap for saying such a thing in the whitesuburbs of 1968 I should know better. *You know she got big, well, she's gonna get bigger*—

This was my only experience of nigger until I went to Blue Mountain girls' camp in summer 1969. We lined up to go on a hike through the hills and next to me in line was a black girl. *Baby got her hand got / Her finger on the trigger*— We were hiking in the buddy system so we had to hold hands and I grew white with fear and shame because I thought my hand would turn black from her wet palm I could feel. I feared our sweaty palms would dissolve her black stain mine blue we walked the Blue Mountains hand in hand, sweaty-palmed. *Baby, baby, baby is a rock 'n roll nigger.*[5]

Track 7

Sound of police siren rising and falling ... Burn Hollywood, burn / I smell a riot goin' on / First they're guilty, now they're gone / Yeah, I'll check out a movie / But it'd take a black one to move me / Get me the hell away from this TV / All this news and views are beneath me / So all I hear about / Is shots ringin out / About gangs puttin' each other's head out / So I'd rather kick some slang out / Alright fellas, let's go hang out / Hollywood [thinks] they might / make us all look bad like I know they have / But some things I'll never forget, yeah / So step n' fetch this shit / For all the years we've looked like clowns / The joke is over—smell the smoke from all around ... BURN HOLLYWOOD, BURN, HOLLYWOOD BURN, HOLLYWOOD BURN, HOLLYWOOD BURN, HOLLYWOOD BURN, HOLLYWOOD BURN ... — Public Enemy (New York, 1990).[6]

Track 8

A subversion of the colonizer's ability to represent colonized cultures— Recent critiques of the politics and practice of ethnography emerging within feminism, postcolonial studies, anthropology, and cultural studies, focus on the inescapable complicities between ethnographic discourse and colonial and colonizing forms of representation and authority. —*can only radically challenge the established power relations*— As the "science" perhaps most directly charged with navigating the methodological routes for researching and representing cultural differences, ethnography has come under attack for reproducing institutional and historical forms of social hierarchy and exploitation[7] —*when it carries with it a tightly critical relation with the colonizer's most confident characteristic discourses.*[8] A critical, and critically different, practice of ethnography must inscribe itself within the very forms of representation, or language practices, of the fieldworker-writer. Thus, a reflexive deconstruction of ethnographic practice necessarily entails the creative reconstruction of a different discursive field. The practice of an intentionally troubled language, of a disordered and disturbing uncommon language, seems to me a necessary corollary to any serious methodological intervention within the fields of ethnography.

My partial aim is to attempt to re/signify ethnography as I try to signify some of the possible meanings, social organization, and political significance of blackurban rap music in Oakland. I want to pursue the possibility of *un*making the disciplinary, disciplining discourse binding dominant forms of ethnographic knowledge in violent relations to dominant social powers—a discourse that reproduces racist exclusions from domains of knowledge even as it exploits the bodies and histories of marginalized "Others" transformed into research(ed) "Objects." If such a possibility is constantly constrained, certain to fail in its *un*becoming desire to open and propagate productive uncertainties, then it's worth recalling The Sociologist's observation, "The relation to what is possible is a relation to power."[9] Is it possible, in this research on rap, to resist reproducing another Masterful discursive account of young blackurban men in the ghetto? And will such *un*constructive efforts be recognized as ethnography?

The fires in Los Angeles are for many of us no longer a hot memory. The ruins may still smoke, but not on the TV screen. Do you remember that the armed forces of law and order, including a National Guard operating under direct command of the U.S. military and 4,000 U.S. Marines and infantry, were deployed on the streetcorner, bunkered down in empty shopping malls?[10] Do you know that closer to home, the city of San Francisco operated for two days under a state of emergency declared by newly elected mayor and former police chief Frank Jordan, with a citywide curfew set from 9 P.M. to 6 A.M.? In Berkeley, the curfew began at 7 P.M.

On Friday night, May 1, 1992, the two rap events I'm scheduled to attend, one in Berkeley, one in San Francisco, are canceled due to the curfews.[11] I stay at home. In Oakland. By 8 P.M. the streets are mostly empty. I watch a police car drive slowly past. The cop on the passenger side holds a rifle between his legs.

My field is in a state of emergency. Certain imperatives are suddenly suspended. Other, powerful imperatives arise—to at least attempt an urgent rewriting of how ethnographic knowledge might produce different meanings and forms of knowing. Can ethnography reconstruct the meaning of cultural and racial differences less lawfully, more disordered, in the face of the fiery demands from Los Angeles? Can the im/possible desires compelling the rebellions in L.A. be met by something less disciplined and punishing than a police boot, something other than a martial display of paramilitary state power? Black sky. Black, black sky. White noise. *Do you know what's happening?*

Track 9

I head in my car to T's Wauzi, Saturday afternoon in late January 1992, 65 mph down 580 with a tape of Benny B's rap show (KALX) on my boom box. *The Underground Selector* goes out every Saturday morning from 10:30 A.M. to noon. I've just come from the radio station and a conversation with Benny B and DJ Joe Quixx. Their take on the local Oakland rap scene is critical—lotsa people trying to make money and lotsa low-quality music. But if I'm interested in hearing Oakland rap, they advise me to visit T's Wauzi, a "mom and pop record store" at the Eastmont Mall with the widest selection of local rap music.[12]

I arrive at the Eastmont Mall. This is new. My mall experience is straight outta suburbia, layered now with an urban knowledge of ritzy, downtown galleries. But this I've never seen. To my eyes, this is a ghost town mall. Not a lot of people for a Saturday afternoon, the peak of suburban shopping frenzies. Not much sound. No bustling buzz of bodies and rolling strollers and chatter set against a background echo of voluminous space—my aural memory of Ridgedale, Rosedale, Brookdale, and Southdale, the malls that mark the four suburban corners of Minneapolis and bound my teenage memories of shopping. At the Eastmont Mall in Oakland, the echo reaches into the foreground, the quiet sounds of moving bodies outweighed by the empty aural zones.

The wing of the mall I've entered opens out into a broad indoor plaza. The store space that looks like it should hold a major department store—three large window displays running along for 300 or so feet of unbroken retail space—is empty. The window displays are boarded up, the entrance filled in by a false wall. Three Latino kids are playing with a tennis ball against the bricks. Bounce. Chase. Laughter. The sound of the ball hitting the wall. Erratic echo.

I walk further down the mall and now notice that every fourth store is either vacant or having its Grand Opening. Several stores don't have permanent signs above the entrance. Instead, temporary banners of computer printout paper name the store and announce a Grand Opening, or a Going-Out-of-Business sale.

"T's WAUZI." The sign over the store is big, permanent, brightly colored. Next to the store name is a logo—the African continent striped red, black, and green. In the upper-right corner of the continent is a black record disk.

The salesclerk, a tall, thin black man named Moses, comes over to help me. I ask him for hard-core rap, maybe something political, has to be an Oakland group. He pulls out a tape, *Righteous Black Guerillas* by The Ansars. He thinks they're good and might go far. The image on the cassette is both familiar (black-and-white photo of four young black men, unsmiling, in hooded jackets) and, to me, unreadable (a red crescent moon and star centered at the top of the image, the black man in the middle holds forth a thick book like an offering). More local groups—Black Dynasty, *Eight Ball in the Corner Pocket;* No Money, *To Live or Die in Oakland;* Spice-1, *Let It Be Known* (he's just signed with Jive Records—the salesclerk thinks he's real good and is already on his way); M.C. Ant, *The Comeback '91.*

I pay for The Ansars tape at the register. The price is $4.99. Then the salesclerk laughs and introduces me to two guys from Righteous Records, producers of The Ansars, who just walked in. They look a little surprised that I'm buying their tape. Gino and Earl tell me Righteous Records recording studio is just about a mile down the street. I ask about that name, The Ansars, and they tell me it's a real common name. In Chicago, there's as many Ansars as there are Jones. I still look bewildered. It's a common Muslim name, they finally spell out for me. Oh, and what's this red moon and star? "The symbol of the Muslim nation."

I leave T's Wauzi holding a red bag with a black outline of the continent of Africa with a record disk somewhere in the Sudan. I take the long way home, driving up Foothill Avenue instead of the highway. Watching the streets I drive through. Small storefronts. A comicbook store. Churches. A few men half-lit leaning inside a doorway. I put The Ansars on my boom box. It's hard to say exactly when I leave the field.

Track 10

Police sirens wail. Crowd voices. A man's laugh. A knock on the door. Voices rise over a busy noise, a sustained screech like a tape being rewound, or fast forwarded. It's gettin' critical ... [Rifle fire.] Silly ass niggers ... It's gettin' critical ... Situation serious ... Government delirious ... It's gettin critical ... prepare for destruction ...silly ass nigger tryin to run ... there ain't no time, you know what I'm sayin ... niggers keep dancin if they want to ... A single voice sounds out against a background of Public Enemy samplings, scratching, a hard-drive bass beat—"Ah yeah, this is the Brotherhood tapped into X. We're broadcasting live underground at RBG headquarters number nine. I'm feeling tapped in you niggaz' frequencies. All you drop top riders, high siders, high rollers, rock dealers and cop killers, big wheel Oaktown Righteous Black Guerillas, sons of brothers, fathers, mothers, daughters, sisters."

The rap rhythmic comes in strong as the speaking voice fades ... Niggaz comin' up dead / Bright sunny day forecasting rain / It's a drought y'all / Light shines through the atmosphere of pain / Makin it plain so y'all can understand / Less heat on the street, please / The black man's curfew's changed from nine to seven / o'clock once the sun go down / I'm with the Underground / Daddy's on the exit, brother's [in a face net] / Who in the place be strapped / In a concentration camp / I ain't goin out like this / I'm bringin' hope despite / All my people tryin' to fight this ...

Word to the niggers in the street ... Better trip cause this is not a dance tune record / Listen close to the deli ass message / Niggers gotta know before they hauled off / Killed in the streets by the enemy at all costs /... Niggers that I miss with the lyrics / Check it out, play it back and you will hear it. [Background, multiple voices chant] Niggers don't die ... Niggers don't die ... Niggers don't die —The Ansars (Oakland, 1991).[13]

Track 11

If we take seriously the music industry's evocation of "The Hip-Hop Nation," Oaktown (aka Oakland) is indisputably a key city-state. After New York City and Los Angeles, Oakland is arguably the next most proliferate site for the cultural and musical production of rap. One of the industry's biggest national and international rap superstars, MC Hammer, is a West Oakland boy, and well-known artists Too Short, Digital Underground, MC Pooh, 2Pac, and Oaktown's 3.5.7. are all Oakland-based. In the past several years, the image of Oakland as a hip-hop town that's "gettin busy," ready to "blow up" on the national scene, has encouraged an explosion of new rap groups circulating their first tape or rap single, looking for airplay and record industry attention. Of the 150+ rap labels reportedly in the Bay area,[14] the bulk of them are Oakland-based, with dozens of other groups coming out of surrounding San Francisco, B-Town (Berkeley), Richmond, San Jose, Hayward, or Vallejo. The geographic distribution of hip-hop "juice" has even disrupted San Francisco's nominal standing as "The City" in the Bay area, with hip-hop critics referring to the scene in the "Oakland-Bay Area."

Stories of how and when Oakland rap emerged circulate magnetically around the figure of Too Short. His image—tough, short, nasty, money-loving ghettoboy with a gold chain around his neck—shaped for years the imagination of Oakland rappers. His sound—slow, heavy bass beat, laid-back, with lyrics that story-tell everyday life of fucking off, fucking up, fucking—exemplifies one local rap producer's characterization of Oaktown rap: "It's like when you're frying food in grease, you gotta let it fry, it's gotta stay there in that grease for awhile to really

taste right. You don't take it out too soon."[15] Local legends of Too Short's persistent self-promotion, selling tapes out of the back of his car and on public buses,
taking $20 commissions from folks for rap songs about themselves that he'd rap
out in his bedroom with a beat box hooked up to the turntable on his stereo, are
as well known as his music.

A more specific story of Oakland rap's origins comes from local rap producer-
promoter Lionel Bea, founder of Bay Area Productions and one-time manager of
Too Short. A 1982 graduate of Oakland High, Lionel Bea said he got into the business of promoting by going to a dance in high school—they paid to get in, looked
around at the DJs, the technicians, the people taking money at the door, the
crowd, and said, "Hell, *we* know all these people ..." So they started producing
for-profit dances.

In 1984, Bay Area Productions (BAP) was just getting off the ground and de-
cided to organize the first all-rap show in the Bay Area, featuring an East Coast
group called Run DMC. When Run DMC became an overnight success a few
months later (one of the first rap groups to gain a nationwide audience), it was
gold for Lionel Bea and BAP. "I became a legitimate promoter overnight," Lionel
Bea says, smiling.

Lionel Bea met Too Short on the back of a bus sometime in 1985. He'd heard his
music, liked it, and promised Too Short he'd put him on a show. BAP was now
hooked up with music industry giant Bill Graham and was producing most of the
major music concerts in the East Bay. In March 1985, Lionel Bea scheduled Too
Short to open a show at the Henry J. Kaiser auditorium. It was an incredible moment, Lionel Bea remembers, when Too Short came onstage and shouted into the
sold-out audience, "WHERE ARE ALL THE NIGGERS FROM EAST OAKLAND!?" The
crowd went wild.

But the real breakout of Oakland rap came in October 1987, when Too Short
opened for a Def Jam tour featuring the Beastie Boys, Houdini, Public Enemy,
and Run DMC. Too Short, a local lightweight in a heavy lineup of national rap
stars, is given a strict 12-minutes-only on the stage. Twelve minutes into his performance before a sold-out Oaktown-Bay Area crowd, Too Short is in the middle
of his new, soon-to-be released song "Freaky Tales." It's a pretty nasty song, Lionel
Bea explains. The production manager says "get him off the fuckin stage" and
cuts the power and turns off the stage lights. The crowd thinks they're cutting Too
Short off cause he's singing dirty raps and they're furious, hissing and booing. A
few months later when Too Short drops his new album, *Born to Mack,* featuring
the song "Freaky Tales," it takes off. The album sells 50,000 copies regionally because everybody wanted to hear him finish the song. "Timing is everything,"
Lionel comments. And that was the moment Oakland rap was born.

Lionel Bea has a definite date for the death of major live rap concerts in the Bay
area—October 13, 1989. There was a riot during a rap concert at the Oakland Coliseum produced by Al Hammond, featuring MC Hammer with Heavy D, Cool

Moe D, and The Boys. No major venue would book rap shows after that. A few years ago, he says, Oakland was so happening you could just take a group and put 'em in the Coliseum and get 4,000 or 5,000 people there. And there were smaller clubs—Scottish Rite, Kisha's Inn. But nothing's happening there now.

Track 12

Long, sleek black car against a white background. The hood is down. Maybe it's a Cadillac. A black man in a black shirt, white pants, a thick gold chain around his neck, sits on the backseat of the car. The hood is down. T-O-O $-H-O-R-T is spelled out in black letters against the white background—the money sign stands out big and green. Attached to the plastic wrapper, the price tag for the cassette tape reads $8.99.

The beat starts up slow against a syncopated scratching, a percussive bell. Without a doubt I'm comin back and I will do it again / You can take away my beat but don't touch my pen / My name is Short but that's okay because I rap so long / Other rappers hip-hop / I put funk in this song / Young tender on the floor, wiggles it all/ Homeboy keeps tellin her to give him a call / He's been on her since ten, and it's almost two / Walkin through the party with his dick on the roof ... The party started jumpin five hours ago / The mix don't stop til it's way past four / At three A.M. / I hit the scene / Buck two freaks 'bout three fifteen / Cut out with one, ditch the other / I jump in my ride and I burn rubber—Partytime! Get busy! —Too Short (Oakland, 1988).[16]

Track 13

A commodity, she thought, *is* a mysterious thing.[17] Perhaps more mysterious than she'd ever thought before.

The relation between processes of commodification and contemporary cultural production was for her the theoretical field in which she encountered rap. Within the noise of this field, two questions emerged; probably they'd been there all along. First, *what is the oppositional or resistive potential of rap music, as a black cultural practice, in our time?* And second, *to what extent is it legitimate to designate rap as a postmodern cultural practice?* These questions, appropriated from Cornel West's reflections in "Black Culture and Postmodernism," circled for her around the mysterious experience of purchasing several $9 cassette tapes and having access to radically different wor(l)ds of articulate and rhythmic rage directed at violent hierarchical structures of whitesupremacist power, sometimes syncopated by celebrations of goldstuff and green money. Or buying a $22 ticket to attend a rap concert where, shoulder to shoulder with a multiracial, multicultural, and mostly middle-class crowd of men and women, she would hear the blackurban rap performers from the streets of Newark shout, "WHERE ARE THE REAL MOTHERFUCK'N

NIGGERS IN THE HOUSE?!" and the crowd would roar, waving their hands in the air with a weird and heterogeneous pride.[18]

The question of the oppositional potential of rap converges with broader considerations of culture as a site of resistance and, in particular, how contemporary culture is articulated in relation to mass commodification and commercialization. For Cornel West, ultimately, black music is oppositional only in "the weak sense." While insisting on the specificity and inseparability of the relation between culture and politics for African Americans, and recognizing cultural practices as the historical form in which "black resistance is channeled," West critically measures the domesticating effects of commodification.[19] Packaged for leisure time pleasure, fetishized within Euro-American markets capitalizing on consumer tastes for the exotic and primitive, black music has been deployed and circulated in a post–World War II economy where the cultural, military, and political hegemony of the United States has extended a transnational reach. From West's theoretical vantage point, whatever resistive potential rap might offer is recontained within structures of commodification and capital.

But West's analysis is curiously unsettled by the historical significance of what literary critic Henry Louis Gates Jr. calls "signifyin(g) practices." Recounting a rich and various tradition of "signifyin" within African American vernacular culture, Gates describes how signifyin(g) practices turn language inside out, doubling and sidestepping dominant meanings to create shared rhetorical strategies of survival and celebration.[20] Oral storytelling, everyday conversations, the street game called the Dozens, and literary and musical texts are sites where African Americans have created a "poetry of signification," reconstructing cultural meanings out of a hybridity of languages, syntax, images.[21] Signifyin(g) exploits the meaningful fact that the *form* in which a thing is signified can undercut, double, and reinflect the overt meaning signified by *content*. Gates's account of signifyin(g) as a *subversion from within* dominant white culture, a practice that could be deployed publicly across the dominant social field where the Master literally could not hear its figurative significations, raises difficult questions about how to understand rap as a commodity form. If the formal deconstruction of meaning is taken seriously as a historical strategy of subversion among African Americans, then can rap's presence within commodified markets SIGNal a popular generation of new, subversive signifyin(g) forms? Do all commodity forms share the same SIGNs of political neutralization and hegemonic incorporation?

Dick Hebdige's work on the meaning of subcultural styles among contemporary British youth converges with Gates's insights.[22] Hebdige analyzes, across variables of race and class, practices of remaking meanings, or signification, as a form of cultural subversion. Reading the semiotics of style written by a diversity of youth subcultures ranging from rasta to reggae to punk, Hebdige tells a story of semiotic guerrilla warfare conducted through the creative redeployment of commodified objects and meanings, disassembled and rearranged through the syncretic subcultural cut and paste of dominant religious, cultural, political, and national signs. The social consensus through which hegemonic culture legitimates its own power, naturalizing its own representations to produce a consensual hallucination called reality, is disrupted by the shattering styles and deviant significations circulating within these subcultures in an attempt to re/present or re/signify possible meanings and social practices.[23]

But for Hebdige, as for West, the symbolic disorderings of subcultural re/significations are destined to be incorporated into dominant systems of meaning. Subcultural "noise" is recuperated through the commodity form, defused through the "production, publicity and packaging" of its style.[24] From semiotic guerrilla, then, to commodified clown, Hebdige's theoretical story turns back on its subversive intent to acknowledge the power of hegemonic asSIGNments of meaning.

Here, in the persistent uncertainty of how to read the multiple significances of rap as a form of subcultural resistance *and* as a commodity form, the question of historical moment and postmodernism emerge. Recent theorists have suggested postmodernism marks not only a shifting aesthetics of style or a new practice of literary and philosophical criticism, but a radical deconstruction and reconstruction of contemporary social relations and subjectivities engineered by increasingly abstract, accelerated, transnational and technological forms of capital and SIGN circulation.[25] Within this new and disembodied economy, cultural and racial differences are commodified and deployed as SIGNs of difference that reproduce the same old story of hierarchical power and profit. In this economy of profitable INdifferences, rap can be read as the perfect, postmodern example of rage, resistance, and racialized Otherness becoming commodified and circulated for an indifferent diversity of consumers.[26]

The question of postmodernism—the debate over historical periodization that asks WHAT TIME IS IT? because the answer just might count—is complicated by Cornel West's observation that it may not be the same time for everybody.[27] Seemingly present in the same space, peoples may be embodied in significantly different historical times, subject to different cultural, economic, and social relations. WHAT TIME IS IT? emerges as a radically racialized determination.

Her questions spin out of analytical control. WHAT TIME IS IT? Is it the same time for everybody? Why does Public Enemy's Flavor Flav always wear a huge ticking clock around his neck? How to measure the uncertain time between "This Is Not a Dance Tune," sung by The Ansars on the edge of apocalypse, and Too Short's "Partytime," played for a high-funk, low-down ghettodance body, beating with an insistent partytime present?

WHAT IS RAP? Does rap subversively circulate through multiple channels of (diss)communication?[28] Or is it something less dangerous, more tuned into fully capitalized frequencies? How to construct a story of the significance of rap as a form of cultural resistance *and* as a commodity form? Can this story be told without history? Then, WHAT TIME IS IT? What if the significance of commodified cultural practices is a different story depending on where you are in history? What if a *text* gets re/signified in relation to different *contexts?* And if there's a *con* **in** your *text,* then who are you ever gonna trust for sure?

WHAT (TIME) IS RAP (IN)? WHAT (CON)TEXT IS RAP (CO)MODIFYING?

Track 14

The historical emergence of rap music often begins with a party—two turntables, a mixer, a DJ over a microphone, and a crowd of bodies moving, breaking, stepping, freestyle dancing. The party may be at a park in Harlem,[29] sometimes at an uptown club like the Audobon Ballroom in Manhattan,[30] or at a punk rock club on the Lower East Side.[31] The DJ is Kool DJ Herc from the Bronx via Jamaica or perhaps Afrika Bambaataa or Grandmaster Flash. The two turntables are worked over by an ear directly tuned to a mixed, multiple-frequency archive of funk, soul, rock 'n roll, or reggae and by a pair of genius hands that can play the two rotating "wheels of steel" like some musical mutant born of a percussive rhythm and a high-pitched, electronically wired zipper. The mouth at the microphone is emceeing "shout outs" to folks "in the house" or performing vernacular acrobatics of boast and challenge, remixing the toasting element of reggae. The crowd of bodies is black and brown, young, sometimes punk. The dress code is funky, creatively enforced. The collective, wildly colored signature of the emerging culture is the graffiti art on subways, fences, bridges, and borderlands of Manhattan. It's called hip-hop, sometimes beat; nobody's calling it rap yet, but it's only 1975.

For several historians of rap, the sounds of hip-hop are without doubt an embodied opposition, a sonic war call against the hegemonic beat of disco invading the airwaves in the mid-1970s.[32] Black radio stations that had catered to the sounds of R & B, soul, and the energetic P-funk pioneered by George Clinton were now caving in to the "form of record industry sabotage dubbed 'disco'—or .. disCOINTELPRO, since it destroyed the self-supporting black band movement which P-funk (jez) grew out of."[33] Turning to the tools of "disCOINTELPRO oppression into a new form of black vernacular expression," hip-hop reads in this story as a radical cultural counterinsurgency; the context of this counterinsurgency is black culture's historical ability to continually resist through reinventing capitalism's "cannibalization and commodification" of revolutionary ideas.[34]

Houston Baker remarks how the early hip-hop party emceeing radically transformed the possible relations between humanbodies and hightechnology by re/signifying the two-turnable technology of disco DJs. By adding a beat box, amplification, headphones, and a pair of very deft hands, "discotechnology was hybridized through the human hand and ear—the DJ turned wildman at the turntable. The conversion produced a rap DJ who became a postmodern, ritual priest of sound rather than a passive spectator in an isolated DJ booth making [disco] robots turn."[35] And the bodies listening to the re/signified technosounds began to break new ground as well—breakdancing, one of the early forms of hip-hop dance style, becomes a new blackurban form of B-ing.[36]

Rap's "seizure of the means of reproduction" triumphed through the deployment of several musical-technological innovations.[37] Scratching and sampling, the constructionist grounds of hip-hop sound dismembered the meaning of a musical "recording." Scratching, the DJs rhythmic scrape of the needle across a rotating record disk, re/signified the grooved surface of a recording as itself the musical material of percussive play and searing sound. And sampling, the fragmenting and remixing of pieces of prerecorded music, found sounds, cartoon voices, TV news, movie soundtracks, high-pitched screams, industrial noise, gunfire, sirens, or canned laughter, re/signified the entire world of recorded and recordable sound as meaningful elements in a technomix that constructs, out of disassembled/reassembled soundbytes, a musical text with a contagious rhythm that captured the body like a heartbeat.

The political economy of this re/signifying practice of scratching and sampling threw an innovative "fuck y'all" in the face of expensive musical instruments, training, and electronic equipment. Rap was composed, parasited off the backs of all the sounds already circulating in relatively cheap, accessible commodity form. The musical creation rests not in knowing how to put mouth to brass and blow, or how to throw your fingers across the familiarity of a black-and-white keyboard, but rather in how to assemble prerecorded music into unprecedented mixes—how to make unheard-of sounds scratch across a vinyl history of harmonies turned into technonoise. This method of reproducing sound is not only, then, a musical creation but a political, economic, and cultural discovery of how to compose a cheap, unforgettable dance party. Make the record speak not by making another record but by putting the old record on the turntable and making that your instrument. Your drum machine. It doesn't take a manufacturing process to groove a record so that the needle can read and amplify the music, it takes a musician with a different intelligence in the fingers to scratch new grooves across the old, right there live, emitting a rhythmic and irritable, innovative insistence that this is a sound you want to move to.

And the voice, above all else the rapper's voice, emerges over the top of the sampled and scratched construction, splitting off from the voice of the DJ emcee at the turntables, appearing downstage center as a separate figure of sustained, high-velocity vocality.[38] The voice of the rapper is the final, hybrid element to define rap's distinctive cultural recomposition. Variously traced through a genealogical remixing of a black oracular tradition of African griots-storytellers, black Christian preachers, black street-corner males' signifying, the rhetorical ovations of the Nation of Islam, and bad-ass ghettoboy slang,[39] the rapper's voice sounds out as the final texture re/signifying what it can possibly mean to sing anthems to obscenity, illegality, pimping, hoeing, sexing, partying, fucking the police, playing in the panic zone, busting out of prison, being chased by a fat girl, racing toward the apocalypse, or being the greatest mack in the motherfuck'n world.

The technological breakthrough that makes rap materially reproducible, a recorded product that can circulate beyond the here and now of partytime, is called "multitracking." The mode of reproducing rap into a final, recorded mix of sampling, scratching, and voice depends on this recent technology for mixing multiple sources of prerecorded sound into a single master track. Multitracking offers the possibility of recording and then being able to play back—simultaneously on parallel tracks—up to 24 different soundtracks.[40] Pieces of melody, rhythm, spoken words, found sounds are recorded on separate tracks and then sourced into a master mix, enabling the performer-producer to mix, listen, remix, listen again, adding tracks, reworking rap textures, until the sound finds its music and moves.

Track 15

Freeze-frame. A black-and-white image, blurred. It's dark out. There's a white cop car parked against a horizon of black, a pool of light from headlights shining outside the frame. A man in white pants is on his knees, torso twisted. You cannot see his face. Surrounding him are four cops, dressed in black. Three of the cops have arms raised outward, shoulder level, toward the man on his knees. You cannot see their faces.[41] *In Euro-American analytical systems, knowledge has been obtained by extracting the object of attention—* Reportedly, one of the courtroom strategies used by the defense in the trial against four white police officers accused of beating Rodney King was the "dissection" of an 81-second videotape of the scene *from its ongoingness within a fluid environment*—jurors saw the tape forward and backward, in fast forward, and freeze-framed—*where the fluidity itself is controlled in research regimens that decide what is extraneous or insignificant to the identified area of functioning in question.* One of the key frames isolated and analyzed by the defense occurred in the first five seconds of the video, when King was still standing on his feet. Focusing on the movement of King's feet, the radical uncertainty of whether the movement should be interpreted as a step or a charge, introduced the significant question of how the police could know whether King was about to attack.[42] *In many respects, to know is to freeze, to stop the mobility of the organism by isolating it.* The defense repeatedly argued that King could have ended the violence at any time by "assuming the position"—lying on the ground, face down, legs spread, arms outstretched, not moving. *So far, magnification of the organism and its components, dissection, measurement, and attribution have necessitated stillness.*[43] Further evidence of the dangerous indeterminacy of King's movements, and the probability that he was on PCP, rested in the fact that he laughed at police officers and turned his back to them, wiggling his ass.[44] This behavior occurred, the defense lawyers reminded jurors, before the first frame of the videotape.

Track 16

What is rap? *Man, you must don't know who I am—I'm the sweet peeter jeeter the womb beater / The baby maker the cradle shaker / The deerslayer the buckbinder the woman finder / Known from the Gold Coast to the rocky shores of Maine.* I first learn of H. Rap Brown reading Henry Louis Gates's account of African American "signifyin(g) practices," where Rap Brown appears as the embodiment and achievement of rap, which meant, before rap music, the ability to humorously, dexterously, usually insultingly, play black vernacular rhetorical games. *Rap is my name and love is my game / I'm the bedsucker the cock plucker the motherfucker / The milkshaker the record breaker the population maker / The gun-slinger the baby bringer / The humdinger the pussy ringer / The man with the terrible middle finger.* Quoting from Rap Brown's 1969 autobiography, *Die Nigger Die!*, Gates emphasizes Rap's rejection of the book-learning offered in school and his celebration of the poetry-making he learned in the streets playing the Dozens: "I learned to talk in the street, not from reading about Dick and Jane going to the zoo and all that simple shit. ... If anybody needed to study poetry, my teacher needed to study mine. ... We played the Dozens like white folks play Scrabble."[45] *They call me Rap the dicker the ass kicker / The cherry picker the city slicker the titty licker / And I ain't giving up nothing but bubble gum and hard times and I'm fresh out of bubble gum.*[46]

Rap Brown begins to run through my field like a figure just outside the frame—I can never quite catch up with him but I keep hearing his voice. At T's Wauzi record store I meet Muhammad, a Vietnam vet and resident historian of black history and U.S. government atrocities. "I'm a student at Berkeley studying rap." "H. Rap Brown?" he asks. "No, the music." "H. Rap Brown happened before the music," Muhammad says, shaking his head. "A lot happened that was rapping before the music you call rap. People don't know their history, they gotta do their homework. Have you heard of The Last Poets—'Ghettos of the Mind'—they were happening before Grandmaster Flash and all that gang?" "No, I never heard of them," I admit and ask if he has a copy of *Die Nigger Die!* He doesn't. "Well, I'll look for it at the UC library." Muhammad laughs and gives me the name of several bookstores in Oakland.

I check the computerized listings at the UC Berkeley library for *Die Nigger Die!* The green message on the black screen reads MISSING/WITHDRAWN. I look the title up in *Books in Print;* it's out of print.

The Key Bookstore in downtown Oakland is run by a gray-haired black man who tells me he hasn't seen a copy of *Die Nigger Die!* for some time. I browse through the collection of mostly used books, many black authors, with an eclectic selection of black history, fiction, poetry. In the paperback section I leaf through a copy of Angela Davis's *If They Come in the Morning.* In the section on political prisoners, there is a brief entry on H. Rap Brown. Synchrony. I read. I learn that along with being a poet and storyteller, Rap Brown was chairman of the Student Non-Violent Coordinating Committee (SNCC). In 1967, he was indicted in Maryland for inciting to riot and arson after a schoolbuilding burned down three hours after he delivered a speech in the neighborhood. In 1968, he was charged with a felony nobody had heard of before—transporting weapons through interstate commerce—for having twice checked his gun at an airport, after which it was transported with the pilots in the cockpit of the plane. Released on bail after the felony charge, he was rearrested after traveling to Oakland, California, and appearing on the podium of a Black Panther meeting at the Henry J. Kaiser Center. His bail was posted at $50,000. For forty-six days he fasted in prison to protest the use of bail as ransom to gag Black activists. He was sentenced to five years in prison, and while he was out of jail and his case on appeal, two SNCC members and friends of his were killed in a car bomb and he disappeared, went underground. Davis concludes: "It is not known whether Rap is dead or alive."

Track 17

"Microcomputation, multitrack recording, video imaging, and the highly innovative vocalizations and choreography of blackurban youth have produced a postmodern form that is fiercely intertextual, open-ended, hybrid ... revis[ing] a current generation's expectations where 'poetry' is concerned. ... I query my students in a course devoted to Afro-American women writers. 'What,' I asked, 'will be the poetry for the next society?' To a man or woman, my students responded 'rap' and 'MTV.'

"My student's responses, however, are not nearly as natural or original as they may seem on first view. In fact, they have a familiar cast within *a history of contestation and contradistinction governing the relationship between poetry and the state.* The exclusion of poets from the republic by Plato is the primary Western site of this contest ... in Afro-America it is the Preacher and the Bluesman.

"Plato argues the necessity of a homogeneous state designed to withstand the bluesiness of poets who are always intent on worrying such a line by signifying and troping irreverently on it and continually setting up conditionals. *'What if this?'* and *'What if that?'* ... If the state is the site of what linguists call the constative, *then poetry is an alternative space of the conditional.* If the state keeps itself in line ... through the linear, empty space of homogeneity, then poetry worries this space of line with heterogeneous performance. If the state is the place of reading the lines correctly, then poetry is the site of audition, of embodied sounding on state wrongs such as N.W.A.'s 'Fuck tha Police.'

"*If poetry, like rap, is disruptive performance, ... an articulation of the melancholia of the people's wounding by and before the emergence of the state line, then poetry can be defined, again like rap, as an audible or sounding space of opposition.*"[47]

Track 18

A red convertible with the hood down, parked under a street sign reading "Westminster." Five black men in baseball caps and T-shirts or sweatshirts, jeans, sur-round the car. The man in the driver's seat is holding a cellular phone to his ear. Blue sky. The price tag stuck to the plastic wrapping says $4.99.

Let the drums fall where they may / I'm the prophet, the poet-king / Production and birth of a dark ebony soul / I come forth with the truth for black youth on a round stool / Out of the jungles of concrete and black asphalt / I taught many lessons and sessions / Just like a seminar / Poetry and poverty relate to my mortal state / My essence is the word the poet came with—I'll demonstrate / Scars and scrapes from hoppin' so many gates / Selling drugs, like a thug, you know my pockets got green stuff / The hell with the pale boss-man of the evil plan / Brothers in the pen never sold out to Uncle Sam / I'm the ghetto-dweller storyteller of dirt I did / Mellow'd at the base of the economic pyramid / Quiet is kept, suckers were trailin' my footsteps / I crept when they slept leavin' them searchin' for intellect / From the pathway of the lost land / Unknown regions get involved with the Legion of the dope-man / Righteous I stand like an Islamic man / Living in the age of a wanderin' hypocrite / Come show me your whip, punk, you claim a ghetto gang / Fly as you wanna be in this urban society / You killin' in the village of the east central city / Ain't that a pity—dumb suckers wanta get some of this / I'm from the Oaktown—Don't forget where you came from.

Black dynasty Black unity Black people Black power Black rhythm Black soul Black poetry Black magic Black male Black female Black wisdom—Let the drums fall where they may—I'm the prophet, the poet-king —Black Dynasty (Oakland, 1991).[48]

Track 19

What if, she asked, *the story of rap is read in the context of the history of H. Rap Brown?* I return to the Key Bookstore and reintroduce myself to the owner, Lumukanda. "I stopped in last week. I'm a student at Berkeley and I'm studying rap." "Rap Brown?" he asks. "No, the music." Have I ever heard of The Last Poets? he asks. They were the first to really rap, he says, "everything after that is meaningless blather." He says rap today is shallow, superficial. Not backed by any profound analysis. No knowledge of the Black Power movement, nobody's reading *Revolutionary Suicide.*[49] They have no understanding of militarism, the structured organization of oppression, the need for organized response. "Capitalism," I offer, "there's almost no critique of capitalism. They're *in* capitalism, not against it." "Yes," he nods, "they want to be entertainers. They write stuff that's clever." He knows 'cause his son's a rapper, writes lyrics. Maybe he'll do okay with it someday.

He hasn't found a copy of Rap Brown's autobiography. But he thinks he has a copy of *The Berkeley Barb* that I'd be interested in. I leaf through a box of fragile, browned newspapers to find it, a local weekly underground newspaper dated February 23–29, 1968. There's a photo of Rap Brown standing between two other black men, in sunglasses, a beret, with both fists raised face level. The headline above the photo reads, "Beside the empty seat of the Minister of Defense, Prime Minister Carmichael, Minister of Justice Brown and Foreign Affairs Minister Forman rise in honor of Huey Newtown and promise to set him free."[50] Lumukanda gestures out the bookstore window, "Rap Brown came to Oakland and spoke there at the Kaiser, just down the street. He joined the Black Panthers that evening."

I buy the old newspaper. It costs $10.81. I read:

> Rap Brown, who had come despite a court order confining him to the New York City area, jarred his listeners with a series of blasts at them as "chumps" for their acceptance of white culture and concessions.
>
> "Concessions are not progress," he rapped out. "They give you a nigger astronaut. I said they would lose him in space, but they haven't even let him go up. They gave you Thurgood Marshall on the Supreme Court—a Tom of a high order."
>
> It was nearly 11:30 P.M. and Brown said he would sit down and let Carmichael speak. The crowd called to him to "keep talking" and he gave them:
>
> "You enjoy being lied to. You believe in Santa Claus—a white honky who slides down a black chimney with presents for black kids.
>
> "The only politics relevant to black people is the politics of revolution. The only thing that is going to free Huey Newton is gunpowder."[51]

A small boxed article on the same page with the headline "Rap Brown Arrested" relates that Black Power leader H. Rap Brown was arrested in New York by federal marshals and city police. The warrant for his arrest charged him with making a trip to Oakland in defiance of a court order limiting him to New York unless he received prior permission to travel.

Track 20

Let me tell you a story. Once upon a time, lots of different people started to publicly say, in lots of different ways, that whitemale Western and warrior history is not the only story. *When history separated itself from story, it started indulging in accumulation and facts.* They started trying to listen to the historical stories of people who've been silenced, deviant-ized, genocided, enslaved, patholog-ized, woman-ized, or ignored by whitemale Western warrior history. But reconstructing historical stories when the makers and the subjects of that history have been structurally dispossessed of most public, institutional spaces for remembering their selves, is not a simple task. *It thought it could build up to History because [it thought] the Past, unrelated to the Present and the Future, is lying there in its entirety, waiting to be revealed and related.* The most powerful resources for remembering may become fragments of oral story, artifacts of memory or imagination often stored "underground"—in buried traces of the Underground Railway, women's networks of safe houses, witches' rituals in Salem, the sanctuary of local church basements, or in unconscious, underground spaces of dream, vision, disease. All these resources for remaking history are marked in whitemale and Western culture with the "taint" of fiction, ambiguity, secrets, subjectivity, uncertainty, of non-reliable, non-verifiable non-information. *But the act of revealing bears in itself a magical (not factual) quality—inherited undoubtedly from "primitive" storytelling.* The deeply political, highly policed boundaries between what counts as a historical fact and what can be discounted as fiction function to keep these "outlaw" memories and "unreliable" stories contained, difficult to access and dangerous to pursue. *History ... thus manages to oppose the factual to the fictional (turning a blind eye to the "magicality" of its claims). ... If we rely on history to tell us what happened at a specific time and place, we can rely on the story to tell us not only what might have happened, but also what is happening at an unspecified time and place. No wonder that in old tales storytellers are very often women, witches, and prophets. The African griot and griotte are well known for being poet, storyteller, historian, musician, and magician—all at once.*[52]

Track 21

I understand that time is running out—tick tock tick tock tick—I understand that time is running out!—tock tick tock—running out as hastily as niggers run from The Man ... Time is running out on lifeless serpents reigning over a living kingdom. Time is running out on talks marches tunes chants and all kinds of prayers. Time is running out of time. I heard someone say things were changing—changing from brown to black. Time is running out on bullshit changes. Running out like a bush fire in a dry forest. Like a murderer from the scene of a crime. ... *Run nigger!* whippin your ass— *Run nigger!* stealin your culture— *Run nigger!* takin your life— *Run nigger!* killin your children ... *Run nigger cause time is running. Run like time ... is running running running tick tock tick tock tick tock tick time's gone run out* —The Last Poets (New York, 1971).[53]

Track 22

What if the text of rap is reread in the context of H. Rap Brown? The trail of Rap Brown leads her into unfamiliar fields, where certain knowledge is missing, withdrawn, out-of-print. Certain histories are not well documented by the archives to which she had immediate access. She's led to middle-aged blackmen storytellers, bookstores, yellowed newspapers, and to a history of Oakland as a once-upon-a-time site of militant political and cultural rebellion. Stories of Rap Brown's evening with the Black Panthers at the Kaiser Auditorium, where some twenty years later Lionel Bea produces major rap concerts, sets her ethnographic imagination spinning. She confronts the difficult question of how the boundaries between imaginary and material resistance get set, how the construction of those boundaries, always a theoretical and political achievement, sets the stage for how "culture" as a site of resistance will be read.

She knew it was theoretically possible to tell a story based on both Muhammad and Lumukanda's genealogy of rap through figures like Rap Brown and The Last Poets, of contemporary rap as a depoliticized black cultural practice—its resistance purely rhetorical, its message commodifed, lacking any relation to organized political action. But she wanted to tell a different story, a different reading of the history of rap/Rap, that insisted on the theoretical fiction of the *materiality of imaginary and rhetorical structures,* of the possibility of poetry as a form of (social) movement. She wanted to argue that the materiality of fictions, poetic forms, and rhetorical gaming also has its density, its intelligent abilities to hold the line, to keep political possibilities open, to keep political im/possibilities imaginable.

This spin of imaginings led her back to the question of "signifyin(g) practices" as resistant rituals of *un*making meanings, of doubling and tricking up the SIGNS of dominant culture. What is the meaning and political significance of rap when poets like Rap Brown were once arrested for giving a speech that led to fire? What if Rap Brown's double(d) identity as black rhetorical acrobat *and* as political militant is recognized? What if his going underground at a particular moment in the story is acknowledged as a necessary survival strategy at a specific historical moment when assassination became a U.S. government policy for dealing with organized, aboveground black political resistance?[54] What if Angela Davis's uncertain conclusion, "It is not known whether Rap is dead or alive," is re/signified with this double(d) meaning: the uncertainty of Rap the man—who embodied both the fire of rap's rhetorical heat and a politically militant, organized resistance—being dead or alive *and* the uncertainty of rap the music as a dead or alive oppositional force. What if these two uncertainties are intimately entangled at this moment in history, knotted by the radical impossibility of a determinant answer?

What if, at this point in the story, the uncertainty of whether Rap/rap is dead or alive as a form of political resistance becomes itself a politically threatening question, the answer necessarily subterranean? The empiricity of Rap/rap's political potential or effects at this historical moment may be precisely, and for good socio/logical reason, an *underground* phenomenon. And what if a provisional closure to the question is available only by appeal to a historical and socio/logical story whose own "ending" will itself circulate, like rap, in the imagination of its readers? Perhaps leaving the question itself undecided, an open question, is a sustaining gesture of subversion through uncertainty. Perhaps. Perhaps this is a socio/logic of and in the postmodern?

And so she knew, for the time being, … that she would come down on the uncertain side of suggesting that the circulation of rap could be a powerfully resistive social fiction, or social fact—the difference between these two words no less or more than life or death or the im/possibility of transforming suffering for many of the embodied stories that moved materially, and with music, in and out of her field ... And all of this, really, was quite difficult for her to imagine.

Track 23

Sound of police sirens wailing. Ambulance. A firetruck in the distance coming closer. Crowd noises. Laughter. A line of cops in black short-sleeved uniforms standing, with clubs drawn, from sidewalk to sidewalk across Market Street. Behind them, nine black-and-white police cars, parked three abreast. Behind the police cars, she could only see black smoke rising from the middle of Market Street. It was Thursday, April 30, 1992. Los Angeles was still burning and dusk was just going dark when she walked out of the subway into downtown San Francisco. She had come too late for the protest march, which began in the late afternoon. She found herself somewhere else, perhaps a war zone, perhaps a riot, perhaps a party—but she immediately recognized it as her field. By the sound. Police sirens wailing all around.

Glass splinters in the upper register, a crash of paned glass slivers the soundwalk. Shrieks, multiply pitched, a rush of sound and maybe five or six young people run into the hole that was a storefront. *Once it is no longer bought, the commodity lies open to criticism and alteration*— Then out. *—whatever particular form it may take.* Running fast up the block. The streets are littered with shoeboxes. Several small storefronts have already been shattered, the insides ransacked. *Only when it is paid for with money is it respected as an admirable fetish.* More bodies run toward the store, gather in an excited crowd, run on just before two or three police on white motorcycles turn the corner, hop the curb, chase the sounding crowd now up the block and around. *Looting, which instantly destroys the commodity as such, also discloses what the commodity ultimately implies*— People stroll past or watch together in small groups gathered in entryways—*the army, the police and the other specialized detachments of the state's monopoly of armed violence.* She searched the faces, the strolls, the style of dress for signs. Asian Americans, blacks, Chicanos, some whites, punks, hippies, mostly young, mostly black, mostly looking happy, interested, some ecstatic, some slightly fearful, curious. A crowd gathers on the streetcorner near the black hole of a storefront, four cops on motorcycles turn the corner, jump the curb, the crowd scatters. *What is a policeman? He is the active servant of the commodity ... whose job it is to ensure that a given product of human labor remains a commodity with the magical property of having to be paid for.*[55] Two black women on the corner hold hand-painted signs with N.W.A.'s lyrics F-U-C-K T-H-E P-O-L-I-C-E waving over their heads, chanting. "Fuck the Police! Fuck the Police! Fuck the Police!"

More noise from somewhere out of sight, shouts, the sound of breaking glass, people running toward the sound. Cops following.

She has never been here before, this place they will call "riot." She is neither scared nor ecstatic. She is totally engaged. What is this field? How did everybody get here? She strolls, watching, through the narrow streets just off of Market. Filled with moving people.

A Chicano man in a bright yellow-and-red–striped shirt runs toward a cop on a motorcycle, swings a bat furiously at the windshield, the cop body. He tears up the street. Cheers on the sidewalk. Ten seconds pass before two, then three, then a dozen cops on white motorcycles in a chaos of pursuit up the block. She watches them out of sight, fading dissonance of angry siren.

A minute later, she turns the corner and a bare-chested brown man runs across the street. Terror on his face she cannot fully recognize. Cops run on foot, four from the bottom of the block, another six on motorcycles at the top of the block. The man, cornered, runs back across the street. A cop on motorcycle catches the back of his left foot under the front wheel he lunges for the sidewalk a few feet from where she stands. Frozen next to the car. Watching this. A cop runs to grab the brown man on the sidewalk he lunges across the hood of a parked car then caught arms pinned face smashed into car metal cops appear from everywhere pull batons swing across the air scream get back she tries to run through the cops now moving in now baton against armflesh quick pain cops on motorcycle crash into sidewalk running bodies she turns back now jumps across hood of car scrambles over top into street across from siren screams from everywhere *do you know, do you know what's happening?*

She walks down the next block. On.

The mouse king and queen stand six-foot tall, soft graywhite fur, a red cap on the queen's mousehead, next to each other in the window display of the high-ceilinged toy store. Train tracks circle upside down across the ceiling. The voluminous space is filled with stuffed animals velvetsoft spotted orange giraffes chocolatebrown gorillas pinkelephants goldenbears with green neckbows. Staring, absorbed, into the abundant jungles of animal, human-sized doll, a rocking horse, she is surprised to see three people, one in a cushioned wicker chair, one on a gold-edged trunk, seated in the middle of the store. Three white people watching a TV perched on the checkout counter. She takes out her notebook, writes while staring through the pane. "F.A.O. Schwartz. Corner of Stockton and O'Farrell. 8:40 P.M." The three people notice her standing outside the dark glass windows. Walk on.

8:50 P.M. Five cops approach her sitting on the curb, writing. There's a curfew at nine. State of emergency. Please get off the streets hey make it easy for us okay? 9:05 P.M. Three blackmen workers barricaded inside Carl's Jr. restaurant. Trash cans against door. Signs read "Carl's Jr. Roast Beef Deluxe. Chicken Strips." She writes it down. "Hey, write this down," a shout through the glass doors. "Three black men inside Carl's Jr. does not mean it's a robbery! Now, *four* black men—

that would be a robbery. Two guys for the cash register. One guy for the lights. And one guy on the music." Laughter. 9:15 P.M. A huge garbage dumpster burns, flames orange. Black smoke. Woman in a red scarf rides by slowly on a bicycle, talking into a microphone. 9:18 p.m. Matthew Shell, general contractor. Union wages. Carpenter's Local 22. Boarding up huge windows for The Limited Express. "Put me in your story—good for business." Laughs. Looks at windows—"If it were up to me I'd just let 'em in." 9:25 P.M. Twenty-six riot police in bright blue suits from Alameda County, lined across an empty Market Street. "Sieg Heil!" the young whiteman yells furious, crossing in front of the police line. The fourth cop from the end videos him. 9:40 P.M. Quiet city except for sirens. Streets empty except for cop cars every block down Market Street. Next to the cops black and brown men on their knees against the wall. 9:45 P.M. Civic Center.

After a few minutes he said his name was carl which she wrote down since she had pulled out her small notebook as soon as he said he knew of h. rap brown. "i may be drunk / but i got the spunk" she had to write that down and he said yes music comedy entertainment i was once engaged in quite a baroque profession and how about yourself? She noticed it was dark but from the coplights the streetlights the lights from helicopters moving low in the nightsky she could see to scribble it all down he said it's happening, yes, the war of the worlds get drunk and enjoy the movie. They sat still for a moment among sirens, smoke. Yes he said everything was going fine everyone sitting orderly in their desks and then somebody, yes, the class clown, yes Bush the Bozo, the clown had to get everybody excited are you taking all that down?

He was slight, black-skinned, with a manner polite and measured as if they'd just met at the theater a brown bag wrapped loosely around a beer can. After some time he said you will move to the suburbs but don't you burn no cross on that lawn he said smiling you seem to admire black men? She said yes a little slow she said yes I learn from them and he smiling said you learn from them you are in bondage, smiling, oh, yes, you learn that women are niggers too. This was before she'd pulled out her notebook and

he said smiling still i will take you to the other side of the mirror.

Exactly when he asked for the first dollar she didn't remember maybe that's when she pulled out the notebook after she asked about rap brown and he asked about the dollar and she gave him one from the inside of her suitcoat pocket and then said she felt terrible he said what you cannot pay a black scholar? So then she could laugh and he said yes i'm beating the drum as i'm speaking to you now you really won't understand you can't you won't get it by writing it down word for word you see i'm a rapper and i am here. Get drunk and enjoy the movie. Now i got popcorn. He waved the bill once in the air. Exactly when he asked for the second dollar she remembers cause she wrote it down he was saying again yes you'll move to the suburbs but don't you burn no cross on the lawn smiling still and right then she wrote down "here's a dollar" so it must have been then she handed him the second bill.

By then she was out of dollars and he soon got up, walked a few steps away from the parkbench, turned, beckoned her to follow. She sat scribbling "you can't get it by writing it down word for word." And he walked off

under the black sky. Black, black sky. Noise. Noise. The dark buzz of white noise.

Track 24

A week after the fires in Los Angeles I receive a message on my answering machine from Premo, an Oakland rap artist I interviewed in mid-April. "Well, isn't that radical" he says with a little laugh into the machine after listening to my message—BURN HOLLYWOOD BURN HOLLYWOOD BURN.

"This is Premo, just calling to say I told you so." Premo told me a lot. But one thing I wrote down, so I remember it well. Premo told me, "If I think of what's the most important thing to tell you, for whatever story you're going to write, it's this. The most intelligent black men today are in prison now. Cause you look around and you want things now, the American Dream. You want that 40 acres and a mule and there's no other way you're gonna get it."

Premo says he just called to see how my project was going. And then he starts rapping into the machine. He raps all the words from his latest song, "Triple K Frat Party." It's about the Rodney King beating, and he'd given me a copy of the words when we met. He'd been working on it for a few months. But he's added a few verses. He leaves them on my machine. For free.

> Folks got to learn / That the P-the R-the E-the M-O- won't let ya burn / You got to know your past to know your future / And if you don't well Premo gonna school ya / What I got is so true believe me / Don't believe what they show you on TV / Playin Nintendo / Drunk like Endo / Trying to be the star of the latest rap video … I'm not asking for your money / I need your time / I'm not asking for your body / I need your mind / I can't do it by myself but I'll damn sure try / And if you're with me, Homey, it's hoe or die / It's hoe or die …[56]

Click. The whrrrr of the answering machine. Rewind. Click. Do you know what's happening?

A Postscript on Methods

As a radical critical intervention, cultural studies … can be a site of meaningful contestation and constructive confrontation. … Of course we must enter this new discursive field recognizing from the onset that our speech will be "troubled," that there exists no ready-made "common language." Drawing from a new ethnography, we are challenged to celebrate the polyphonic nature of critical discourse, to—as it happens in traditional African-American religious experience—hear one another "speak in tongues"...

—bell hooks

Polyphonic, troubled, critical, contesting—bell hook's evocation of a "new discursive field" marks the potentially disruptive and unusually demanding style of much writing done under the contemporary sign of cultural studies. Ethnography as both a research and representational practice has been a particularly rich site for elaborating the possibilities of new fields of writing, thinking, and representing culture and its study. In this brief postscript, I want to suggest some of the intellectual and historical contexts for the methodological disruptions and desires informing my ethnography of rap. While explicitly experimental in its form, this text—like any experiment—has its antecedent inspirations and shaping contexts. Most important, I want to insist that the question of writing style or textual form is not simply an issue of intellectual fashion but also a sign of consequential struggles over the epistemological and political borders between science and literature, fact and fiction, between the Subject of Reason and its racialized, gendered, classified, and sexualized Others. Within the polyphonics of style and the troubled excess of "speaking in tongues" lie the uncertain truths of new objects and methods of study whose meanings are powerfully bound up with material struggles over history, memory, and the possibility of subversive (social) movements.

"Re/Sounding Race, Re/Signifying Ethnography" is based on five months of fieldwork studying rap music in Oakland, California. In many ways, my methods followed the usual pattern of participant observation. I attended Bay area rap concerts; hung out at local record stores; interviewed Oakland rap musicians, rap producers, radio DJs, and record store managers; listened to local rap radio programs; and spent hours inside a Walkman listening to rap from Oakland and elsewhere. But from the beginning my ethnographic ear was attuned to multiple frequencies and the montage of contradictory and sometimes just simply confusing sounds in my field: I listened for noise as well as melody, pursued static and interference as well as coherence, studied ambivalence and uncertainty as intently as analytic "through-lines." These static frequencies are not tuned out or backgrounded—they form a central theme of the work, a place from which to write not only *about* but *within* the complexities of cultural and racial differences, *within* the historical materiality of an ethnographic ear that, initially, could barely make out many of the words in rap lyrics. And the more I was able to hear, the more I could listen to what I continued to not know: Everyday experiences and practices of language and representation that are local and historical, racialized and gendered, melodic and violent. These charged tensions fusing around the limits of my listening and the ever-widening range of what I came to hear as a part of my "field" became the material with which I composed a piece of writing that engages with rap as a language or signifying practice, a politics, a commodity, and an effect of local histories of resistance and music.

In writing the text, I looked to the form of rap itself as a source of formal principles for constructing my analysis. The technology of "multitracking"—where
up to twenty-four samples of sound are mixed into a musical artifact (the rap recording)—became the constructivist principle upon which I built a collage essay
composed of twenty-four tracks, or textual fragments. By playing off the structure of a rap recording, I wanted to raise questions about the correspondences between rap and ethnography as constructed and aesthetic forms. I wanted to evoke
recognition of ethnography as a stylized form of representation, but I also wanted
to emphasize how rap operates as a sophisticated method for constructing and
communicating social knowledges. The collage form allowed me to juxtapose
theoretical discourse and samples of rap lyrics, offering a way to *formally* pose the
question of how different styles of representation affect what social reality
"sounds" like. The openness introduced by the collage form—in which analytic
claims are evoked rather than argued, suggested rather than spelled out—can for
some readers weaken or render unreadable any analytic focus. The effectiveness of
the form depends on how carefully the collage is crafted, analytically and aestheti-
cally, and on the particular ear and eye of the reader.[57]

My experiments with style emerge out of a critical mix of contemporary re/
soundings of what it means to produce ethnography. Recognition of knowledge-
production as itself a cultural practice, located within specific institutional, gender, national, class, racial/ethnic, and philosophical contexts, and bearing the formal and coded signs of its own social positioning, has encouraged a reading of
ethnographic discourse as the telling inscription of the social-material relations of
those who produce it. The ethnographic gaze has bent back upon its practitioners, compelling a reconsideration of the situated politics and epistemological
partialities of all attempts, including and especially those of "science," to represent cultural worlds.

A well-known early effort to define and respond to the question (some would
say crisis) of representation within ethnographic discourse is James Clifford and
George Marcus's anthology *Writing Culture: The Poetics and Politics of Ethnography* (1986). In his introductory essay, Clifford announces the "historical predicament" of contemporary ethnography faced with radically transformed understandings of culture, science, politics, and poetics. The factual basis upon which
ethnography builds its knowledge claims is reconceived as a powerful artifact:
The fictive effect of forceful, culturally specific economies of what is (and is not)
visible, what is (and is not) speakable, what is (or may never be) representable.
Within this destabilized ethnographic field, the materiality of poetry as an alternative economy of truth-telling, as a political strategy for foregrounding the ethical arts of all evidence-making, is reevaluated: "Poetry is not limited to romantic
or modernist subjectivity: it can be historical, precise, objective."[58]

The possibilities of a poetic politics of ethnography, although announced by
Writing Culture, is nowhere materialized in its own textual practices, conducted

in the usual academic cadence of argumentation and authority.[59] A more provocative coupling of critique with experimental ethnographic author-izing is found in the work of Trinh Minh-ha, feminist theorist and filmmaker. In *Woman, Native, Other: Writing Postcoloniality and Feminism* (1989), Trinh's analysis of anthropology as a conversation between Man and Man about Them—a form of gossip given the self-congratulatory title of Science[60]—is woven into a textual montage of voices that confounds the traditional ethnographic attempt to represent a sovereign and authoritative telling of the "real" story. Her break with the explanatory depths of a masculine Western ethnographic discourse is accomplished through a carefully composed textual surface that performs the slippery, uncertain reversals of a subject writing its (other) self. Her shifting ethnographic "I" aims at the moving truth of a story that is always situated somewhere in between—between the West and its exoticized Others, between enlightened reason and its excess. Her target is the elusive, repetitious operations of the "real," as it dis/continuously represents its self through the play of Otherness, difference, and dream.

Experimental ethnographic writing and critical reconceptions of ethnography's "subject" and "object" are an active, cross-disciplinary interest of much recent intellectual work, but it would be a mistake to call such interests "new." Within what I pose as "antitraditions of ethnography" lies a history of innovative interventions into the dominant traditions of ethnographic method and style. In France, this antitradition emerged between the world wars in the form of "ethnographic surrealism" and the related work of the Collège de Sociologie, inspired by the teachings of Marcel Mauss and the later writings of Emile Durkheim; in the United States, it can be found in the ethnographic writings of Zora Neale Hurston in the 1930s and in the work on Haitian voodoo by artist-ethnographer Maya Deren in the late 1940s. The ethnographic methods, ambitions, and textual styles of these authors by no means form an integrated "antitradition," but they can be configured as a moving historical ground of heterogeneous practices *within* ethnography—a ground that supports, however invisibly, contemporary rethinkings of ethnographic method.[61]

"Ethnographic surrealism"—a term deployed by James Clifford to describe a method of visual or written montage that gives notice to the ideologically constructed nature of our un/conscious perceptions of reality—emerged within creative exchanges between the human sciences and the cultural avant-garde in France after World War I.[62] According to Clifford, ethnographic surrealism pursued the "analytic decomposition of reality" through the composing of texts and visual work that operate in a "continuous play of the familiar and the strange," aiming at a simultaneously aesthetic, moral, and political engagement with reality and its *sur*real elements (the French *sur* meaning "over," "into," "toward").[63]

The sociohistorical context of ethnographic surrealism was not only the provocative conversation between modernist avant-garde artistic concerns and social science methods but also the pervasive cultural and moral shell shock of post–World War I societies. The everyday world had been radically defamiliarized through the violent moral and technological economies of industrial warfare; this cultural shattering set the social stage for aesthetic and political responses of an equally intense *dis*order. Within this historical moment, ethnographic surrealism's vision of reality as deeply in question—as an artificial archi-texture of coded representations *that could be rearranged*—was an act of profound critique but also of radical hope. The ethnographic and aesthetic turn to "primitive" Others as a source of this *sur*realist hope was, I would suggest, a contradictory response to France's destabilized relation to its African colonies and to rearticulations of race and racism within popular culture and politics.

The Collège de Sociologie (1937–1940), whose membership included Georges Bataille, Michel Leiris, Roger Callois, and Walter Benjamin, provides an exemplary instance of the ethnographic surreal taken up as a collective intellectual and political project.[64] The ambitions of the college have been traced back to the ethnographic and ethical project of Emile Durkheim in *The Elementary Forms of Religious Life,* and forward (largely through the influence of Bataille) into the poststructuralist critiques of Jacques Derrida, Roland Barthes, Julia Kristeva, and the *Tel Quel* group.[65] Among the explicit aims of the college's "sacred sociology" was a commitment to experiment with the "contagious effects of the collective representations it studies"—to conduct a form of rigorous ethnographic research in the style of Durkheim but not to recoil as he did (in the name of science) from the potentially effervescent powers of its *own* collective representations of ethnographic sur/realities.[66] Collage writing became a representational strategy employed and theorized by members of the college. "The ethnography as collage," Clifford writes, "would leave manifest the constructivist procedures of ethnographic knowledge; it would be an assemblage containing voices other than the ethnographer's, as well as examples of 'found' evidence, data not fully integrated within the work's governing interpretation."[67] The juxtapositions and fragmentation characteristic of collage offered its practitioners a formal and aesthetic tactic for constructing their ethnographic claims about social reality as a "naturalized" assemblage of familiar representations that could be interrupted and interrogated through collage's denaturalizing alchemy.

In the United States there also exists a history of productive, if less chronicled, border-crossings between artistic avant-gardes and the social sciences. The ethnographic writings of Zora Neale Hurston and Maya Deren were intimately tied to avant-garde culture and community: for Hurston, the Harlem Renaissance and for Deren, a post–World War II avant-garde influenced by European and Latin American surrealism and the emerging field of independent filmmaking, of which she was an early organizer.[68]

The ethnographic career of Zora Neale Hurston produced two texts—*Mules and Men: Negro Folktales and Voodoo Practices in the South* (1935) and *Tell My*

Horse: Voodoo and Life in Haiti and Jamaica (1938). Described as "simultaneously a travelogue, a piece of journalism and political analysis, a conventional ethnography, part legend and folklore with art criticism and commentary thrown in,"[69] Hurston's *Tell My Horse* bears some of the genre-blurred marks of collage without displaying the precise sutures of its multiple voicings. Reading with the ease of a story, Hurston's texts inhabit a discursive field where the popular and the scientific, imagination and analysis, are sympathetically fused into a new ethnographic form.

Maya Deren's *Divine Horsemen: The Living Gods of Haiti* (1953) also signals a stylistic and methodological break with dominant ethnographic traditions. Deren traveled to Haiti in 1947 for an eight-month stay, originally intending to make a film "in which Haitian dance, as purely a dance form, would be combined (in montage principle) with various non-Haitian elements."[70] Her failure to make the film turned into a 300-page ethnographic text analyzing the rites and meanings of Haitian voodoo culture.[71] By her own account, the challenge to understand the "form" of Haitian dance necessitated the much broader study of the history, mythology, and syncretic religious practices of voodoo.[72] From her particular positioning as artist turned ethnographer, Deren writes a scholarly and poetically intelligent ethnography of Haitian culture and mythology. Insisting on a methodological approach and cultural understanding that refuses Western dualisms of mind and body, Deren embraces an embodied spiritual materiality as a necessary ethnographic stance. "The White Darkness," the last chapter of Hurston's ethnography, narrates her experience of voodoo possession, the ecstatic ritual around which Haitian dance, as religious practice, is organized.[73]

This brief overview of ethnographic antitraditions in the work of Deren, Hurston, and the Collège de Sociologie offers an account of the productive margins of the "field" called fieldwork. It also, I hope, suggests a historical and intellectual context for reading contemporary efforts to re/signify ethnography as a contested, heterogeneous, and unsettled cultural practice.

In addition to this intellectual history, a very immediate conjuncture of institutional and political events profoundly shaped my work. These events pushed me toward an affirmation of the resistive potential of rap, which came to constitute a central claim of my research. During my fieldwork, the institutional site in which I was working exploded into an organized and angry protest by sociology graduate students against the faculty's hiring decision in the field of race/ethnicity. Motivated by graduate students' collective critique of the institutionalized racism within our own department, I partially abandoned the original theoretical context for my work (focusing on racial and cultural differences as a new, capital-friendly commodity circulating within an indifferent landscape of transnational hyperconsumption) and began to read more social theory by and about African Americans, including critiques of "postmodernism" that racialized and complexified notions of historical context. This shift theoretically tilted my guiding questions and final in/conclusions toward a more hopeful, ambivalent, and historically informed reading of rap as potentially resistive.

The second event that radically affected my analysis was the uprisings in Los Angeles—and Las Vegas, Seattle, San Francisco, Berkeley, Atlanta—after the acquittal of four police officers charged with the beating of Rodney King. My involvement with the mass protests, which frames the beginning and end of my ethnographic story, was a transformative experience. When I sat down to begin writing this text, San Francisco was still operating under a curfew and state of emergency. The sound of police sirens in my Oakland neighborhood increased tenfold and continued to mark the soundscape throughout the spring of 1992. The daily media spectacle of "looting"—and the confused efforts among leftists to critique or defend it as a form of protest—heightened my commitment to explore the racialized mystifications of the commodity-form. Media and other metacommentary on the supposedly "chaotic" situation, and the virtual lack of local public outcry over the declaration of a state of emergency and the deployment of paramilitary state forces that took to the streets in a far more extensive display of power than any group of "rioters," made the forms of knowledge and calls for racial justice (or, simply, "less heat on the streets, please") circulating in rap culture seem all the more ethnographically significant and historically astute. This text was a partial attempt to respond to and chronicle the urgencies of that conjunctural moment—which has not passed.

NOTES

I would like to thank Natasha Kirsten Kraus, Michael Burawoy, and members of the participant observation seminar who engaged—sometimes critically, always carefully—this work as it took shape.

1. The breaks between lines (marked by a /) are taken from Premo's own written version of this song. Premo, "Triple K Frat Party," *New World Order* (Oakland: Strong Arm Records, 1992).

2. I borrow this accelerated word construction from Houston A. Baker Jr.

3. Loic Wacquant, "Interview with Pierre Bourdieu," *Berkeley Journal of Sociology* 34 (1989), pp. 1–30.

4. Timothy Maliqualim Simone, *About Face: Race in Postmodern America* (New York: Autonomedia, 1989), p. 152, emphasis mine.

5. The song lyrics, in italics, are from "Rock 'n Roll Nigger" by Patti Smith (New York: Arista Records, 1975).

6. This and all following rap lyric quotes are based on my transcriptions. The break between lines (/) is where I "heard" a break. Words inside brackets are words I'm not sure I heard right. Definitely, there are words I didn't hear right but think I did. So these transcriptions are my best translations of what I can hear. These lyrics are from Public Enemy, "Burn Hollywood, Burn," *Fear of a Black Planet* (New York: Columbia Records, 1990).

7. See Trinh Minh-ha, *Woman, Native, Other: Writing Postcoloniality and Feminism* (Bloomington: Indiana University Press, 1989); bell hooks, "Culture to Culture: Ethnography and Cultural Studies as Critical Intervention," in *Yearning: Race, Gender, and Cultural Politics* (Boston: South End Press, 1990), pp. 123–134; James Clifford and George Marcus, eds., *Writing Culture: The Poetics and Politics of Ethnography* (Berkeley: University of California Press, 1986); and Avery Gordon, "Feminism, Writing, and Ghosts," *Social Problems* (November 1990), pp. 485–500.

8. Fragments of phrase in italics are a quote from Trinh, *Woman, Native, Other,* p. 71.

9. Pierre Bourdieu, *The Logic of Practice* (Stanford: Stanford University Press, 1990), p. 65.

10. See *Oakland Tribune,* May 1–3, 1992, for one account of the arrival and deployment of U.S. military forces. On May 3, 1992, a local rap radio program, *The Sunday Morning Show* on KALX, provided details of the troop deployment not available in the mainstream news, based on the eyewitness account of a phone caller from Los Angeles. The caller described the bunkers of dirt built by soldiers on street corners, bolstered by piles of bricks and other materials. "It's a war, you can see it with your own eyes."

11. Shot 'O Soul was scheduled to perform in a talent show in Wheeler Hall on the Berkeley campus at 7 P.M., then to open later that evening in San Francisco for the rap group Black Sheep. Both events were canceled. As I wandered around the campus and Bancroft Avenue Friday night after curfew, the only African Americans I saw were driving around in cars or were cops. The actual wording of the Berkeley City Council's curfew notice specified that people "with a destination and purpose" would be permitted on the streets. My own observation, wandering around Berkeley without any particular purpose, was that the curfew was selectively enforced according to race, age, class, and, probably, gender specificities.

In San Francisco that same night, two hours before the 9 P.M. curfew, over 400 people were arrested in a police sweep that took place as protesters of the King verdict were assembling for a peaceful march through the Mission District. Everyone on the street was arrested without warning by the police, including a reporter from *Business Week* and people, many of them Chicanos who live in the neighborhood, who had no knowledge of the protest but happened to be out on the streets. All people arrested were taken to Santa Rita jail, forty miles outside the city, and held for over thirty hours. With the exception of protest organizers (the leadership of Roots Against War, the group organizing the protest) and "illegal aliens," most people were released without charges and bused back to San Francisco, arriving at 3 A.M. Sunday. Since the curfew was not yet in effect and the police had not declared the gathering an illegal assembly, the Friday night arrests seem to indicate that during a state of emergency, the possibility of a peaceful protest against racism is a threat to the state. Several lawsuits were filed against the San Francisco mayor's office and the San Francisco Police Department for the apparently illegal actions of the city police that Friday evening.

12. Unlike larger record stores or national chains, T's Wauzi is willing to take a small number of tapes (say twenty-five or thirty), often brought in by the rappers themselves, and sell them in the store on commission. The Eastmont Mall store was awarded the Best Independent Store in the Nation Award at the 1992 Gavin music industry convention.

13. The Ansars, "This Is Not a Dance Tune," *Righteous Black Guerillas* (Oakland: Righteous Records, 1991).

14. This figure was cited at the music industry's 1992 Gavin convention. Nobody knows the exact number, and it fluctuates monthly as groups disband, start up, or reconfigure themselves with different names and different sounds.

15. Reginald McKnighten of Night Time Management, producer of rap and R & B, offered this great description.

16. Too Short, "Partytime," *Born to Mack* (Oakland: Zomba Recording, 1988).

17. Karl Marx was perhaps the first to notice this. He observed, "A commodity is therefore a mysterious thing, simply because in it the social character of men's labour appears to them as an objective character stamped upon the product of that labour." *Capital,* vol. 1 in *The Marx-Engels Reader,* ed. Robert Tucker (New York: W. W. Norton, 1978), p. 320. I am not sure this is at all how rap producers experience the commodity-object called rap. Some things yet remain to be demystified.

18. The scene here is a rap concert, January 31, 1992, at the Warfield in San Francisco. The group is Naughty by Nature, a popular hard-core rap group from Newark, New Jersey.

19. Cornel West, "Black Culture and Postmodernism," in *Remaking History: Discussions in Contemporary Culture,* ed. Barbara Kruger and Phil Mariani (Seattle: Bay Press, 1989), pp. 94–96.

20. Henry Louis Gates Jr., *The Signifying Monkey: A Theory of Afro-American Literary Criticism* (New York: Oxford University Press, 1988).

21. See Gates, *The Signifying Monkey,* pp. 51–64. In particular, Gates cites the figure of the Signifying Monkey, a popular character in a wealth of black vernacular stories, as exemplary of the operations of signifying practices: "The ironic reversal of a received racist image of the black as simianlike, the Signifying Monkey, he who dwells at the margins of discourse, ever punning, ever troping, ever embodying the ambiguities of language, is our trope for repetition and revision, indeed our trope of chiasmus, repeating and reversing simultaneously as he does in one deft discursive act" (p. 52).

22. Dick Hebdige, *Subculture: The Meaning of Style* (New York: Methuen, 1979).

23. Ibid., p. 17. Following Hebdige, blackurban rap artists' appropriation of the hegemonic image of the bad-ass ghettoboy becomes readable as a hyperacceleration of the black male "gangsta" image, a collective self-representation presented in rap with a theatrical, rhetorical velocity that pushes the image into caricature, simultaneously professing the truth *and* giving the lie to dominant images of the dangerous black man. If the discourse on the dangerous black man is really controlled by a hegemonic racist discourse, how to account for rap's appropriation of it to glorify and consolidate an affirmative black male identity? I thank Danyel Smith, then music critic for the *San Francisco Bay Guardian,* for suggesting to me that "gansta" rap is often resignifying gangster images from "blaxploitation" films.

24. Ibid., p. 95.

25. See Stephen Pfohl, "Welcome to the Parasite Cafe: Postmodernity as a Social Problem," *Social Problems* 37, no. 4 (1990), pp. 421–442; Donna Haraway, "A Manifesto for Cyborgs: Science, Technology, and Socialist Feminism in the 1980s," *Socialist Review* 80, pp. 65–107; and Jean Baudrillard, *Simulations* (New York: Semiotext[e], 1983).

26. Timothy Simone raises the concern that in a postmodern U.S. culture in which difference is homogenized through an "overproduced plurality" of choices, blacks may be identified as the only social group that "continues to experience real difference" and is po-

sitioned in a new form of racist demand: "Instead of picking cotton for us, blacks will make *our* culture for us" (*About Face,* pp. 92–93).

27. Cornel West, *Prophesy Deliverance! An Afro-American Revolutionary Christianity* (Philadelphia: Westminster Press, 1982), p. 44. West suggests this paradox of African American history: Just as African Americans fully enter the modern world, the postmodern period commences; after they gain a foot in the modern industrial order, it is succeeded by postindustrialism. Thus, "At the same time, the Afro-American underclass and the poor working class exhibit the indelible traces of their oppression in modernity and their dispensability in postmodernity" (p. 44).

28. "Dissin" or "diss" is a common black vernacular expression meaning something like "to insult" (maybe connected to "disrespect"?). A whitesuburban translation of dissin I grew up with was the cheap shot "Your mother wears army boots."

29. Havelock Nelson and Michael A. Gonzales, *Bring the Noise: A Guide to Rap Music and Hip-Hop Culture* (New York: Harmony Books, 1991), pp. xvi–xvii.

30. Greg Tate, *Flyboy in the Buttermilk: Essays on Contemporary America* (New York: Simon and Schuster, 1992), p. 156.

31. Interview, Afrika Bambaataa, "On the Line With…," *KMELJAM'S Beat Report* (San Francisco: KMEL, December 1991).

32. For this version of music history, see Tate, *Flyboy in the Buttermilk,* p. 154; or Houston Baker, "Hybridity, the Rap Race, and Pedagogy for the 1990s," in *Technoculture* (Minneapolis: University of Minnesota Press, 1991), p. 198.

33. Tate, *Flyboy in the Buttermilk,* p. 154, is signifying on COINTELPRO, the U.S. government-sponsored, FBI-organized operation that was reportedly responsible for infiltrating, discrediting, and assassinating members of the Black Panther Party, the American Indian Movement, the Peace and Freedom Party, the Puerto Rican Independence movement, and other groups of political resistors.

34. Ibid.

35. Baker, "Hybridity," p. 200.

36. Ibid., p. 198.

37. Tate, *Flyboy in the Buttermilk,* p. 154.

38. I'm referring here to the division of labor that develops out of the early role of the DJ at the turntable as simultaneously emcee, master technician, and rap voice in the mike to the current role of the DJ as primarily the music mixer, with the vocals (and microphone) now embodied in the rapper—who moves out from behind the turntables to "come downstage" as the central vocal figure in the group. There are certainly DJs who also perform vocally, mixing with the rapper. But largely the DJ's job has shifted to techno-mixmaster. It was pointed out to me at my first rap concert, by a more experienced fan, that the two giant turntables that were placed onstage for the performance were actually never used. All the sound, including the disk scratching, was prerecorded.

39. For this particular genealogy, I thank Houston Baker ("Hybridity," pp. 201–202).

40. Mark Costello and David Foster Wallace, *Signifying Rappers: Rap and Race in the Urban Present* (New York: Ecco Press, 1990), p. 55.

41. The image I read here is from *Newsweek* magazine, May 11, 1992, p. 36, in a photo layout and commentary titled "How the Defense Dissected the Tape."

42. I am responding here to the richly suggestive analysis made by Avital Ronell in "T.V. Trauma: Rodney King—Twelve Steps Beyond the Pleasure Principle," a paper presented at

the California College of Arts and Crafts, Oakland, May 4, 1992. For a published version of the paper, see Avital Ronell, "Video/Television/Rodney King: Twelve Steps Beyond the Pleasure Principle," in *Culture on the Brink: Ideologies of Technology*, ed. Gretchen Bender and Timothy Druckery (Seattle: Bay Press, 1994).

43. The phrases in italics are a quote from Simone, *About Face*, p. 164.

44. *Newsweek* reports the laugh; Ruth Wilson Gilmore, in her paper "Terror Austerity Race Gender Excess Theater," presented at the University of California–Berkeley, March 6, 1992, described King's ass-wiggling as reported in the Los Angeles press coverage of the trial. King was not on PCP during the beating. For a published version of the paper see Ruth Wilson Gilmore, "Terror Austerity Race Gender Excess Theater," in *Reading Rodney King/Reading Urban Uprising*, ed. Robert Gooding-Williams (New York: Routledge, 1993).

45. H. Rap Brown quote in Gates, *The Signifying Monkey*, p. 72.

46. All lines in italics are a quote from H. Rap Brown's poetry in *Die Nigger Die!* as quoted in ibid., p. 73.

47. Entire passage is a quote from Baker, "Hybridity," pp. 204–205, emphasis mine.

48. Black Dynasty, "Don't Forget Where You Came From," *Eight Ball in the Corner Pocket* (Oakland: Flammy Flam Productions, 1991).

49. By Huey P. Newton. It's out of print.

50. Huey Newton, who was raised and went to school in Oakland, cofounded with Bobby Seale the Black Panther Party in Oakland in 1966. In 1967 he was charged with murdering a policeman, convicted of manslaughter, and sentenced to prison for 2–15 years. Protests against his conviction and imprisonment were nationwide. In 1970, the conviction was reversed by the California Court of Appeals. Newton was shot dead in Oakland in August 1989. (This information was taken from the CD insert of Paris's rap album *The Devil Made Me Do It.*)

51. *Berkeley Barb*, February 23–29, 1968, pp. 3, 6.

52. All passages in italics quoted from Trinh, *Woman, Native, Other*, pp. 119–120.

53. The Last Poets, "Run Nigger!" *The Last Poets* (New York: Douglas Records, 1971).

54. I'm referring to COINTELPRO and U.S. government–sponsored overt and covert actions to destabilize and dismember the Black Power movement.

55. The lines in italics are quotes from Guy Debord's analysis of the Watts riots, "The Decline and Fall of the Spectacle-Commodity Economy," in *Situationist International Anthology*, ed. and trans. Ken Knabb (Berkeley: Bureau of Public Secrets, 1981), pp. 153–159. Debord was a founding member of Situationist International, whose critique of the society of the spectacle helped shape the insurrections in France in 1968. Debord's analysis situates "looting" as an erasure of the exchange value of the commodity and a seizure of the eternally deferred satisfaction that commodity culture will promise but never (can) deliver.

56. "Hoe or Die" is also the title of one of Premo's songs on his album *New World Order*. He told me it was an expression going around Oakland, a kind of re/signifying of "Do or die." He said it means you got to give it your all, you just can't give up.

57. And since unconscious structurings are at play in the composition of a collage, the unconscious responses of readers may involve resonances or resistances that are not fully articulable or clear to anybody. This often makes reading (a good) collage disturbing.

58. James Clifford, "Introduction: Partial Truths," in *Writing Culture: The Poetics and Politics of Ethnography*, p. 26.

59. That is to say, the anthology is at best a contradictory attempt to re-vision ethnography. Nowhere are its contradictions more clear than in Clifford's introductory explanation for the editors' exclusion of feminist perspectives, accounted for by the "fact" that "feminism had not contributed much to the theoretical analysis of ethnographies as texts" (ibid., p. 20). The arti-factuality of this fact is left unexplored. For an analysis of the exclusion of feminists and scholars of color from this anthology, see hooks, "Culture to Culture," pp. 125–129.

60. Trinh, *Woman, Native, Other,* pp. 57–58.

61. I owe a particular debt to Stephen Pfohl, Avery Gordon, and the work of the Parasite Cafe, where I was first acquainted with elements of these antitraditions and with rethinking ethnography as a method in/of the postmodern. See Stephen Pfohl and Avery Gordon, "Criminological Displacements: A Sociological Deconstruction," *Social Problems* 33, no. 6, pp. 94–113; Gordon, "Feminism, Writing, Ghosts"; and Stephen Pfohl, *Death at the Parasite Cafe: Social Science (Fictions) and the Postmodern* (New York: St. Martin's Press, 1992), pp. 74–103.

62. James Clifford, "On Ethnographic Surrealism," in *The Predicament of Culture: Twentieth Century Ethnography, Art and Literature* (Cambridge: Harvard University Press, 1988).

63. Ibid., pp. 540–541.

64. Ibid., pp. 559–561. For more developed accounts of the college's ambitions and cultural productions see Denis Hollier, ed., *The College of Sociology (1937–1939),* trans. Betsy Wing (Minneapolis: University of Minnesota Press, 1988).

65. See Pfohl, *Death at the Parasite Cafe,* pp. 135–153; and Michele Richman, "Anthropology and Modernism in France: From Durkheim to the College de Sociologie," in *Modernist Anthropology: From Fieldwork to Text,* ed. Marc Manganaro (Princeton: Princeton University Press, 1990), pp. 183–214.

66. Richman, "Anthropology and Modernism in France," p. 199.

67. Clifford, "On Ethnographic Surrealism," pp. 563–564.

68. From a public lecture by Marilyn Fabe at a showing of Deren's short films (Pacific Film Archive, Berkeley, June 26, 1991).

69. Deborah Gordon, "The Politics of Ethnographic Authority: Race and Writing in the Ethnography of Margaret Mead and Zora Neale Hurston," in *Modernist Anthropology: From Fieldwork to Text,* p. 154.

70. Maya Deren, *Divine Horsemen: The Living Gods of Haiti* (New York: McPherson, 1953), p. 5.

71. After her death, footage Deren shot while doing fieldwork was edited into a remarkable film, titled after her book *Divine Horsemen.*

72. Ibid., p. 7.

73. Ibid., pp. 258–262.

12

Aliens in the Corpus:
Shakespeare's Books
in the Age of the Cyborg

ELIZABETH PITTENGER

Writing is pre-eminently the technology of cyborgs,
etched on the surfaces of the late twentieth century.
Cyborg politics is the struggle for language and
the struggle against perfect communication,
against the one code that translates all meaning perfectly,
the central dogma of phallogocentrism.
That is why cyborg politics insist on noise and advocate pollution,
rejoicing in the illegitimate fusions of [organism] and machine.

A machine wrote this.

I am myself a writing-machine.[1]

FOR THOSE OF US who write on Shakespeare, or who reproduce him by teaching his books, I think it's safe to say that we are by now accustomed to (attacking) the assembly of cultural investments that privilege this particular corpus as the embodiment of the essence of humanity. I use the parentheses contentiously in order to suggest the possibility that two antagonist projects might occupy a similar point of departure, for if what romantic and modernist projects have desired to grasp is Shakespeare's hand, now warm and capable, critical projects have struggled by and large to loosen the power of the very same grip. An emphasis on the common ground opens up the possibility that a pre-postmodern notion of "the human" continues to operate, perhaps by tacit complicity, in what I prefer to call posthumanist critiques of more traditional assumptions about essential humanity. To grapple with these issues, I would like to divert our eyes to something else, to glance at something I call "alien." From my perspective what emerges from the pages of Shakespeare's books is not his hand, his corpus, or his mind, but something rather less familiar. Even when, in examinations of Shakespeare's literal books, what emerges from the inky black is not perfected genius but something more like the brain that wouldn't die or maybe a hand forged by the mechanical press, both hybrids of technology and human—though that's never quite what the interested parties seem to disclose. I hope to draw out the noisy, polluted, illegitimate aliens that occupy Shakespeare's corpus by looking directly at his books, both in the literal and material sense and, by extension, in the reproduction of his books in editorial, critical, and cultural practices.

My concern with these issues radiates from a core interest in the technology of writing, especially the materiality of texts in the many senses that the phrase indicates. Underlying this is an investment in materialist and feminist positions, an alliance that ultimately motivates my use of Haraway's manifesto. In an essay on Shakespearean texts and print technology, I investigated the ways in which the female body is produced as a blank in order to reproduce the dominant ideologies of patriarchical culture of early modern England.[2] I argued that the technology of the printing press introduced a specific set of fantasies advantageous to various projects, a set of fantasies revolving around the notion of "mechanical reproduction" operating in textual standardization, pedagogical transmission, and psychic regularization, as well as in patriarchal naturalization. Though the feminist agenda will be less explicit in these pages, I hope that the gendered and sexual implications are evident and that the initial gesture toward Haraway resonates off and on, to use a cybernetic metaphor. I will concentrate on a range of bibliographic approaches that figure the technology and materiality of writing even as they mystify Shakespeare's books.

The Hand in Shakespeare's Corpus

Pre-cybernetic machines could be haunted; there was always the spectre
of the ghost in the machine. They were not man, an author to himself,
but only a caricature of that masculinist reproductive dream.[3]

I shall not undertake the search for aliens in the heart of the Shakespearean corpus but will begin on the fringes with the illegitimate *The Book of Sir Thomas More*. Because the text is literally composite, produced from the collective labor of anonymous hands, it raises unavoidable problems of attribution, authorship, and agency. (Its subject, a humanist intervention in an alien uprising, raises these questions as well.) The bibliographic projects that swarm around the text have stakes in the same million-dollar question: Can we call it one of Shakespeare's books? And if so, how much of it is from his hand?[4] It's a million-dollar question because "hand" here is also meant literally (a usage that tugs at the boundaries of what is meant by "literally"): Shakespeare's hand indicates both his hand in writing *The Book of Sir Thomas More* and his handwriting in the manuscript of the play. Agency and the traces of character—how are these figured in the conflation of hand in writing/handwriting? How is handwriting a fantasmatic object, itself presenting the alluring prospect that both agency and character are the same?–– or rather, that both support what Jacques Derrida aphoristically calls the "structure of maintenance and manuscription," in which the individual emerges in "the punctual simplicity of the classical subject."[5] "The space of such an individual is suggested," as Jonathan Goldberg just as aphoristically puts it, "by the image of the detached hand."[6]

The Book of Sir Thomas More consists of twenty leaves of paper marked by the script of six hands, primarily of English character and conventionally designated by the letters A, B, C, D, E, and S. More important to bibliographic studies than analyzing the labor of the hands is their assignment to the appropriate bodies: the predominant Hand S belongs to Anthony Munday, A is Henry Chettle, E is Thomas Dekker, B is questionably Thomas Heywood, and C is vaguely "a playhouse functionary."[7] The three pages of Hand D are ascribed, with much titillation, to the Shakespearean corpus. These pages script a scene that represents the intervention of humanist Sir Thomas More in preempting the violence of an uprising of apprentices against the aliens resident in London (riots that did occur in 1517, though More's role is significantly expanded and idealized). It's important to add that the pages are appendages to the body of the text—they are called "Addition II"—and are usually thought to be written separately, if not completely in the dark, since they display a lack of awareness of the other hands of the play and especially of the hand of the censor, Edmond Tilney, who prohibited the use of "straungers" (used repeatedly by Hand D) because of brewing anti-alien sentiments contemporary with the writing (erupting in 1593 and again in 1595).[8] More could be said about this nexus vis-à-vis the initial claims of the essay, but for now I want to stick with the issue of the hand.

According to an often-repeated anecdote, when eminent paleographer Sir Edward Maunde Thompson opened the book to the pages by Hand D, he "threw up his hands and cried, 'Shakespeare!'"[9] The instantaneous recognition conveys the compelling urgency of the editorial investment in the authorial hand and the mystified immediacy with which editors claim to identify Shakespeare. This extends beyond the hand to questions of value, for "Addition II" is also judged to be worthy of Shakespeare's corpus because of the "high merit of its composition."[10] Functioning from the basic equation that Shakespeare is the proper name for the hand of genius, the editorial machinery programmatically discerns what properly belongs in the corpus while excising lines, speeches, and even whole compositions as illegitimate corruptions. In mystification of value, the traits of the hand indicate not the agency of Shakespeare but the character of genius, connected not to a mundane historical body but to a miraculous bardic brain, one that lives beyond the page. The holograph projects a hologram.

An exception to "all the solemnity that has over the generations gone into proving that Hand D was Shakespeare," Scott McMillin's study of *The Book of Sir Thomas More* resists tracing the hand to the agency of the bard.[11] Though he confesses that his work may not have "dislodged" the identifications attached to this hand and body, he labors to estrange them. Primarily, he challenges the extent to which the bibliographers are certain that D was a playwright and C was a "transcriber only," for their hands are quite similar: "I cannot discountenance the idea that Hand C was joined to this mysterious body" (154). McMillin quotes W. W. Greg, who also edited the play: "[Hand D] writes 'other' and leaves it to C to assign the speech to whom he pleases."[12] "Other" is a "leaving" to be assigned by another, a forgoing of the agency of speech in a forgoing of the agency of writing, both coincidentally marked by "other." The example marks the subversion of agency, which McMillin suggests in a slightly different way: "Greg writes in the full confidence that D and C were different, that one 'left' things for the other to 'clear up.' This is the master-slave relationship, but on the radical assumption that D and C were the same, Greg's passage can be read without change, and with the uncanny effect of reminding us how one person's writing actually is done—writers have masters and slaves in themselves" (157). If I play out the implications of his suggestions, the mysterious body to which he adds Hand D contains an alien hand; the body is bifurcated by the two hands that then embody the agencies of "functionary" and "genius"; finally the self-divided writer represents an allegory of production along the lines of master/slave, an allegory open to analysis, especially of the Lacanian sort. Contrary to Haraway's suggestion that precybernetic man is author to himself, the writing body envisioned may be as much a caricature of production as the machine is of reproduction. And it may be just as haunted.

What emerges between the hand and its other in the editorial project is the specter of the authorial presence, a ghost: "We always seem to be dealing with ghosts when troubling over an author's identity" (149). McMillin speculates that "the writer is often at odds with himself,"

> faced with clearing up his own leavings whether or not he will eventually be called a genius, and although in the collaborative work of the theatre for which *Sir Thomas More* was composed and revised, it is possible that C and D were different, in the scholarly work of authorial identification it is advisable to consider them the same, at least until the ghost disappears. For the ghostly identification of Shakespeare has not been laid to rest here. Shakespeare may well have collaborated on the original *Sir Thomas More* for Strange's men in 1592–1593, and the secret charm that will lay that spectre to rest is the counteridentification: not Shakespeare as Hand D, but Hand D as Hand C. What can a literary scholar say about that? There are no letters between D and C, no ground for the ghostly name to take shape. (158)

McMillin frames the editorial story as an uncanny replay of the plot of *Hamlet*, the ghostly paternal presence motivating the desires of dutiful yet ponderous sons. But McMillin may not be able to sidestep the scenario he sets, since he continues ambivalently to invoke the ghost he seeks to lay to rest. Even as he demystifies the skeletons in the closet of bibliographers, he concludes mysteriously, "If the master and the slave can be seen as one, the distance between C and D becomes an interior space, a space known to you and me as well as the others, and our need for ghostly authors should disappear once and for all" (159). I myself do not know what he supposes you, me, and the others to know. If there is no letter between the letters, no ground for the ghostly name, then what kind of space are we asked to imagine? Would the distance between the letters be none other than *différance*? How would this spacing make the ghostly author disappear? How is this related to the self-divided master/slave? What kind of interiority would this be? "Once and for all" are the final words of his book. While he puts himself to rest, he leaves this space to other hands to clear up.

To do so, we might follow his hint that the subversion of the agency of the hand leads to a subversion of the agency of authorial presence: "That one Hand is the same as another eliminates the very synecdoche by which authors are thought to be seen behind manuscripts. ... For the Hand is really a trope of another kind— not a synecdoche for the writer but a metonymy for the writing, the actual handwriting on the paper; and the handwriting does not come out of a grave, it comes out of the stack in the Manuscript Division of the British Library, where nothing apart from some of the Supervisors is to be feared" (158). With the ghost put back in the grave, McMillin moves away from the specter of the hand in writing toward a disembodied handwriting, gesturing toward the materiality of Shakespeare's book. And what's on the pages for the most part is not script, but printed characters, the typographic marks of the mechanical press.

Mechanical Hands

Although I write by hand,
with a connected script of the sort which is called cursive,
it is not the flow of it which interests me, but the instant
when a character singles itself out: my model is a
typographical one, the process of printing—
I am myself a writing machine.[13]

The internalization of the collaborative efforts of production, the master/slave relationship as McMillin calls it, leaves open the possibility that the agency of the hand is in fact not in step with the imagined sovereign agency of the human; for instance, the agential character of differing hands might belong to the same body, and that same body might "belong" to differing hands. At times Shakespeare's "other" hand takes over the writing of his own hand. As I suggested, editorial projects tend to portray this "other" hand as corrupt, illegitimate, and alien, as the agency tied to the meddling of functionaries, even though the scenario described by McMillin provides some resistance to this tendency.

These issues are not confined to the unusual case of the handwritten play-text, for the assumptions about Shakespeare's hand and the meddling of others are *commonly* reproduced in ordinary textual commentary, especially the introductory material of *popular* editions. I emphasize "common" and "popular" because I want to move away from the bibliographic stacks toward more widely circulated reproductions of Shakespeare, ones that influence readers and students the most. For example, I recently assigned to my students the Arden edition of *Two Gentlemen of Verona*.[14] *Two Gentlemen* might arguably be considered a run-of-the-mill play, but this very quality constitutes it as strange precisely because it is from the genius's hand. Editor Clifford Leech, noting the lapses of time and space, confesses that when "we consider the number of such minor oddities in the play, we are bound to grow suspicious of the text" (xxi). Although Leech does not indulge his suspicions directly, they reappear in the mouths or hands of others. For instance, he mentions John Upton, who in 1746 saw *Two Gentlemen* along with *Love's Labour's Lost* as non-Shakespearean in manner and style (xxv). Non-Shakespearean plays by Shakespeare? Though an interesting case could be made for exactly this "oddity," it would exceed the imagined possibilities, since what is non-Shakespearean is by definition not by Shakespeare.[15] Leech maintains these limits when he defers to the tradition of giants Rowe, Pope, Hamner, Theobald, Malone, and even Coleridge marshaling in more raised eyebrows (lii). "Hamner thought," Leech reiterates, " 'It may well be doubted whether *Shakespear* had any other hand in this play than the enlivening it with some speeches and lines thrown in here and there' " (liii). Again we have the presence of the authorial hand and alongside it an alien, an illegitimate Shakespeare. The suspicions and shuffling of hands work to consolidate in concrete terms more familiar to editors the floating anxiety that the play doesn't really belong with Shakespeare's books, that it's an alien in his corpus.

Leech is not alone. The concretization around the issue of the hand fits into most bibliographic projects, old and new. The New Bibliography differs in its claim to be "scientific" because it attends to the material properties of the book rather than editing according to taste or aesthetics. But the difficulty of separating the two is clear in the case of *Two Gentlemen,* since the suspicions of another hand are introduced precisely to address issues of taste and aesthetics; it is non-Shakespearean, whatever that might mean, and it is bad, something that it might mean. Even when editors step beyond the limits of the authorial character to discover the meddling of others, they are still compelled to embody and characterize these effects. Thus, in studies such as Eleanor Prosser's *Shakespeare's Anonymous Editors,*

the typographic marks yield mysterious agents, some with names like Compositor B and the Literary Scribe.[16] Although Prosser should be commended for her
emphasis on the agency of Compositor B (whose position bears an uncanny resemblance to that of Hand C), she continues to hold onto the individual nature of
the hand, an investment that amounts to a displacement of the author function
onto another agent as a kind of multi- and mini-bardology. In place is still a notion of "what Shakespeare wrote," and her compositorial study, unfortunately,
leaves open the possibility that these many corrupting hands can be excised from
the text in order to find the real Shakespeare.

Margreta De Grazia's criticism of the New Bibliography shows how a claim to
be "new" instead works in the service of a surreptitious repetition of the "old," the
unscientific search for the authentic Shakespeare and his essential genius.[17]
Though it's easier to stay within the field of textual criticism, and I will for the
most part adopt this protective cover, De Grazia ventures to indict interpreters as
well by sketching the parallel paths taken by both editors and critics: "For what
bibliographic treatments of Shakespeare resist is non-authorial writing; that is, a
play text recording a wide array of collective and extended contributions and
transformations. And what critical treatments evade is non-authorial meaning;
that is, discourse representing an interplay of the cultural and economic activities
in which performance and publication are involved" (82). The space of collective
production and the interplay of cultural and economic in performance and publication provides a more specific and less-mystified description of *Sir Thomas
More, Two Gentlemen,* and other Shakespearean as well as non-Shakespearean
texts. If, then, we can agree with De Grazia and McMillin to lay to rest the specter
of the ghost, how do we handle nonauthorial writing?

De Grazia calls for an analysis of the "material processes of book-production"
(69). Of course, several branches of bibliography focus on the "wide array of collective and extended contributions and transformations" that constitute Shakespearean texts. Compositorial study, for example, analyzes the processes of early
modern publication in terms of typesetting, printing house styles, orthographic
variations, copy texts, and so on. Here we would expect to leave the realm of the
ghostly hand and body behind to enter the space of labor and machines. And yet
the processes of mechanical reproduction continue to be haunted with mystifications; the machine prints an "incarnational text," as De Grazia incisively puts it,
"material in form, immaterial in essence" (82). On the one hand, because editors
continue to search for "what Shakespeare really wrote," they inevitably subscribe
to the view of writing as technological vehicle, a mechanical channel of the living
logos. Therefore, their scientific investigation of the materiality of the printed text
results in a suppression and abjection of the mechanics that produced the material text.[18] On the other hand, mechanical reproduction figures as a principle of
textual property; in the most concrete—yet markedly mystified—sense, texts are
reproduced mechanically, that is, by machine and the printing press and by the
manual labor of "mechanical" operators, the compositors, the pressmen, the

proofreaders. This principle of mechanical reproduction has affected and continues to affect editorial and critical evaluations of Shakespearean texts because it is
so inextricably bound up with determining what the Shakespearean text *is* in the
first place.

The Language of Mechanical Noise

*Data-storage machines are much too accurate to make the classical
distinctions between intentions and citation, independent thought and
the mere repetition of something already said. They register
discursive events without regard for so-called persons. Thus the
pretext of being able to distinguish between mental ownership,
citation, and parapraxes became as superfluous as in psychoanalysis.*[19]

When we attend to the "material processes of book-production," we start to see
things, not specters of hands and ghosts but the errant and variant forms of
nonauthorial writing. For example, compositorial study in its scrutiny of mechanically reproduced pages is fascinated with typos; in fact, this field might be
renamed the grammar of "noise," since it involves accounting for typos and accidents by parsing them according to categories of error. Bibliographers rarely offer
systematic or theoretical discussions of error, yet most of their studies presuppose
and depend upon distinctions of various types. Since these categories help maintain assumptions about (non)authorial writing and meaning, I want to analyze
them, even though my aim is to call the categories into question. Bibliographic
studies presume the ability to detect and reveal the following distinctions:

1. "Gross error"—typos due to the mechanics of setting type, for example,
   upside-down letters and substitution of letters next to each other in the "lay
   of the case."
2. Contingent error—typos due to accidents in the print shop, for instance,
   type shortages, broken characters, loosened chases during printing.
3. Compositorial error—mistakes and slips made by typesetters, for example,
   misreading the copy text due to some difficulty such as revision or foreign
   languages or missetting due to the compositor's own errancy.
4. Accidentals—variants due to orthographic habits, for example, of compositors, manuscript scribe, authors, or characters.
5. Slips—motivated errors attributed to characters or discourses by authors,
   for example, malapropisms and misquotations.
6. Mistakes—errors not located in the printing house or in the representational space, for example, memorial reconstructions, pirated plays, scribal
   pretensions, authorial revisions.

Each category stands in relation to another so that, for example, among the possible printing errors, some have to do with typesetting (1) and others with mechanical or economic problems of the printing house (2). Each category exists as a plausible explanation, but only in the realm of possibility. The plausibility of the categories disguises the fact that they are merely genetic hypotheses and as such are suspect. In addition, the rather technical, logical, and historical gestures encoded in these explanations give the appearance of scientific accuracy, which often disguises ideologically motivated choices. Hence, several problems arise. First, the categories, even in the abstract, are not firmly distinct. Second, they are treated as existing prior to or outside the text, when in fact they are created from and by the "text" through the material marks on the page. Thus, they are reified and codified. Third, the distinctions begin to evaporate in textual analyses that do not presuppose and maintain them.

To illustrate this I'll look to *Love's Labour's Lost,* one of the texts suspected as non-Shakespearean. The Pedant, better known as (though not always called) Holofernes, cites Mantuan, *"Facile precor gelida quando pecus omne sub umbra Ruminat* and so forth" (4.2.90); editors point out that the line is misquoted, thus an error. But whose error? Here the distinction between compositorial error, character slip, authorial lapse, or even actor-memorial failure (3, 5, 6, respectively) depends on factors other than technical discernment, factors pertaining to bibliographic and editorial assumptions such as class alignments (who knows Latin and who does not) and cultural-authorial investments ("A line so well known … could hardly be misquoted by Shakespeare").[20] I think this example goes far to demonstrate the possible motivations that might produce distinctions among types of error in order to reproduce distinctions of class, literacy, and creative genius.

There are other kinds of motivations at work as well. On the page, many errors look identical to each other, except perhaps for the most mechanical types such as upside-down letters, but even here it's a task to determine from the printed page whether the letter was set this way (1) or whether it was dislodged during the printing (2). Misprints could be 1, 2, or 3. Misspelling could be 3, 4, 5, or 6. Misprints and misspellings are hard to tell apart; therefore, all six explanations could apply. Add misquotation, corrupt foreign phrases, malapropisms, misattributed lines, repetition, unmetrical verse, and nonsense, to name a few of the textual problems treated as error, and the situation rapidly gets out of hand. How could one possibly give individual and distinctive causes for these "errors"? How could one begin to explain how one decides when something is "intentionally corrupt"?[21]

Some editors acknowledge for a fleeting moment that they stand on the edge of chaos and might even agree with E. K. Chambers that "the disintegration of Shakespeare is an open career for talent." Nevertheless, the textual pollutions are swiftly swept under the rug or at least disguised with prettier faces or uglier

hands, always with the pretext of being able to distinguish between mental ownership, citation, and parapraxes. That error signifies character through lapse is
something editors share with Freud; but more important, they share in their
mapping of misprints a tendency to invoke "an autonomous interdependent system of reified atemporal, nonhistorical terms, where the space and time for contingent events has vanished."[22] The editorial machine demarcates the printed text,
containing and fixing accidents on a determinate map of systematized meaning.
This might be called a modernist discourse network, yet it yields a network that
determines and is determined by both meaning and noise.

As soon as noise enters into the textual situation, otherness becomes a possible
and likely producer of the writing. Once this happens, the fortunes of textual
mastery and bibliographical knowledge become the misfortunes of accidents.
These errant particles of language become legible within a symptomatic reading
not because they contain inexhaustible meaning but rather because of their "remarkable insignificance."[23] As re-markable marks, they depend on the possibility
of repetition and iteration, but this repetition does not reproduce the same. The
accident insists on the "capacity for diversion" within the structure of the mark.
The structure determines the necessity of accident and is determined by it. In the
theoretical fiction of textual critics, the expectation of a ghostly authority for the
word prevents a recognition of accidents, which are only misrecognized as cor-
ruption, lapse, error, noise; and yet the project depends upon a characterization
of accidents in order to construct the authority it seeks and attempts to reproduce. One thing postmodernism has taught us is that reproduction is never "mechanical" in the fantasmatic sense of reprinting high-fidelity copies without error,
since it is always reproduction with a difference and a reproduction of difference.

The Corpus of Mechanical Reproduction

Immediate mediation like originary reproduction
also must resituate the originary scene of subject and object;
activity and life, being, begin in those duplications.
Originary prints. Everything begins with reproduction.[24]

The intrusions of accident and error introduce other noisy aliens to
Shakespeare's corpus. In accepting nonauthorial writing, we might go a little far-
ther and accept the possibility of what might be called nonagential writing. With
a notion of nonagential writing, either the drift of error, the interruptions of
noise, or the hardwiring of discourse, even if we found "what Shakespeare really
wrote," we would not be in a position any different from the one that didn't
bother to look, for nonagential writing would already structure "what
Shakespeare really wrote" just as much as it structures the media that constitute
the system of marks.

The print of the mechanical press is an etched surface that bears the marks of the processes of language, history, and intersubjective discourse that in this case might be tied to particular moments of the period we now call early modern, but this marking exceeds character, author, and editor, exceeds embodied and agential delimitations. Typographical "errors" might instead be read in light of technological change, for example, produced by the interference or "noise" of two separate media, a stage-centered speech transcription impacting with print conventions not accustomed to logographic style. The "errors" produced in this case do not belong to an individual, functionary or genius, but instead to a historically specific moment in which performative speech and theatrical handwriting meet a nascent technology and try to effect a translation into print conventions that have a different, although not completely separate, relation to writing.

Among Shakespeareans, the analysis of the "mediality" of writing and texts finds brilliant expression in the work of Randall McLeod, or Random Cloud, as he also calls himself. Like De Grazia, McLeod uncovers editorial contradictions that stem especially from "setting art above its material manifestation" and calls instead for the study of "the conditions of creation, production, and reception of literary art in the Renaissance."[25] He suggests a material foundation for editing: "since the reprinting of a book required the recomposition of its entire text, it is understandable that editors themselves saw transmission as an occasion for re-composition (to use the word in a different sense). ... All I wish to suggest by linking it with typesetting is that editing is consonant with the means of physical reproduction, and may be influenced by it."[26] McLeod counteracts the standard notion of transmission with the concept of "transformission" and says, even more strongly, that "we [must] recognize this transformissional dynamic not as some airy adjunct to textual study, but as running down so deep in text of the period, that it is ineradicable (unless, of course, you edit them) because, simply, it *is* text."[27]

Emphatically asserting the transformative traces in a text, textual nonidentity, he looks primarily at the "pure letters," especially at the setting of words as ligatures, not as letters, arguing that Renaissance readers would have governed their readings "by the mediation of the text by its types."[28] Yet as he scrutinizes the tiniest features, ligatures, catchwords, hyphens, he exhibits a fascination with the "pure play of letters"—as Charles Melman describes it, "a pure play of the symbolic, without any voice, without any link to the imaginary."[29] Melman pushes the metaphor even closer to McLeod's position: "It would be necessary, if I were to pursue this narrow path, to conceive of something like a typography in the unconscious, working unbeknown to the subject, producing his ideas. In the obsessional we see that the unconscious writes its messages letter by letter, exactly as a typographer would" (132). I cite Melman not to psychoanalyze the editors but to show a suggestive link between the technology of writing and what might be called the "technology of the subject." Along these lines, Friedrich Kittler has argued that the Lacanian orders themselves arise in a historically specific "discourse network" formed by typewriter, film, gramophone.[30] The symbolic is the world of the machine; the imaginary, the mirror image of the body; and the real, the disorder and accidents of bodies. He argues that Lacanian psychoanalysis is both the theory and the "historical effect of the material and technical differentiation" (114–115).

One could reconstrue the examples I've run through in these terms as well: the language of noise and error as the realm of disorder and accidents; the hand in Shakespeare's corpus as the realm of imaginary identifications, ghostly reflections, and the mirroring of the body; and the machine of mechanical reproduction as the voiceless typographic letters of the symbolic. Of course the problem is that the orders do not exist concretely like solid and distinct technological objects; they are entangled and simultaneous. If we extend this to my examples, we see a resistance to the material of the real and the symbolic marked by the recurrence of corporeal shapes in a play of identity.

Even McLeod's attention to the materiality of texts printed by the machine is haunted by specters and ghosts. When he contrasts the essential text fashioned by editorial tradition to the "existential" text reproduced by photofacsimile, McLeod still complains that even in the facsimile text, "our education inclines us to look upon the existential text as stripped rather than merely naked."[31] If the editor's desire is to strip the veil of print, the "un-editor's" desire is to see the print naked. In order to get down to the existential text, McLeod must strip the editorial clothing of the essential text; in so doing, he essentializes the veil of print, giving it full-bodied meaning. Although his investment in materiality is explicit, his orientation is skewed by a fantasmatic desire for a denuded page, one imagined as blank and as female. As Luce Irigaray writes, "Commodities, women, are a mirror of value of and for man. In order to serve as such, they give up their bodies to men as supporting material of specularization, of speculation. They yield to him their natural and social value as a locus of imprints, marks, and mirage of his activity."[32] The marks of the machine reflect the specularity of the ghostly identifications; now we have traced our way back to the hand in the corpus of Shakespeare's books.

This very long stick was a prefiguration of my pen: you can imagine
it as large as you wish, you may conceive it as infinite.
You can write with a stake:
what happens on the paper as a result is of no consequence
so long as this makes you understand that the figures behave
in the same way as the power.
They are communicated naked. You must conceive nudity
as the stripping away of the body: its disappearance.
I measure the motion of the mind in the body

by that of the fluid which flows through the entire body,
similar to the ink in the calamus.[33]

The fantasy of this configuration of writing and body should no longer surprise us. We see similar mystifications perpetuated and celebrated even in the most unlikely places. Look at the deliberately postmodern *Prospero's Books,* which might have taken its epigram from the hand of Nancy. Peter Greenaway's film fetishizes the book and the hand in writing even as he indulges in the high-tech pyrotechnics of high-resolution video insets and the hypertextuality seen in other projects. The blue, black, and brown fluids of writing are the liquids of the island realm—pools, drops, drips, and dribbles; water, ink, wax, and urine. His perfected technique communicates a phantasmagoria of naked bodies, books, food, fancy—all revolving around one thing, the mind behind the production, the magisterial presence of the creator, which is at once the voice of Gielgud, the vision of Greenaway, the vitality of the Bard. Even this hip high-tech cybernetic postmodern is haunted by the ghosts of the early-modern human. The living folios of *Prospero's Books* enact a humanist fantasy, not only a bibliophilic disinterment of the past but the extreme concretization of discourse into an encyclopedic curiosity closet, a becoming literal of the literary, words becoming flesh. To play with favorite themes from the hand of this auteur, *Prospero's Books* is a pageant of hunger for drowning by knowledge. In the end Prospero drowns his books, saving "Thirty-Five Plays" for dessert. In the folio are a handful of blank pages, for a little more writing by another auteur. How handy.

NOTES

1. This essay was first circulated in March 1992 at a Shakespeare Association session, "Postmodern/Early Modern: Critical Theory and Cultural Practice." I would like to thank in particular Don Wayne for organizing the group and Linda Charnes for her comments as a respondent. The proposed aim of the essay is to address the historically specific discursive technologies that constitute early modern literature as an object of study for postmodern cultural theory and critical practice. I selected fragments from recent figures who have focused on the materiality of written production, in this case, Donna Haraway's "A Cyborg Manifesto: Science, Technology, and Socialist-Feminism in the Late Twentieth Century," in *Simions, Cyborgs, and Women: The Reinvention of Nature* (New York: Routledge, 1991), 176; Jonathan Goldberg, *Writing Matter: From the Hand of the English Renaissance* (Stanford: Stanford University Press, 1989), 318; Jean-Luc Nancy, *"Dum Scribo," Oxford Literary Review* 3 (1978): 8. The limits of the format preclude a full-fledged discussion of these and other important writers (Michel Foucault, Jacques Derrida, Walter Benjamin, and Marshall McLuhan), but I hope that the fragments resonate in ways that are productive for further discussion. These theorists and critics often overlap with more historically oriented scholars interested in media change, literacy, and print technology, including Elizabeth Eisenstein, Walter Ong, Lucien Lefebvre, and Natalie Zemon Davis. In order to focus on

the materiality of Shakespeare's books, I have narrowed the examples primarily to the bibliographic field.

2. Elizabeth Pittenger, "Dispatch Quickly: The Mechanical Reproduction of Pages," *Shakespeare Quarterly* 42 (1991): 389–408.

3. Haraway, "A Cyborg Manifesto," 152. We will see this fantasy repeat. I prefer to stand it on its head: There was always the specter of the machine in the human. Precybernetic man was haunted by mechanical reproduction.

4. See, for instance, two important collections of bibliographic essays: *Shakespeare's Hand in the Play of Sir Thomas More*, edited by Alfred W. Pollard (Cambridge: Cambridge University Press, 1923); and *Shakespeare and Sir Thomas More: Essays on the Play and Its Shakespearean Interest*, edited by T. H. Howard-Hill (Cambridge: Cambridge University Press, 1989).

5. Jacques Derrida, "Freud and the Scene of Writing," in *Writing and Difference* (Chicago: University of Chicago Press, 1978), 226.

6. Goldberg, *Writing Matter*, 239. With some alterations for the context, my argument about the hand in *Sir Thomas More* (*STM*) agrees with Goldberg's sense that "rather than delivering an individual by writing in the proper hand, the proper hand delivers the individual within the socially marked spheres that differentiations in handwriting signify" (238–239).

7. The formative work to mention here is W. W. Greg's "The Handwriting of the Manuscript," in *Shakespeare's Hand*, 41–56. In addition to the essays already mentioned, see Edward Maunde Thompson, *Shakespeare's Handwriting* (Oxford: Clarendon Press, 1916), especially p. 30ff.

8. Alfred Pollard's "Introduction" to *Shakespeare's Hand* discusses the "Ill May Day" scenes, and he prints an appendix of accounts of "anti-alien disturbances of 1595, 1586, and 1593" (1–40). In the volume edited by T. H. Howard-Hill, William Long's "The Occasion of *The Book of Sir Thomas More*" discusses the role of the Officer of the Revels and censorship in the context of social upheaval and instability (45–56).

9. Recounted by J. Dover Wilson, "The New Way with Shakespeare's Texts, III," *Shakespeare Survey* 9 (1956): 73.

10. Thompson, *Shakespeare's Handwriting*, 30. With this and most of my examples, I don't mean to single out a critic but merely select a convenient exemplification of a particular, usually widely shared, tendency.

11. Scott McMillin, *The Elizabethan Theatre and The Book of Sir Thomas More* (Ithaca: Cornell University Press, 1987), 154. Subsequent references to this book are in the text.

12. McMillin, 158, citing W. W. Greg, Malone Society Reprint, xiii.

13. Nancy, "*Dum Scribo*," 8.

14. Clifford Leech, ed., *The Two Gentlemen of Verona* (New York: Methuen Press, 1969).

15. For instance, I could imagine an argument emphasizing the "discursive agency" of these texts, that is, the predominance of other discourses borrowed from earlier writing, Lyly for example, or intruding from the extensive rhetorical training that "hardwired" pedagogical subjects. In these plays, the characters do not own or operate discourses but are owned and operated by them.

16. Eleanor Prosser, *Shakespeare's Anonymous Editors* (Stanford: Stanford University Press, 1981).

17. Margreta De Grazia, "The Essential Shakespeare and the Material Book," *Textual Practice* 2 (1988): 69–86. Further references are cited in the text.

18. The metaphysical investment in the opposition between living spirit and dead letter is by now familiar from various Derridean writings.

19. Friedrich A. Kittler, *Discourse Networks, 1800/1900,* trans. Michael Metteer (Stanford: Stanford University Press, 1990), 300.

20. Arden editor, R. W. David, *Love's Labour's Lost* (New York: Methuen, 1951), 81, n. 90. The line "Fauste precor gelida" is described as "the one tag that even the worst of Grammar School dunces might be expected to remember."

21. R. W. David in *Love's Labour's Lost* continues in the note on the mistaken line "*Facile precor gelida*" that surely "the blunder is Holofernes'; and this raises the question of how far the other quotations from foreign languages are intentionally corrupt" (81, n. 90).

22. William Warner, *Chance and the Text of Experience: Freud, Nietzsche, and Shakespeare's Hamlet* (Ithaca: Cornell University Press, 1986), 42–47.

23. For a discussion of otherness and the "syntax of chance," see Barbara Johnson, "The Frame of Reference," in *The Purloined Poe,* eds. John P. Muller and William J. Richardson (Baltimore: Johns Hopkins University Press, 1988), 248–249. See Derrida's analysis of marks and re-marking in "My Chance/*Mes Chances,*" in *Taking Chances: Derrida, Psychoanalysis, and Literature,* edited by Joseph H. Smith and William Kerrigan (Baltimore: Johns Hopkins University Press, 1984), 15–17.

24. Goldberg, *Writing Matter,* 315, and Derrida, "Freud and the Scene of Writing," *Writing and Difference,* trans. Alan Bass (Chicago: University of Chicago Press, 1978), 199.

25. Random Cloud, "The Marriage of Good and Bad Quartos," *Shakespeare Quarterly* 33 (1982): 425.

26. Randall McLeod, "UnEditing Shake-speare," *Sub-stance* 33–34 (1982): 37.

27. Randall McLeod, "Information upon Information," paper presented at the International Shakespeare Conference in Stratford-upon-Avon, August 1988, typescript, 26.

28. McLeod, "Information," 9.

29. Charles Melman, "On Obsessional Neurosis," in *Returning to Freud: Clinical Psychoanalysis in the School of Lacan,* ed. Stuart Schneiderman (New Haven: Yale University Press, 1980), 134. Further references are cited in the text.

30. Friedrich Kittler, "Gramophone, Film, Typewriter," *October* 41 (1987): 101–118.

31. McLeod, "UnEditing," 37–38.

32. Luce Irigaray, "Women on the Market," *This Sex Which Is Not One,* trans. Catherine Porter (Ithaca: Cornell University Press, 1985), 177.

33. Nancy, "*Dum Scribo,*" 10–11.

13

The Cyborg Body Politic and
the New World Order

CHRIS HABLES GRAY & STEVEN MENTOR

*The union of the political and the physiological ... has been a major source of ancient
and modern justifications of domination, especially of domination based on differences seen as natural, given, inescapable, and therefore moral. ... We have allowed the
theory of the body politic to be split in such a way that natural knowledge is reincor-
porated covertly into techniques of social control instead of being transformed into
sciences of liberation.*

—Donna Haraway[1]

I N THE WORLD OF burgeoning transnational corporations and disintegrating
nation-states, why begin theorizing the body politic with Hobbes? Earlier Western bodies politic emphasized the analogy of the organic body to the social body,
usually with strict hierarchies of status and function. Head, heart, stomach, legs
and arms—all corresponded to groups and warranted their placement in a system
of difference enforced by might. From Plato and Plutarch through St. Paul and
John of Salisbury to Shakespeare writers attempted to lend coherence to the diversity of actual political and social situations by means of organic and physical analogy. This sought-for coherence, however, was illusory even on the textual plane,
as various political writers and actors manipulated the body metaphor for their
own ends. An organic conception of the state was often used to justify social in-
equality, but it also was used to justify the necessary cooperation of parts of society and contest the collapse of parts into the "head," be it Henry VIII's or the imperial pope's.[2]

For Hobbes, however, the "Body Politique" is not as much an organic metaphor as a mechanistic one: the robot body politic but *with a soul.* The state is a

Nature (the Art whereby God hath made and governes the World) is by the *Art* of man, as in many other things, so in this also imitated, that is can make an Artificial Animal. For seeing life is but a motion of Limbs, the beginning whereof is in some principall part within; why may we not say, that all *Automata* (Engines that move themselves by springs and wheels as doth a watch) have an artificiall life? For what is the *Heart,* but a *Spring;* and the *Nerves* but so many *Strings;* and the *Joynts,* but so many *Wheeles,* giving motion to the whole Body, such as was intended by the Artificer? *Art* goes yet further, imitating that Rationall and most excellent worke of Nature, *Man.* For by Art is created that great LEVIATHAN called a COMMON-WEALTH, or STATE, (in latine CIVITAS) which is but an Artificiall Man; though of greater stature and strength than the Naturall, for whose protection and defense it was intended; and in which, the *Soveraignty* is an Artificiall *Soul,* as giving life and motion to the whole body; The *Magistrates,* and other *Officers* of Judicature and Execution, artificiall *Joynts; Reward* and *Punishment* (by which fastned to the seate of the Soveraignty, every joynt and member is moved to performe his duty) are the *Nerves,* that do the same in the Body Naturall; The *Wealth* and *Riches* of all the particular members, are the *Strength; Salus Populi* (the *peoples safety*) its *Businesse; Councellors,* by whom all things needfull for it to know, are suggested unto it, are the *Memory; Equity* and *Lawes,* and artificiall *Reason* and *Will; Concord, Health; Sedition, Sicknesse;* and *Civill war, Death.* Lastly, the *Pacts* and *Covenants,* by which the parts of this Body Politique were at first made, set together, and united, resemble that *Fiat,* or the *Let us make man,* pronounced by God in the Creation.

—Thomas Hobbes, *Leviathan*
(original emphasis, 1651, 1985, pp. 81–82)

machine, its people parts, all in imitation of the "Body Naturall." Only the sovereign is significantly more, since he or she is a divinely created "Artificiall Soul." The soul, and God, are crucial parts of Hobbes's commonwealth, as the bulk of *Leviathan* is at pains to argue. The correspondence of this conceit to Rene Descartes's description of the human individual as a mere automaton with a divine soul is no accident. Today, Hobbesians and Cartesians certainly don't talk much about souls or the gigantic absence left in the commonwealth and in Cartesian man if their soul is missing. Yet as Michel Foucault explains, "It would be wrong to say that the soul is an illusion, or an ideological effect. On the contrary it exists, it has a reality, it is produced permanently around, on, within the body. ... This real, non-corporeal soul is not a substance; it is the element in which are articulated the effects of a certain type of power and the reference of a certain type of knowledge, the machinery by which the power relations give rise to a possible corpus of knowledge, and knowledge extends and reinforces the effects of this power. ... The soul is the effect and instrument of a political anatomy; the soul is the prison of the body."[3] Today, the "effect" and the very political "instrument" is the control system—cybernetic, informatic, defining, determining. Information, impatterned and wild, is the very context of life as well as the simulacra of essence, whether it is called consciousness, personality, individuality, or a unique cognitive system. Having machines, or seeing oneself as a machine, is one thing. Controlling machines, and oneself, is another. In hindsight it seems as if the machine age inevitably had to give way to the control revolution, but the machine was sovereign a good while.

By the end of the seventeenth century the Machine Age had triumphed in much philosophical and political thinking, at least rhetorically. By the nineteenth century it was hegemonic, in the form of Western imperialism, on land and sea and was taking aim at the sky. The Machine Age is now coming to an end, and with it the domination of machine metaphors. We now live in the Information Age, and what metaphor could be more fitting than that of the organism as an information system linked to prosthetic machines—the *cybernetic organism* also known as the *cyborg*. If the webs of information and power/knowledges incarcerate the organism today, they sustain and move it as well, just as Hobbes and Descartes felt that the soul sustained (and vitalized) the automaton body and the artificial body politic in a larger whole.

From our particular vantage in North America at the end of the twentieth century, the postmodern nation-state is certainly more of a cyborg than it is a machine with a divine soul. The postmodern state is a strange and still powerful creature that mixes humans, ecosystems, machines, and various complex softwares (from laws to the codes that control the nuclear weapons) in one vast cybernetic organism, linked itself in many ways to the rest of the polities and other forms of life on the earth.

And this Leviathan is not only soul and machine—it is also clearly text, as was the monster Hobbes imagined. The burden of Hobbes's introduction to *Leviathan* is to show how to read the text of the body politic. Hobbes chides those whose notion of political reading consists of gossip and censure; instead, he advises, "Nosce teipsum; Read thy self." That is, read the self as if it were a state with passions that are similar in all men (and all actual states). It is not enough to read men's actions, or the objects of their desires: "He that is to govern a whole Nation, must read in himself, not this, or that particular man, but Man-kind."[4] The only way to understand this strange machine-body of the state is to read the actual machine-body of the human being.

The famous title page of *Leviathan* fittingly bridges two different orders of body political discourse. On the one hand, the king's enormous form unites the citizens in an apparently organic unity, an image familiar to Hobbes's contemporaries. On the other, his body is not made up of organs, of different parts with very separate functions, but of a multiplicity of bodies, each of which contains a similar multiplicity. The king must read his own motivations, passions, and conflicts in order to comprehend the state of his subjects, in order to read the text of the state. As the natural body is a model for the automaton and for the machine-body of the state, so too the individual's thoughts are regulated by desire, which helps give Hobbes a picture of the way political thinking is regulated by desire as well. He textualizes desire for future goods as a fiction and suggests that discourse—words and speech—parallel the sovereign's function, to lend the body motion.

So even in Hobbes's time, we have an intersection of mechanical/scientific, discursive, and natural/organic metaphors for the state, which seems to be grounded on the discourse of actual bodies. From the Greeks on, theorists use the actual body and bodily functions to explain problems or loss of control or harmony in states. How can or ought the state to work? What controls the automaton or machine and how might one decipher this control? This in turn splits actual humans into natural and artificial bodies, individuals and decidedly "di-viduals," humans split between citizen and person, person and self, machine and organic life.

The answers Hobbes came up with are authoritarian to us—but they are certainly not foreign. The same questions bedevil our own times and structures; if anything, the invasion of the body by discourses of science and politics has accelerated beyond all imagination. We live in a society of cyborgs, of machines tightly coupled with "organic" bodies themselves denatured and reassembled, discursively as well as literally, under the knife of the surgeon or the hand of the prostheticist. The process that Hobbes saw and helped institute, the proliferation of selves, the joining of machine to natural image to make a hybrid, is with us with a vengeance. Hobbes joined the discourses of Galilean physics and Christian eschatology with the figures of the automaton and of the king; we confront the discourses of post-Einsteinian physics, cybernetics, and democracy with the figures of the cyborg citizen and the cyborg body politic.

Contemporary informatics make the postmodern state logistically workable, just as modern technologies made the modern state possible. Modern states, as well as modern science, the Machine Age, modern war, and European imperialism all developed simultaneously in a messy, bloody conversation and confrontation.[5] This is all the more sobering when we realize that today we are in the midst of a similar conversation, or more likely an elaboration of the same "modern" one, as technoscience and politics make another staggering transition, this time under the sign/trope of the cyborg instead of the soulful automaton.

A Proliferation of Cyborg Bodies

A cyborg, or cybernetic organism, is an organic creature (animal or human) intimately connected to the machine, exchanging information and perhaps energy in a homeostatic system. There are many actual cyborgs among us in society. Anyone with an artificial organ, limb, or supplement (such as a pacemaker), anyone reprogrammed to resist disease (immunization) or drugged to think/behave/feel better (psychopharmacology) is technically a cyborg.[6] But even if many individuals in the industrial and postindustrial countries aren't full cyborgs, we all live in a "cyborg society."[7] Machines are intimately interfaced with humans on almost every level of existence, not only in the West and Japan but among the elite in almost every country of the world.

The range of these intimate human-machine relationships, however, is just as significant. There is no one kind of cyborg. To borrow from the future/present world of science fiction, where most cyborg theorizing has taken place, cyborgs can range from the barely organic Terminator, merely a human skin over a complete robot, to Chief Engineer Geordi of the liberal United Nations/Planets multicultural fantasy *Star Trek: The Next Generation* with his simple visual prosthetic visor (and our colleague with the myloelectric prosthetic arm). Cyborgs can be rugged individuals, but they are usually trapped in intense corporate settings, for example, the "six-million-dollar man," who works for U.S. intelligence, and "Robocop," who is with the Detroit police (both are in TV series of the same names). This is only fitting, as real cyborg technology requires incredible institutional support. Future institutional cyborgs include the fighter-bomber pilot in the state-of-the-art cockpit who can target enemies with his eyes, fire missiles with his voice, and use computers to monitor his own body and to create a disembodied God's-eye view of the battle. They also include the potentially billions of humans, yet unborn, who are the products of genetic engineering. Or the cyborg can become the institution itself, as with the group-mind totalitarian civilization of the Borg, inhabitants of *Star Trek: The Next Generation*. There is a proliferation of these cyborg creatures, real and imagined, and in some subcultures they are ubiquitous: the military, medicine, computer science, science fiction.

Cyborgology is not simple. The range of human-machine couplings is immense. Even just looking at contemporary existing cyborgs we note how they range from the quadriplegic patient totally dependent on a vast array of high-tech equipment to a small child with one immunization. The patient on a kidney machine twice a week or the combat pilot attached to his warcraft with sensors and complex interfaces for flights are both intermittent cyborgs, and yet between them there is a tremendous difference. The patient uses cyborg technologies to maintain his or her human body; the pilot cyborg is an enhanced human, a man-plus. Other distinctions become readily apparent, and it is easy to note differences between neo-, ultra-, semi-, meta-, hyper-, retro-, mega-, and many other types of cyborgs. There is no simple correlation between the different permutations of actual and potential cyborgs and the possible cyborg citizens and cyborg body politics of today and the future, but there are striking similarities, some of which we explore here.[8]

Science fiction also offers us a complex collection of incredibly militarized cyborgs, unsurprising, since most existing cyborg technology has military origins;

civilian medical research is another important source.[9] The other major centers of actual cyborg research are entertainment and work (the computer industry, certainly, but also the cyberneticization of industry). Together, these four cyborg-ology centers map another set of distinctions between types of cyborgs. Cyborg technologies can be restorative in that they restore lost functions and replace lost organs and limbs, as most are in medicine, or they can be enhancing, which is what most of the military and industrial research aims for. These latter projects seek to construct everything from factories controlled by a handful of "worker-pilots" to infantrymen in mind-controlled exoskeletons to the realization of that very important dream many computer scientists have of downloading their consciousness into immortal computers. Cyborg advances in entertainment offer the possibility of more ambiguous changes that neither enhance nor restore humans but just alter them, or perhaps even degrade them into addicts of direct neuro-stimulation or more virtual thrills.[10]

Body Politics:
Thesis, Antithesis, Synthesis, Prosthesis

Contemporary images of the body politic continue to reflect the mappers' desire for coherence and readability, for the reduction of social conflicts to bodies or units capable of control, and for the containment of new technologies (of self as well as science and industry) that have broken traditional boundaries and threaten the figures and metaphors of political discourse. This is painfully obvious in the case of contemporary technoscientific policies.

To give but one out of many possible examples, the Office of Science and Technology Policy has put out two glossy reports called *Grand Challenges: High Performance Computing and Communications*.[11] Both reports feature covers on which eight computer-generated graphics circle a map of the United States; on the first (1992) cover a startling set of graphics is connected by relatively crude dots to a network inscribed on the U.S. map. The United States is meant to contain these radically different screens and the discourses they represent—a numerically modeled thunderstorm, a space vehicle, an image of the earth's biosphere components, and prototypes of a wafer and a multichip. That these projects are connected by Hobbes's bloodline of wealth and capital is clear—all are in need of the funding that the producers of such reports are in search of. But also, the country is literally turned into a cybernetic network, of which these images are moments, produced by nodes on the network and in communication (ideally) with all other nodes. This is the discourse that must be controlled; in a sense, these are images of a sublime body politic capable of containing and organizing the ultramicroscopic (cells, wafers) and the gargantuan (the biosphere, space).

The second *Grand Challenges* report (1993) goes further in mapping the landscape of the cyborg body politic (see Figure 13.1). Again, eight computer-generated images, all full color, wildly different, and of widely differing scales, are ar-

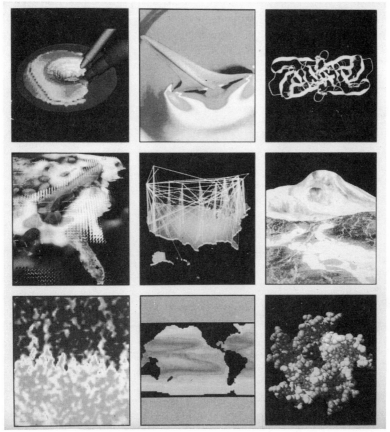

FIGURE 13.1

ranged around a U.S. map. But now the map is included as a figure in the text proper and named "Network Connectivity" (Figure 13.2). Like its predecessor, this U.S. map is strangely sovereign—there are no other countries next to it, and it glows blue and three-dimensional in a black void. Above it hovers a bright yellow network of what look like telecommunication lines, fiber optic webs; the caption makes use of both body and network figures: "The image represents the interconnected 'backbone' networks of NSF, NASA, and DOE, together with selected client regional and campus area networks. Nodes of the backbones are represented as connected spheres on a place above the outline of the United States; the client networks are represented as dendritic lines from the backbone nodes to the geographical locations where the client networks attach." "Backbone" must be in quotes at first, as it is strange to anthropomorphize such an image; yet by the second sentence, it is already naturalized. There is no Hobbesian kingly head (though it is implicitly in Washington, D.C., where NSF, NASA, and DOE net-

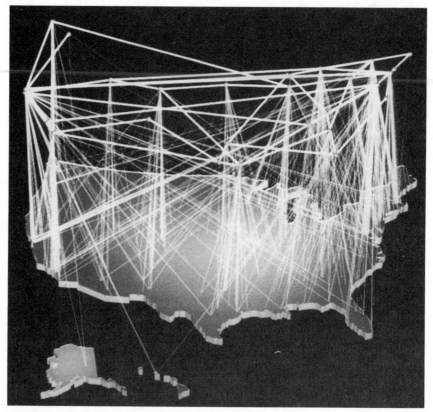

FIGURE 13.2

works converge), yet "backbone" signifies strength as much as Leviathan's gargantuan sword, and this image, too, hovers over the more familiar geography of
the nation. A dendrite is, of course, a branching figure or marking; the trees that
still dotted England's green and pleasant land in 1651 are here replanted as neu-
rons, conducting their impulses toward the cellular nodes. This anatomy is one of
power; it is the body of the artificial man who will confront the "grand challenges" to national power and sovereignty and unify the divided and contentious
bodies (here, competing scientific discourses and the people who represent/are
represented by them) in an ideal form.

What does a citizen of this body politic look like? Figure 13.3, "Network Applications," again presents the U.S. map, but this time nodes of the network are
themselves represented: data (not financial) banks, libraries, research institutions. These "real" geographic institutions are brought together and contained
not by the map itself but by a screen on which the institutions are shown as overlapping displays. Hobbes argued that only the king could set the whole machine
in motion and that the king must control this discourse; here the screen reads

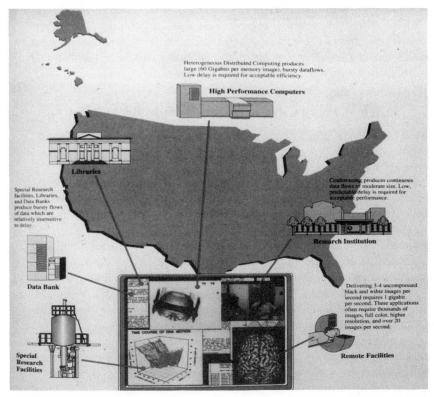

FIGURE 13.3   Network Applications

"Time Course of DNA Motion," linking the discursive text of databanks with the "bursty flows" of high-performance computers, an image of an individual brain, and a real-time conference between scientists using the screens.

Despite the obligatory technologese (the network will "promote enhancements in networking infrastructure"), what we are looking at is a mininarrative of the new Frankenstein's cyborg. The remote-facility graphic shows a human lying prone, presumably undergoing a CAT scan; the individual subject may be ill or even dying, but the viewer (who is in the position of operating the screen) can literally unlock the motion not just of political subjects but of individual minds through talking to machines and humans through a machine connected to other humans and/at machines. Notice the proliferation of different body images— photoimage of brain; computer graph of brain data; forehead bound by straps; video of actual humans, faces, torsos, clothes—all shrunk to fit a corner of the screen.

Older body political maps were based on organic and machine models. Subjects are bodies and, like bodies in Newtonian physics, are subject to certain laws and predictions. Political machines made use of these laws, gauging ways to strike the bodies in order to produce the desired chain of actions and reactions. Every action produced an equal and opposite reaction—revolutions turned Thermidorian; pendulums swung; increasingly mass societies behaved like Newtonian masses, obeying laws of inertia and motion, of thesis, antithesis, and then synthesis. Today, however, synthesis is followed by prosthesis.[12]

The Cyborg Citizen: Mapping Multiple Subjects

Rumors of my death have been greatly exaggerated.

—The Political Subject (with apologies to Samuel Clemens)

Who are the subjects of such a cyborg body politic? Hobbes's notion of the commonwealth's citizen-selves was based on a new powerful link between real bodies and a real (governing) machine; but machines were then in their infancy, and the state was correspondingly feeble. Who is the subject of today's incredible (political) machinery controlled through the theories of mainstream political science, scientific management, systems analysis, and strategic studies—all types of information theory fundamentally based on that hypothetical automaton *without* a soul, the "rational man," and on cybernetics with its feedback loops and learning curves, its network dynamics, its number crunching, its modeling and simulating, and its machines based on the integrated circuit?

Contemporary attacks on humanist notions of self-aware identity and clear boundaries of self parallel the development of cybernetic and information metaphors in discourse. Derrida and Lacan attack the presence/absence determinations of difference in language, subjecting linguistic technologies (a key type of prosthetic and one of the earliest enhancing technologies) to arguably infinite regresses of deconstruction and antifoundational critiques. By now it is a commonplace to assert that the speaker is not the origin of meaning of her utterance, that it is only through language, with its system of difference, that speakers can constitute themselves as subjects. Derrida insists that "the subject (self-identical or even conscious of self identity, self consciousness) is inscribed in the language, that he is a 'function' of the language. He becomes a speaking subject only by conforming speech … to the system of linguistic prescriptions taken as the system of differences."[13] As the child enters the symbolic order, she learns first to identify with "I," the subject of her sentences, and then with a series of other subject positions in signifying systems. Catherine Belsey argues, "'Identity,' subjectivity, is thus a matrix of subject-positions, which may be inconsistent or even in contradiction with one another. Subjectivity, then, is linguistically and discursively constructed and displaced across the range of discourses in which the concrete individual participates."[14]

This critique has caused great distress in political circles, much as the powerful techniques of sixteenth- and seventeenth-century skepticism undercut political stances of that day. It is easy to see why. If political discourse depends on talking about self-present subjects who can know their own interests, can enter into covenants as Hobbes believed, or mobilize bodies of resistance and self-protection as Kropotkin, Gramsci, and countless other leftist theorists have argued, then undercutting the ability of the individual to do this apparently eliminates or cripples political agency. For example, feminists who argue that women as women can unite as a body, can assume identities based on biology, fear that the poststructuralist critique leaves them without a strategic place from which to battle patriarchal Leviathans, whether liberal democratic, state socialist, or fundamentalist.

This is what makes the cyborg subject so interesting; on the one hand, it participates in a decentering of traditional subjectivity, of the metaphysics of presence, of the organic or essential identity and body; on the other, it offers a physical and bodily experience of what some feminists call strategic subjectivities. The promise and the danger of the cyborgs we are becoming bear striking resemblance to what various feminists argue we need: experiencing difference without opposition, rejecting a science of origins and telos, and embracing and exploring multiple, overlapping subjectivities. The subject, as Foucault reminds us, comes into play as the subject of law, of the Father's symbolic order tied to political power; if the cyborg confronts a law, it is likely to be the law of the machine, of interface with other machines and cyborgs. Without a clear origin, the cyborg does not dream of being outside of representation, outside the politics of representation; but the bodies, the voices, and the mutable boundaries of cyborg representation offer radical possibilities.

These possibilities, we want to argue, are not just potential sites for enacting the new subjectivities that some political theorists say are crucial to political agency; they are also internships and embodied practices in the modes of operation and power of material bodies politic of the late twentieth and twenty-first centuries. For example, it is no longer enough to feel represented by a government (if it ever was); now a citizen of the cybernetic political world inhabits various bodies interfaced more or less intimately with various prosthetics, all models for political structures that subject and partially construct us. Manipulating these bodies, in concert with others so embodied, is crucial for learning to reconstruct political bodies.

The Subject Is Dead! Long Live the Subject!

Man has, as it were, become a kind of prosthetic god. When he puts on all his auxiliary organs, he is magnificent; but these organs have not grown on him, and they still give him trouble at times.

—Sigmund Freud[15]

Just as discourses about the state and its machinery filtered down to the human body, inscribing it with a certain subjectivity and allowing us to see it doubled and complicated, so too the discourse of cybernetics—discourse embedded in the knowledge of all networks, including but not limited to the state and economic powers—becomes a way to resee the body itself, reconfigure its boundaries and possibilities.

The cyborg citizen is the meeting site of two important but often opposed orders of discourse. On the one side are those who want to keep humans in their place in the great chain of being. According to this analysis we can think only in and through the human body as organic whole; yet our current language for dealing with birth, death, livelihood, and government is dominated by metaphors of system, structure, field, and technology that make it difficult or impossible to speak about real human needs. At this site, small is beautiful, and the human scale is reasserted as a way of rebuilding societies so that real humans could potentially manage them and so that real democracy would have a chance of flourishing. On the other side are those who believe only in the chain of reason and the long march of rational man. They see a political landscape of technosciences and bureaucracies, the intricate modern state, the multinational corporation, and the complex technologies of energy and waste treatment as the inevitable forms for managing contemporary societies. To them, human scale is an impossible nostalgia, an irresponsible Luddism, a politically naive standpoint.

Cyborgs embody these contradictions. As Haraway points out, cyborg bodies can take pleasure in machine skill and thus have embodied reasons not to demonize it in favor of some mythical organic origin or unity; but they also have "an intimate knowledge of boundaries, their construction and deconstruction" crucial to reconstructing the boundaries and technologies of daily life and the networks of power. If "our bodies are maps of power and identity,"[16] then cyborgs offer a new map, a new way to conceive of power and identity, one potentially more effective in understanding, confronting, and reshaping the actual networks of power in late capitalism and its mutations.

Indeed, speaking of "the" body, "my" body, is in some ways a strange thing for a cyborg to say. The cyborg body politic is at times a web, a shifting chain of interrelated bodies, some human-machine, some machine. The cyborg is, by definition, one homeostatic system, but it is also interconnected to many networks. From one perspective it is just one node in a vast network, and as that net becomes an image of a political body, it certainly reconfigures what we mean by political machine, and by political community. In an age where power is multiply enacted and bodily dispersed, the cyborg citizen can claim multiple bodies and multiple communities, thanks to its multiple connections. This isn't just a case of linking traditional bodies, getting "bodies" to the demonstration or voting booth, though that happens; it is relearning what a community might feel like as gender becomes ambiguous (which sex[es] am I linked up with?), as persuasion and argument are made more, not less, available, and as information can be amassed from diverse points and concentrated at one location.

As the geography of the body is shifted, so too is the sense of what constitutes a political body or group, and so are the skills and resources that are made available. It is one thing for a progressive company to picture a telephone over the caption "political machine," implying that calls to your Congress creature represent the apex of influence; it is another to conceive of oneself intimately connected to machines and cyborgs, learning the codes of net power, composing and recomposing "prosthetic aesthetics" in the form of teleconferencing, information and argument dispersal, and accessing "official" nets for purposes educational and interceptive. Cybernetics is all about feedback loops and adjustments; we don't know what social and political potential humans have when they are (arguably) freed from the more insidious interpellations of identity, gender, and one-way representation.

This is a political myth, of course, one with plenty of possible dystopian endings as well, from humans going insane inside completely mechanical prostheses to the creation of superhumans with ambiguous relations to "normal" humans.[17] Andrew Gordon has made a useful analysis of these two tendencies in cyborg sci fi. Following Patricia Warrick, he notices a tendency toward either closed-system models (dystopian "visions of destructive technology based on extrapolation from current trends) or open-system models (utopian notions of man-machine symbiosis and evolution).[18] Both visions are being enacted today. Gordon goes on to challenge open-system models in order to deal with and suggest ways to overcome the real fears of the closed-system stories. This may be the real grand challenge for twenty-first-century cyborg citizens.

If, as most argue, the current forms of the nation-state—the "sovereign" state and its correlate, the sovereign individual—are hopelessly incapable of confronting the new sources and configurations of power or of limiting the boundary-shifting forms of multinationals, then we are in an important period of transition, one not dissimilar to Hobbes's time. To what extent will these emergent bodies politically terrify their subjects, tying them to technologies as the lesser half, thrusting implants and software past the boundaries of the organic body in the psychic and emotional equivalent of the bodily horrors of the industrial revolution? How successful will average citizens be in resisting the most noxious forms this will take at the level of government, work, even home and sexual life? We feel that this will depend on choosing to inhabit this new world, exploring cyborg subjectivity as a form of pleasure and power, building new political bodies and bodies of bodies across the nets, and learning the various new boundaries and limitations, learning indeed what might count as action and agency in the age of information.

The cyborg comes after the overstated "death of the subject"; the cyborg is an answer to the question, Who comes after the subject? The cyborg is a meeting place between those unwilling to give up notions of strategic subjectivities and those bent on the liberatory projects that assume the destruction of masterly, coherent selves, "achieved (cultural) or innate (biological)."[19] And the cyborg, especially, can be a place to learn a new conception of agency, what Judith Butler calls "an instituted practice in a field of enabling constraints."[20] Field, network, web—these "inhuman" metaphors, these apparent antitheses to an organic "bodily knowledge" and scale—are not just the arena in which we must bring our bodies and selves to act. They are the new geopolitical territories to be inhabited and contested; they are sites of both current and potential imperialism; of racism, oppression, and multiply-gendered games; of reasonably sophisticated resistances to aforementioned aggressions; and of new possibilities for engaging inappropriate/d others and dispersed bodies of community and power. Cyborgs are trapped in patriarchal and late-capitalist agencies, dependent on institutions while transforming them utterly, and involved in the crucial enactment of new forms of agency negotiating with and confronting central intelligence through dispersed, diverse bodies of information and communication.

The sites of these negotiations and confrontations are multiple and diverse, and they are all cyborg body politics.

Two, Three, Many, Cyborg Body Politics

Recall that it is not only that men make wars, but that wars make men.

—Barbara Ehrenreich[21]

The age of the hegemony of the nation-state is ending. For Hobbes, the world was ideally a community of Leviathans, autonomous nation-states with clear borders and stable sovereigns. Today, the world map is certainly less clear. There is a proliferation of political forms that overlap and even contradict each other; as postmodern states struggle against devolution from below and empire from above, their bodies are drained of sovereignty by multinational corporations on one side and nongovernmental organizations and international subcultures sustained by worldwide mass telecommunications on the other.[22]

The crude and bloody prosthetic surgery being performed on Yugoslavia and on various limbs of the former Union of Soviet Socialist Republics is replayed daily on TV as various retro-cyborg body politics struggle for survival. Similar tendencies to reconstruct the past out of the bodies of today can be seen on the same newscasts, whether it is the proto-retro-cyborg body politics of Europe and Central Asia delimited by language or dialect (Catalans, Welsh, Basques, Scots, Walloons, Quebecois, Kurds), the tribes of Ethiopia and the Sudan, or the clans of Somalia. Movements that we might judge pseudo-retro-cyborg body politics in the form of Christian fundamentalists seeking to establish ideal Christian states or the somewhat more successful movements of Hindus (in India) and Muslims (in Iran) can also achieve state power. But nationalist and religious systems are not the only ones vying for the right to define the dominant body politic in contemporary nation-states; there are economic conglomerations as well.

Many cyborg theorists disguised as writers of cyberpunk SF see nationalism declining[23] and predict that the body politic of the future will be those cyborg industries that meld great skill at information processing and personnel management into tremendous profits and powers. Already today corporations are legally individuals in the United States, and a company such as ITT is as much a sovereign state as Luxembourg, perhaps more so; Gulf and Texaco, British Petroleum (BP) and SoCal, are more involved in foreign policy negotiations and diplomacy than many U.N. members.[24] Not only do multinational corporations seem to be accruing sovereignty, but they are forming great alliances of corporations that seriously challenge all but the most powerful countries. These corporate bodies are spread over vast areas, linked by nets, faxes, and fiber optics communications technologies. Along these nets real power flows.

And these nets, woven by technoscience and cast by power, have changed the very nature of late capitalism. John R.R. Christie, commenting on William Gibson's cyberpunk classic *Neuromancer,* suggests that its fictional cyberspace helped readers see the new "space" of capital:

> Questions beginning "where" and "when," with reference to the location, timing, and operation of the instruments especially of finance capital, moved impressively out of mundane apprehension in the eighties, and *Neuromancer's* cyberspace was a by-no-means negligible devise for revisualizing such operations in networked electronic space, in terms that clarified the bankruptcy of classic and modern conceptions. Such space became increasingly metaphoric in nature, for literally it is no space, no place at all. All it requires is the actualization of information potential at points of access as indefinitely extendible as the supraglobal electronic signaling network. ... the money bank become the memory bank, where the wild time blows.[25]

If the field of capital, and its mechanisms of control, are increasingly virtual, the configurations within that supraglobal network are also capable of strange shape-changing. Richard Gordon argues that more and more companies are being "forced into strategic alliances." He describes it as "the competitive socialization of capital ... across national groupings of competitive corporate blocs."[26] He has charted these developing networks of European, Japanese, and North American transnational corporations as they form into alliances to compete with other European, Japanese, North American transnational alliances, and they are clearly a powerful and fast-growing force in the world political economy.

This has led to a reversal of roles with the state. The axis of competition is shifting from nations to these corporate alliances, and so is economic initiative and power. Richard Gordon marks four major aspects of this "new world economy":

> The importance of telematics. In other words, *information,* especially in terms of the telephones, faxes, modems, and computers that make transnational corporate alliances possible.

The liberation of investment and the liberalization of credit.

The globalization of production.

The shifting material logic of production. Specifically the increasing R&D costs, the shortening of production cycles, the change in demand structures toward diversity and variation, and the convergence of much production technology.

And yet, as the corporations form mega-alliances, networks of economic mega-cyborgs, the capitalist class (yes, those people who control capital) unites on a different level in a number of different political bodies, often disguised as private clubs or public service organizations. One of the most interesting of these is the Trilateral Commission, a group of leaders from industry, government, and academia representing Western Europe, Japan, and North America. This group is particularly interesting because it has been heralding the decline of the nation-state for over fifteen years. "The public and leaders of most countries continue to live in a mental universe which no longer exists—a world of separate nations—and have great difficulties thinking in terms of global perspectives and interdependence. ... The liberal premise of a separation between the political and economic realm is obsolete: issues related to economics are at the heart of modern politics."[27] The Trilateral Commission exercises its power in many ways, including some that would give joy to any conspiracy theorist. But its most potent weapons are its most public: economic and political influence. In both these realms money and physical force are important, but so is rhetoric, known by many as marketing today. Holly Sklar points out, "Marketing—the art of repeatedly displacing and creating new "needs"—is the key to expanding consumption. But it is more. Marketing, like militarism, is a means of *managing social change*."[28]

Where political or economic marketing fail, militarism is available to remake the body politic, and it has been applied lately internally (in Burma and Haiti) and externally in Kuwait (by Iraq), Panama, Iraq, and Somalia. The U.S. military, being one of the most advanced cyborg bodies in the world, has been particularly prolific in its political role in the postmodern era. Now, with the end of the capitalist-Communist Cold War, the possibility of a world dominated by the United States, a Pax Americana, seems quite real.

The incredible U.S. cyborg military, designed around superlative command, control, communications, intelligence, and computers,[29] is the main reason the United States has achieved at least temporary hegemony in the world, although it is far from omnipotent. But in true cyborg fashion, U.S. power isn't based just on its military bodies or on the economic corps that underlie, precede, and succeed the military. Equally important is the cultural influence of the United States. Political power is a combination of military/economic and cultural power. Power (coercive, constructive, and potential) in society is determined by the social and cultural norms that are accepted as given by most of the participants. These represent the rules of public discourse and include ideas of what is appropriate for each gender, what is beautiful, what is moral, and what is not. Whether it is the tax system or the TV show *Life Styles of the Rich and Famous,* the institutions and individuals that make up society are shaped by these rules and the metarules that regulate them.

When considered in this way, the hegemony of the United States seems even more secure than ever. This is a world surprised by the proliferation of liberal-capitalist representative democracies, impressed by the wonders of U.S. science, stunned by the expansion of U.S. culture, frightened by the destructive force of the U.S. high-tech military, and stupefied by the spread of U.S. styles of consumerism and consumption.

Cyborgs are also the children of war, and there is a real chance that the dominant cyborg body politics of the future will be military information societies much like the United States. For now, in the "new world (dis)order" we can see the proliferation of cyborg body politics and polities within a general frame that seeks to continue the basic competitive structure of the modern world system, which is to say that war and rumors of war seem likely.

This is exactly what some nervous Western analysts predict: economic, maybe even real, war between the competing powers of the future. Regis Debray, for one, openly proclaims, "The twenty-first century will resemble the nineteenth."[30] What a horrible thought. However, it does seem that there could well be a proliferation of power blocs and bloc conflicts. These might include conflicts among such mega-cyborg body politics as the "pentarchy" of China, Japan, the United States, Europe, and the former USSR; American, European, and Japanese blocs; the Fifth Reich and everyone else; American/Pacific and Eurasian alliances; the West and the East; or the North and the South.

It is important to notice the development of an Asian common market linking Japan and the four tigers/little dragons and Australia. There is now a united Europe around a united Germany, and an American bloc is developing, incorporating the United States, Canada, and the dominated economies of Latin America. These blocs are growing, but at the same time there are other alliances—OPEC, the Arab League, and the OAS—as evidence that the general economic advantage of the West and Far East over the rest of the world is hardly permanent.

Paul Kennedy sees this as an inevitable shift: "There will be a shift, both in shares of total world product and total world military spending from the five largest concentrations of strength to many more nations; but that will be a gradual process, and no other state is likely to join the present 'pentarchy' of the United States, the USSR, China, Japan, and the EEC in the near future."[31]

However, just as possible is something considerably more benign than a new round of world war, even if it is cold. If Thomas Hobbes is at all right and people must be protected from each other, it is even more true that the people of the world must be protected from their state governments, and those governments from each other. Ever since the astronauts looked down upon the earth, the idea that it is one system or organism (or both) has been gaining currency. The utility of the notion of Gaia,[32] the truths behind the glib idea of "spaceship earth," and the existence of the global market all argue that there will be an increase in world-wide coordination. Perhaps that strange cybernetic organism, that loose network with a growing number of battalions in the field, that dream of a world body politic, the United Nations, might evolve into something that can reconcile many different large political bodies, from nation-states to multinationals, with the many small ones, communities and persons.

In fact, the proliferation of U.N. peacekeeping missions (fourteen since 1988) has led to a changed conception of this "world body." In his already much-quoted article in *Foreign Affairs*, Secretary General Boutros Boutros-Ghali negotiates the paradoxes of national sovereignty in a world of competing networks and bodies. Consider the contradictory language within Boutros-Ghali's rhetoric. The entrance of various new countries such as Bosnia-Herzegovina and Uzbekistan into the United Nations "reaffirms the concept of the state as the basic entity of international relations and the means by which peoples find a unity and a voice in the world community."[33] But right away he qualifies this and also indicates a changed notion of sovereignty: "It is undeniable that the centuries-old doctrine of absolute and exclusive sovereignty no longer stands, and was in fact never so absolute as it was conceived to be in theory. A major intellectual requirement of our time is to rethink the question of sovereignty ... to recognize that it may take more than one form and perform more than one function."[34] He goes on to say that states and their governments can't solve today's world problems alone.

What will help? Note his cyborgian concern with information and communication: "Nothing can match the UN's global network of information-gathering and constructive activity, which reaches from modern world centers of power down to villages and families."[35] He goes on to sketch a very complex, hypercyborg body politic on the world level involving many different political embodiments. He mentions the huge network of NGOs (nongovernmental organizations; there are over 1,000 active NGOs in the United Nations) as the locus of new possibilities for interactive contributions to world organization. This trend, he says, is deep: "Relationships among nations are increasingly shaped by continuous interaction among entire bodies politic and economic. Such activity almost resembles a force of nature. ... Governments increasingly prove ineffective in efforts to guide or even keep track of these flows of ideas, influences, and transactions."[36] Cyborg body politics may abound in our view, but how does that help us understand, and influence, today's politics?

The Work the Cyborg Metaphor Can Do

In their remarkable book on the philosophical debates between Thomas Hobbes and Robert Boyle, *Leviathan Versus the Air-Pump*, Steven Shapin and Simon

Schaffer point out that Hobbes and Boyle had very different ideas about the nature of the body politic. "In the body politic of the Hobbesian philosophical place, the mind was the undisputed master of the eyes and the hands. ... In the body politic of the experimental community, mastery was constitutionally restricted." For Hobbes, the king (Leviathan's soul-mind) had to be supreme to prevent chaos. For Boyle and his fellows in the Royal Society, the mind was merely, to quote one member, part of a "chain" made up of "links" from "Hands" and "Eyes" to "Memory" and "Reason" and about again in "a continual passage round from one Faculty to another." In other words, the soul of Hobbes (and Descartes) is replaced by the cybernetic "chain of links" going "round" and round, one controlling metaphor replaced by another.[37] To the members of the Royal Society, perhaps the human was an automaton, as Hobbes and Descartes imagined, but instead of a soul this automaton was animated by a will to knowledge inflamed by epistemophilia and the desire to bear brain-children.[38] All this is framed by a great and old promise, the Promethean promise of freedom.

As Shapin and Schaffer remark, "Hobbesian man differed from Boylean man precisely in the latter's possession of free will and in the role of that will in constituting knowledge. Hobbesian philosophy did not seek the foundations of knowledge in witnessed and testified matters of fact: one did not ground philosophy in 'dreams.'" But it was not a dream of total freedom. In contrast to Hobbes's absolutism (Leviathan), the scientists wanted some "middle way" between tyranny and democracy. Liberal technocracy doesn't seem a bad label. Shapin and Schaffen indicate this when they mention that many have noticed "an intimate and an important relationship between the form of life of experimental natural science and the political forms of liberal and pluralistic societies." But times change. "Now we live in a less certain age. ... We regard our scientific knowledge as open and accessible in principle, but the public does not understand it. Scientific journals are in our public libraries, but they are written in a language alien to the citizenry. We say that our laboratories constitute some of our most open professional spaces, yet the public does not enter them. Our society is said to be democratic, but the public cannot call to account what they cannot comprehend."[39] Along with Shapin and Schaffer we also justly doubt both "liberal rhetoric" and the "traditional characterization of science." Actually, for some, as for us, the "questions of politics and science are not separate, but simultaneous and similar."[40] At the least both are askable. "As we come to recognize the conventional and artifactual status of our forms of knowing, we put ourselves in a position to realize that it is ourselves and not reality that is responsible for what we know. Knowledge, as much as the state, is the product of human actions. Hobbes was right."[41]

Hobbes may well have been right about the social production of knowledge, but his arguments for Leviathan are not convincing. The automaton with a will of the Royal Society, where the system reigns supreme under the sign of science, triumphed clearly over the automaton with a soul. Now, however, with the cybernetic/organic body politic there is a creature beyond a body-as-machine or machine-with-a-will synthesis; now these synthetic creations are attached to an organic body as prosthesis, or perhaps it is the other way around. In either case, the result is a cyborg of some sort. Just as some claimed the subject was disappearing, the body, sweating and farting, dying and breeding, working out, worked over, and overworked, has made its shocking reappearance. Not that the body really left; it just wasn't so noticeable there for a while, but it remained as important as ever.[42] Now it is just cyborgized. Understanding this reminds us of several things:

The Notion of the Cyborg Citizen Helps Us Read Postmodern Subjectivity. Through this reading we can see how some contemporary conceptions of identity aren't simply relativistic, leveling, or nihilistic but actually serve as pragmatic rehearsals of the selves we well may have to become in order to contest and inhabit the world we are continually (re)constructing.

The Cyborg Is Not Pure, and This Is an Important Ecological Insight. Nature is not pure wilderness and the Disneylands are not purely artificial. We will not live in harmony with the earth until we develop a more realistic notion of ways we create nature as a category and until we have more respect for the complexity of the natural world and can see a rain forest as a living organism and as a cybernetic system that includes "natural" and "artificial" elements with complex feedback and with homeostatic and data-manipulation structures that sustain it.

The Cyborg Metaphor Changes Possible Notions of Resistance. Agents of change might do well to move beyond identity politics toward various politics of affinity and association. It is clear that the sovereign nation-state is not the only important body. Transnational nets and local micropolitical systems are also key sites for "empowerment" and negotiations with power. The decline of state sovereignty, the emergence of hybrids mixing "archaic" formations with new technologies—fundamentalists with AK-47s, Somali youth driving trucks with antiair weapons (cyborg "technicals"), Pakistanis with Soviet nukes—and the proliferation of body politics all call for the forming of new alliances and new associations (and therefore new cyborg body politics) wherever viable and open networks spread.

So cyborgs will perhaps be more open to heterogeneous genderings and identities based on situations; they will also be more able to expand what we think of as resistance and enact new forms of power based on the new forms of power: nets, information, complex systems, multivocal games and rituals, open sets, negotiations between entropy and noise as productive and destructive.

The Cyborg Body Politic Is "Realistic." It is an important and pragmatic figure for calculating current political configurations. The world is interpenetrated by technological developments; in the face of this, contemporary appeals to holism and natural lifestyles ultimately mystify the extent to which we are dependent on and meshed with technology, even if such appeals provide important counterbalances to dystopian "closed system" visions of technology. You can't understand how to deal with modern conflicts and dilemmas of development and progress by appealing to notions of natural, organic people or societies, if there ever were any.

Acknowledging this interpenetration will help us move beyond the paralyzing dualism of humans as inviolable, natural individuals with independent "lifestyles" and humans as resources for social machinery, as cogs in wheels or as operators serving the net. Neither of these is accurate because while we are interpenetrated by technologies that include discourse, humans also make collective and elite decisions that determine the scope and impact of technologies.

Multiply selved doesn't have to mean schizophrenic, as opposed to a paranoid, insane defense of the fictional mirror self; it can mean, rather, the practical application of cyborg rules of order and operation, a cyborg competence based on how we have already come to grips with a variety of cyborgian elements in daily life. Can this competence generate a different kind of subjectivity, one perhaps also transferable to issues of race, class, gender—or rather, transferable from these discourses and practices, because they are so complex now, as more (de)humanized, postpure examples of border crossing and boundary confusion?

Cyborg language has to acknowledge both of these because it has to notice that what animates technology is our inhabiting of it, and what is true about each of us as "cogs" is that society and culture are complex technologies no matter how we think we escape into our individual and isolate selves.

Certainly, confusing, even horrible, things can happen in a cyborg future. Gender may become less important, new genders might be invented. Less titillating is the possibility that class could become real (embodied) as the cyborg rich live longer, even forever, and become a race of the rich.[43] There might be whole races of cyborgs built around income and position or maybe occupation. Specially bred cyborgs for war or space (or both) are common SF themes. Perhaps cyborg tribes or clans will develop around environments (such as the sea or air) or fascinations. And it is hoped that perhaps it will get so confusing and subjectivity will be so clearly constructed that we will become tolerant of difference. John Brenkman admonished that difference shouldn't make all of the difference: "The body politic has to be reimagined as an arena in which political participation stimulates social change rather than confirming existing relations and institutions. Citizenship has to embrace equality without demanding homogeneity, in keeping with the diversity of social roles characteristic of modern societies." As Brenkman goes on to argue, we must go beyond the simple self-definitions of race, class, and gender and

go beyond the abstraction of "positionality" in "determining the socially and politically relevant aspects of identity-formation" because it misses "the crucial difficult and productive tension within every position ... namely, that we are always
at one and the same time a member of _____ (or participant in _____) *and* a
citizen. Moreover, gender-race-class positionality too easily misses the conflicts
that arise *within* every identifiable social group and manifest themselves in *its* po-
litical-cultural debates over its identity, its guiding values, its strategies of struggle, its visions of the community's most desired and its most feared destiny."[44]
The cyborg metaphor offers a unique validation of different identities and the social construction of same. There is a strong tradition in cybernetics that extends
from Norbert Wiener through Gregory Bateson to Francisco Varela and that is
self-conscious and politically committed. Even further back in the genealogy of
cybernetics there are many interesting ancestors, including strong African and
Hispanic influences.[45]

Maybe, eventually, we will all realize, as Audre Lorde realized, that we are all
multiple selves. "Each of us had our own needs and pursuits, and many different
alliances. Self-preservation warned some of us that we could not afford to settle
for one easy definition, one narrow individuation of self. ... It was a while before
we came to realize that our place was the very house of difference rather than the
security of any one particular difference ... and that we could appreciate each
other on terms not necessarily our own."[46] But with all of this said and done, the
idea of the cyborg, as body politic or as anything else, is only a tool, and only as
good as the work it can do or the pleasure it can bring.

Contradicting Our Selves, Issuing New World Orders

There is an arrogance to making these kinds of arguments because they pretend
to a coherence that is, at the most, only contingent. The sovereignty of any metaphor, including the cyborg body politic, is illusory, subject to proliferation, hy-
bridization. For us, it should not be prescriptive so much as descriptive and productive of possibilities, utopian or pragmatic.

The cyborg body politic is a myth, not truth; we acknowledge the presence of
other figuring discourses within these sciences and current bodies politic—discourses of war and mastery, of command and control, of disease and pollution, of
liberation, of autonomy, of gender and race and class. Refiguring the body politic
is one way to raise questions of how progressive forces can be more effective, and
indeed of what might count as progressive given complicated interrelationships
of technology, social groupings, discursive practices, and economic models.

The cyborg body politic is also a metaphor within the powerful prosthetic technology we call discourse. In cybernetics, a small amount of energy runs the control mechanism; that mechanism is flexible, capable of redesign, and in turn it has
powerful effects on the large-scale machinery the controls run. So too with dis-

course, whether Hobbes's seventeenth-century attempt to resolve the crisis in the nation-state or current responses to the Information Age and the increasing interdependence of economies, whether commercial, military, or symbolic. Perhaps we may imagine a nonlinear, noncontinuous shift taking place between Cartesian and cyborgian body-politic metaphors that parallels similar shifts in technological, economic, and political practices. These shifts reflect tensions in the discourse that have material effects on lives and bodies throughout the world.

Two examples may serve. Joseph Nye characterizes the new world order as a dialogue between national and transnational; although the United States maintains hegemony in military affairs, "military prowess is a poor predictor of the outcomes in the economic and transnational layers of current world politics."[47] Instead, a second layer of economic power is tripolar (and changing, as we previously showed), and a third layer is quite diffuse in terms of power. At this level are lumped problems such as drug trade, AIDS, migration and refugee displacement, global warming, and nuclear proliferation, which permeate state boundaries and resist unilateral or even tripolar solutions. Nye imagines an older, Newtonian political discourse ("the mechanical balance of states") giving way before postsovereign notions of multiple bodies of power.

Likewise, Gerald Helman and Steven Ratner suggest the bankruptcy of the sovereign nation-state as an adequate measure of power and solution to civil war and social collapse. States like Somalia and Bosnia, they suggest, have failed to live up to the stringent standards of national selfhood—they are failed nation-states. These states should be treated like a state treats a "failed" individual. "In domestic systems when the polity confronts persons who are utterly incapable of functioning on their own, the law often provides some regime whereby the community itself manages the affairs of the victim. Forms of guardianship or trusteeship are a common response to broken families, serious mental or physical illness, or economic destitution."[48] Both the Nye article and the Helman and Ratner article confront the complexity of world power, a complexity that involves layers of economic, military, and political structures. Both cite the information revolution and the impact of new technologies that cross borders and redefine territories. Both reimagine a United Nations that intervenes in the affairs of nations like Somalia or Bosnia. And yet both speak unselfconsciously from a position of identity and coherence; if problems are transnational, this does not threaten the First World's sense of identity as nation-states, or the major economic powers as some sort of community. None of the centrifugal forces that threaten nation-state coherence around the globe can affect our nation-state, these articles proclaim; and yet this notion of ideal Western hegemony and self-identity is perhaps at the root of many transnational, boundary-permeating "problems." The proposals of these writers, and others, are riddled with metaphors not only from cybernetics and information technology but also from discourses on politics, addiction, race, class. The speakers imagine that they are at the center of a potentially coherent body, a we who share their concern for American power and security. Yet the very forces they begin to unravel and distinguish riddle our own country and those of emerging economic blocs; the powerful technologies of cybernetics and communication are shaping their own state, subjecting it to its own confusing centrifugal forces. Neither article questions the role of political bodies like the World Bank and the International Monetary Fund—like Helman and Ratner's First World nations, these are normative and normalizing institutions, catering to the abnormal, the failed, the somehow-less-than. Neither article imagines that if the world is more and more transnational, interdependent, then policies and technologies emanating from the First World must have something to do with the impact of policies and technologies in the "failed" or "too slowly developing" countries. A case could be made that the anthropocentric metaphor of developing bodies, of parents and children, matches poorly the complex dynamics of proliferating bodies politic. *In loco parentis* may prove difficult and counterproductive if the parents themselves, like the protagonists of many cyborg stories, end up *todo loco*.

We live in a time when bodies, and bodies of thought and language, are undergoing a dramatic and often violent sea change. Whether the products will be rich and strange or impoverished and strange remains to be seen. But the products will most certainly be new bodies and new bodies politic. As Katherine Hayles points out, "When people begin using their bodies in significantly different ways, because of either technological innovations or other cultural shifts, changing experiences of embodiment bubble up into language, affecting the metaphoric networks at play within the culture. At the same time, discursive constructions affect how bodies move through space and time, influence what technologies are developed, and help to structure the interfaces between bodies and technology."[49] The articles we've just cited indicate the extent to which political discourse is affected by new technologies, and also the extent to which it still relies on traditional notions of self, self-interest, successful, and coherent selves. To that extent, they are cyborg discourses, yet naively so. These discourses and others like them vie in a field of power and must be contested by other discourses based on other experiences of body, power, and interfaces with technology. These interfaces must be more self-consciously cyborg; these bodies will be shaped by the resultant discursive constructions of bodies political and cybernetic, will confront new pleasures and powers, new terrors and dangers.

The screen as a theater of representation seems only to enlarge. We watch *Star Trek*'s Captain Picard taken by the Borg, forced to be part of a deindividualized, cyborg society/spaceship/organism that "assimilates" what is other to it by destroying or consuming it. Its cybernetic design gives it massive power; its mantra is "Resistance is futile." Picard, the symbol of human free will, agency, intelligence, is reduced to a mere mouth; his language system and brain are used to communicate threats to the merely human, and he is "responsible" for many deaths in his role as Locutus. This technological rape takes its toll on the body and psyche; for two episodes (an eternity on TV) he wrestles with the shame, the sense of having lost his integrity and self: He says, in effect, they took everything I had.

Certainly rape is a powerful way to imagine the dystopian effects of the new technologies, as well as their seeming unconcern for gender. Cybernetic systems helped pilots kill tens of thousands of Iraqi draftees fleeing Kuwait and determine flows of information capital that have material effects on women semiconductor workers in the Philippines and rubber tappers in Brazilian rain forests, and indeed on the ecosystems of those countries.

And yet there are other stories, other narratives, embedded within cybernetics. We communicate to each other, to friends and activists across the globe, on networks that belie the official organs of news. The notion of who is in one's community, of which community one is part of, changes; whole relationships are conducted across the fiber optics, genders are adopted or switched, games are constructed in which situations and actions are played and replayed and lives and choices are rehearsed and enacted. The same technology that will hardwire a pilot into the computer that flies the jet and enables the missiles will allow our friend, hit by a speeding truck, to walk again. There is no choice between utopia and dystopia, Good Terminator or Evil Terminator—they are both here. Every day we are hit, run over, grazed, or cried over, just as we drive, compute, ingest, and breathe. We are learning to inhabit this permeable body, whether the one we walk around in or the one we are told to vote in, and to experience a range of virtual realities, some of which we can imagine enjoying, passing on to our cyborg children. Perhaps, after all, we just need to learn cyborg family values—good maintenance, technical expertise, pleasures dispersed and multiple, community R&D, improved communication.

NOTES

1. Donna Haraway, *Simians, Cyborgs and Women: The Reinvention of Nature* (London: Free Association Books, 1991), pp. 7–8.

2. The body has long been considered a basis for epistemological reflection. As Leonard Barken points out in *Nature's Work of Art* (New Haven: Yale University Press, 1975), his history of the body as metaphor, it has been used to justify ideas in metaphysics, politics, and aesthetics for millennia. In all of these the body is seen as a microcosm of the world. Barkan argues that when this "equation between man and the world is assumed, then the subject-object problem becomes identical with the problem of self-knowledge" (p. 46). Politically, this has the most profound implications when we realize that for many people today, the image of the human body is no longer the body in nature (the noble savage of Rousseau) or the automaton with a soul (Hobbes and Descartes). Today, many actual and metaphorical human individuals are cyborgs, and so to the extent that the body is used as a "key" to knowing, it is a cyborg epistemology.

3. Michel Foucault, *Discipline and Punish: The Birth of the Prison*, trans. Alan Sheridan (New York: Vintage, 1977), pp. 29–30.

4. Thomas Hobbes, *Leviathan or the Matter, Forme, and Power of a Common-Wealth Ecclesiatsticall and Civill* (London: Penguin, 1965, first published in 1651), p. 83.

5. Chris Gray, *Postmodern War* (London: Free Association Press, 1993).

6. The term "cyborg" was first coined by Manfred Clynes and Nathan S. Kline in "Cyborgs and Space," *Astronautics,* September 1960, p. 27.

7. The distinction between a society of cyborgs and cyborg society was first brought to our attention by our colleague Joe Dumit.

8. One mapping, among many, might be:

- Large cyborg entities are *mega-cyborgs,* including infantrymen wearing gigantic mind-controlled exoskeletons (a Los Alamos labs project), gargantuan human-machine weapons systems (such as Star Wars in some of its more grandiose formulations), or even the worldwide (an empire or the United Nations) or galaxywide (the United Federation of Planets or the Borg) cyborg body politics, good or evil.

- *Semi-cyborgs* are organisms that are only intermittently cyborgs, like dialysis patients linked to the life-giving machine thirty hours a week or like some small semi-industrial countries that are only part of the world economy and world telecommunications culture at only a limited number of specific places and moments.

- *Multi-cyborgs* are combinations of various types of cyborgs or have the ability to shift among flavors of cyborgs.

- *Omni-cyborgs* make a cyborg of everything they interface with, such as the omni-cyborgian theory of articles such as this one.

- A *neo-cyborg* has the outward form of cyborgism, such as an artificial limb, but lacks full homeostatic integration of the prosthesis.

- The *proto-cyborg* lacks full embodiment.

- The *ultra-cyborg* is an enhanced cybernetic organism, greater in its realm than any mere machine or all-meat creature, such as soldier cyborgs literally and some athletes and megastars transformed through drugs, foods, the body sculpting of exercise, cosmetic surgery, and digital enhancements of voice and image metaphorically.

- A *hyper-cyborg* might be one where cyborg embodiments were layered or in some other way cobbled together into greater and greater cyborg bodies.

- A *retro-cyborg* would be one whose prosthetic-cybernetic transformation was designed to restore some lost form, in the case of a *pseudo-retro-cyborg,* a lost form that never was.

- The *meta-cyborg* is the noncyborg citizen in cyborg society; it is cyborg society itself. It isn't a cyborg in the strict definition of the technical term, but in context and process it is most certainly cyborgian.

9. See Chris Gray, "Medical Cyborgs," in Chris Gray, ed., *Technohistory: Using the History of American Technology in Interdisciplinary Research* (Melbourne, Fla.: Kreiger, 1985).

10. See Chris Gray and Mark Driscoll, "What's Real About Virtual Reality? Anthropology of, and in, Cyberspace," *Visual Anthropology Review,* vol. 8, no. 2, Fall 1982, pp. 39–49.

11. Office of Science and Technology Policy, *Grand Challenges: High Performance Computing and Communications* (Washington, D.C.: Government Printing Office, 1992, 1993).

12. A prosthetic process, such as aging today, is much different than a synthesizing one, such as reproduction. Enhancements and replacements are never fully integrated into a new synthesis, rather they remain lumpy and semi-autonomous. The postmodern state is

clearly a prosthetic creature cobbled together out of various organic and cybernetic sub-units such as bioregions, cultures, markets, myths, histories, communities, and so on. Of course, synthetic and prosthetic processes can be combined, as with genetic engineering and political revolution.

13. Jacques Derrida, *Speech and Phenomena,* trans. David B. Allison (Evanston: North-western University Press, 1973), pp. 145–146; quoted in Catherine Belsey, *Feminisms,* p. 595. See note 14.

14. Catherine Belsey, "Constructing the Subject: Deconstructing the Text," in *Feminisms,* ed. R. Warhol and D. Price Herndl (New Brunswick, N.J.: Rutgers University Press, 1991), p. 597.

15. Sigmund Freud, *Civilization and Its Discontents,* trans. and ed. James Strachey (New York: Norton, 1962), pp. 38–39.

16. Donna Haraway, "A Manifesto for Cyborgs: Science, Technology, and Socialist Femi-nism in the 1980s," *Socialist Review,* no. 80, 1985, p. 125.

17. Ambiguous is just putting it nicely. Cyborg technologies have the potential to reify in material bodies class and caste distinctions that were only social constructions up to now.

18. Andrew Gordon, "Human, More or Less: Man-Machine Communion in Samuel Delany's Nova and Other Science Fiction Stories," in *The Mechanical God* (Westport, Conn.: Greenwood Press, 1982), p. 196.

19. Haraway, *Simians, Cyborgs and Women,* p. 135.

20. Ibid., p. 135.

21. Barbara Ehrenreich, "Foreword," in Klaus Theweleit, *Male Fantasies, Volume 1: Women Floods Bodies History* (Minneapolis: University of Minnesota Press, 1987), p. xvi.

22. Such as the international associations of scientists, anarchists, lawyers, therapists, prostitutes, and many other self-selected groups of various levels of importance. Improved worldwide communication and travel will make such contacts, and individual relation-ships across borders and other boundaries, more politically important year after year. Such cybernetic inputs as faxes from Tiananmen Square and E-mail from besieged Sarajevo al-ready play an important political role in shifting the relative importance of various politi-cal bodies.

23. We see a paradox here; as nationalism(s) proliferates (add to the list southern Osse-tians in Georgia, ethnically Turkish Gagauz in Moldova, and Serbians in eastern Ger-many), "nationalism," whose traditional vehicle is the united nation-state, may lose some (but not all, or even most) of its power.

24. A situation that doesn't please everyone. Peter Gloz complains in "Forward to Eu-rope: A Declaration for a New European Left," *Dissent,* Summer 1986, pp. 331–332, that "The second [crucial] worldwide development has been a loss of power by individual na-tions—that is, their political bureaucracies have lost out to central banks, banks operating internationally, transnational finance markets, and multinational corporations. There is a name for this: *the collapse of a central pillar of nationhood, the Lebanonization of the eco-nomic function of the modern industrial state*" (original emphasis).

25. John R.R. Christie, "A Tragedy for Cyborgs," *Configurations,* vol. 1, 1992, p. 183.

26. Richard Gordon, personal communication, 1989, his emphasis.

27. Trilateral Commission Task Force, *Towards a Renovated International System* (New York: Trilateral Commission, 1977), p. 1.

28. Holly Sklar, ed., *Trilateralism* (Boston: South End Press, 1980), p. 20, original emphasis.

29. Officially they are what contemporary war is all about. See Chris Gray, "Excerpts from Philosophy and the Human Future: The Implications of Postmodern War," *Nomad*, vol. 3, no. 1, Spring 1992, pp. 31–39; and Chris Gray, "Kuwait 1991: A Postmodern War," *Nomad*, vol. 3, no. 3, 1993, pp. 25–32.

30. Regis Debray, "Startling New Predictions: 'The Twenty-first Century Will Resemble the Nineteenth,'" *New Patriot*, April 26, 1990, p. 4.

31. Paul Kennedy, *The Rise and Fall of the Great Powers* (New York: Random House, 1987), p. 538.

32. The scientific-pagan principle of a single biosphere, Gaia, can certainly be defined as a cyborg, especially if one unites all of its/her definitions into one idea(l). With Gaia, one can avoid Donna Haraway's hard choice and choose to be (part of) both a cyborg and a goddess.

33. Boutros Boutros-Ghali, "Empowering the United Nations," *Foreign Affairs*, vol. 72, no. 5, Winter 1992–1993, p. 98.

34. Ibid., pp. 98–99.

35. Ibid., p. 99.

36. Ibid., p. 101.

37. Steven Shapin and Simon Schaffer, *Leviathan Versus the Air Pump: Hobbes, Boyle, and the Experimental Life* (Princeton: Princeton University Press, 1985). All quotes are from p. 338. Original emphasis.

38. See, for example, Zoe Sofia, "Exterminating Fetuses," *Diacritics*, vol. 14, no. 2, Summer 1984, pp. 47–59; Chris Gray, "The Culture of War Cyborgs: Technoscience, Gender, and Postmodern War," *Research in Philosophy and Technology* (special issue on technology and feminism), Joan Rothschild, ed., vol. 13, 1993, pp. 141–163; and the work of Donna Haraway.

39. Shapin and Schaffer, *Leviathan Versus the Air Pump*, pp. 338, 343–344. Here the concept of the "technopeasant" meets the demand for a cyborg literacy.

40. John R.R. Christie commenting on Henry Adam's statement that "politics or science, the lesson was the same." Christie traces many interesting cyborgian themes of "women, science, technology, politics, and the future" in his "A Tragedy for Cyborgs," *Configurations*, vol. 1, no. 1, Winter 1993, pp. 171–196.

41. Shapin and Schaffer, *Leviathan versus the Air Pump*, p. 344.

42. See especially Elaine Scarry's *The Body in Pain: The Making and Unmaking of the World* (New York: Oxford University Press, 1985), which shows how central bodies are to such archetypal political acts as war and torture; and N. Katherine Hayles, "The Materiality of Informatics," *Configurations*, vol. 1, no. 1, Winter 1993, pp. 147–170, which makes a rich argument for understanding postmodern subjectivity in cyborgian terms.

43. For fictional accounts, see Roger MacBride Allen, *The Modular Man* (New York: Bantam, 1992); and Roger Zelazny, *Lord of Light* (New York: Avon, 1979).

44. John Brenkman, "Multiculturalism and Criticism," unpublished ms., 1992, pp. 20, 26, original emphasis.

45. Ron Eglash has brought much of this history to light. See especially his article "Towards a Black Cybernetics: African Traditions and the Cyborg Citizen," to be published in Chris Gray, ed., *The Cyborg Handbook*, forthcoming from Routledge. Many key cyberneti-

cists have been from Spain or Latin America, such as Arturo Rosenblueth, Jose Delgado, Fernando Flores, H. R. Maturana, and Francisco Varela.

46. Audre Lorde, *Zami: A New Spelling of My Name* (Trumansburg, N.Y.: Crossing Press) 1982, p. 12.

47. Joseph Nye, "What New World Order?" *Foreign Affairs,* vol. 72, no. 5, Winter 1992–1993, p. 88.

48. Gerald Helman and Steven R. Ratner, "Saving Failed States," *Foreign Policy,* no. 89, Winter 1992–1993, p. 12.

49. Katherine Hayles, "The Materiality of Informatics," *Configurations,* vol. 1, no. 1, Winter 1993, pp. 164–165.

14

Eyephone, Therefore I Am: Miki Kiyoshi on Cyborg-Envy in *Being and Time*

MARK DRISCOLL

HEIDEGGER´S MEDITATIONS ON TECHNE and technology have occasioned some interesting secondary discussions of the relation and constitutive cross-switchings among "machine," "mind," and "body."[1] These readings—along with most other readings of Heidegger as the quintessential, if at times ambivalent, technophobe[2]—have been motivated by the assertion that Heidegger's work represents the most sustained critique of the Western technological drive as the violent Cartesian legacy of the splitting of self from world. This split, initiated by Greek philosophy's fall into metaphysics, culminates with the deadly technological *Gestell*—the technological fixing and framing of the world—as the modern mode and mood of a productionist metaphysics that freeze-frames and reifies the world and entities in the world. This argument continues with the frequently cited proposition that for Heidegger, the essence of technology contains nothing technological. Technology is derivative of the will to enframe and fix the natural world as a standing reserve (*Bestand*) waiting to be put to use by the *Bestand* and the brightest toward the telos of the instrumental drive to produce.

My reading of *Being and Time*,[3] influenced by Michel Haar's *Le chant de la terre*,[4] led me to the conclusion that this early text contradicts and fundamentally glitches the canonical reading of Heidegger's technophobia. Heidegger's extended meditation on Nietzsche demonstrates the ways in which the "subject/object digital" grounds the Western reification of everything as the object of technology. The existential analytic offered in Division 1 of *Being and Time*, however, would appear to oppose the technological understanding of being, as it offers the most thorough critique of the subject/object digital in Western philosophy available in 1927. Heidegger's main argument in Division 1 is that ready-to-hand (*zuhanden*) objects are more fundamental and prior to present-at-hand (*vorhanden*) objects.

Zuhanden objects are characterized as entities that exist in the world of equipment. Being present-at-hand characterizes the mode that is operational in objective and reifying representational logics, which are themselves causal effects of the subject/object distinction. Heidegger wants to demonstrate that although the relationship between present-at-hand and ready-to-hand is usually thought of whereby the logic of present-at-hand detachment must initially calculate and frame the objects that it will use, this is actually derivative from a constitutive mode of the ready-at-hand, which Heidegger describes as the technical manipulation of objects in the world. Heidegger wants to privilege the program of ready-to-hand as fundamental, and he theorizes that being present-at-hand only results from a system error in the more ontologically fundamental program of being ready-to-hand. He contends that the manipulation of ready-at-hand objects takes place within a larger background he calls the "equipmental totality." Through use, we realize that the instrumental function of *zuhanden* entities signifies only within a matrix of "references and assignments." This matrix hard-drives the background of equipmental totality within which each function is placed. The totality of equipment might be configured as the toolshed that houses *Zuhandenheit* as its own mode of being.

My argument turns around a few simple questions, and I ask them partly through an explicitly implicit critique of Heidegger offered by Japanese hermeneutic-Marxist philosopher Miki Kiyoshi. Miki was the first Japanese philosopher to incorporate the protocols of a fundamental ontology into his work, and with his mature software package of the early and mid-1930s he attempted to deal with a *Dasein* analysis from within a more explicitly materialist methodological hardware. I mobilize his reflections on techne and being to bring out some of the deep contradictions of the Heideggerian analysis of things technic and techno.

Miki helps us explore whether the representation of the being of equipment in the early Heidegger can in fact be mobilized as a critique of technology. Miki's analysis supports the claim that an aporia of readiness-at-hand (*Zuhandenheit*) fundamentally scrambles the later analysis of technology as the culmination of the violent *Gestell* of a productionist metaphysics as Western techno-will to power. By pressing the rewind button on Heidegger's theory of technology and reading metaleptically, it is easy to demonstrate that his way out of the problematic of technology as the effect of the subject/object digital—as expressed after 1935 in the Nietzsche books and in the first version of "The Question Concerning Technology"—is the analysis of *Zuhandenheit* in *Being and Time*. Listening to Heidegger in reverse allows us to sample the contradiction and to resequence him.

Dasein Left to Its Own Devices

The analysis of equipment in Division 1 seems to invert the hierarchy of subject/object as it puts this infamous Western binary into serious crisis. *Zuhandenheit,* grounded in the equipmental totality, allows Heidegger to get out of the problem of a digitalized subject/object. Unfortunately, the double bind of this move grounds the ontology of *Zuhandenheit* in technical equipment, instruments, and devices. This aporetic only displaces the problem of technology and regrounds it in *Zuhandenheit*, which then becomes operational as the support system for an ontologically more fundamental involvement in things technic and techno. The fallout from the wasting of the metaphysical subject in Heidegger's project goes in two ways. Initially, it might sketch out what he calls situation/*Lage* as a "situated" knowledge of Heidegger's necessarily overdetermined by the equipmental totality. His emphasis on what Henri Lefebvre—after Heidegger—called the ontological structure of "everyday life" (Lefebvre has commented that his thinking on the ev-eryday was thoroughly morphed by Division 1 of *Being and Time*) has aided and abetted some of the most famous advances in social theory—from Marcuse to Foucault—in this century. The accepting, however, of this equipmental totality without anything resembling what we could call with the Frankfurt School the "social totality"[5] could lead to the passive involvement in an increasingly totali-tarian and hypertechnologized state, although I want to press the pause button on this reading and allow it to remain undecidable for now.

I will begin to examine this aporia by appealing to the notion of the cyborg, a notion that has become something of what Barthes called a "metaphor without brakes" at my school, the University of California at Santa Cruz.[6] My analysis con-cerns something called Heidegger's "cyborg envy."[7] It is hoped that this theory will help bury the canonical interpretations of a Heideggerian Luddism by ex-tending and advancing[8] the theory that *Being and Time* articulates a ground of technology as constitutive for the disclosure of *Dasein*. This technophilia is dis-avowed somewhat by the deployment of the tropes of a preindustrial workshop, but at other points in the text Heidegger unambivalently praises things technical. This praise, however, does not extend to the attempts getting under way at the time of the composition of this text in the mid-1920s to, in effect, download the contents of "the human" into machines. Heidegger stood violently opposed to the newly developing disciplines of cognitive science and artificial intelligence. But his opposition to AI does not prevent him from articulating a *Dasein* as the being-with of equipment and organisms within the integrated circuitry of the equipmental totality.

Equiprimordial/Equip(ped) Primordially

The being of *Dasein* is characterized by being-with (*Mitsein*) and being-in-the-world (*In-der-Welt-sein*). The ways in which *Dasein* fundamentally carries itself in the world are all characterized by modes of caring (*Sorge*); "Dasein's facticity is such that its Being-in-the-world has always dispersed itself or even split itself up into definite ways of Being-in. The multiplicity of these is indicated by the following examples: having to do something, producing something, attending to something and looking after it, making use of something ... All these ways of Being-in have concern (*Besorgen*) as their kind of being" (83/56). As an existential—which concerns itself with a primordial and ontological understanding of being as opposed to a derivative and ontic understanding—this concern is constitutively relational and is fundamental to *Dasein*'s being. The existential mode of being-in-the-world toward Other entities is called solicitude (*Fursorge*). Therefore, *Dasein* is care (*Sorge*) because care's relationship to the world is constituted by the totality of equipment; that is, the relationship involves concern (*Besorgen*), and care's relation to Others in the world is one of solicitude (*Fursorge*).

Although Heidegger tries to make a distinction between entities as equipment and entities as Others having the potential for the being of *Dasein,* there is an etymological hookup in German that is lost in English and that can help us see the blurring of the distinction and disclose Heidegger's cyborg envy. He writes, "But those entities towards which Dasein as Being-with comports itself do not have the kind of Being which belongs to equipment ready-to-hand; they are themselves Dasein. These entities are not objects of concern, but rather of *solicitude/* Fursorge" (157/112). Heidegger is trying to articulate his hierarchy of beings through the specific mode of being that is constitutive for them. Equipment does not have the potential for the being of *Dasein*. We can begin to show, however, that the implicit hierarchy of modalities of dealing with concern/*Besorgen* toward the *Dasein*-positive Other and dealing with solicitude/*Fursorge* toward *Dasein*-negative equipmental entities in our technical world begins to blur in Heidegger. This interfacing and blurring produces the readout of a parataxis of things given for manipulation (*zuhanden*), things objectively given (*vorhanden*), and being-with-others (*Mitdasein*).

Dasein as Software Package/*Dasein*(er) Software

There is a curious democratic circuitry here whose inauthentic chips are nevertheless driven by the authenticity of the existential care. The care package and the packaging of care occur within the delimited confines of inauthentic everydayness. Heidegger warns again and again, though, about the mutual parasiting and contamination of the authenticity of *Dasein* with its inauthenticity in everydayness. He suggests that there is an essential looping of *Dasein* from authentic to inauthentic and that the vehicle for this looping is the existentials, hence the importance of them in my treatment. Although inauthentic/authentic falls into the more important digital of "ontic" (or the mode of entities that are secondarily derived from a more primordial and constitutive "ontological") and "ontological," Heidegger—unlike those who police the necessary border between ontic and ontological—treats the inauthentic/authentic digital as a difference *in degree,* not a difference *in kind,* although he never states the difference as such.

There is considerable disagreement over this problem, and the textual evidence itself is contradictory. In Section 27 he offers the inauthentic "they" as a ground: "The originary phenomenon is the 'they,' *das Man*" (167/129). Putting a search on authenticity, then, would produce the readout that the authentic can only be the effect of an existential upgrade of the primordial *das Man*. Elsewhere, the flipside of this rules. In Division 2, the claim, "The 'they' … is an existential modification of the authentic self" (365/317). In Section 27, again he writes that "the authentic self … can be only an existential modification of the 'they,' which has been defined as an essential existential" (168/130). I would like to appropriate these aporias for my thesis of the desire for jacking in that is textually potent in the early Heidegger. He asks us to always consider authenticity with *Dasein*'s inauthenticity in a freeze-frame on the same screen, that is to say, always in the tension of its lived differentiality. Likewise, inauthenticity is always one side of the necessarily split screen of *Dasein*, with authenticity on the other side of the split screen. The encrypting of the authentic in the inauthentic and the reverse point to the being-in-the-world of *Dasein* and its existential quality of infinite interfaceability. In Division 1, this interfacing is grounded in the tool-tality of equipment, and from my reading I would recode this as a desire for machine hookups; a symptom of cyborg envy.[9] The Heideggerian cyborg would be coded following Haraway: "No longer structured by the polarity of public and private, the cyborg defines a technological polis based partly on a revolution of social relations."[10]

This discussion might be helped by a detour through Section 38, which in some sense is a preparation for Division 2 and its articulation of the authentic projection of the transcendence of *Dasein*. Heidegger claims the existential of falling as the second aspect of being-in, after care, and he writes in Section 38 that "falling reveals an essential ontological structure of Dasein itself" (224/179) and that "through the Interpretation of falling, what we have called the 'inauthenticity' of Dasein may now be defined more precisely" (220/176). In his discussion of falling, he offers his most lucid explanation for the necessarily supplemental nature of inauthenticity with authenticity; "'inauthenticity' does not mean anything like Being-no-longer-in-the-world, but amounts rather to a quite distinctive kind of Being-in-the-world—the kind which is completely fascinated by the 'world' and by the Dasein-with of Others in the 'they.' Not-being-its-self functions as a positive possibility of that entity which, in its essential concern, is absorbed in a world. This kind of *not-Being* has to be conceived as that kind of Being which is closest to Dasein and in which Dasein maintains itself for the most part" (220/176). Haraway describes her feminist cyborg as "wary of holism, but needy for connection."[11]

The existential mode of falling describes the way in which *Dasein,* by means of its essential quality of being-in-the-world, is pulled away from its primordial sense of what it is. But in this pulling away, Heidegger suggests that the "framework/*Gerust*" that is the constitutive background for "the kind of Being which is

Dasein's" (221/176) can be glimpsed for the first time: "It must have seemed that Being-in-the world has the function of a rigid framework, within which Dasein's possible ways of comporting itself towards its world run their course without touching the 'framework' itself as regards its Being" (221/176). The existential of falling clears the framework that "makes up" the kind of being that is *Dasein's*. This notion of the framework/*Gerust* that makes up *Dasein* comes very close to Heidegger's later critique of the essence of technology, whose main feature is an enframing *Gestell* that reifies and fixes entities to be objectified. Except here, the German *Gerust*—which means scaffolding as well as frame—is read as producing the conditions for the possibilities of *Dasein's* being-in-the-world. That is to say that the notion of the frame, which is very close to the ground for the critique of technology that would be mobilized eight years later,[12] is here articulated as the existential midperson responsible for clearing both *Dasein's* being-in-the-world and the possibility for *Dasein* to first realize that its being is an issue for it. That another technical metaphor of industrial scaffolding—*Gerust*—should be deployed to articulate this crucial bridge between Division 1 and 2 of *Being and Time* can further contribute to my reading of cyborg envy. The tropes of technical machinery—*Zeug* and *Gerust*—are operational as the hardware *and* software of the ontological structure of *Dasein*.

Show Me That You Really Care

The worldhood of the world will emerge through the existential analysis of *Zuhandenheit*. The representative entities of this mode of being-in-the-world are equipment, tools, and devices, and *Dasein's* involvement with them is grounded in use. The most basic character of equipment, tools, and devices is instrumentality. The mode of being of these particular entities is that they must be employed for something. "Equipment is essentially 'something-in-order-to'" (97/68). Through use we realize that the instrumental function of *zuhanden* entities signifies only within a matrix of "references and assignments." This matrix constitutes a background within which each function is placed. The in-order-to of equipment and its assignment is always for *Dasein*. But *Dasein* is not only an entity that makes use of equipment and its instrumentalities appearing in the world; it also constitutes the "for-the-sake-of" that makes it possible for entities in the world to have the instrumental character that must be theirs as *zuhanden* entities.

The world is also said to have as its grounding characteristic the "for-the-sake-of." Although it is not clear what the world needs for-the-sake-ofs *for*, *Dasein* needs for-the-sake-ofs in order to be what it is: "*Dasein* has assigned itself to an 'in-order-to,' and it has done so in terms of an ability to be for the sake of which it itself is" (119/86). *Dasein* both receives assignments from the equipmental totality and is capable of assigning roles itself. Where would *Dasein* get the input for determining these roles? It could only acquire this information from always already being-in-the-world. Heidegger calls this acquiring of assignments of information through input and output "significance" (*Bedeutsamkeit*). He writes, "The 'for-the-sake-which' signifies 'an in-order-to,' this in turn, a 'towards-this'; the latter an 'in-which' of letting something be involved; and that in turn, the 'with-which' of an involvement. These relationships are bound up with one another as a *primordial whole;* they are what they are as this signifying in which Dasein gives itself beforehand its Being-in-the-world as something to be understood. The relational whole of this signifying we call 'significance'" (120/86, my emphasis).

Just as Otherness is presupposed in equipment, *Dasein* and world seem mutually presupposed in the workshop as equipmental totality. *Dasein's* heretofore distinct activities of manipulating equipment (*Fursorge*) and coping with Others (*Besorgen*) is very close in the German. Dealing concernfully with the Other and dealing with solicitude toward equipment in our technical world can't be distinguished for Heidegger, as both *Dasein* and world seem to receive their assignments of for-the-sake-of from the equipmental totality. Equipment was supposed to be an in-order-to, for the sake of *Dasein* and the world, but read this way, they all seem to be equiprimordial. "Primordial" signifies for Heidegger the most direct and fundamental way of involvement with entities. *Dasein,* world, and the equipmental totality/tooltality all stand in an equiprimordial relation. *Dasein* and world therefore can be taken to be equip(ped)rimordial.[13]

Tooltality/Totality

Although being-in-the-world is supposed to be constitutive, there is really no priority, and *Dasein*/Other/equipment/machine/world all become scrambled for Heidegger. The world, equipmental tooltality, and *Dasein* are all interfaced by the same for-the-sake-ofs. *Dasein* needs the assignments from the equipmental tooltality to be what it most essentially is. For its part, the equipmental whole is driven by the for-the-sake-ofs that are ways of being *Dasein.* The tooltality has significance only because it is organized as the for-the-sake-of *Dasein's* becoming what it is. *Dasein* and, implicitly, the world get their assignments and gather the for-the-sake-ofs that are the components of the tooltality. All through the discussions in Division 1 there is a blurring of machines/equipment and *Dasein.* Heidegger's cyborg envy is retroactively supported by Donna Haraway's claim that "we are all chimeras, theorized and fabricated hybrids of machine and organism; in short, we are cyborgs."[14]

Dis(sing)severance on Remote Control

Heidegger introduces the notion of dis-severance to articulate *Dasein's* concern toward spatialized equipment. This is *Entfernung*—"remoteness" in German—although Heidegger uses the word with a hyphen, which emphasizes the privative ent. Thus the word comes to have the sense of negating a remoteness/controlling a remoteness/wiping out a distance and is translated as "de-severance" by the people who brought you *Being and Time* in English. Heidegger uses *Ent-fernung* not only in his discussion of the way equipment appears spatially but also in a somewhat introductory function in his large discussion of publicness that follows. Here I read the term as contributing crucially to the problematic of publicness *and* as supporting a thesis underdeveloped by Heidegger, that *Dasein* is always already *Mitsein*. As I am attempting to connect this to my theme of cyborg envy, I'll start with a general introduction to the term and then try to use it to jack into the latencies of Heidegger's technophilia.

Although *Entfernung* hasn't been deployed often in Heideggerian criticism, it has been central for some of Jacques Derrida's readings of Heidegger. In a piece on Maurice Blanchot called "Pas" he makes the claim that "all 'Heideggerian' thought proceeds in its decisive 'turnings' by the 'same' approaching the de-severance of the near and far. *Entfernung* desevers the far which it constitutes; the approach then brings it closer in keeping it at a distance."[15] This is close to Heidegger's gloss on the term: " 'Desevering' amounts to making the farness vanish—that is, making the remoteness of something disappear, bringing it close. Dasein is essentially de-severant: it lets any entity close by be encountered as the entity which it is" (139/105). De-severance seems to be setting up his discussion of disclosedness that becomes linked with thrownness and projection, thereby grounding his crucial discussion of temporality that appears in Division 2. As such, de-severance is something like the condition of proximity in which the temporality of the event transpires. This proximity of de-severant *Dasein* becomes not so much a place as the always timely (timely because ordered by assignments from the equipmental totality) comings and goings of being-in-the-world.

For now, the ways in which de-severance is always already the software for the hardware of the equipmental totality need to be unscrambled. Heidegger starts his short discussion of de-severance by warning us that the fact of de-severance, and care, being existentials—a fundamental characteristic of *Dasein*—must be kept in mind. De-severance as an existential, or primary characteristic of *Dasein*'s comportment, offers *Dasein* the quality of "bringing-close—bringing something close by, in the sense of procuring it, putting it in readiness, having it to hand" (140/105). Heidegger follows this with an emphasized sentence: "*In Dasein there lies an essential tendency towards closeness.* All the ways in which we speed things up, as we are more or less inclined to do today, push us on towards the conquest of remoteness. With the 'radio,' for example, Dasein has so expanded its everyday environment that it has accomplished a de-severance of the 'world'" (140/105). Heidegger's quotes around "radio" seem to invite the obvious reading that new technological media in their de-severance become existentials—or simulacra of existentials—of *Dasein*. Not only does de-severant technology bring the world close for *Dasein*, it also discloses other technical media; namely, ready-to-hand equipment. De-severance does not disclose equipment and its embedded relation of nearness and farness in a present-at-hand way. This to say that de-severant *Dasein* has its own mode of measuring and disclosing nearness and farness: "Everyday Dasein maintains itself. … Though these estimates may be imprecise and variable if we try to *compute* them, in the everydayness of Dasein they have their own definiteness which is thoroughly intelligible" (140/105, my emphasis). *Dasein* thus comes with its own customized supercomputer, whose high-tech tracking system scans the tooltalized world of low-tech equipment.

Karaoke Heidegger

Dasein's existential of de-severance demonstrates how a mode of being discloses a world where things in general can be either near or far, in addition to showing the de-severance of specific pieces of equipment. "That which is presumably 'closest' is by no means that which is at the smallest distance 'from us.' It lies in that which is desevered to an average extent when we reach for it, grasp it, or look at it. Because *Dasein* is essentially spatial in the way of de-severance, its dealings always keep within an "'environment' which is desevered from it … , accordingly our seeing and hearing always go proximally beyond what is distantially 'closest'" (141/106–107). De-severed ready-to-hand entities have the qualities of this closeness that is not supposed to be a quantifiable closeness. And because the ready-to-hand is configured as always already caught up in equipment and its tooltality, de-severance not only seems to have as its principal quality a technological aspect, but the entities with which it carries itself in its worldly concern are primarily technical equipment. We should replay here the fact that Heidegger theorizes *Dasein* as comporting itself with/toward equipment in the mode of concern: "Circumspective concern decides as to the closeness and farness of what is proximally ready-to-hand environmentally" (142/107).

As Heidegger seems to blur the ontico-ontological distinction between *Dasein*'s de-severance, bringing *specific* things closer to *Dasein,* and de-severance *in general,* concernfully disclosing entities for *Dasein,* he offers the examples of eyeglasses and the telephone to further flesh out his cyborg envy. "Seeing and hearing are distance senses not because they are far-reaching, but because it is in them that *Dasein* as deseverant mainly dwells. … Equipment for seeing—and likewise for hearing, such as the telephone receiver—has what we have designated as the inconspicuousness of the proximally ready-to-hand" (141/107). In terms that evoke the image of the virtual reality eyephone,[16] Heidegger completes the looping of *Dasein*'s de-severant technology that brings ready-to-hand equipment closer into the purview of *Dasein*'s concern. But is this a closeness that can be quantified? If so, then this would have to be an ontic separation because ontological separation as dis-severance cannot change and cannot be subjected to any mathesis.[17] An aporia of dis-severance is evident in the blurring of ontic distance, which changes, and ontological distances, which do not. Is Heidegger guilty as charged for collapsing ontic distance with ontological dis-tance? Or is this an effect again of his cyborg envy, where the blurring between ontic and ontological would be constitutive despite the efforts to delimit them? Could the cyborg be precisely what holds open the place where the pairs ontic and ontological and figural and literal implode into each other?

This blurring, as the mode of being "wary of holism, but needy for connection," could be cleared a little for Miki Kiyoshi by introducing Deleuze and Guattari's discussion—crucial for any theory of cyborg envy—of the difference between human-machine and humans-machines. Human-machine is the situation of work stations and corresponds to what they call "machinic enslavement."[18] Humans-machines are compounds of open systems that hook up human and nonhuman elements in a less repressive structure they call "social subjection": "There is enslavement when human beings themselves are constituent pieces of a machine that they compose among themselves and with other things (animals, tools), under the control and direction of a higher unity. But there is subjection when the higher unity constitutes the human being as a subject linked to a now exterior object, which can be an animal, a tool, or even a machine. The human being is no longer a component of the machine but a worker, a user. He or she is subjected to the machine and no longer enslaved by the machine."[19] They emphasize the interactive qualities of the new cybernetic and informational machines and emphasize the contemporary media shift to "recurrent and reversible 'humans-machines systems' that replace the old nonrecurrent and nonreversible relations of subjection between the two elements."[20]

On the Way to Language via Ex-press Bullet Train

Philosopher Miki Kiyoshi was the first Japanese to develop a serious relationship with a Heideggerian fundamental ontology. He studied with Heidegger in Marburg from 1923 to 1924 and then composed his *Pasukaru ni okeru Ningen no Kenkyu* (The Study of the Human Being in Pascal) in Paris in 1925. Published in Japan the next year, this text was the first published account of the problematics of an analytic of *Dasein*, as *Sein und Zeit* didn't appear in print until a year and a half after Miki's Pascal book. Miki's existential analysis of human existence configured the human being (*ningen*) as being between—*nin* is the character for "person" in Japanese, and the character for *gen* means "in between"—with a foundation of radical instability in a precarious state of thrownness across a void. Miki called this instability of being in process, in a between state, *chukansha*.[21] His key concept in this text, however, is his notion of fundamental experience (*kiso keiken*), which is a rough analog to Heidegger's being of *Dasein*. *Kiso keiken* is a ground for the being-in-between of human subjectivity because it exists at the caesura separating symbolic *logos* from what Miki called *pathos*, similar to Lacan's pathemes.

Miki's *kiso keiken* at once destroys and creates. It respects the logos that is always ahead of it as it necessarily cuts into and reconfigures this logos in its *pathos* of affective thrownness. He theorized this hybrid of *logos* and *pathos* in a sympathetic critique of what he saw to be Heidegger's undertheorization of a social theory still recovering from the hangover from a Cartesian/Husserlian subjective individualism.

When Miki returned to Japan in 1926, he quickly became a Marxist and for the next ten years or so attempted to alloy the protocols of a *Dasein* analysis with his own hermeneutical Marxist signature, some fifteen years before this methodology would become popular in Western Europe. In 1932 he published *The Philosophy of History* (*Rekishi tetsugaku*).[22] Here, Miki distinguishes what Hayden White would call three historical tropes. History as actual event is nominated history-as-being (*sonzai*), and this corresponds to something like an intelligible, though reified, ontic history.[23] History as the constellation of symbolic laws, codes, and events he calls history-as-logos (*rogosu*). Miki's third category is an upgrade of the earlier *kiso keiken*, which he calls history-as-facticity (*jijitsu to shite no rekishi*). I translate *jijitsu*—usually rendered as "fact" or "truth"—as facticity to give the sense of ontological primordiality to this historical trope. Miki is trying to articulate the sense of a lived materiality as event that is constitutive for history-as-being and history-as-logos, and in this sense it is an algorithm of sorts for Heidegger's *Dasein*. History-as-facticity, or history-as-the-Real—as William Haver recodes the Japanese—gets at the brute material fact of history, which is not to be accessed by either of the ontic historical modes. Miki argues that *jijitsu to shite no rekishi* would ontologically (*ontologischteki*) mediate *logos* and *pathos*. As a Heideggerian, Miki argues for the primacy of the ontological—or what Lacan would nominate as the Real after reading Heidegger. Although read as an intervention into Marxist historiography, it can and has been configured as an argument for the movement from existence as material history into the social.[24]

Reading Miki as a Heideggerian Marxist needs to be carefully qualified before turning to his analysis of technology. Miki's attempt to put the facticity of the fundamental experience before the ontico-ontological divide necessitates our placing him in relation to Nishida's notion of "absolute nothingness." With this notion, Nishida tried to combine the ontic and the ontological and, rewinding our earlier discussion of Heidegger, the authentic and the inauthentic. Absolute nothingness is located in the self-development of this dialectical self-determination.[25] The development from nothingness would be the absently present site of a pure or fundamental experience in Miki's sense. His notion of *jijitsu* and his emphasis on activity allows one to get out of the problem of a tilt toward either the ontic or ontological. Haver tries to argue that "what 'action' means for Miki is the condition of possibility for that very differentiation or rupture between the ontic and the ontological. ... For Miki the ex-pressivity of signification, a material practice, founds those differences which decenter our being in the world."²⁶ This drive to "ex-press" comes from a place Miki calls "demonic."

However, this demon is not so demonic as to transcend historical materiality, unlike the demon that one could construct from both Heidegger's and Nishida's texts. Miki's facticity/Real as ex-pression cuts the social as it is cut and inscribed by the social. What he called a "dialectical ontology" would implicitly critique both the reading of the early Heidegger that was prominent among the major Japanese philosophers in the late 1920s and 1930s (that Heidegger's *tetsugaku* was still too subjective and that *Dasein* had some of the same characteristics as the good old Cartesian *subjectum*) *and* the reading of *Being and Time* that I share with Michel Haar and that has been previously sketched (that the early Heidegger was leaning too much toward the being of a technic/techno-determinist). Miki's dialectic of ex-pressivity, which cuts the social as it is cut by the social, needs only to be read against one of the few mentions of the body in *Being and Time* to bring out this point.

Right at the beginning of the important Section 26, where Heidegger briefly discusses the crucial notion of Mitdasein/Being-with, there is a brief mention of the kind of being that is involved with zuhanden/ready-to-hand entities and the way in which this kind of being receives its determining assignments from the equipmental totality. This kind of being receives "an essential assignment or reference to possible wearers ... for whom it should be 'cut to the figure'" (153/117). Putting a search on "cut to the figure" in Heidegger's German produces the readout "Leib zugeschnitten," which can also be translated as "cutting into the body." This cutting into the body and tattooing it with the symbolic codes of the equimental tooltality sounds very much like the Taylorist ideologies of upgrading human bodies and readying them for the increasing panic over exigencies of industrial capitalism in the 1920s. The sciences of ergonomics and human engineering—which, of course, would become hegemonic in Germany a few years after the publication of *Being and Time* in 1927—are just two examples of the industrial sciences that concerned themselves exclusively with the most effective ways to get docile bodies to harmonize with the dictates of both industrial machinery and increasingly competitive world markets. The putatively pastoral Heidegger—whom some configure today as a proto-Green—sounds very much like a modern primitive in 1927.

In my discussion of Heidegger's notion of dis-severance, I tried to quickly sketch the aporia in the basic structures of *Dasein's* being-in-the world, which is its quality of breaking down distances and bringing what is far near; technical equipment also seems to have this existential structure. The point is not to attempt to keep straight the hierarchy of who or what gets to dis-sever who or what, as Heidegger himself is making the first serious attempt this century to get out of the violent digital of subject/object and active/passive. What I am attempting to make clear is that one of the modes that Heidegger employed to take his step back out of metaphysics was to accessorize *Dasein* with some of the same structures as technical equipment. In his haste to do this—and along the way splatter the subject/object digital—he subjectivizes *Dasein*, which was the dominant critique of *Being and Time* in Japan. He also depends on the matrix of *zuhanden* equipment in a mode very close to a technological determinism that would have as its allies both the hegemonic scientific socialism grounded in a forces-of-production argument in the Soviet Union of the late 1920s and 1930s and the North American Taylorist and Fordist industrial engineers—Heidegger's two most famous enemies. I have been alloying this troubled aporia of an equipmental totality and the reliance on equipment that is ready-to-hand and calling it cyborg envy. The desire for a fluid interfacing with and nonreifying relation to the objective world was Heidegger's telos. His deep hatred for the Cartesian subject of consciousness led him to some astonishing and brilliant meditations on the problems of ontology and temporality. It also initially forced him to put the old subject of consciousness into a modernized and technologized world on automatic play, and this mode of autoplay was hard-drived in the early Heidegger by *equipmental* desires and exigencies.

Miki Kiyoshi Presses the Pause Button on Heidegger

Miki's *Ningen sonzai no Hyogensei* (The Representation of Human-being),[27] written in the mid-1930s, doesn't mention Heidegger at all. This was the case in all of Miki's important texts after 1930. Heidegger functions very much in the mode of a ghostly interlocutor, an absent presence[28] who haunts all of Miki's works. I read this text as responding directly to some of the problems I have sketched in *Being and Time*, although it is difficult to say if this was the referent for his signifier. One of the most interesting points Miki makes in his implicitly explicit critique of Heidegger is his notion of a "mutual dis-severance" (*fudan no kogo*). What he calls *homo faber* is operational in a thrown dialectical movement toward language, and that language as a social technology brings close and is thrown toward *homo faber*. The structure of this mutual dis-severance is such that it is difficult to distinguish the digital, if there is a digital at all; "to say it more concretely, language and manual labor exist in the deseverance of mutual use, difficult to separate."[29] What Miki means here by "language" is intended to both quilt the digital labor/language and technology and displace it. Donna Haraway writes that "there is no fundamental, ontological separation in our formal knowledge of machine and organism, of technical and organic."[30] I would put Miki and Haraway on line together as they read what could be called the zone of interfaciality or the cyborg as that which both joins and separates, both condenses and shatters, the limits of organic-technical interfacing.

Miki has what he calls two definitions of technology. The first one is the delimited meaning of technology, the second is the fluid meaning of technology, that which he calls demonic: "This notion of the material production of technology—the narrow meaning of technology—exists in order to attain the end result of changing nature. Technology, on the other hand has a demonic nature (*demonisch na seikaku*)."[31] He characterizes the first meaning as purely instrumental and the second as something akin to what Julia Kristeva calls the "semiotic," the realm where all drives and pulsions are effected and the originary site of their dissemination. Miki wants to emphasize the expressive (*hyogen*) nature of the demonic mode of technology. *Hyogen* means both representation and expression, but the sense employed here is the pulsating drive that the demonic has to press out and beyond the site of its production, in the sense of Haver's translation *ex-pression*. He also uses *pathos* to describe this structure of desire as drive, or what Lacan would call ten years later the pathemes. This movement will then be recoded and contained by the first mode of technology, which he also nominates as *logos*. Miki emphasizes over and over the mutual complicity of the two technological modes. His claim is that "the essence of technology must be understood from the dialectical construction of logothetic (*rogosteki*) and pathematic (*patosteki*) of human *Dasein* (*sonzai*)."[32]

As a necessary supplement to this dialectical structure, Miki adds a third term. He calls this nothingness, and it grounds everything groundlessly. "Human subjective existence is grounded in the thing that is built on human nothingness. Even if the technological demon is the one/single activity, this is not objectively regulated interest, rather it is the pathos regulated by fundamental nothingness."[33] Miki sets up a triangulated system involving nothingness as ground which in turn drives pathos, which in turn drives logos. This trinitarian system also works the other way, operational in an open feedback system. This works very much like a trilateral dis-severing, though Miki doesn't say this explicitly.

A triangulated structure would also disallow the purportedly uncontaminated Heideggerian distinction between ontic and ontological, a distinction that becomes blurred at times, though most often the border police guarding against contaminants between ontic and ontological are on round-the-clock duty. It would be useful to extend his trinitarian structure to his discussion of tools. For Miki, human existence, things in the world, and the body—as a composite of organs—are all theorized as tools. He begins his discussion of techne/technology (*gijitsu*) by playing on the slippage in Japanese between *kikan* and *kiki*. *Kikan* means "organ," as in an organ of the body. It can also mean "instrument" or "prosthetic." The Chinese character that is read *ki* in Japanese and that is the first character in the two-character word for "body organ" means "instrument" or "device" by itself. This character is the second character in the Japanese word for machine, *kiki*. The Chinese character *ki*, in Miki's usage, condenses both the organic and the technical/technological. To extend this a bit, *ki* combined with the second character in the Japanese word for tool, *dogu*, gives us the readout *kigu* as implement/device/appliance. Miki suggests that the metonymic displacement from *kikan* as body organ to *kigu* as technical device or implement occurs through tools, *dogu*. He writes, "The uniqueness of tools and their importance are situated in a zone belonging to the object and at the same time belonging to the subject. ... In this modality, tools mediate the subject and object."[34] The tool as both body and machine mediates what Miki calls the zone between subject and object: "The thing that mediates subject and object is the essence of all systemic activity and the systemic activity is generally tool-like, rather it is technological."[35] Here the technological as tool is the master trope for the interfacial zone of subject and object and opens on the becoming-cyborg.

"What You Need Is a Big Strong Hand ... Ex-press Yourself" —Madonna

Miki won't let us forget, though, that the movement from organ to machine through tools always loops us back to the body, as he argues that the hand is always a tool and technological prostheses are always only doubles of the hand.[36] To highlight this he argues that reason as the symbolic and the hand as a tool are equiprimordial: "So not to separate hand and tool, the coming to existence of the hand and the materialization of reason can't be separated."[37] We need to remember that Miki wants to theorize the human, *ningen*, as "being between," or the entity that is both the production of material difference *and* the effect of her expressive activity and the expressive activity of the Other. This zone of betweenness/*ningen* is driven by the organism as body and it is steered by the material trace of the social. *Ningen* produces/writes/expresses by the hand as always already technological. This hand carries the triple responsibility of being, making, and using tools and expression/*hyogen*, and production is only possible as the result of the hand both making and using tools. Miki's ground of the hand that is the tool and that makes and uses tools might be offered as a partial retroactive response to Judith Butler's critique of the hegemony of the phallus in Lacan. Butler writes in "The Lesbian Phallus and the Morphological Imaginary"[38] that symbolic structures of mirroring—as Lacan articulates in his "Mirror Stage" article—unify all organs and body parts under the name and law of the male penis/phallus: "Lacan claims that the organs are 'taken up' by a narcissistic relation, and that this narcissistically invested anatomy becomes the structure, the principle, the grid of all epistemic relations. In other words, it is the narcissistically imbued organ which is then elevated to a structuring principle which forms and gives access to all knowable objects. In the first place, this account of the genesis of epistemological relations implies that all knowable objects will have an anthropomorphic and androcentric character. Secondly, this androcentric character will be phallic."[39] Miki argues that the law of the hand will necessarily decenter a phallic androcentrism and privilege social labor and technical prostheses. His answer to the Lacanian—and in my reading of *Dasein* as phallus, Heideggerian—aporia as articulated by Butler echoes Madonna's "What you need is a big strong hand"— the most effective line of flight from the precincts of penis/phallus.

The (Heideggerian) Nerd Is a Noeud[40]

To come to closure here, we seem to have arrived at a provisional definition of the Heideggerian nerd. By way of locating this figure, we could begin with the morphed picture of an atomized subject still hung up on the Cartesian need for a subject/object binary—again, the dominant reading of Heidegger in Japan in the 1920s and 1930s and Nishida's take on him—and disavowing this hang-up, immersing *him*self in what McLuhan called "gadget love." This Heideggerian nerd thinks that gadgets and the right software programs will help him to get out of the violent closure of the subject/object digital. The nerd seems to be aware of the problems of the old metaphysics of identity that wants to fully differentiate itself without contamination from Others. This nerd seems to be "wary of holism, but needy for connection"; this nerd wants to be jacked in. The process of accessing is not separate from the process of being accessed, the nerd knows well. The nerd is aware of his programming of cyborg envy, and he knows that this is not a *fallen* mode but one that is constitutive for human *Dasein*. Miki Kiyoshi suggests that human *Dasein*'s being is being-between. The nerd calls this "being-a-cyborg." The Heideggerian nerd would trope and swerve the essence of *Dasein* until, swerving, it crashed into the cyborg; the cyborg would terminate it. As this morphed *Dasein*, *Dasein* terminated, the cyborg would have the highest degree of issueness/ presence, as it is always being thrown/placed into the abyss of nonpresence/ issuelessness. Is the nerd, however, stage-managing his own defacement, though merely to regather subjective power at a higher, phallic level, at a place where the nerd would tip over into the noeud?

Eyephone, Therefore I Am

Miki's emphasis on the history and production of technology as expression won't allow for the reified and determinist modes of technical equipment articulated in *Being and Time*. When both agency and the social receive their assignments and references from the totality of equipment—which, although looped through *Dasein* and its constellations of concerns, still seems to position and interpellate *Dasein* on its terms—the effect is a certain, closed world. This closed world, in many ways like the closed-off universe of a militarized virtual reality environment or the experience of being hardwired to computer programs through "eyephone" technology, seems to be constructed to immunize the socialized self from material contradictions and the real traces of a history. As the Rodney King trial winds down and we wait for the verdict here in California, the ISA and RSA solutions to the social and economic problems that the King situation were only an effect of are becoming mobilized around technical solutions and technological quick fixes. No money has been spent on inner-city social problems, R&D, or job creation, but lots of money has been spent on the technologized modes of social control. The structure of equipmental totality assigning its police new high-tech tracking gear and more powerful electronic stun guns is providing answers to the serious problems of the urban space that is Los Angeles. These answers are lacking completely in any concern or analysis of labor, race, and violent structures of social history. An equipmental totality that drives Southern California's law-enforcement panopticon looks for answers and solutions only in terms of technical equipment and new high-tech gadgetry.

NOTES

I'd like to thank the following friends and mentors for discussing this essay in part or whole with me: resident Hoy Polloi Scott Mobley, Diane Nelson, Sue Ratour, Andrew Haas, Naoki Sakai, and Jacques Derrida, whose graduate seminar at Irvine in spring 1992 provided an encouraging space for me to initially stumble through—I'd rather think of it more in terms of a Nietzschean stammer—some of these thoughts. I take all blame, of course, for the necessary fuck-ups and misprisions.

1. Recently, the two most interesting works—and the ones that I will be offering sympathetic critiques of—are Avital Ronell's *The Telephone Book* (Lincoln: University of Nebraska Press, 1989), and Michael E. Zimmerman's *Heidegger's Confrontation with Modernity* (Bloomington and Indianapolis: Indiana University Press, 1990). Ronell has offered the most brilliant and thorough analysis of the early Heidegger around the notion of the technologization of the call that comes from an uncanny place of the Other, or the *unheimlich* site of an Other nondifferentiated from *Dasein*'s own being-for-itself. Ronell installs the telephone in a place that Heidegger—in her analysis—would supposedly want to hold open exclusively for poetry and art. This installation demonstrates the ways in which the telephone in cyberspace, "somewhere among politics, poetry, and science, between memory and hallucination" (p. 3), scrambles the purity of the limit marking thinking and technology. In what is coming to be accepted as one of the most seriously provocative readings of the technological since Heidegger, she demonstrates how the telephone is the instantiation of the constitutive poisoning of thinking by technology. She argues that a two-way street as feedback loop is operational as a continuum between subjectivity and technicity that puts into crisis Heidegger's thesis that the essence of technology is nothing technological. Her proposition that "no fundamental distance establishes itself between the technical, natural, human, or existential worlds, no purity or exteriority of any one of these to the other," is, in my reading, precisely what Heidegger is trying to articulate in *Being and Time*. Ronell's breathtaking deconstruction, then, is itself partially undone-better; it is supplemented—as my reading is supported, leans on, and is inspired by hers—by a close look at the sections on equipmentality in Division 1 together with key parts of Divi-

sion 2. My thesis is simply that Heidegger lays the groundwork himself for the existential analytic of *Being and Time,* that "no fundamental distance establishes itself between the technical, natural, and human worlds." I was surprised to discover that my thesis, drawn from only two close readings of the text with help from Michel Haar, contradicts pretty much all of the secondary commentary on this issue, including Zimmerman's book. To his credit, Zimmerman fully sketches the problematic.

2. See *Philosophy Today* (Summer 1987) for a long list of these readings. For example, Simon Moser concludes a long essay on Heidegger and technology with the hysteria of this warning shot: "The situation of man becomes tragic, for ultimately Being itself provokes man to provoke nature and he cannot extricate himself from this situation under his own power." "Toward a Metaphysics of Technology," *Philosophy Today* 15, no. 2 (Summer 1971), p. 148. The unproductive digital that gets set up in most of these discussions between a have-a-nice-day antitechno "liberation" on one hand and "technological determinism" on the other can perhaps best be answered with the Not! of the Foucaultian/Nietzschean laugh programmed into all children of power/knowledge, like me. See also discussions by Zoe Sofoulis, "Through the Lumen: Frankenstein and the Optics of Re-origination" (University of California–Santa Cruz, Ph.D. thesis, 1988); the intelligently sober discussion offered by Andrew Ross, *Strange Weather* (London: Verso, 1992); and Chuck D., the lead singer for the rap group Public Enemy. Chuck D. suggests in the rock monthly *Spin* (October 1992) that African American aesthetic culture has been enabled by technological advances, and he says that the white-boy totalizing paranoia about an evil technology is a bullshit ivory tower privilege; Public Enemy says that African Americans have much more immediate modes of domination to deal with. My reading of the 1927 Heidegger would put him in total agreement with Public Enemy, at least on this point.

The moral universe that mobilizes a "just say no to technology" position seems to be a symptom of a resentful and tragic white-male anxiety that can only proclaim apocalyse now—instead of a more responsible Foucault/Haraway answer of "apoco-ellipsis," emphasizing the continuation after the technological intervention and the necessity to intervene politically in the process from beginning to end instead of *white-wine*ing about it—at every technological innovation. The long list includes luminaries like Marcuse and Vattimo as "misreading" Heidegger, usually a misreading that ignores *Being and Time* as laying the ground for the discussions of technology that will take place later; discussions that will often elicit the disavowal of this ground of technical equipment in the earlier work. This "misreading" is absolutely consistent among the right-wing, or nondeconstructive, Heideggerians who privilege the later work on language and read him as a proto-Green who finds in poetry and nature a mystical access code to being. By "right-wing, nondeconstructive," I would of course include most of the white-male New Left (now undead) interventions of the 1960s, mainly inspired by Marcuse, though they are not as complexly undecidable and sophisticated as Marcuse's own meditations on these matters. As perhaps the most symptomatic of this position, Paul Colaizzi's book on technology employs the standard misreading of Heidegger. He defines technology's origin as "that endeavor which in bad faith seeks to surmount death," *Technology and Dwelling: The Secrets of Life and Death* (Pittsburgh, 1978), p. 10. Later, he discusses ways to avoid a technologically determined being and locate a mode of existence that would be more humanly liberating. His textual cum shot actually says the following, coming close to a parody of the machismo of the white-male Undead Left, "Feeling the world and fucking the world is the

only *preparation* for death. Authentic embodied existence is making love to the world. …
Ecstasy, self-transcendence, love-making—they all go together. This way of going is our alternative to bad faith, technology and death-evasion" (p. 92).

3. Martin Heidegger, *Sein und Zeit* (Tubingen: Max Niemeyer Verlag, 1986), and *Being
and Time*, trans. John Macquarrie and Edward Robinson (New York: Harper and Row,
1962). All citations give the English page number followed by the German page number.

4. Don Ihde has an excellent work that I discovered after my essay here had been proof-
read. It fiber-optic-cables *Being and Time* to "The Question Concerning Technology," as it
offers a smart reading of tools in the 1927 text and their constitutive infacings with the later
notions of technology. See his *Existential Technics* (Albany: State University of New York
Press, 1983).

5. Lucien Goldmann has an interesting reading that makes the claim that *Being and
Time* is an answer of sorts and almost a sympathetic critique of Lukacs's *History and Class
Consciousness*. The similarity between Heidegger and Lukacs has been frequently demon-
strated. Both philosophers were obsessed with overcoming the subject/object digital,
Lukacs by appealing to social praxis, Heidegger by a ground of cyborg envy. *Lukacs and
Heidegger* (London: Routledge and Kegan Paul, 1977).

6. "For the exogenously extended organizational complex functioning as an integrated
homeostatic system unconsciously, we propose the term 'Cyborg.' The cyborg deliberately
incorporates exogenous components extending the self-regulatory control function of the
organism in order to adapt it to new environments. If man in space, in addition to flying
his vehicle, must continously be checking on things and making adjustments merely in order to keep himself alive, he becomes a slave to the machine. The purpose of the Cyborg, as
well as his own homeostatic systems, is to provide an organizational system in which such
robot-like problems are taken care of automatically and unconsciously, leaving man free to
explore, to create, to think, and to feel." Manfred Clynes and Nathan S. Kline, "Cyborgs
and Space," *Astronautics* (September 1960), p. 27. It is fitting that the term "cyborg" (from
cybernetic organism) was coined in this technical article on the development of man-machine systems in space, for the very possibility of cyborgs is predicated on militarized high
technology, or in Heidegger's (space) case—the hypertechnologized state of a national socialism. When Manfred Clynes and Nathan S. Kline first articulated the word in 1960, they
defined cyborgs as "artifact-organism systems" that would be integrated on an unconscious level. Cyborgs appeared in science fiction decades before the term was constructed.
Stories such as "Solar Plexus" by James Blish (1941), "No Woman Born" by C. L. Moore
(1944), and "Camouflage" by Henry Kuttner (1945) all have fully realized cyborgs. Cruder
cyborgish creatures were written about in the 1930s and, of course, in the discourse of fundamental ontology of the 1920s.

My deployment of the term will speak to the notion of a subject essentially thrown into
a world determined by what Heidegger calls in *Being and Time* the devices and instruments
of an "equipmental totality." This overdetermination of the human *Dasein* by its involvement in technologized equipment will have to stand as my first preliminary definition.
These days the term is fashionably deployed as both a celebration and a critique of the situation Heidegger described in a very positive fashion in 1927, and Donna Haraway articulates in a somewhat less enthusiastic—though celebratory as to the role of contemporary
technologization in the decentering of the white-male subject of Western reason—mode in
1985.

A cyborg can be anything from a human with a neurocontrolled prosthesis to a computer made up of organic biochips to a robot with a thin veneer of human skin, as in the Terminator movies. Lewis Mumford talks of the astronaut, and all humans today, as "encapsulated man," existing only within and connected to complex mechanical systems, exemplified by the astronaut's pressure suit. Donna Haraway agrees. In "A Cyborg Manifesto: Science, Technology, and Socialist-Feminism in the Late Twentieth Century," in *Simians, Cyborgs, and Women* (Routledge: New York, 1991), she writes that "by the late twentieth century, our time, a mythic time, we are all chimeras, theorized and fabricated hybrids of machine and organism; in short, we are cyborgs." Most of this information has been provided by my friend and colleague Crystal Gray.

7. I borrow the term as I partly refunction it from my friend and fellow Santa Cruz grad student Joe Dumit. He is the editor of the forthcoming *Visual Anthropology,* which will deal with "cyborg anthropology." All of this is inspired by Donna Haraway, of course.

8. See Hubert Dreyfus, "Heidegger's History of the Being of Equipment," in *Heidegger: A Critical Reader* (Oxford: Basil Blackwell, 1991). I came upon this text while trying to work out my argument from a reading of Heidegger that is indebted to Philippe Lacoue-Labarthe's distinction between onto-typology and typography in his work on *typos* in Heidegger. See his "Typographie," in *Mimesis des articulations* (Paris: Flammarion, 1975); and "L'obliteration," in *Le Sujet de la philosophie* (Paris: Aubier-Flammarion, 1979). I discuss some problems I have with Dreyfus in my Ph.D. dissertation, University of California–Santa Cruz, forthcoming.

9. To offer a provisional definition of cyborg envy here, I would have to locate a movement—developed further in my dissertation—from the pre–World War I Freudian penis envy to the postwar cyborg envy, a movement I will try to locate in Gertrude Stein, the Mexican Communist painter J. C. Oroszco, Japanese proletarian women's writing of the 1920s and 1930s, and Georges Bataille as well as here with Heidegger. The shift has everything to do with the ways in which gender and the subject undergo major retoolings as effects of the devastations brought by World War I and the globalization of technological goods and the philosophies of industrial management proliferating in the world system of the 1920s and 1930s. One of the effects of all this was to irreparably obliterate the patriarchal humanist subject of 1900 and recollect it differently in a desire for hookups with machines and technical gadgets, with the attendant shifts in gender called out by these transformations.

10. Haraway, "A Cyborg Manifesto," p. 151.

11. Ibid., p. 150.

12. Lacoue-Labarthe, in "Typographie," criticizes this notion of *Gestell* in the Heidegger of the 1930s as something that Heidegger attempted to situate beyond relations of mirroring and mimesis. This notion of a depoliticized *Gestell*—depoliticized because it is outside of the politics of representation and social positioning—is no longer configured in the social world of the Heideggerian "They" or in the mode of a social being-with.

13. See Hubert Dreyfus, *Being-in-the-World* (Cambridge: MIT Press, 1992), pp. 97–99, for support for this and an extremely clear and helpful analysis of what he calls "The Interdependence of *Dasein* and World."

14. Haraway, "A Cyborg Manifesto," p. 150.

15. Jacques Derrida, *Parages* (Paris: Galillee, 1986), p. 27. My translation.

16. Eyephones are small video monitors—like small television screens—that are placed over each eye in some virtual reality systems. These eyephones are attached to the virtual software program and provide visual information fed from larger computers. The technologically enhanced "freedom to explore" is overdetermined by the programmer's gender and power markings and remarkings, of course. Karaoke is similarly a technological environment that allows one to "have fun" and "express oneself." I am not foreclosing on the resistive possibilities of new technologies—I have tried both karaoke and virtual reality and love them both—but merely readying the warning systems as to their undecidability. On a more progressive note, see Susie Bright's work on virtual reality and virtual sex in her *Virtual Sex Reader*, and the newly formed group of software engineers, Digital Queers. Tom Reilly, founder of Digital Queers, says that the goal of his group is to empower the queer movement to disseminate information rapidly: "We'll connect the gay groups around the country—the idea is to have gay individuals connected to gay groups and the groups connected together, all part of one big on-line queer universe." *Advocate*, March 9, 1993, p. 17.

17. See Dreyfus, "Heidegger's History of the Being of Equipment," p. 135.

18. Gilles Deleuze and Felix Guattari, *A Thousand Plateaus* (Minneapolis: University of Minnesota Press, 1987), p. 456.

19. Ibid., p. 457.

20. Ibid., p. 458.

21. See Naoki Sakai, "Return to the West/Return to the East," in *Japan in the World*, special issue of *Boundary 2*, 18, no. 3 (Fall 1991).

22. Miki Kiyoshi, *Rekishi tetsugaku*, in *Miki Kiyoshi zenshu* (Complete Works of Miki Kiyoshi), ed. Ouchi Hyoei et al., 19 vols. (Tokyo: Iwanami, 1966–1968), vol. 6. *Miki Kiyoshi zenshu* will hereafter be cited as *MKz* with the volume number following. All translations from Japanese are mine.

23. See William Haver, "The Body of This Death: Alterity in Nishida-Philosophy and Post-Marxism" (University of Chicago, Ph.D. diss., 1987), pp. 54–60, for a stunning discussion of Miki's historical tropes. My thinking on Miki has been deeply influenced and tattooed by Haverian inscriptions.

24. See Yasuo Yuasa, "The Encounter of Modern Japanese Philosophy with Heidegger," in *Heidegger and Asian Thought*, ed. Graham Parkes (Honolulu: University of Hawaii Press, 1987).

25. See Nishida Kitaro, *Nishida Kitaro zenshu* (Tokyo: Iwanami Shoten, 1965–1966), vol. 11, pp. 441–442.

26. Haver, "The Body of This Death," p. 71.

27. *MKz*, vol. 18, pp. 297–355. Again, all translations from Japanese are mine unless otherwise noted.

28. Naoki Sakai made this point to me in personal correspondence, and I am grateful.

29. *MKz*, vol. 18, p. 313.

30. Haraway, "A Cyborg Manifesto," p. 178.

31. *MKz*, vol. 18, p. 310.

32. Ibid., p. 312.

33. Ibid., p. 306.

34. Ibid., p. 301.

35. Ibid. p. 302.

36. Heidegger, by contrast, wants to cut off organs from *Dasein*. The protocols of a Heideggerian fundamental ontology hold that humans don't have eyes in order to see, rather it is because we see that we have eyes. The same applies to hands; readyness-at-hand is an authentic mode of *Dasein,* but the facticity of hands as such falls from this mode and derives from it. My sneaking suspicion is that the deprivileging of organs may be operational as the disavowal of the main organ for Heidegger, the phallus/penis. Consider for a moment the similarity in the language describing the phallus in Lacan as that which "gathers and collects" and Heidegger's description of *Dasein* as that which "gathers entities and clears a space for them."

37. *MKz*, vol. 18, p. 302.

38. Judith Butler, "The Lesbian Phallus and the Morphological Imaginary," *Differences* 4 (Spring 1992), pp. 133–171.

39. Ibid., p. 152.

40. *Noeud* is the French word for "cock," which Lacan uses sometimes in place of and as supplement—plenty is needed to keep the undead Old Man propped up—for phallus. Its French pronunciation is a homophone for the word "nerd." *Noeud* also means knot, as that which ties and gathers together, again exactly like *Dasein*. The Lacanian pun on the "Father's noeud" as the (1) father's cock, (2) father's ability to gather and unite under his law, and (3) the father's Not as the castrating No of the father as punitive, is becoming a bit clichéd. I repeat it here only to set up my wordplay: The (Heideggerian) nerd is a noeud, Not!?

15

The Best of Both Worlds:
On *Star Trek*'s Borg

JULIA WITWER

<<Cultural Worker's Log, Stardate 5432.1.>>

SITTING BEFORE ME on my desk is a little figure about four inches high, known as an "action figure." It's Captain Jean-Luc Picard, a rather good likeness, with veins on his hands and little worry lines on his high forehead. He is jointed and fully poseable, ready for "action," but his expression is tranquil. One hand makes a catchall open fist, the other a strange gesture, two fingers extended, like the signal of the hierophant. For giving orders, perhaps. "As the Symbolic Order, civilization (in its modern version at least) is a vast unconscious. But no 'unconscious' can force the consciousness to work for it, it can extract no energy or labour from it *without having an executive arm*, without, that is, appearing in (twisted) form to that consciousness."[1]

As Picard, in his incarnation as the Borg mouthpiece Locutus, forms the center of my meditation, I will take this little figure as my mascot and guide and consider, as I look at him, the nature of the order that is to be executed.

▮○⸏⸏↦▮▮▮ ▮⸏▮ℓ⤛ ⸏⤜▮▮↦↦▮ℏ⤞ℓℓℓℓℓ⸏⸏‿‿‿‿▮▮é ⁎ ⁎ ⁎ ⁎

éäℓ▮▮ℓ▮○⸏▮◖▮▮ℓ⸏○○⤛↦⸏▮⤜▮▮ℏ▮ ö § §s, ¢∞ wü⸳⸳⸳u [[[▮◖▮⤞▮▮○◖▮▮[[[[[[[[[[[

make it so

#⸏⸏▮`▮▮⸏▮▮⸏▮▮⸏▮ ▮åaˆøπ4$S ▮○⸏⸏‿‿▮▮↦ ▮▮ø•¥⸳ʃ8▮ ▮↦↦▮▮⸏ᵃe 8ˆ⸳⸳

▮·˙▮▮   åaros ååååååˉ«««««««««««««««««««««««««««««««««««Let's begin with the enemy.

Science fiction has always been distinctive for its enemies. It departs from the tedious sameness of the Red, Yellow, or Brown Menace one finds in "realistic" adventure fiction, giving us green, atemporal, or amorphous menaces instead. It is rather refreshing to fight nightmares instead of people every so often, to let one-self go, to externalize all that is hateful to one in some wildly original fashion and have at it with lasers.

(As a rule, we humans seem to like having enemies. It relieves our minds.)

Enemies from outer space are familiar to us. Grendel and his mother, creeping out of the lake, were some of the first aliens. Of course, their ancestor was Cain, the one who was banished to the Outer Darkness, thousands of light-years away. Today we know better than to be afraid of lakes. Today we even shoot craft into the sky. Not much, but enough to make us understand that the Outer Darkness is also to be inhabited, that it simultaneously recedes and cedes to us its terrain—space: "The Final Frontier."

Our dreams of outer space are vivid and uneasy; we cohabit with a startlingly vast array of other sentient beings, to which we can no longer readily relate as "en-emies." We are not allowed to stigmatize the green races. The Klingons cannot be the repository of atavistic nightmare anymore, and nowadays it's considered dis-respectful to refer to Vulcans as "pointy-eared devils." Each race, we have been forced to acknowledge, has its own "culture." (The best, the ideal, enemy has no culture and no aim but its own supremacy, your own destruction.)

Star Trek: The Next Generation (hereafter referred to as STTNG) is an uneasy dream about human variety and human virtue. It treats gingerly these other kinds that, we have been taught, are much like "us" (white Americans of the middle class, STTNG's projected core viewing audience). The dream is careful not to of-fend; it has changed its motto to embrace the female spacefarer ("to boldly go where no one has gone before"). The Eurocentric, androcentric, anthropocentric model has been buffeted around on campuses, in the workplace, out here in space. STTNG has moved with alacrity to make the proper changes. A Klingon serves on the *Enterprise*. A woman is a doctor. A black man is chief of engineering.

Did we feel some relief when the enemy, after its long sojourn in the outer darkness, finally found us?

ßå¨ød9p‿◁∘∎ **∎‿∎∎ ∎∎∎**∘≻__ ___∎∎↦ ///////////////a ¨å [3o‿∎∎↦↦ℓ∎__⇕ ⇕

⇕∎ℏ‿◀∘↦↦é 8ª7 • • • {}

No one knows for sure what kind of people the Borg were before they became their own technology. Nowadays it would be impossible to tell; the Borg (best re-ferred to in a singular form, as the plural to Borg has long fallen out of use) has assimilated countless races in its migration across the galaxy. Its path is devastat-ing, emptying entire planets, leaving huge craters where cities used to be. The people are destroyed outright or incorporated into the computer network. The Borg does not take prisoners—cultures who survive the Borg's assault survive only as bodies. They become new members through a process of neural-net con-tagion, as though their minds had been ransacked by a computer virus.

The huge spaceships of the Borg are cube-shaped—a form that exemplifies total functionality. (In space the streamlined look our ships have is really for show, to give us an impression of motion that we earth-based ones can understand.) Each cube is a hive full of pure white "worker bodies." It is difficult even to say that these bodies have been modified to accept the interpolated Borg technology, the wiring, the chips, the sensors and hookups. It is what they are, what they are for. The Borg body is a kind of living corpse; dead-white skin hints at an uncanny animation; *it lives,* though it should not.

The Borg is not one "mind" spread out over a computerized network of information; or rather, one must not think of the Borg as *an entity.* Nor, as we have seen, is it a race. The Borg is a function. The Borg's powerful weaponry and advanced technology assure its "functioning." You could say that the Borg is very good at what it is—eater of worlds, raptor of cultures; the Federation's run-in with the Borg is a terrifying encounter with a pure drive that evidently exists only to exist: "A drive is precisely a demand that is not caught up in the dialectic of desire, that resists dialecticization. ... Drive ... persists in a certain demand, it is a 'mechanical' insistence that cannot be caught up in dialectical trickery: I demand something and I persist in it to the end."[2] The Borg is utterly foreign: It doesn't even hate. It goes about its grim purpose, affectless, mindless as cancer.

▮↦ ▮_▮▮⤝⤜⤟⟨○▮ℓℓℓ▮ℓℓℓℓℓ▮▮↦_?ajl[[[

The Borg is sighted in Federation space: "Further readings indicate the Borg vessel to be headed to Sector 001 [the Earth Sector] at high warp speeds."[3] The *Enterprise* is dispatched to "engage the Borg in advance of the fleet"[4] while the muster goes out: Here comes trouble. The *Enterprise* encounters the Borg ship, which appears, ominously, to have been waiting for it. Amid the chaos of the Borg attack, Picard is lost in the shuffle: Borg units appear and abduct him straight off the bridge of the *Enterprise.* It becomes clear that the sole purpose of the assault has in fact been to acquire this man.

The capture of Jean-Luc Picard, captain of the starship *Enterprise,* by the Borg, his subsequent modification and incorporation into the Borg, and the devastation his knowledge wreaks on his Federation make up the first half of one of the more bracing season cliffhangers of STTNG. When Picard is inserted into the net, the Borg absorbs his access codes, his knowledge of the Federation's fighting numbers, and his vast strategic powers, all of which it makes efficient use of. The Borg also acquires his memories, his experiences, those things that are surplus, unnecessary, that make him human.

The choice of Picard as the one who becomes Locutus is fitting and horrible. We have had all our hopes pinned on Picard, prized representative of the United Federation of Planets, captain of Starfleet's flagship. Like Beowulf, Picard is the greatest man of his time. And above even his high status, it is his "surplus" that so marks him; of all the characters on STTNG, Picard has the most "character," the most culture. (This may have something to do with why on his little doppelganger, the action figure, his face has been reproduced with such haunting accuracy.)

Picard has been portrayed as a Renaissance man. There is a "Picard-ness" that extends beyond his duties. He quotes Shakespeare from memory (in the world of popular culture, Shakespeare is *the* indicator of high culture, no matter what sector of the galaxy you're in). He plays Mozart on his flute. He drinks Earl Grey tea. He thinks clearly and abstractly and never acts rashly. He is a diplomat and a negotiator, not a conqueror: Picard is the one they send when there is a tricky "first contact" to make with a new people. His intuitions are not rough and fiery, like Captain Kirk's were, but subtle: Still water runs deep, we say, looking at his sober face.

How awful to have this man, champion of the cultivated individual, the best liberal human of them all, suddenly tell us, "Resistance is futile. Assimilation is inevitable."

▄▌▄▄▄█████▄▌█ℏ℧ * * ›fifl432§ å¨åååååååååååååååååååååååååååå a a a * ^(-=
▃▄███∪∩▌λ ▌∩....·▌ ▌▌   {}   ◁ ==== ▌▌‹

If we consider the Federation as a unified culture and study its boundaries, we find that the greatest threat is not a raw, untamed wilderness of space. That "empty" space is actually highly advantageous to the Federation. It provides elbowroom: This is space as container, background, blank canvas. Deep space, far from being the enemy, is the Federation's best friend. The Federation's opposite number is not empty space but "filled," ruled, hyperbolically ordered space. These days, the Federation defines its edge by the Borg, which was described on the show (by an amusing omniscient being called Q) as being "much more than you humans can handle."[5] Indeed, the battle against the Borg takes a grievous toll (the casualties: 39 starships, 11,000 lives). What Q is saying is that the Borg, despite a harrowing absence of what human beings might recognize as culture, is a more complex civilization. What moves the Borg inexorably across the galaxy is what Lacan called a *cultural drive,* the drive behind the symbolic order. Juliet F. MacCannell is helpful here: "The drive of culture is neither benevolent nor malevolent; it is a mindless, inexorable drive towards division, splitting. It is aimed, but only at producing, through this fission, the energy and power to perpetuate itself" (151).

How does this splitting action relate to the terrible oneness the Borg threatens? As cogs relate to the machine: There is one vast apparatus, but the cogs are "ridged," articulated, highly specialized. The Borg is even more specialized, actually, than free, individual, specific human beings.

This is the cultural drive stripped of its lineaments of "culture": just white bodies and black machinery, a particularly meaty allegory.

Of what?

This operation reminds me of something.

▙▁▟▋▋λ▊▊▊▊▊ ··' ·. 90¥¶ᵃ08w= [[[[[f=   o◁▊▊▊▊∩'·.▊···▊▊···▊U▊·'▊▊'·.U∩▁▟

* { ========0w£▊▊ §

The passage that follows is not about science fiction. It does not purport to describe the Borg.

> Symbols set us apart from all other sentient beings since they require a common interhuman recognition for their existence, and a mutual, "conventional" agreement about their significance. Speech is the primary example, as are other forms of social intercourse. But in their tendency to dominate all other modes (e.g. imaginary and real) symbols also have an inherent tendency to move beyond the realm of recognition and conscious agreement. *Unconscious,* they become powerful systems that transcend, pre-date and pre-order those humans who now can be seen less as the makers and masters of the symbol than its servants, less users of symbols as tools than themselves mere instruments for perpetuating the existence of symbols: "speech" cedes priority to language as a general system. (124–125)

Black wires and white bodies suggest the machinery of the black text on a white page. It is on this formal level that the Borg can be seen as a language. Or rather the Borg is *language per se:* When it finally gets to you there can be no plurality of symbolic systems. It is this monadal character that gives the Borg its allegorical resonance. If the Borg is language per se, it is *our* language as well; it cannot be exteriorized as "foreign." That it is profoundly alien at the same time is not a contradiction: It is the language that exists prior to us. It is the incomprehensible Babel into which we are born, and through which we comprehend ourselves.

Juliet F. MacCannell describes "the scene of culture" as "the scene of alienation, order and negation" (157). The Borg is a monoculture that is predicated on a binary split. The Borg units themselves are not isolated from each other: they are locked into the net with no precise sense of self. But the net is built of incredibly intricate *binary codes,* an infinite set of little on/off switches that enables an entire Borg star-cube to function flawlessly with effectively *no* chain of command.

The Borg's goal is homogeneity, but it is neither pure nor impure in its ultimate manifestation, it simply *is.* The Borg realized is the symbolic with nothing left to tame. The drive to order, fulfilled, reverts to sheer undifferentiation.

∂π´▁▁▊▊79q8∫∫∫oyq * *   ü ▁▊▊▊▊▊▊▊▊ℓ ▊▷▊ℓℓℓℓℓℓℓℓ o▊▊

Of course, this all-inclusive Borg is the perfect "impure" against which the Federation can close its doors. The Borg may be a manifestation of symbolic law, predicated on binary distinctions (the Borg understands on and off), but it also presages the end of difference as we know it, the end of "individuality." The "benign" United Federation of Planets wants to dissociate itself from the nasty alien-ating aliens, the Borg. Yet symbolic law is also behind the making of the social hu-man being as we (in "my" culture) understand it. The U.S.S. *Enterprise* is in part a surveyor ship, going "where no one has gone before." The *Enterprise* charts the limits of consciousness, maps its territory, delineates the off-limits neutral zones: It patrols the border, the edge of the dark mere of the unconscious, ostensibly ex-tending Federation knowledge and territories but also protecting the Federation's integrity against the Outside.

Picard, as ship's captain, is the local representative of Federation law; he per-forms marriages and carries out delicate diplomatic functions. He is the adjudica-tor par excellence. His characteristic order is not "Do this" but "Make it so." "Make it so" is not an invasive or tyrannical command, rather it suggests the abil-ity to adjust and to go with the flow: It is eminently reasonable. As captain, Picard governs democratically, quick to integrate the suggestions and insights of his team into his agenda. ("Engage," another characteristic order, is somewhat myste-rious; demanding no specific direct action, it is merely an injunction to *hook up*, to get going.) Juliet F. MacCannell remarks: "In this most benign, 'civilizing' in-terpretation, the Symbolic Order stands in the role of the mediator: as the law, it restricts desire; as the mediator who must also assure procreation, it also—selec-tively—accommodates desire to the law which denies it" (128).

Finally, STTNG operates with a paradigm of self as ineffable, indestructible center, the structure of which is established by an essentialized, post-romantic hu-manism, along with a friendly overlay of twentieth-century pop psychology. Cul-ture is the locus of what is "best" and "most human" about us (should they really be elided?). Michelangelo's David, as Picard explains to Lieutenant Data in a later episode, speaks to us all "individually." Various interpretations will show surface differences—say, if you're a woman or an android or an Organian energy-being—but it's okay, that means you're "unique," the way people are supposed to be. Un-derneath this lovely variety, then, is a formidable vision of unity. *Of course* David speaks to us all. True culture transcends the "trivial" differences. This is "good," friendly, reassuring unity, a common tongue. It is not like the unchecked spread of the Borg's undifferentiated "bad" unity at all.

Is it?

↦▮ where no öne has go§¶•ªö e ‹‹

Despite—or perhaps because of—the haunting similarity between the two, there is a border between Federation and Borg that must be maintained. Locutus is the Federation tainted by the Borg, and therefore the end of the Federation. As-similation is annihilation when you are an autonomous self, Federation style. We'd almost rather see Picard dead. Dead, at least he would still be able to have opposed the Borg, body and soul. Instead, the border between the Federation and its enemy is effaced; the blurring of the critical difference takes place within the body of Jean-Luc Picard, but it has repercussions beyond the loss of a single man. The entire structure of the individual, the subject under Federation law, is what is at stake.

Locutus is an orifice, a hole in the protective wall that defines the Federation-issue subject, like the "narrow breach" through which Freud accessed the unconscious and through which the unconscious—in the form of the nightmare Borg— now has access to us. This access is structured around Locutus's formal function. As "he who speaks," Locutus articulates the Borg's drive to assimilate. The interpretive function of Locutus reminds us that law is not just externals, behavioral proscriptions and prescriptions: The law is the law of language first and foremost. The structure "I" is above all a linguistic one, enmeshed in an intricate web of preordained linguistic connections, a "net" of relations and differentiations wrapped around a formal binary that establishes "the being who speaks" through a severance and a closing off from an undifferentiated "outside" that is coalesced into the Other*___██◄█████t∘≺≺w£™ ██ ███████ a

As MacCannell points out on the first page of this chapter, Locutus is well understood as the executive arm of the unconscious symbolic. He is the articulated limb that allows the Borg to "give an order" to the Federation: "Prepare to be assimilated." But this limb, strangely enough, is not fully under the control of the order it represents. Its special articulation sets it apart in clear ways from other units of the Borg. Most significantly, Locutus speaks in the first person. "I am Locutus of the Borg." No self-respecting Borg component refers to itself as "I." The Borg units number themselves, referring to themselves as "third of five," and so on. And unlike any other Borg unit, Locutus has a name, Latin for "he who speaks." Either we can take this in the original *Star Trek* spirit, in which alien planets frequently mirrored aspects of earth culture, or we can assume that "Locutus" was drawn from Picard's own, presumably capacious, store of Latin. Our assumption has been so far that the Borg has totally "possessed" Picard. Why the Latin term? Why not "third of five," or something more relevant to Borg organization?

Locutus is a hybrid, a function of the edge between the two that "differ." He is not strictly Borg. If he were, he would no longer be of use to it. How else could the Borg speak to the Federation, if there are no speaking subjects in its immense decentralized netweb? But that Latin, and the vestige of Picard's "human" culture that it represents, make him a double-edged weapon. Locutus's liminal status gives him freedom to move and makes him very dangerous to both sides. The danger resides precisely in Locutus's existence out there "on the edge."[6]

As a border function, Locutus is unstable; some amount of bleedthrough between his parts is inevitable. Picard's old nickname for Riker is "Number One" (or Third of Five?). Locutus, in his moment of triumph, makes a verbal "slip" and calls Riker "Number One." It is a strange moment, equally interpretable as the nadir of hope and the Federation's last chance. It could mean that Picard has been fully atomized and incorporated into the Borg, that it has penetrated his most deep-seated affections. Or perhaps it is a message from Picard "himself," speaking through the "slip" or break in Locutus's guard. Picard's crewmembers hope that he is still "in there" somewhere, alive in the netweb, if powerless. This hope is what drives Riker to make a desperate bid to abduct Locutus from the Borg, a move Locutus himself did not foresee and was not prepared to resist. The android Lieutenant Data is able, with great care, to rescue Picard by making use of Locutus as a remote terminal for accessing the Borg. He runs the order down Locutus's two-way speaking pipe: Picard's imbrication in the Borg makes him into the Federation's weapon X. The perfect reversal, the kind of thing good TV is made of.

(Is it coincidence that Data tells the Borg, the emissary of the unconscious symbolic, to "go to sleep?" And is it any coincidence that the netwide shutdown causes the Borg's spaceship to explode? Out of mind, out of sight.)

=0 ------------* ///////§¢• =-slée p sppp [[[[[====▮▮▮▮▮   *

<<Cultural Worker's Log: Analysis, Stardate 5934.1>>

A final note from the final frontier

The Federation (the "benign" differentiations that permit the human subject position to exist) and the Borg (unconscious, "alienated/alienating" symbolic order) are interwoven, not warring—despite what you may have heard via the Federation propaganda machine. The Borg operates as the "nightmare lining" of our Federation's dream of a beneficial and necessary order. They are not separable; in fact, at the point of convergence, the hybrid Locutus, they are not distinguishable.

The U.S.S. *Enterprise* patrols the borders of Federation space to protect it from infection, but the strongest link—Captain Picard—became the weakest when he suddenly manifested the repressive and destructive properties of the symbolic order, which are only latent in his role as agent of the benign law. Captain Picard became the hinge, the thoroughfare that refused to let the Federation close its borders. Locutus appeared as a breach, a break in the border-forming activity of the *Enterprise* as vehicle of the law.

We first saw what was going on when one of the Borg units on our viewing screen, the one whose face we couldn't see, slowly turned around. The "turn," a great moment for television, was an appearance of that moment when the abyss looks into us. We caught a glimpse of our own reflection in Picard and saw that we were the Borg. This horrific, transgressive moment was what Locutus was all about: This was the precise moment when the difference that kept us ourselves unraveled.

The rescue operation performed by Riker and Data involved the re-formation of the boundaries of Picard's Federation-issue subjectivity. This could only be achieved by their literally making the Borg unconscious, pushing it back "outside" our beloved captain, to be safely our enemy once again. The "turn," which made such good television, is a moment in Jean-Luc Picard that must be repressed. We had to try and freeze the "turn" before it became a "return."

The conclusion of the double episode, curiously enough titled "The Best of Both Worlds, Parts I and II," was an attempt to return the ego to supremacy. Federation high technology enabled us to disentangle the Borg machine from Picard's central nervous system. We were able to salvage Picard (when the first part of the show aired, there were rumors that Patrick Stewart, the actor who plays Picard, was bailing out and the character really was going to die). We stuffed the Borg back into the empty night that has ever befriended us as our own personal receptacle. We hope it won't ever come back.

We keep having this problem with our enemies, you see, they keep coming back.

And I return to the initial object that sparked my meditation, the miniaturized Picard on my desk: the joints and articulations of the subject, the head that turns from side to side, the knees that bend, the arms that lift up and down, the hand that points, giving a sign; the two fingers of the hierophant that remind me of the two-sided powers of the mediator; the word given as the order "speaks us"—as it hails us into being we recognize its power over us, in a sickening moment. We are structured and undermined by the same gesture, the raised arm, the two fingers extended in the gesture of commanå¨å8 3™£§¢ • ᵒᵃ qw (åa¶   wq9 .▪▪_▪ ▪▪▪_▪▪⊁→∪▪_▪▪▪▪◁▪ ▪▪_▪_▪▪_▪ ▪_▪▪λ∩∪¨·.▪ _▪λ▪▪_▪▪.·˙.·˙.·˙

NOTES

1. Juliet Flower MacCannell, *Figuring Lacan: Criticism and the Cultural Unconscious* (London: Croom Helm, 1986), p. 125, my emphasis. Further citations to this work are in the text.

2. I have taken my definition of drives from Slavoj Zizek's *Looking Awry: An Introduction to Jacques Lacan Through Popular Culture* (Cambridge, Mass.: MIT Press, 1991), p. 21.

3. Michael Okuda and Denise Okuda, *Star Trek Chronology: The History of the Future* (New York: Pocket Books, 1993), p. 124.

4. Ibid., p. 124.

5. The Q Continuum, an "advanced lifeform" that occasionally manifests as an obnoxious humanoid (brilliantly played by John deLancie), deserves its own paper.

6. Allow me to engage in a little fanciful speculation on earth mythology: Locutus operates under the auspices of Hermes. Hermes is the god of language, technology, transgression, thievery; he is the lord of the ways, of paths and networks. He is the genius behind the

personal computer revolution and the intersection of "soft" and "hard" technologies such as Locutus embodies. Hermes is an ambivalent servant of law and order and almost certainly generated the first computer viruses, those little pieces of hyperbolic order that bred chaotically and quickly shut down the net. No realm is closed to him; his own realm is always the edge.

16

Recline and Crawl
of Western Civilization:
An Interview with Arthur Kroker

GABRIEL BRAHM JR.

On the whole our present situation more or less resembles that of a party of absolutely ignorant travelers who find themselves in a motor-car launched at full speed and driverless across broken country. When will the smash-up occur?

—Simone Weil[1]

SIMONE WEIL WAS HARDLY a postmodernist and might seem like an odd choice to quote at the start of an interview with Arthur Kroker (although, for one thing, Catholicism looms large in the background of the political thought of both). Yet oddly enough, what Kroker terms "crash aesthetics" does have resonances with Weil's utopian pessimism—seeming to echo both its dread and its revolutionary embrace of the smashup,[2] as well as its commitment to unflinching clear-sightedness. Compare her metaphor of the merry-go-round,

> Power ... in order to maintain its position, must stir up conflicts with rival powers; and so on once again. Thus it is that the most fatal of vicious circles drags the whole society in the wake of its masters in a mad merry-go-round (66),

with the same image as interpreted by him,

> Postmodern politics begins with [painter] Mark Gertler's *Merry-go-round*. ... The horses are genetically pure, beyond mutation, beyond the cancerous errors of nature poised for the viciousness of the war to come—a ready automated machine. Yet what is this, the protruding buttocks, rounded open fleshy white? The solar anus open to the culture of fun/fear ready to receive consummation as the carousel picks up speed.

Politics becomes the flashing anus of promises of the better world constantly present as the carousel becomes the succession of white strobe-like flashes and as the waste system runs in the now of party time.[3]

This latter is surely an updated view of the amusement park, a souped-up carousel, but a harrowing ride nonetheless (all the more). Both thinkers envision a society spinning out of control, though the disorientation this entails may itself prove another ruse of power unless we counter it.

Kroker's thesis is perhaps summarizable in a simple (yet complex), harmless-sounding (but chilling) phrase: Postmodernism is fun. In what follows, the foremost interpreter of Jean Baudrillard (in *The Postmodern Scene*) and (with the publication of *The Possessed Individual*) clearly an important postmodern philosopher and political theorist in his own right insists that his work is itself not at all pessimistic, but rather imbued with faith in "a raging will to political action."

GABRIEL BRAHM JR: We've been hearing a lot about cyborgs lately. In your performance-theory piece, *Spasm,* you're already talking about androids. First of all, what's the difference? And second, how do the two—androids and cyborgs—get along? What do they have to say to each other?

ARTHUR KROKER: Well, androids might be one further advance on cyborg consciousness because androids really are a manifestation of recombinant culture. They have recombinant intelligence, recombinant feelings, and recombinant sensibilities and they no longer represent any kind of interface between machines and human beings. They represent the creation of technology as a living species-existence with its own kind of recombinant genetic logic which moves by a threefold logic of cloning, transcription, and resequencing. Cyborgs, on the other hand, represent the last kind of spasmodic phase of a modernist era of technology and culture. Androids represent something different entirely. They're the point at which machines come alive and begin to speak and you get to know them on their own terms.

GB: Are we androids now, or cyborgs, or both?

AK: We're imperfect androids or android wannabes. I think the great challenge for this decade is to get to know this new species-existence because genetic logic has leapt into a new evolutionary phase. It used to belong to plants—we could speak of the genetic history of plants, the genetic history of animals, the genetic history being inscribed in the evolutionary history of the human race. But now the genes have sort of flowed out of the eyeballs and out of the fingers and really out of your mouth and they've gone directly into technospecies where technology comes alive as a living species-existence with really its own biogenetic logic. And that represents a new evolutionary phase for human beings to begin to relate to technology—not either as an externalized object or as simply having a logic of intelligent machines, but in fact technology (just like animals and plants and human beings before it) does in fact mean a real living species-being with its own evolutionary history which is just beginning.

GB: That hooks up to something I was noticing as I was looking over your book *The Postmodern Scene*. You quote McLuhan and particularly his famous statement to the effect that humans exteriorize their nervous systems in technology, which can be seen as an extension of hands, feet, eyes, and now with information technology, extensions of the brain itself. So McLuhan's subtitle for his book *Understanding Media* is *The Extensions of Man*. But that phrase almost sounds nostalgic now. Would there be more to it than mere wordplay to suggest that now it's the other way around and that we're the extensions of media?

AK: Yeah, we are and we aren't, I would say. It's this kind of doubling situation. McLuhan's a really brilliant theoretician. He saw exactly what would be meant by the inscription into the realm of technological culture of the human nervous system itself. So, McLuhan would say we're living in the age of nasty turtles—they have their soft part on the outside and the hard part, the shell, comes inside. And he says, What's the disposition of turtles who are in a threatened situation? They become anxiety-ridden, disturbed, and very nasty. So he says, you know, like nasty turtles—like Canadian consciousness, where I come from. So in some ways that's really an exact description of that phase of technology. But we're now living in not the age of McLuhan any longer, but really in the age of post-McLuhan. And McLuhan if he were alive would be the first to recognize this. The extension of McLuhan's theory would be to say that it's not the media as extension of human beings or of "Man" in a generic sense, but in fact, a kind of doubling situation in which the machines have come alive and we have existent relation to them in a completely schizophrenic way. We're servo-mechanisms of machines, but at the same time, let's face it, human beings need compensatory technologies even to keep up pace with machines. So we're also this kind of disturbed, emptied remainder that's left over when machines—when technology as living species-being—have sort of come alive and adopted their own life-giving powers. So we're simultaneously compensatory apparatuses of a machinic age and a kind of useless remainder. Between servo-function and uselessness is the human fate. It seems to me to be a happy kind of fate.

GB: A happy fate?

AK: Yeah, well, because it means that you live in a zone—you live in what Burroughs would call an "interzone." You live as servo-mechanism with really demonic, predatory technologies that are eating our bodies every day. We don't have to wait for the twenty-first century because this is the 1990s, and these ways in which the technologies inscribe themselves into our flesh parasite us almost as vampires and then transform us into simply intelligence-functions, feeling-functions, or sight-functions or consumer-functions in the technocracy. This seems to be our daily situation. Your body is spit out of this machinery because it is, for the most part, not needed in this relational apparatus. So the challenge of thinking critically today, in a political fashion, is to think, Well how do you live in this new historical state? What are the possibilities and perils of the interzone? Of what William Burroughs called the interzone. Or what Kathy Acker has written of as the interzone.

GB: That's a very interesting question. What sort of politics *are* adequate to the "interzone"? I was interested to hear you say "happy fate" because you're associated with a strategy which you defend as "hyperpessimism," which you've suggested is the only appropriate mood for contemporary theorizing. You say, in fact, that it's "the only realistic basis for a raging will to political action."

AK: Yeah.

GB: I'd like to ask you several things about that. What sort of political action do you have in mind? is my first question. Although perhaps I need to know a little better what "hyperpessimism" really is.

AK: My general political strategy is what I would call "crash aesthetics." It's a doubling strategy. It simultaneously means that you immerse yourself ironically and fully—ironic immersion in popular culture, the media-scape, and in the power centers of your culture. You drench yourself in them so that you don't try to retreat ahead of this culture but in fact advance with high velocity into the culture itself. Because, after all, if you're going to engage politics you have to engage the material existence of your culture. So one part of the doubling strategy of crash aesthetics is in ironic immersion.

The other part, though, is critical distancing. You don't retreat into techno-fetishism or technological euphoria. But, in fact, you understand that technology is not freedom today. Technology speaks a profound form of human degeneration. So this process—this political strategy of crash aesthetics—consists of a doubling strategy of ironic immersion and critical distancing. And they don't occur at separate moments—they're simultaneous strategies. It's genuinely a schizoid strategy: perfectly relative to the unique historical situation in which we live. That strategy is hyperpessimistic because ... it's crash. Because it recognizes that the situation of technology is that of a simultaneous double movement towards passive nihilism and towards suicidal nihilism. Passive nihilism in the sense that we live in a culture in which the growing majority of human beings haven't learned to think deeply about themselves, take their entertainment culture as the good life or as fun life, and burp. They've never learned to think deeply. And suicidal nihilism because our creative leaders know that there is no longer any substantive purpose to their willing but that they'd always prefer to go on willing rather than not to will at all. So faced with that situation hyperpessimism is, for myself, the only realistic and historically responsible political attitude to adopt. It's thinking without illusions and thinking into life. And for myself that's generally a Nietzschean and Bataillean strategy of life in which you invest your body responsibly in your real material circumstance. But most people associate pessimism with paralysis, and I never have. I always think hyperpessimism is in fact the beginning of real political action. My translation term for pessimism would be just realistic. What other people call pessimistic, I just call realistic thinking. I refuse to think unrealistically. I refuse illusions.

GB: Is hyperpessimism "active nihilism" then? It sounds like something Nietzsche recommends in *The Will to Power*.

AK: Yeah. But it's will to power taken to another stage. Because really, culture today is not about a will to power anymore. It's about a will to powerlessness. That's the great reversal we're living through in the 1990s. The age of technology really has come to an end and technology has disappeared into the will to virtuality. The will to virtuality is not a catastrophe or a decline. The will to virtuality is about reclining—getting rid of yourself as fast as possible. So the disappearance of a body into the technosphere, the disappearance of emotions into a highly elaborated media-scape which processes you through radically as a kind of radical semiurgy of emotion, and getting rid of your relationships because after all what's vaunted, what's celebrated today is becoming like an intelligence function or a cultural function or a social function in a relational database, which is what our culture has become. So that's for me all about the will to virtuality. Where the will to virtuality is about a great relaxation, exhaustion, and logic of disappearances. The disappearances of the body ... you know, of culture—into kind of a posttechnological civilization.

GB: Before we leave the topic of "political action" per se, I think I should ask you the question that people ask me sometimes about your work. Well, it's more of an accusation: This isn't a democratic discourse, this manner of writing and speaking and of doing "performance theory" with a lot of sights and sounds and terminology. What do you say to the charge that it's a nondemocratic or "elitist" discourse?

AK: It's hyperdemocratic. Hyperdemocratic is doubled. It's simultaneously immediately and immensely democratic because it is based on a simple function. That is, what C. Wright Mills said, that you should strive to become (also following

Jean-Paul Sartre) a master of your situation by achieving a kind of critical consciousness of your situation. And for myself the discourse that I have is the discourse that tries to wrest people's minds back. My mind most of all and immediately, but everyone else's mind as well, back from these kinds of totalizing ideologies and totalizing discourses that threaten to exterminate our identities. So it has that strategy to it, and at the other end of things it tries to create a kind of politics of individuation once more. It refuses to surrender its discourse to the totalities of class, ideology, or race. It refuses all discourse of domination and tries, for once, to create a new kind of relationship between morality, a kind of ethics, intelligence, and a really genuinely democratic politics.

GB: Last question on this topic ...

AK: And I would say that that's based in the good old American tradition of John Dewey in some ways. Because after all, think of Dewey's reconstruction and politics in which Dewey said democracy will only come to America when there is a kind of reflexive recombination, like a reflexive union once more of intelligence, ethics, democracy. I've always been influenced by Dewey and James's work—that side of their work. And this work really recovers that tradition but resituates their pragmatism in a new historical situation. Maybe I could say one other thing about that. This discourse—this form of thought, of political action—also could not be spoken about using "democracy" as an abstract thing because in fact the work has some real, some concrete, specificities to it. It's a feminist discourse. Most of our work that I've done with Marilouise [Kroker] has in fact been in rethinking the meaning of feminism in postmodern cultures. In texts like *Body Invaders* we said, What happens today when McCarthyism is no longer political McCarthyism but it's body McCarthyism—a real internal control over the quality of your bodily fluids, a kind of viro-politics. Or in *The Hysterical Male* we examined the grisly follow-up from the breakdown of the unitary male will as it leaches out in these kinds of spasmodic outbursts of grisly, sacrificial forms of male violence. And in the next text that we have coming out, which is *The Last Sex,* we really ask the question: Is an identitarian feminist politics possible or really desirable in light of the situation of the hysterical male? And we answer it in fact, no, that perhaps it's time that the identitarian basis of feminism be shifted on to what we call a kind of third sex, a kind of last sex, in which there is a kind of movement beyond the cult of gender, which is what Kate Bornstein, a San Francisco performance artist, has called this. So our politics now is beyond the cult of ideology, beyond the cult of normal pragmatic politics, and certainly beyond the cult of gender. We're sort of anticultist, I'd say.

GB: Are you concerned about the term "postfeminism" and what it might mean as a danger? Do you see a danger in ...

AK: We never use that term. We use hyperfeminism. It's not post-anything; it's an intensification of tendencies. But feminism surely has to be rethought in terms of the fall of the hysterical male. The really catastrophic consequences for women are becoming more and more severe. But also, the really vicious, Fascistic backlash against any form of sexual difference—against lesbians and gays most of all. And a kind of violence exercised within the domicile of the family against children. These, for us, are really the political problem that I think we're probably most motivated by, trying to think about possible political responses to and ways of organizing. So the feminist position we would adopt has this double tendency to it. Simultaneously recovery of memory, and at the same time it's a recognition—not only a recognition—it's a refusal of the cult of gender. Because for us it is really a profound political mistake to back into a referential illusion. You know, into the church of gender once, which is a stabilized pole-position in modernist discourse and which ultimately allies yourself with the most neoconservative forces in the society. It's a very comfortable position: Neoconservative forces will just take the opposite polar position, and it's a kind of comforting discourse. Well, for us, if a feminism does that, it is a feminism in fact that allies itself tacitly and probably unconsciously with neoconservatism, allies itself with the most regressive political forces in society. A feminism that's not recombinant today is not really a feminism at all. Because it is not really dealing with what is happening to the processing of sexuality and the kind of double spaces that a lot of people live in. I mean a space of all the outlaw bodies, from gays to transsexuals to lesbians to heterosexuals, for example, heterosexual males who are fleeing the cult of gender and who don't engage in sacrificial violence. So why, for once, not a politics of feminism that would not work to create differences but in fact work to create real genuine forms of political reconciliation and forms of sexual coalition against really a Fascistic outbreak of violence on the part of powers that are demonic on sexual grounds, on many other grounds. The general cultural politics of this would be that we struggle against the will to purity. For us the 1990s is marked by a Fascistic outbreak of will to purity on many different fronts. In Bosnia, Yugoslavia, it's marked by ethnic cleansing. In many countries in the world it's marked by racialist cleansing. In South America it's marked the logic of disappearances in Fascist regimes, by simply bodily disappearances. Or in California it's marked by the cultural cleansing of any improper perspectives and things. Well, these are all part of a great fascistic "Recline of Western Civilization," a mark of will to purity. And what we would have to say about the third sex cannot be understood outside of that context of a general struggle against this massive world universal movement towards a will to purity. Will to purity is on one side and we're really for speaking about the creation of differences in a kind dirt once more, I guess. If the world has gone towards a will to purity, then I would say that we would like once more a dirty, street politics, a dirty feminism. And I'd like to be a dirty theorist. That kind of dirt theorist is the basis of our politics.

GB: Well that's fascinating. Speaking of dirt, and excrement …

AK: That's our meat.

GB: I've been struck by the strange continuity between your work and that of Norman O. Brown with regard to implosion, waste, and excess. What do you think of Brown's latest, "Dionysus in 1990," where he posits a link between postmodern potlatch and an amelioration of mass resentment? Check this out: "Gift-giving, a primary manifestation of Dionysian exuberance, might revel in its own intrinsic self-sacrificial nature, instead of being inhibited and distorted, in bondage to primary social institutions of self-assertion. And public joy might manifest itself in carnivalesque extravaganzas uninhibited by the resentment of the exploited, the excluded, the deprived."[4] Would you call that realistic?

AK: I think it's quite wonderful. It's wonderful because Norman's trying to think of the possibilities within the given historical traditions. The transformation of the very worst of tendencies under the sign of a predatory, capitalist economy which is deeply nihilistic in character. Where it reverses itself into its opposite. Where in fact gift-giving isn't exercised as it is today for predatory purposes, and for purposes of sacrificial violence. But, as he says, it begins to revel in its own possibilities of *jouissance*. Well that strikes me as a wonderful mind, which Norman O. Brown has always been. That's why he's been so influential on many of us, as a thinker in fact who really thinks through the body to the possibility of a recovery of a democratic politics, and certainly the recovery of a culture that's animated with a zeal for life once more. And that's Brown. The question of realism or irrealism is really irrelevant. It's in fact an ethical possibility which stands as a furthest frontier on the expansion of the demonic culture that we have today.

GB: You share with Brown an interest in transvaluing political economy. What are the bases for a critique of postmodern political economy? Is the logic of accumulation, and the profit motive, any longer an adequate basis? What is *postmodern political economy*?

AK: Disaccumulation. Well, let me answer in two ways. Not necessarily in opposition, but to represent my position, it wouldn't be anything about the Dionysian. Now this is really a difference in sensibility, of a way of taking the world. And rather than being Dionysian I more think we're zooming down the highway on the way to intensive care. That's our situation. That's what I would think out of. So you ask, What's a postmodern political economy? I would say, What's the entanglement of capitalism and technology? And I would reply to that by saying in fact that capitalism basically has vanished, and it's vanished into technology as a will to virtuality. Because it strikes me, very practically, that (for example) corporations don't use advertising any longer as a way of generating profits. It's what Michael Weinstein, the Chicago philosopher, says in a piece on panic advertising that we once published, which I think is really correct, that now companies operate not on the basis simply of profit motive, but really of historical destiny. They generate as much money as they can in order to buy as much advertising space as they can. And whole corporations seem to have vanished into promotional culture. And promotional culture is not normal capitalism. It's certainly not primitive capitalism, and it's also not organized capitalism. It's sort of lost its systematicity and has become like a relational database. So I would say that we really live in the age of at least panic finance, which is global in character, and which even the medium of money and credit has disappeared into twenty-four hour stock exchange relations. It's really a cybernetic mode of economy that doesn't operate according to normal capitalism. Capitalism is exhausted and really has to be almost propped up by technocenters. It's dispirited and worn out and it's kept alive as sort of a false synergization of things. The real focus of power now is the will to virtuality, and everyone gets into the act because the will to virtuality is immensely seductive. People want to get rid of their bodies as fast as they can, and people want to get rid of their freedoms as fast as they can. That's what technostructures are betting on. That's why it's the logic of seduction, not coercion.

GB: What makes America, as you call it in *The Possessed Individual,* "the first purely poststructuralist society"?

AK: America was born a virtual society. The very principles of the European industrial revolution that couldn't be exercised because of the resistance of feudal structures in Europe always were allowed to be fully played out across the American frontier. The conquest of the American frontier itself. America was born a virtual society. It never had a modernist phase. It never even had a medievalist phase. It went from perfect primitivism to perfect postmodernism or poststructuralism. And it's really poststructuralist because America was born as a sign system. It was born as a sign system which alternates between pure sacrifice, pure energy, pure conquest, pure remembrance. A kind of fictitious remembrance, pure invention and reinvention of the meaning of the American self, and pure exterminism of memory.

GB: I wonder if our deep postmodernism, or poststructuralism as you describe it, had anything to do with the fact that, as opposed to Europe, we did without much of a state for a long time in our history. Hegel said we hadn't even got to that phase of the world spirit yet, you know? Does the different history of the state in America figure into our lived poststructuralism?

AK: That's an important question because in America what formed was a new form of subjectivity outside the colonizing framework of the state. I think that

America, as the world's first postmodern society, was invented in the materiality of the body. It's the de Tocquevillian subject. As de Tocqueville said in his journals, what is most amazing about the American pioneer is that here is a person who is like a seizer of the wilderness, who goes into the wilderness with an ax in one hand but a newspaper in the other. Who is a reflective intelligence while he's appropriating and exterminating and destroying everything in his wake. But de Tocqueville also described not only the forward movement of conquest, the forward movement of technological dynamism as the center of the American self, but also predicted the denouement of the American self when he said, "Well, what happens when the frontiers of conquest have been reached? When you settle California and then you have no more materiality of land to go forward to?" Then de Tocqueville intimated what will happen in the twentieth century is that the process will begin to reverse itself. The American self, the American pioneer, will return back upon the landscape and retrace like a predator-parasite, raping and pillaging and burning everything in its wake. That, I think, describes the history of America in the 1980s and 1990s and certainly has been globalized as the history of America's foreign policy. It's like the history of a serial killer in some ways, raping and pillaging and burning, with appropriation and abandonment as its double principles.

NOTES

1. Simone Weil, *Oppression and Liberty,* trans. Arthur Wills and John Petrie (Amherst: University of Massachusetts Press, 1973), 121. Subsequent references to this edition appear in the text.

2. This is not to ignore the more obvious allusion to J. G. Ballard and perhaps early Lyotard, but simply to suggest another crash site.

3. Arthur Kroker, *The Postmodern Scene* (New York: St. Martin's Press, 1986), iii.

4. Norman O. Brown, *Metamorphosis and/or Apocalypse* (University of California Press, 1991), 191.

About the Book and Editors

Defined as that space of collision between human and machine, where technology and humanity fuse, is the "prosthetic territory" of postmodern existence. Within that territory a new terrain of political and cultural struggle is emerging—a weird place where theory and practice can converge.

This collection of essays maps the newest terrains of political struggle by deploying a range of poststructuralist concepts embodied in phrases such as "technology of writing," "corporeal city," "cartographic self," "geography of the body," "words as ligatures," "battleground of bodily form," "semiotic guerrilla warfare," "veil of print," "textual architecture," and "materiality of the printed text." Such terms allow the authors to approach in innovative ways topics in feminism, Marxism, postcolonialism, queer theory, psychoanalysis, postmodernism, political theory, and the critique of racism and technique.

Prosthetic Territories is the third in an innovative serial—Politics and Culture—under the general editorship of Michael Ryan at Northeastern University and Avery Gordon at the University of California–Santa Barbara.

Gabriel Brahm Jr. teaches politics at the University of California–Santa Cruz. **Mark Driscoll** is a fellow in the Department of Comparative Literature at Cornell University.

Index